The Legal Environment of Contemporary Business

Revised Second Edition

Richard J. Hunter, J.D.
Professor, Legal Studies
W. Paul Stillman School of Business
Seton Hall University

John H. Shannon, M.B.A., J.D.
Associate Professor, Legal Studies
W. Paul Stillman School of Business
Seton Hall University

Henry J. Amoroso, J.D.
Associate Professor, Legal Studies
W. Paul Stillman School of Business
Seton Hall University

Susan A. O'Sullivan, J.D.
Senior Faculty Associate, Legal Studies
W. Paul Stillman School of Business
Seton Hall University

THOMSON
™

Australia · Canada · Mexico · Singapore · Spain · United Kingdom · United States

The Legal Environment of Contemporary Business

Richard J. Hunter, J.D. / John H. Shannon, M.B.A., J.D. / Henry J. Amoroso, J.D. / Susan A. O'Sullivan, J.D.

Editor:
Susan O'Sullivan

**Senior Project
Development Editor:**
Lori Gud

Marketing Coordinators:
Lindsay Annett and Sara Mercurio

**Production/Manufacturing
Supervisor:**
Donna M. Brown

Senior Project Coordinator:
Jennifer Flinchpaugh

Pre-Media Services Supervisor:
Dan Plofchan

**Rights and Permissions
Specialist:**
Bahman Naraghi

Cover Design:
Krista Pierson

Compositor:
Becky Arrants

Printer:
Globus Printing & Packaging

CONTENTS

PREFACE

As this edition of *The Legal Environment of Contemporary Business* was completed, we thought back to the first semester we taught this subject and realized that each successive class of students had two facts to discover. Besides becoming familiar with some legal concepts and terminology, they would realize that as teachers we derive much from the students themselves. As teachers, we look forward to each new group of students, the eagerness and anticipation they bring to the classroom; the expression of their doubts about the law and justice, and their aspirations in making the transition from student thinkers to participants in the working world who would have a positive effect on that world.

We also hoped that they would see that law evolves; that it is dynamic. Each case is the culmination of a series of events involving protagonists and adversaries, some of them even heroic. The law is like a series of plays. The facts preceding the climax of a court's decision are at least as fascinating as the outcome itself. Therefore, by providing students with the information about the people who eventually entered the courtroom, we enliven what some believe is a tedious business at best. It is our responsibility to stoke our students' interests so that they might be encouraged to eagerly consume more knowledge and finally to realize the best of their dreams.

We hope that with this revised edition of *The Legal Environment of Contemporary Business,* we will be able to provide a means for our students to meet their challenging goals.

LAW

=============

"Law is the highest reason, implanted in nature, which commands what ought to be done and forbids the opposite."

Cicero, *De Legibus,* Bk.1

"Law is an ordinance of reason for the common good, made by him who has care of the community, and promulgated."

St. Thomas Aquinas, *Summa Theologica,*
Part II, First Part, Qu. 90 Art.4

"The end of law is not to abolish or restrain, but to preserve and enlarge freedom."

Locke, *Two Treatises on Civil Government,*
Bk.II Ch.VI.

"Law is the sum of the conditions of social life in the widest sense of the term, as secured by the power of the State through the means of external compulsion."

Jhering, *Law as a Means to an End,*
Ch. VIII.

Unit I
Introduction to the Legal Environment

CHAPTER ONE
THE LEGAL SYSTEM

SOURCES OF AMERICAN LAW

For the most part, the roots of our legal heritage can be found in England. Once a British colony ruled by King George III through his appointed governors, the United States adopted the greatest share of its laws and legal traditions from the English. For all intents, English law began with the Norman invasion of England in 1066. William the Conqueror and his successors established the king's court (Curia Regis) to help create a unified nation. Before the Norman Conquest, disputes were settled according to local tribal customs. The king's court began to develop a common or uniform set of customs applicable to the whole population. This evolved into what became known as the common law, named so because it was intended to be common to the entire British kingdom.

As the number of courts and disputes increased, the more important rulings made each year were compiled into the *Year Books*. Judges referred to them as a source of guidance in settling cases similar to those already decided. If a dispute was unique (called a case of first impression), judges had to create new law, but they attempted to base it on previously established legal principles. Today we still rely on this body of judge-made law developed over the centuries. It is called common law or case law.

The common law was carried to the colonies by the first English settlers and used by the courts during the pre-Revolutionary War period. Common law continued to apply after the Revolution and the writing of the U.S. Constitution. It is still a viable source of law especially in tort, contract, and agency law. However, the states have codified some parts of the common law, most often in the criminal area. The states have also passed laws that supersede common law. For example, laws relating to the sale of goods are found in UCC Article 2.

THE DOCTRINE OF *STARE DECISIS*

In cases governed by the common law, courts locate the appropriate legal guidance in prior cases called precedents. The principle of choosing and applying the rulings of previous cases to decide the present case is the doctrine of stare decisis. It literally means "to adhere to decided cases" and holds that similar cases should be decided alike. If a court determines that the facts in the precedent are not really the same as those in the present case and, therefore, should not control the ruling, it distinguishes the precedent. Courts also can, but rarely do, overrule their prior decisions. They strain to avoid overruling earlier cases because it upsets stare decisis and the reliance people place on settled law in planning business and personal affairs.

CONSTITUTIONAL LAW

The United States Constitution is the paramount legal document in this country. A state's constitution is similarly absolute within its borders. Constitutions establish the structure of government for the political unit (federal or state), by providing for the branches and subdivisions of government and by conferring and denying powers to each part of that entity. The U.S. Constitution created three branches of government, the executive, legislative, and judicial. It provides each of them with unique powers that theoretically make each branch equal to the other two. This separation of powers provides a system of checks and balances so that one branch may not prevail over the others. Thus, the Constitution establishes a Congress to make laws, a presidency to enforce the laws, and a judiciary to interpret them. It also delegates to the states certain powers and casts a relationship between the states and the federal government. The relationship created is by definition a federal form of government. Each state possesses a limited amount of sovereignty, but the law of the central government is supreme and applicable to all of the states.

THE U.S. CONSTITUTION
ARTICLES I TO VII
Article I—Creates in the legislature the authority to enact laws. It defines the functions, powers and means for conducting business in Congress. Section 8 relates directly to matters affecting business in the U.S.: the power to lay and collect taxes, to regulate commerce with foreign nations and the states; to promulgate uniform bankruptcy laws; and establish courts having less power than the U.S. Supreme Court. Section 9 also affects business affairs—states may not impose a tax on exports to a country and they may not give preference to one state over another by regulating commerce.

Article II—The subject of this article is the executive power. The President holds the power to enforce federal laws. It establishes the President's term of office, requirements to become President and the presidential election process. It identifies the President as Commander in Chief of the Armed Forces, confers in the President the power to make treaties with the advice and consent of the Senate and to make executive agreements with other nations without the advice and consent of the Senate. At the root of this power is the President's power to speak and act on behalf of the country in matters of foreign relations.

Article III—This article establishes the judicial branch of the government. It confers the power to interpret laws and adjudicate certain disputes in the court. It authorizes the establishment of the U.S. Supreme Court and other federal courts. It provides for trials by jury for all crimes and contains the definition of treason.

Article IV—Concerns the relationships between the states. Each state is bound to recognize the public acts and proceedings of the other states through the "full faith and credit" clause. The power to extradite a criminal from one state to another is found here.

Article V—Lays out the means by which the U.S. Constitution must be amended.

Article VI—Confers supremacy of the U.S. Constitution, federal laws and treaties over all other laws. All officials—federal and state—are sworn under oath to uphold the U.S. Constitution.

Article VII—Includes original acceptance of the U.S. Constitution by the states.

CONSTITUTIONAL AMENDMENTS
The Bill of Rights is the collective name of the first ten amendments to the U.S. Constitution. Included are the freedoms of speech, press, religion and assembly; the requirement that law enforcement authorities must possess a warrant in order to perform a search and seizure; protection

from self-incrimination; establishment of a grand jury for capital offenses; just compensation in eminent domain cases; prohibition of double jeopardy; and due process of law provisions.

The Fourteenth Amendment—While each amendment to the U.S. Constitution is intrinsically and equally important, the Fourteenth Amendment might be considered the first among equals in that it makes all guarantees of the Bill of Rights applicable to the states.

SUPREMACY OF THE U.S. CONSTITUTION

The U.S. Constitution has been interpreted to allow the federal government to take legal action in the conduct of most areas of our daily lives. The governance of some activities may be relegated to the states. Any federal law that conflicts with a state law on the same subject matter takes precedence over the state law, unless, of course the federal action is ruled unconstitutional. Should Congress determine that federal law takes priority; its decision must be accepted. If Congress is silent on the matter, the court of competent jurisdiction applies the following analysis to the federal law to determine whether it takes precedence.

Does the U.S. Constitution permit the federal government to regulate the area of law in which this particular law resides? If yes, the federal law will likely prevail.

Does the federal law violate a right guaranteed by the U.S. Constitution, for example, the right to a speedy trial?

If not, does a state law address the same subject mater? If so, is there an inconsistency between the two laws? If one exists, the federal law prevails.

If both the federal and state laws are not contradictory, the state law is said to be concurrent with federal law.

STATE CONSTITUTIONS

Powers not delegated to the federal government are retained by the states unless prohibited in the states' own constitutions. Therefore, laws on the same subject can differ from one state to another in many ways. Distinctions between federal and state authority is established, but conflicting perceptions appear with respect to the point at which federal power ends and state rights begin.

STATUTORY LAW

Statutes are written laws. They may be enacted by Congress or a state legislature for the purpose of declaring, ordering, or prohibiting something. Counties, cities, and towns may enact laws, as well. They are called ordinances. They cannot violate the U.S. Constitution or the applicable state constitution. Federal and state regulatory agencies (for example, the Environmental Protection Agency and the Federal Trade Commission) enact laws, too. They usually have the same impact as a statute and, therefore, are part of the law, although they are usually called "rules and regulations."

State statutory law varies throughout the country, partly because of cultural and geographical differences, and partly because of diverging needs. For example, eight western states enacted marital property statutes, called community property laws that are derived from the Spanish legal system that exists in Mexico. Louisiana has laws on the books that originated in the Napoleonic Code because the French initially settled that area.

Throughout the text, you will study various state and federal statutes. As you read these laws, you will begin to understand the difficulty in interpreting and applying them. A large portion of the work of modern courts consists of interpreting what the legislators meant when they passed a law and applying it to the current circumstances. In this task, a court may be guided by reading the legislative history of any law, in order to ascertain the intention of the writers of any statute.

EQUITY

Equity is that body of law that carries out justice when the law itself fails to provide a fair or adequate remedy or no remedy at all. It originated in medieval England. During this period, the existing common law rules were highly technical and rigid. The remedies available in the common law courts were scarce. As a result, a prevailing party might not be able to obtain adequate relief in those courts. To rectify this problem, the chancellor, the king's highest-ranking executive, heard cases that could not be settled satisfactorily.

The principles of equity were adopted by the American colonies along with the common law. Eventually, the two became merged so that today, the majority of states have eliminated separate equity and law courts. The same court handles both types of claims. Further, the courts may award both monetary damages and an equitable remedy in specific cases.

Actions of law and suits in equity resolve issues using different procedures. In actions of law, disputes are resolved by the application of current statutes and previously decided cases. Suits in equity are decided by equitable principles and rules requiring no proof or which bear no argument. These are called maxims.

Examples of maxims include Laches and the Clean Hands Doctrine. Laches is the maxim that "equity aids the vigilant and not those that slumber on their rights." This means that if one neglects or omits to do what one should do, it is presumed that he has abandoned his right or claim. The Clean Hands Doctrine means that the court will not provide an equitable remedy to one who has violated conscience or good faith or other equitable principles.

Equitable decisions are called decrees. Unlike legal relief, which involves awards of money or something else of value, equity decrees order the losing party to do or refrain from doing something. For example, the remedy may come in the form of an injunction, either temporary or permanent (prohibiting one party from doing an act or commanding a party to perform an act). Another type of equitable relief is specific performance; the losing party must perform the contractual promise he or she made. It is imposed when monetary damages are insufficient. Example: Ross, a famous artist, promises to paint Joan's portrait. Later, he changes his mind and reneges on his contractual duty. The court may demand that Ross perform, i.e., paint Joan's portrait. Additional equitable remedies include rescission (canceling a contract, thereby putting the parties to the contract in the same position they were in before the contract was formed) and reformation (where the court of equity rewrote all or part of a contract to reflect the parties' actual intentions).

ADMINISTRATIVE AGENCIES

As the United States became industrialized in the latter half of the 19th century, the need arose to create divisions of government that could handle the ever-complex situations that evolved. Congress and state legislatures began to establish administrative agencies. The duties that Congress could not perform in regulating certain activities because of the lack of time and specialized knowledge were delegated to these agencies.

To date, congress and the executive branch have created over 100 administrative agencies to make, interpret and enforce laws. These agencies provide a forum where complex commercial issues and disputes can be adjudicated with efficiency, expertise and fairness. Administrative agencies are authorities in their particular areas of law. Their expertise is critical given the complexities of the law and the complexities of the areas of business the laws regulate.

Administrative agencies exist at every level of the government and they derive their power from the particular branch of the government that created them. For example, Congress creates federal agencies, state legislatures create their agencies and city councils create their cities' administrative agencies. An example of a governmental agency includes the Securities and Exchange Commission (SEC) which is authorized to enforce the federal securities laws that apply to issuers of and persons who trade in securities.

Legislative supervision over agencies usually is minimal; however, administrative agencies are subject to some general laws on the functioning of the agencies. The Administrative Procedure Act (APA) requires agencies to follow certain uniform procedures in making rules and it establishes notice and hearing requirements.

While the vast majority of administrative actions are processed informally, certain administrative agencies have the judicial authority to adjudicate cases through an administrative proceeding. These proceedings are not identical to court trials however; the agency must comply with the Due Process Clause of the U.S. Constitution. In other words, the individual or business must be given adequate notice, a meaningful opportunity to be heard, and fair trial procedures.

Administrative law judges (ALJs) preside over administrative proceedings. There is no jury. The administrative agency and the respondent may be represented by counsel and may call witnesses and introduce evidence. Upon hearing the case, the ALJs render their decision in the form of an order that will state the reasons for their decisions. The order becomes final if it is not appealed. If either party is dissatisfied with the decision, it may seek an appeal that consists of a review by the agency.

TREATIES

Through the U.S. Constitution, a treaty is made by the president with the head of a foreign country. It must be ratified by two-thirds of the Senate. It then becomes "the supreme law of the land." A conflict of law between a treaty and a state or federal law causes that law to become invalid.

BASIS OF COMMERCIAL LAW

The area of law pertaining to commercial dealings is called commercial or business law. It includes all aspects of contract law, sales, corporations, agency, partnerships, and other subjects included in this text.

The American Law Institute developed a number of comprehensive codes of law. Its purposes for doing so includes the creation of uniformity of laws among the states and the reformation of laws to maintain their currency. Beginning in the late 19th century, the National Conference of Commissioners on Uniform State Laws began meeting to draft uniform statutes. As they were written, each state legislature was encouraged to adopt the uniform law. Such adoption is a state matter. Each state may adopt all or part (or none, for that matter) of a uniform law. Therefore, the law on any particular subject is not "uniform" throughout the country. Examples of uniform laws include the Model Business Corporation Act, the Uniform Gifts to Minors Act, the Uniform Arbitration Act, and the Uniform Federal Lien Registration Act. A number of other uniform laws have been written as well. Students of business law will find that the Uniform Commercial Code is the most important of these legal codes.

THE UNIFORM COMMERCIAL CODE

The UCC is a unified body of statutes governing nearly all commercial transactions. Nevertheless, the interpretations of the UCC are found in decisional law (cases), not within the UCC. The UCC encourages the advancement of business by providing assurances and stability among businesspeople that their legal contracts will be carried out.

The UCC did not create severe changes in the basic principles of commercial law. Merchants are still held to a very high standard of performance to act in good faith within the commercial sphere. In UCC§ 2-103, good faith means honesty in fact and the observance of reasonable commercial standards of fair dealing in the trade.

The UCC defines and elucidates commonly misunderstood legal and business terms, assisting parties in the drafting of contracts and aiding courts in their interpretation and enforcement. Courts may rule that certain contracts or terms within a contract are unconscionable and, therefore, unenforceable. The decisional law governing contracts in one state has persuasive value in courts of other states because adoption of the UCC results in "uniformity."

Currently, the entire UCC has been adopted in all fifty states. The District of Columbia, the Virgin Islands, and Guam have also adopted the UCC.

CLASSIFICATION OF LAW

Usually laws are classified into three different groupings. They are: (1) criminal law and civil law; (2) substantive law and procedural law; and (3) public law and private law. Every law fits into one subgroup of each group. Therefore, a constitutional law may be criminal and substantive, public and civil or procedural and public, for example.

CRIMINAL AND CIVIL LAW

Philosophically, a crime may be considered a wrong committed against society. When the government acts as prosecutor by taking legal action against a person for committing a wrongdoing, criminal law applies. The governmental entity may be the state or federal government. In certain instances, a city or municipality may initiate a criminal action, such as charging a person with drunk driving. However, the formal charge is made in the name of the state in which the alleged violation took place. In some cases, "persons" may include corporations and other types of business entities. Crimes are punishable by imprisonment and/or fines.

In general terms, civil law is applied when one party brings an action against another because the latter party did not meet a legal duty owed to the first party. Anyone may be a party to a civil suit—individuals, business entities, and government entities. The party initiating a civil suit is called the plaintiff; the party sued is called the defendant. If the defendant loses the case, the plaintiff is awarded some form of damages (money, property) or equitable relief.

At times, the same wrongful behavior may violate criminal and civil laws. For example, a rapist may be charged for violating a criminal statute and may also be sued in a civil court by the individual that was raped.

SUBSTANTIVE AND PROCEDURAL LAW

Laws that prescribe the rights and obligations of people in their everyday lives are called substantive laws. A statute that makes theft illegal is a substantive law.

Procedural laws establish the means and rules by which substantive laws are applied. For example, in federal civil suits all individuals involved (judge, defendant, jury, plaintiff, etc.) act in compliance with the rules set down in the Federal Rules of Civil Procedure.

PUBLIC AND PRIVATE LAW

Public law is law enacted by an authorized government body. Examples include the U.S. Constitution, state constitutions, federal aviation laws, state laws of incorporation, municipal parking ordinances, and zoning laws.

Private law develops from a relationship between parties and creates a framework of rules to establish rights and obligations of the parties. For example, a contract for employment creates a legal relationship between the employer and employee. The terms of the contract are a type of private law to be obeyed by the parties. The requirements for executing the contract and the means for enforcing the contract are a matter of public law; however, the terms for performance are private law created by the parties to the employment contract.

CHAPTER QUESTIONS

1. How did the common law develop?

2. What is a "case of first impression"?

3. Explain the principle of "*stare decisis.*"

4. Why is the U.S. Constitution so important in this country?

5. Differentiate between courts of equity and law.

6. Name the three classifications of law and explain each.

7. What role do administrative agencies play in government?

CHAPTER TWO:
COURT SYSTEMS

INTRODUCTION

The vast and complex body of American law is based on several components—case law and reasoning that form the common law; statutes enacted at the federal and state levels; federal and state constitutions; legal codes such as the Uniform Commercial Code; and administrative laws promulgated by agencies such as the Federal Trade Commission. The laws alone would have no significance if it were not for the court system that was created for the purpose of interpreting and applying the law.

The principles of law are embued in every aspect of the business environment; government regulations actively facilitate and restrict business operations. It is, therefore, essential for business managers to have a general knowledge of the legal system and understand how the applications of the rules affect their trade. In all likelihood, all businesspeople will be involved, at one time or another, in the court system. Thus, it is important to know the basic structure of the court system and the route a lawsuit takes through that system.

Before examining the federal and state court structures, the chapter will discuss the meaning of jurisdiction. This plays an important part in understanding where and why a suit starts in one court rather than another.

JURISDICTION OF COURTS

The word "jurisdiction" is derived from two Latin words, *juris* meaning "law," and *dictum* meaning "to speak." To hear a case a court must be able "to speak the law," i.e., hold the power to rule on that case. In order to have this power a court must have jurisdiction over the parties and subject matter of the case. Federal courts have subject matter jurisdiction in two types of cases; federal question cases where the application of federal law is necessary to resolve the dispute, and diversity cases where a suit arises between citizens of two or more different states and the amount in question is $75,000 or more.

Diversity cases require that federal courts apply the statutory and case law of the state in which they are heard—not federal law or cases. Federal courts are used to maintain impartiality in deciding the dispute.

IN PERSONAM JURISDICTION

Besides subject matter jurisdiction, courts must have jurisdiction over the parties in a case that is personal jurisdiction. The legal term is *in personam* jurisdiction. A court may obtain *in personam* jurisdiction in any of three ways: 1) Compulsory process—If a defendant is served with a summons, giving notice of the suit and requiring a response in court, within that court's state; 2) The party is a resident or does business in the state where the court is located; and 3) Consent—The party appears in the court without objecting to the court's jurisdiction.

By all three methods, a court always has jurisdiction over a plaintiff who has consented by bringing a case. However, subject matter jurisdiction cannot be obtained merely by consent. Note, though, that nonresident defendants may make a "special appearance" to challenge the court's jurisdiction without consenting to that jurisdiction.

LONG-ARM STATUTES

States protect their citizens from unscrupulous non-residents by enacting laws that grant courts in personam jurisdiction over non-residents having at least minimum contacts within the state. These long-arm statutes allow one party to sue another living in a distant state without bearing the burden and expense of traveling to the defendant's state.

The following case, *International Shoe Co. v. State of Washington*, still provides a perfect example and demonstrates the application of these jurisdictional principles.

International Shoe Co. v. State of Washington 326 U.S. 310 (1945)

The questions for decision are (1) whether, within the limitations of the due process clause of the Fourteenth Amendment, appellant, a Delaware corporation, has by its activities in the State of Washington rendered itself amenable to proceedings in the court of that state to recover unpaid contributions to the state unemployment compensation fund exacted by state statutes,...and (2) whether the state can exact those contributions consistently with the due process clause of the Fourteenth Amendment.

The statutes in question set up a comprehensive scheme of unemployment compensation, the costs of which are defrayed by contributions required to be made by employers to a state unemployment compensation fund. The contributions are a specified percentage of the wages payable annually by each employer for his employees' services in the state. The assessment and collection of the contributions and the fund are administered by respondents. Section 14(c) of the Act...authorizes respondent Commissioner to issue an order and notice of assessment of delinquent contributions upon prescribed personal service of the notice upon the employer if found within the state, or, if not so found, by mailing the notice to the employer by registered mail at his last known address. That section also authorizes the Commissioner to collect the assessment by distraint if it is not paid within ten days after service of the notice. By §§14(e) and 6(b) the order of assessment may be administratively reviewed by an appeal tribunal within the office of unemployment upon petition of the employer, and this determination is by §6(i) made subject to judicial review on questions of law by the state Superior Court, with further right of appeal in the state Supreme Court as in other civil cases.

In this case notice of assessment for the years in question was personally served upon a sales solicitor employed by appellant in the State of Washington, and a copy of the notice was mailed by registered mail to appellant at its address in St. Louis, Missouri. Appellant appeared specially before the office of unemployment and moved to set aside the order and notice of assessment on the ground that the service upon appellant's salesman was not proper service upon appellant; that appellant was not a corporation of the State of Washington and was not doing business within the state; that it had no agent within the state upon whom service could be made; and that appellant is not an employer and does not furnish employment within the meaning of the statute.

The motion was heard on evidence and a stipulation of facts by the appeal tribunal which denied the motion and ruled that respondent Commissioner was entitled to recover the unpaid contributions. That action was affirmed by the Commissioner; both the Superior Court and the Supreme Court affirmed....Appellant in each of these courts assailed the statute as applied, as a violation of the due process clause of the Fourteenth Amendment, and as imposing a constitutionally prohibited burden on interstate commerce. The cause comes here on appeal..., appellant assigning as error that the challenged statutes as applied infringe the due process clause of the Fourteenth Amendment and the commerce clause.

The facts as found by the appeal tribunal and accepted by the state Superior Court and Supreme Court are not in dispute. Appellant is a Delaware corporation, having its principal place of business in St. Louis, Missouri, and is engaged in the manufacture and sale of shoes and other footwear. It maintains places of business in several states, other than Washington, at which its manufacturing is carried on and from which its merchandise is distributed interstate through several sales units or branches located outside the State of Washington.

Appellant has no office in Washington and makes no contracts either for sale or purchase of merchandise there. It maintains no stock of merchandise in that state and makes there no deliveries of goods in intrastate commerce. During the years from 1937 to 1940, now in question, appellant employed eleven to thirteen salesmen under direct supervision and control of sales managers located in St. Louis. These salesmen resided in Washington; their principal activities were confined to that state; and they were compensated by commissions based upon the amount of their sales. The commissions for each year totaled more than $31,000. Appellant supplies its salesmen with a line of samples, each consisting of one shoe of a pair, which they display to prospective purchasers. On occasion they rent permanent sample rooms, for exhibiting samples, in business buildings, or rent rooms in hotels or business buildings temporarily for that purpose. The cost of such rentals is reimbursed by appellant.

The authority of the salesmen is limited to exhibiting their samples and soliciting orders from prospective buyers, at prices and on terms fixed by appellant. The salesmen transmit the orders to appellant's office in St. Louis for acceptance or rejection, and when accepted the merchandise for filling the orders is shipped f.o.b. from points outside Washington to the purchasers within the state. All the merchandise shipped into Washington is invoiced at the place of shipment from which collections are made. No salesman has authority to enter into contracts or to make collections.

The Supreme Court of Washington was of opinion that the regular and systematic solicitation of orders in the state by appellant's salesmen, resulting in a continuous flow of appellant's product into the state, was sufficient to constitute doing business in the state so as to make appellant amenable to suit in its courts. But it was also of opinion that there were sufficient additional activities shown to bring the case within the rule frequently stated, that solicitation within a state by the agents of a foreign corporation plus some additional activities there are sufficient to render the corporation amenable to suit brought in the courts of the state to enforce an obligation arising out of its activities there. International Harvester Co. v. Kentucky, 234 U.S. 579, 587, 34 S.Ct. 944, 946, 58 L.Ed. 1479; People's Tobacco Co. v. American Tobacco Co., 246 U.S. 79, 87, 38 S.Ct. 233, 235, 62 L.Ed. 587, Ann.Cas.1918C, 537; Frene v. Louisville Cement Co., 77 U.S. App.D.C. 129, 134 F.2d 511, 516, 146 A.L.R. 926. The court found such additional activities in the salesmen's display of samples sometimes in permanent display rooms, and the salesmen's residence within the state, continued over a period of years, all resulting in a substantial volume of merchandise regularly shipped by appellant to purchasers within the state. The court also held that the statute as applied did not invade the constitutional power of Congress to regulate interstate commerce and did not impose a prohibited burden on such commerce.

Appellant's argument, renewed here, that the statute imposes an unconstitutional burden on interstate commerce need not detain us. For 53 Stat. 1391...provides that "No person required under a State law to make payments to an unemployment fund shall be relieved from compliance therewith on the ground that he is engaged in interstate or foreign commerce, or that the State law does not distinguish between employees engaged in interstate or foreign commerce and those engaged in intrastate commerce." It is no longer debatable that Congress, in the exercise of the commerce power, may authorize the states, in specified ways, to regulate interstate commerce or impose burdens upon it. Kentucky Whip & Collar Co. v. Illinois Central R. Co., 299 U.S. 334, 57 S.Ct. 277, 81 L.Ed. 270; Perkins v. Pennsylvania, 314 U.S. 586, 62 S.Ct. 484, 86 L.Ed. 473; Standard Dredging Corp. v. Murphy, 319 U.S. 306, 308, 63 S.Ct. 1067, 1068, 87 L.Ed. 1416;

Hooven & Allison v. Evatt, 324 U.S. 652, 679, 65 S.Ct. 870, 883; Southern Pacific Co. v. Arizona, 325 U.S. 761, 769, 65 S.Ct. 1515, 1520.

Appellant also insists that its activities within the state were not sufficient to manifest its "presence" there and that in its absence the state courts were without jurisdiction, that consequently it was a denial of due process for the state to subject appellant to suit. It refers to those cases in which it was said that the mere solicitation of orders for the purchase of goods within a state, to be accepted without the state and filled by shipment of the purchased goods interstate, does not render the corporation seller amenable to suit within the state. See Green v. Chicago, Burlington & Quincy R. Co., 205 U.S. 530, 533, 27 S.Ct. 595, 596, 51 L.Ed. 916; International Harvester Co. v. Kentucky, supra, 234 U.S. 586, 587, 34 S.Ct. 946, 58 L.Ed. 1479; Philadelphia & Reading R. Co. v. McKibbin, 243 U.S. 264, 268, 37 S.Ct. 280, 61 L.Ed. 710; People's Tobacco Co. v. American Tobacco Co., supra, 246 U.S. 87, 38 S. Ct. 235, 62 L.Ed. 587, Ann.Cas.1918C, 537. And appellant further argues that since it was not present within the state, it is a denial of due process to subject it to taxation or other money exaction. It thus denies the power of the state to lay the tax or to subject appellant to a suit for its collection.

Historically the jurisdiction of courts to render judgment in personam is grounded on their de facto power over the defendant's person. Hence his presence within the territorial jurisdiction of a court was prerequisite to its rendition of a judgment personally binding him. Pennoyer v. Neff, 95 U.S. 714, 733, 24 L.Ed. 565. But now that the capias ad respondendum [a writ commanding the sheriff to take the defendant to answer the plaintiff in an action] has given way to personal service of summons or other form of notice, due process requires only that in order to subject a defendant to a judgment in personam, if he be not present within the territory of the forum, he have certain minimum contacts with it such that the maintenance of the suit does not offend "traditional notions of fair play and substantial justice." Milliken v. Meyer, 311 U.S. 457, 463, 61 S.Ct. 339, 343, 85 L.Ed. 278, 132 A.L.R. 1357. See Holmes, J., in McDonald v. Mabee, 243 U.S. 90, 91, 37 S.Ct. 343, 61 L.Ed. 608, L.R.A. 1917F, 458. Compare Hooperston Canning Co. v. Cullen, 318 U.S. 313, 316, 319, 63 S.Ct. 602, 604, 606, 87 L.Ed. 777, 145 A.L.R. 1113. See Blackmer v. United States, 284 U.S. 421, 52 S.Ct. 252, 76 L.Ed. 375; Hess v. Pawloski, 274 U.S. 352, 47 S.Ct. 632, 71 L.Ed. 1091; Young v. Masci, 289 U.S. 253, 53 S.Ct. 599, 77 L.Ed. 1158, 88 A.L.R. 170.

Since the corporate personality is a fiction, although a fiction intended to be acted upon as though it were a fact, Klein v. Board of Tax Supervisors, 282 U.S. 19, 24, 51 S.Ct. 15, 16, 75 L.Ed. 140, 73 A.L.R. 679, it is clear that unlike an individual its "presence" without, as well as within, the state of its origin can be manifested only by activities carried on in its behalf by those who are authorized to act for it. To say that the corporation is so far "present" there as to satisfy due process requirements, for purposes of taxation or the maintenance of suits against it in the courts of the state, is to beg the question to be decided. For the terms "present" or "presence" are used merely to symbolize those activities of the corporation's agent within the state which courts will deem to be sufficient to satisfy the demands of due process. L. Hand, Jr., in Hutchinson v. Chase & Gilbert, 2 Cir., 45 F.2d 139, 141. Those demands may be met by such contacts of the corporation with the state of the forum as make it reasonable, in the context of our federal system of government, to require the corporation to defend the particular suit which is brought there. An "estimate of the inconveniences" which would result to the corporation from a trial away from its "home" or principal place of business is relevant in this connection. Hutchinson v. Chase & Gilbert, supra, 45 F.2d 141.

"Presence" in the state in this sense has never been doubted when the activities of the corporation there have not only been continuous and systematic, but also give rise to the liabilities sued on, even though no consent to be sued or authorization to an agent to accept service of process has been given. St. Clair v. Cox, 106 U.S. 350, 355, 1 S.Ct. 354, 359, 27 L.Ed. 222; Connecticut Mutual Life Ins. Co. v. Spratley, 172 U.S. 602, 610, 611, 19 S.Ct. 308, 311, 312, 43 L.Ed. 569; Pennsylvania Lumbermen's Mut. Fire Ins. Co. v. Meyer, 197 U.S. 407, 414, 415, 25 S.CT. 483, 484, 485, 49 L.Ed. 810; Commercial Mutual Accident Co. v. Davis, 213 U.S. 245, 255, 256, 29 S.Ct. 445, 448, 53 L.Ed. 782; International Harvester Co. v. Kentucky, supra; cf. St. Louis S. W. R. Co. v. Alexander, 227 U.S. 218, 33 S.Ct. 245, 57 L.Ed. 486, Ann.Cas.1915B, 77. Conversely it has been generally recognized that the casual presence of the corporate agent or even his conduct of single or isolated items of activities in a state in the corporation's behalf are not enough to subject it to suit on causes of action unconnected with the activities there. St. Clair v. Cox, supra, 106 U.S. 359, 360, 1 S.Ct. 362, 363, 27 L.Ed. 222; Old Wayne Mut. Life Ass'n v. McDonough, 204 U.S. 8, 21, 27 S.Ct. 236, 240, 51 L.Ed. 345;

Frene v. Louisville Cement Co., supra, 77 U.S.App.D.C. 133, 134 F.2d 515, 146 A.L.R. 926, and cases cited. To require the corporation in such circumstances to defend the suit away from its home or other jurisdiction where it carries on more substantial activities has been thought to lay too great and unreasonable a burden on the corporation to comport with due process.

While it has been held in cases on which appellant relies that continuous activity of some sorts within a state is not enough to support the demand that the corporation be amenable to suits unrelated to that activity, Old Wayne Mut. Life Ass'n v. McDonough, supra; Green v. Chicago, Burlington & Quincy R. Co., supra Simon v. Southern R. Co., 236 U.S. 115, 35 S.Ct. 255, 59 L.Ed. 492; People's Tobacco Co. v. American Tobacco Co., supra; cf. Davis v. Farmers' Co-operative Equity Co., 262 U.S. 312, 317, 43 S.Ct. 556, 558, 67 L.Ed. 996, there have been instances in which the continuous corporate operations within a state were thought so substantial and of such a nature as to justify suit against it on causes of action arising from dealings entirely distinct from those activities. See Missouri, K. & T. R. Co. v. Reynolds, 255 U.S. 565, 41 S.Ct. 446, 65 L.Ed. 788; Tauza v. Susquehanna Coal Co., 220 N.Y 259, 115 N.E. 915; cf. St. Louis S. W. R. Co. v. Alexander, supra.

Finally, although the commission of some single or occasional acts of the corporate agent in a state sufficient to impose an obligation or liability on the corporation has not been thought to confer upon the state authority to enforce it, Rosenberg Bros. & Co. v. Curtis Brown Co., 260 U.S. 516, 43 S.Ct. 170, 67 L.Ed. 372, other such acts, because of their nature and quality and the circumstances of their commission, may be deemed sufficient to render the corporation liable to suit. Cf. Kane v. New Jersey, 242 U.S. 160, 37 S.Ct. 30, 61 L.Ed. 222; Hess v. Pawloski, supra; Young v. Masci, supra. True, some of the decisions holding the corporation amenable to suit have been supported by resort to the legal fiction that it has given its consent to service and suit, consent being implied from its presence in the state through the acts of its authorized agents. Lafayette Insurance Co. v. French, 18 How. 404, 407, 15 L.Ed. 451; St. Clair v. Cox, supra, 106 U.S. 356, 1 S.Ct. 359, 27 L.Ed. 222; Commercial Mutual Accident Co v. Davis, supra, 213 U.S. 254, 29 S.Ct. 447, 53 L.Ed. 782; State of Washington v. Superior Court, 289 U.S. 361 364, 365, 53 S.Ct. 624, 626, 627, 77 L.Ed. 1256, 89 A.L.R. 653. But more realistically, it may be said that those authorized acts were of such a nature as to justify the fiction. Smolik v. Philadelphia & R. C. & I. Co., D.C., 222 F. 148, 151. Henderson, The Position of Foreign Corporations in American Constitutional Law, 94, 95.

It is evident that the criteria by which we mark the boundary line between those activities which justify the subjection of a corporation to suit, and those which do not, cannot be simply mechanical or quantitative. The test is not merely, as has sometimes been suggested, whether the activity, which the corporation has seen fit to procure through its agents in another state, is a little more or a little less. St. Louis S. W. R. Co. v. Alexander, supra, 227 U.S. 228, 33 S.Ct. 248, 57 L.Ed. 486, Ann.Cas.1915B, 77; International Harvester Co. v. Kentucky, supra, 234 U.S. 587, 34 S.Ct. 946, 58 L.Ed. 1479. Whether due process is satisfied must depend rather upon the quality and nature of the activity in relation to the fair and orderly administration of the laws which it was the purpose of the due process clause to insure. That clause does not contemplate that a state may make binding a judgment in personam against an individual or corporate defendant with which the state has no contacts, ties, or relations. Cf. Pennoyer v. Neff, supra; Minnesota Commercial Men's Ass'n v. Benn, 261 U.S. 140, 43 S.Ct. 293, 67 L.Ed. 573.

But to the extent that a corporation exercises the privilege of conducting activities within the state, a procedure which requires the corporation to respond to a suit brought to enforce them can, in most instances, hardly be said to be undue. Compare International Harvester Co. v. Kentucky, supra, with Green v. Chicago, Burlington & Quincy R. Co., supra, and People's Tobacco Co. v. American Tobacco Co., supra. Compare Connecticut Mutual Life Ins. Co. v. Spratley, supra, 172 U.S. 619, 620, 19 S.Ct. 314, 315, 43 L.Ed. 569, and Commercial Mutual Accident Co. v. Davis, supra, with Old Wayne Mut. Life Ass'n v. McDonough, supra. See 29 Columbia Law Review, 87-195.

Applying these standards, the activities carried on in behalf of appellant in the State of Washington were neither irregular nor casual. They were systematic and continuous throughout the years in question. They resulted in a large volume of interstate business, in the course of which appellant received the benefits and protection of the laws of the state, including the right to resort to the courts for the enforcement of its rights. The obligation which is here sued upon arose out of those very activities. It is evident that these operations establish sufficient contacts or ties with the state of the forum to make it reasonable and just according to our traditional conception of fair play and substantial justice to permit the state to enforce the obligations which appellant has incurred there. Hence we cannot say that the maintenance of the present suit in the State of Washington involves an unreasonable or undue procedure.

We are likewise unable to conclude that the service of the process within the state upon an agent whose activities establish appellant's "presence" there was not sufficient notice of the suit, or that the suit was so unrelated to those activities as to make the agent an inappropriate vehicle for communicating the notice. It is enough that appellant has established such contacts with the state that the particular form of substituted service adopted there gives reasonable assurance that the notice will be actual. Connecticut Mutual Life Ins. Co. v. Spratley, supra, 172 U.S. 618, 619, 19 S.Ct. 314, 315, 43 L.Ed. 569; Board of Trade v. Hammond Elevator Co., 198 U.S. 424, 437, 438, 25 S.Ct. 740, 743, 744, 49 L.Ed. 1111; Commercial Mutual Accident Co. v. Davis, supra, 213 U.S. 254, 255, 29 S.Ct. 447, 448, 53 L.Ed. 782. Cf. Riverside & Dan River Cotton Mills v. Menefee, 237 U.S. 189, 194, 195, 35 S.Ct. 579, 580, 581, 59 L.Ed. 910; see Knowles v. Gaslight & Coke Co., 19 Wall. 58, 61, 22 L.Ed. 70; McDonald v. Mabee, supra; Milliken v. Meyer, supra. Nor can we say that the mailing of the notice of suit to appellant by registered mail at its home office was not reasonably calculated to apprise appellant of the suit. Compare Hess v. Pawloski, supra, with McDonald v. Mabee, supra, 243 U.S. 92, 37 S.Ct. 344, 61 L.Ed. 608, L.R.A.1917F, 458, and Wuchter v. Pizzutti, 276 U.S. 13, 19, 24, 48 S.Ct. 259, 260, 262, 72 L.Ed. 446, 57 A.L.R. 1230; cf. Bequet v. MacCarthy, 2B.& Ad. 951; Maubourquet v. Wyse, 1 Ir.Rep.C.L. 471, See State of Washington v. Superior Court, supra, 289 U.S. 365, 53 S.Ct. 626, 77 L.Ed. 1256, 89 A.L.R. 653.

Only a word need be said of appellant's liability for the demanded contributions of the state unemployment fund. The Supreme Court of Washington, construing and applying the statute, has held that it imposes a tax on the privilege of employing appellant's salesmen within the state measured by a percentage of the wages, here the commissions payable to the salesmen. This construction we accept for purposes of determining the constitutional validity of the statute. The right to employ labor has been deemed an appropriate subject of taxation in this country and England, both before and since the adoption of the Constitution. Steward Machine Co. v. Davis, 301 U.S. 548, 579 et seq., 81 L.Ed. 1279, 109 A.L.R. 1293. And such a tax imposed upon the employer for unemployment benefits is within the constitutional power of the states. Carmichael v. Southern Coal & Coke Co., 301 U.S. 495, 508 et seq., 57 S.Ct. 868, 871 et seq., 81 L.Ed. 1245, 109 A.L.R. 1327.

Appellant having rendered itself amenable to suit upon obligations arising out of the activities of its salesmen in Washington, the state may maintain the present suit in personam to collect the tax laid upon the exercise of the privilege of employing appellant's salesmen within the state. For Washington has made one of those activities, which taken together establish appellant's "presence" there for purposes of suit, the taxable event by which the state and to suit to recover the tax. Equitable Life Assur. Society v. Pennsylvania, 238 U.S. 143, 146, 35 S.Ct. 829, 830, 59 L.Ed. 1239; cf. International Harvester Co. v. Wisconsin Department of Taxation, 322 U.S. 435, 442 et seq., 64 S.Ct. 1060, 1064 et seq., 88 L.Ed. 1373; Hoopeston Canning Co. v. Cullen, supra, 318 U.S. 316-319, 63 S.Ct. 604-606, 87 L.Ed. 1722, 145 A.L.R. 1113; see General Trading Co. v. State Tax Com., 322 U.S. 335, 349, 64 S.Ct. 1028, 1030, 88 L.Ed. 1309, 1319.

AFFIRMED.

In Rem Jurisdiction

In rem jurisdiction pertains to the fact that the property that is the subject of the dispute is located within a given state. This gives the state courts the power to determine rights in that property even though any persons whose rights are affected are outside the state's in personam jurisdiction. For example, a New Jersey court would have in rem jurisdiction to hear a dispute involving ownership of real property, even if one of the disputing parties lived outside the state.

A second type of in rem jurisdiction is called quasi in rem jurisdiction. In this case, a plaintiff who obtains a judgment in one state may attach the defendant's property in another state in an attempt to collect the judgment.

VENUE

Venue determines which trial court is the appropriate one in which a case will be heard. Do not confuse venue with subject matter jurisdiction. State statutes prescribe what the proper venue is for a case. It is a matter of geographic location usually based on the defendant's place of residence, the property location if that property is the subject of the dispute, or the place in which the incident occurred that is the subject of the dispute. If multiple defendants reside in various geographical locations, the plaintiff may usually select the venue from any of these locations. If the court's location is inconvenient to a party, he or she may request, under the doctrine of *forum non conveniens*, to move the case from that court. The judge in the case decides whether to move the case to a different location after a hearing on the motion.

THE FEDERAL COURT SYSTEM

The federal judicial system was created by the U.S. Constitution in Article III. It is structured in a three-tiered format consisting of trial courts (federal district courts), intermediate courts of appeal (circuit courts of appeal), and the United States Supreme Court.

U.S. DISTRICT COURTS

The district courts are at the trial level in the court system. Each state has at least one federal district court that serves a certain prescribed geographical area (i.e. district). Currently there are 96 federal district courts. If a suit is within the federal jurisdiction, it is usually initiated in a federal district court. The court has both a fact-finding and law determining function. The jury or judge may perform the finding of fact; however, the judge always determines the law.

The jurisdiction of federal district courts is based on diversity jurisdiction and federal question jurisdiction. Diversity jurisdiction exists when a suit arises between (i) citizens of different states; (ii) a citizen of a state and a citizen of a foreign country; or (iii) a citizen of state and a foreign country where the plaintiff is the foreign country. The amount in controversy must exceed $75,000 or else the action must be brought in the appropriate state court.

A corporation is considered a citizen of the state of its incorporation and the state in which it has its principal place of business. A partnership (general or limited) is a citizen of every state in which a partner is a citizen.

In a diversity case, the federal district court resolves all issues according to the law of the state in which it sits. This is based on the decision handed down by the Supreme Court in *Erie Railroad Co. v. Tompkins* (304 U.S. 64 (1938)). Federal procedural rules apply, however.

Federal question jurisdiction is applied when a case arises under the U.S. Constitution or federal laws or treaties. For example, if a federal bank is robbed (thus, violating a federal statute) or if a U.S. treaty with a foreign nation requires interpretation, the case will be heard in a federal district court.

Federal district courts have sole or exclusive jurisdiction over certain matters, such as cases involving federal crimes, antitrust, bankruptcy, patent and copyright cases, suits against the United States, and admiralty cases. State courts are not permitted to hear these cases. However, both the federal courts and state courts have concurrent jurisdiction over certain matters, more particularly, cases involving diversity of citizenship and federal questions. When concurrent jurisdiction arises and the plaintiff chooses to have the case heard in a state court, the defendant may remove the case to a federal district court.

U.S. COURTS OF APPEALS

The U.S. Courts of Appeals are the federal court system's intermediate appellate courts. There are thirteen circuits in the federal court system. These courts perform no fact-finding function; their purpose is to review only the legal conclusions reached by lower federal courts.

The first eleven Courts of Appeals have jurisdiction over several states in a particular geographical area (i.e., a circuit). For example, the Court of Appeals for the Third Circuit, located in Philadelphia, hears appeals from the district courts located in their circuit, namely, Delaware, New Jersey, Pennsylvania, and the Virgin Islands. The courts at this level also hear appeals from the Tax Court, the Bankruptcy Court and decisions from several administrative agencies.

The twelfth court of appeals is located in Washington, D.C., known as the District of Columbia. The thirteenth court of appeals is called the Court of Appeals for the Federal Circuit that is also located in Washington, D.C. The Federal Circuit Court of Appeals hears specialized appeals concerning patent and trademark issues and appeals from the Claims Court and the Court of International Trade.

THE U.S. SUPREME COURT

The U.S. Supreme Court is the only court explicitly established by the Constitution. It is the highest court in the land and serves as an appellate court. Nine justices make up the Supreme Court. As are all federal judges, Supreme Court judges are nominated by the President, must be confirmed by the United States Senate, and serve a life term.

The Supreme Court generally hears appeals from the federal circuit courts of appeals and the highest state courts. At times, a case may be appealed directly from a federal district court to the Supreme Court. The Supreme Court does not accept evidence nor does it hear testimony. It simply reviews the lower court's record and determines whether there has been an error that warrants a reversal or modification of the decision. The Supreme Court's decision is final.

Appeals to the Supreme Court are not automatic. A request for review of a lower court decision must be made by filing a petition for *certiorari*. Four of the nine justices must agree to hear an appeal in order to grant *certiorari*. A *writ of certiorari* is issued if the Court decides to hear a case. This is an order issued by the Court requiring that the lower court produce the certified record of a case heard in that court.

The Supreme Court also has original jurisdiction in certain cases, meaning that it acts as a trial court. The Court has original and exclusive jurisdiction over all controversies between two or more states; over cases involving foreign ambassadors and ministers; controversies between a state and the United States; and cases involving a state and a citizen from another state or an alien.

THE STATE COURT SYSTEMS

State courts are organized much like the federal court system. They differ in specifics such as number of courts, their names, and jurisdiction. At the base of a state's judicial system are courts of limited jurisdiction. These include municipal courts, justice of the peace courts, and small claims courts. They hear minor criminal matters and civil controversies involving small amounts of money. Court proceedings are relatively informal and often no transcript of the testimony and proceedings is kept. The parties to a case frequently represent themselves and the presiding judicial officer is not required to be an attorney.

State trial courts perform the same functions as the inferior courts. However, they handle cases of greater significance and there is no limit to the dollar amount that may be awarded or the penalties meted out in a criminal case. Also, unlike the inferior courts, a detailed record of the proceedings of a case is kept. A judge or jury may perform the fact-finding duties at this level; however, the judge always determines questions of law.

The state appellate courts review questions of law only. As in the federal court system, no juries are involved in an appeal. Some states have only one level of appellate court while others have an intermediate level and a supreme court.

CIVIL PROCEDURE

The judicial system has developed detailed and complex rules on how, when and where a legal dispute can be brought to court. For civil suits, the rules of civil procedure apply. A different set of rules pertain to criminal cases. These rules of procedure are necessary to obtain an orderly and impartial determination of a trial that is consistent with prior decisions based on similar facts. The procedural rules are not uniform among the states; however, there are basic similarities.

In the following sections, we will outline the primary steps of a civil lawsuit. Note, not every component is employed in every case because parties often settle out of court or they may not want to raise every issue possible. As a general rule, attorneys will try to settle cases before beginning the process of initiating a trial. A recently issued Federal Executive Order requires attorneys to pursue alternative methods of dispute resolution in attempts to obtain out-of-court settlements prior to instituting suit. These procedures will be discussed later in the chapter.

THE PLEADINGS

Pleadings are the papers filed with the court to institute and respond to a lawsuit. To initiate a lawsuit, a litigant files a complaint with the clerk of the appropriate court. This formal document states the litigant's (the plaintiff) claim against the opposing party (the defendant) and includes sufficient facts to show that some legal remedy is necessary to right the harm done.

The defendant is served with process, usually in the form of a writ, notice, summons, or the actual complaint. This puts the defendant on notice that an action is pending against him and that he is subject to the particular court's jurisdiction.

The defendant must respond to the plaintiff's complaint by filing an answer. The defendant, through his answer, either admits or denies the plaintiff's allegations or states that he lacks the information needed to evaluate the veracity of the plaintiff's allegations; this amounts to a denial.

The answer may also include affirmative defenses to the claim asserted in the complaint. An affirmative defense is a rule of law enabling the defendant to prevail in the case even though all of the plaintiff's allegations are true. For example, if a plaintiff sues a defendant after the time within which to bring the action has expired; the defendant may raise this point as an affirmative defense.

At times, the answer may include a counterclaim. This is a separate claim being asserted by the defendant against the plaintiff that arises from the same facts as stated in the complaint. A counterclaim is the defendant's means for obtaining legal relief; it is not merely an attack on the plaintiff's claim.

If the defendant fails to file an answer to the complaint, a default judgment is entered against him. The default judgment establishes the defendant's liability; however, the plaintiff still must prove damages.

Some jurisdictions allow or require the plaintiff to respond to the defendant's affirmative defenses or counterclaim by means of a reply. It is a point-by-point response to the elements introduced in the defendant's affirmative defense or counterclaim. If the particular jurisdiction does not allow a reply to an affirmative defense, the defendant's new assertions are automatically denied. However, a plaintiff who wishes to contest a counterclaim must file a reply.

PURPOSE OF THE PLEADINGS

Historically, pleadings defined and limited the questions to be decided at the trial stage. Issues raised in the pleadings were considered part of the case; all others were excluded from further consideration. On rare occasions, amendments to the pleadings were permitted. Once the litigants admitted to allegations they were bound by their admissions. Allegations that were denied would be included in the dispute between the parties. This stage of the case also included several technical pleading rules that, if violated, could jeopardize a party's chances of winning a suit.

Some jurisdictions continue in this tradition. Others have used this stage to provide notice to each litigant of the claims being asserted by the other litigant(s). Additionally, these jurisdictions are more inclined to decide cases on the merits rather than on the technical defects of the pleadings. Frequently, amendments to the pleadings are allowed. In addition, they may be used to introduce issues to be considered at trial that were not initially raised in the pleadings.

MOTIONS

Once the pleadings have been filed and reviewed, it may be evident that the plaintiff has no case. In such a situation, to pursue the litigation would be a waste of the court's limited time and resources. The procedure for disposing of the case is a motion to dismiss. It may be made after the plaintiff has filed the complaint. A similar procedure is used to dismiss a case after the pleadings are completed. This is a motion for judgment on the pleadings.

Motions for dismissal may be made to attack inadequate service of process or a particular court's lack of jurisdiction over the parties, subject matter or both. However, the most important type of motion to dismiss is a demurrer. This motion is used to assert that the plaintiff has failed to state a claim upon which relief can be granted. In other words, even if every allegation made in the plaintiff's complaint were true, the plaintiff could not recover because no rule of law exists entitling him to win on those facts.

DISCOVERY

Discovery is the process used to exchange relevant information between the litigants. Its purpose is to aid the litigants in preparing their arguments and to narrow and clarify the issues to be decided at trial. The costs of obtaining discovery can be substantial depending on the extent to which the litigants carry out the process.

Written questions called interrogatories may be directed to each party and they are legally bound to answer them. Further, depositions may be taken whereby individuals (the parties in the case and witnesses) are questioned under oath before a court reporter. Other forms of discovery include requests for documents and other evidence such as the litigants' files and records; mental and physical examinations; and requests for admissions, one litigant's written demand that the other party agree to certain statements of fact or law.

SUMMARY JUDGMENT

Once the discovery process is completed, it is common for one party to make a motion to the court for summary judgment. If the party making the motion prevails, the case will not go to trial. In order to succeed, the movant must show that there are no genuine issues of material fact, and that he is entitled to judgment as a matter of law.

PRE-TRIAL CONFERENCE

The participants in a pre-trial conference include the judge and attorneys, only. It may or may not be mandatory, at the trial judge's discretion. They discuss the issues that must be tried, the length of the trial, and the possibility of settlement. If the case cannot be settled, the judge enters a pre-trial order including all the attorneys' stipulations and other agreements. Typically, the terms of this order bind the parties throughout the rest of the case.

THE TRIAL

A trial may be held with or without a jury. The jury is the trier of fact, meaning that they determine the veracity of the facts alleged in the case. The judge on the other hand acts as the trier of law. If neither party requests a trial by jury, the judge will assume both roles as trier of fact and the trier of law. Note, the jury can never make findings of law.

The U.S. Constitution guarantees the right to a jury trial for cases at law in federal courts if the amount in controversy exceeds $20. Most states have similar guarantees in their own constitutions, but impose a higher minimum dollar amount. One does not have to exercise the right to a jury trial. Either party may request a trial by jury or it is presumed to be waived.

In civil cases, the plaintiff has the burden of proving the case by a preponderance of the evidence. This means that the greater weight of evidence must favor the plaintiff. To sustain that burden of proof, the plaintiff must convince the judge or jury that the facts probably bear out what the plaintiff alleges.

JURY SELECTION

Clearly, the selection of a jury, if the case is to be heard by one, is extremely important to the parties in the case. A panel of possible jurors is selected at random from the citizens residing within the court's venue. The selection process is called "*voir dire*," a French term meaning "to speak the truth."

The judge, attorneys or both, question potential jurors to find out whether or not they could decide the case without bias.

A potential juror may be removed "for cause" if the attorney questioning the person believes he or she could not be unbiased. Attorneys have an unlimited number of challenges for dismissing potential jurors for cause. Attorneys may also eliminate potential jurors without providing any reason for doing so. These peremptory challenges are very limited in number. Peremptory challenges are allowed because the judicial system recognizes that to a limited extent an attorney's instinctual feelings play a part in the jury selection process. Today, potential jurors may not be eliminated from participating on juries solely because of race or gender.

Petit Jury

The petit (meaning small) jury is selected to hear the proceedings of the trial. It usually is made up of six or twelve individuals. A petit jury may hear either civil or criminal cases.

Grand Jury

A grand jury is so named because it is comprised of more jurors that a petit jury. A federal grand jury must have at least sixteen but not more than 23 persons. A grand jury is used only in criminal actions. Its purpose is to determine, after hearing the state's evidence, whether probable cause exists for supposing that a crime has been committed and whether a trial should be held. If the grand jury finds probable cause, it returns a bill of indictment. If it does not find probable cause, it returns no bill.

Trial Proceedings

Each trial begins with the plaintiff's attorney making an opening statement about the facts that he or she expects to prove during the trial. The defendant's attorney may make his opening statement at this point or reserves the right to make it after the plaintiff presents his or her case-in-chief.

Presenting the Plaintiff's Case

After the opening statement(s), the plaintiff calls his or her first witness for examination (questioning). This is the direct examination. The defendant's attorney is then permitted to cross-examine this witness. If the defense attorney cross-examines the witness, the plaintiff's attorney has another opportunity to question the same witness. This is redirect examination. The defense attorney may then follow with recross-examination. This process continues with each witness.

Directed Verdict

After the plaintiff calls all of his or her witnesses, the defendant's attorney is permitted to ask the judge to direct a verdict for the defendant on the ground that the plaintiff has presented no evidence that would justify the granting of the plaintiff's remedy. This is a motion for a directed verdict. It takes the case away from the jury and gives a judgment to one party before the jury has an opportunity to decide the case. The moving party makes an assertion that, even upon reading the evidence in a light most favorable to the nonmoving party, such evidence leads to only one result and it need not go to the jury for deliberation. Motions for a directed verdict are seldom granted at this stage of the trial.

THE DEFENSE

If the motion for directed verdict is not granted, the defendant's attorney presents the evidence and witnesses for the defendant's case. The same procedure applicable for the plaintiff is employed by the defendant. When the defendant rests, either attorney may again move for a directed verdict. If not granted, the plaintiff is allowed to present a rebuttal. This may include additional evidence to refute the defense's case. The defendant can rebut this evidence in a rejoinder.

CLOSING ARGUMENTS

Once all the evidence is presented, each party's attorney gives a closing argument. The plaintiff goes first. Each attorney urges a verdict in favor of his or her respective client. The judge instructs the jury (if a jury is hearing the case) in the law that applies to the case. These are often called charges.

VERDICTS

The jury begins its deliberations in an effort to reach a verdict on which the court's judgment is based. The jury's deliberations may result in one of several outcomes. It may issue a general verdict. In this case, the jury declares which party prevailed and the relief (if any) to be awarded. It gives the jury the freedom to ignore the judge's charge and follow its own inclinations because it does not have to state its factual findings or its application of the law to those findings.

Alternatively, and at the discretion of the trial judge, a special verdict may be rendered. In this situation, the jury only makes specific findings of fact; essentially it answers questions submitted to it. Based on its answers, the judge determines which party obtains the judgment by applying the law to the jury's findings.

On rare occasions, a judgment notwithstanding the verdict (in Latin, *non obstante veredicto*) may be issued. The party against whom the verdict was rendered moves for a judgment in his favor because, based on the weight of evidence, the party receiving the favorable judgment should not have prevailed. Unless the jury was clearly lax in the performance of its duties, courts will not grant a Judgment N.O.V.

MOTION FOR A NEW TRIAL

The losing party does not have to accept the judgment rendered, but may make a motion for a new trial. Such a motion will be granted if the judge erred in some way during the trial, misconduct by the jury or attorney was evident, new evidence was found, or the plaintiff was awarded excessive damages.

APPEALS

A losing party may appeal the decision of the lower court if no reason exists for granting a motion for a new trial. The winning party also may appeal if the award is not as much as was expected.

An appeal is not a second trial. Therefore, no jury is required. The judges of the appellate court read the written record of the lower court's proceedings. Then they make their determination as a matter of law whether or not there was error in the trial and judgment.

Appealable matters include the trial judge's decisions on the pleadings or motion to dismiss, on admissibility of evidence, a motion for summary judgment, directed verdict, judgment n.o.v., or motion for a new trial. Further, a party may make an appeal based on the trial court's rulings on service of process, its legal findings in a nonjury trial, its instructions to the jury in a jury trial, and the damages or equitable relief awarded.

The appellate court has several options at its disposal. It may affirm the ruling of the lower court, reverse the lower court's decision, or affirm one part of the decision and reverse another part of it. If the appellate court does not agree with the application of the law made by the lower court, it may set aside or modify the action of the lower court and enter a judgment that the lower court should have entered. It may set aside the action of the lower court and send the case back to it with directions to hold a new trial or it may enter a new judgment in accordance with the opinion rendered by the appellate court. In this situation, the appellate court reverses the decision of the trial court and remands the case back to the lower court. If a higher appellate court exists, the case may be appealed to that level.

ENFORCEMENT OF JUDGMENTS

It is one thing for a plaintiff to be awarded a favorable judgment and another to collect on that judgment. If the losing party fails to comply with the rendering of a judgment of monetary damages, the prevailing party has to obtain a writ of execution that enables the sheriff to seize certain property in order to satisfy the judgment. The judgment may be satisfied by garnishment of the losing party's salary, wages or other funds held by a third party. If the successful party is awarded an equitable remedy such as an injunction and the losing party fails to obey the order, he or she may be held in contempt of court and punished by fine and/or imprisonment.

ALTERNATIVE DISPUTE RESOLUTION

Two factors impact negatively on our legal system: delay and cost. The heavy volume of lawsuits, the highly formal and technical procedures involved in all stages of a suit contribute to this problem. The legal system has developed several alternative means by which to streamline the process and settle conflicts.

MEDIATION

The process of mediation involves an intermediary to assist parties in resolving their dispute. The intermediary, a mediator, has no legal power to enforce a solution. It is the mediator's ability to persuade, assist the parties in understanding each others' position, present the strengths and weaknesses of each person's side, and assess the benefits of settlement and cost of proceeding toward a trial that provide a viable alternative to a lawsuit.

ARBITRATION

In this process, the arbitrator is empowered to issue a decision that is binding on the parties. The parties agree to arbitrate or statutes may be enacted to compel it. Such agreements are usually made before any disputes arise through the inclusion of an arbitration clause in a contract. However, it may commence after a dispute arises.

Arbitrators need not be attorneys. They are usually professionals with expert knowledge of the subject matter in dispute. Arbitration is an informal proceeding that does not require the meticulous conformity to rules of evidence and procedure governing a lawsuit.

MEDIATION/ARBITRATION

The combination of the above two means for resolving a dispute is called med/arb. This alternative to a lawsuit involves a third party who first acts as a mediator. All issues not resolved through mediation are then subjected to binding arbitration. The mediator and arbitrator may be two different people.

COURT-ANNEXED ARBITRATION

In this case, arbitration is ordered by a judge after a lawsuit has been filed. Jurisdictions allowing court-annexed arbitration provide that the judge's decision to order it depends on the subject matter of the dispute and the amount of money at issue. The losing party does not lose his or her right to a conventional trial.

OTHER MEANS OF ADR

Minitrial

A legal dispute is processed through an informal, abbreviated, private "trial" in which the attorneys present their side to a panel of business executives of the disputing companies that have the power to resolve the dispute. Time limits are agreed to in advance. A neutral "advisor" acts as the judge and presides over the hearing while offering opinions and proposals to the executives.

Summary Jury Trial

A limited time is given to each side to present its best case to a jury. Each party meets with the jury to discuss the strong and weak points of its case and a settlement conference results.

CHAPTER QUESTIONS

1. In *International Shoe,* how did the Court balance the due process rights of the corporation against the rights of the state of Washington to collect taxes from it?

2. How was process served on the shoe company?

3. Did the issue of interstate commerce have any impact on the case? Explain.

4. What are "minimum contacts"?

5. Discuss in rem and quasi in rem jurisdiction.

6. How does venue differ from jurisdiction?

7. In the federal district courts civil jurisdiction is based on diversity and federal question jurisdiction. Explain what these terms mean.

8. Describe exclusive and concurrent jurisdiction.

9. Provide an example of a situation in which the U.S. Supreme Court exercises original jurisdiction.

10. What is a *writ of certiorari?*

11. Explain the process of bringing a civil suit through a typical state court system.

12. What is the function of the grand jury? The petit jury?

13. Define general verdict, special verdict, and judgment notwithstanding the verdict.

CHAPTER THREE:
CONSTITUTIONAL PERSPECTIVES

INTRODUCTION AND OVERVIEW

As the "supreme law of the land," the U.S. Constitution influences all aspects of our government, its operation, and the people that it serves. It provides us with the structure of our government by creating the three main branches of government through the allocation and separation of power among them, and it prevents government from taking certain actions, most particularly those actions restricting individual rights, including those rights of artificial individuals such as corporations.

The United States has a federal system where the national government and the government of each of the states coexist. The federal government is one of limited, enumerated powers where the three branches of the government can only assert those powers specifically granted by the U.S. Constitution. Thus, whenever the constitutionality of congressional legislation is at issue, some relationship to a specifically enumerated power in the constitutional text must be shown.

On the other hand, the state governments hold a general "police power," i.e., a broad power to promulgate legislation for the health, safety, morals, and general welfare of state residents. Thus, any action by a state government is valid under federal law provided it does not violate some specific limitation imposed by the Constitution. In contrast, in order for a federal action to be deemed valid, it must fall within one of the specifically enumerated powers listed in the Constitution.

At first glance it may seem as if the federal government has very "limited-power"; however, in addition to the specific powers given by the Constitution, the Congress is given the power to "make all laws which shall be necessary and proper for carrying into execution" the specific powers. Accordingly, if Congress is seeking an objective that is within the specifically enumerated powers, then it can use any means that is rationally related to the objective it is trying to achieve (assuming that it does not violate any specific prohibition in the Constitution).

EXAMPLE:

The Supreme Court, relying on the "necessary and proper" clause, held that Congress had the power to create a bank even though such a power was not specifically granted in the Constitution. The Court found that this power was incidental to the carrying out one of the constitutionally enumerated powers, specifically Congress's power to raise revenue. *McCulloch v. Maryland,* 17 U.S. 316 (1819).

DOCTRINE OF SEPARATION OF POWERS

The Constitution provides for the allocation of distinct powers to three branches of government. Article I of the Constitution created the legislative branch that established a Congress made up of two bodies, the House of Representatives and the Senate. Congress has the sole power to legislate, that is, make laws, at the federal level. Article I establishes the means by which legislation is passed and states, in Section 8, most of the specific ways Congress can make law.

The second branch of government, created in Article II, is the executive branch. It establishes in the President, the executive power to enforce or execute laws passed by Congress. Some of these powers include the power to command the country's armed forces and the power to make treaties and appoint ambassadors. However, even these powers are not unrestricted.

Article III created the judicial branch that grants the Supreme Court and other federal courts the power to interpret laws. Article III also delineates the scope of the federal judicial powers, such as the types of cases the federal courts may decide.

CHECKS AND BALANCES

In addition to providing three branches of government and enumerating specific powers to the federal government, the Constitutional Convention set up an inherent system of checks and balances within Articles I, II, and III. While the states gave up certain powers for the greater good of the nation, they provided insurance for themselves to ensure that the central government would not evolve into a dictatorship. Therefore, for example, the President can veto legislation, but the Congress can override that veto. In addition, the President, vice president, and other federal officials may be impeached, treaties made by the President must be approved by the Senate, and the President may appoint certain individuals (e.g. federal judges) but only with the "advice and consent" of the Senate. In effect, the independent checks prevent Congress and state governments from overstepping the limitations of their granted power.

SUPREMACY AND PREEMPTION

Article VI, Clause 2 of the Constitution is called the Supremacy Clause. It provides that the Constitution, statutory law enacted by Congress, and treaties of the United States are the supreme law of the land. It is the keystone in establishing the order of state and federal relationships. This clause provides that when a direct conflict exists between a federal law and a state law, the state law becomes invalid. To this extent, the clause is easy to understand.

However, some powers are shared by the states and the federal government. These are called concurrent powers and occasions arise where it is necessary to determine which law should prevail. When concurrent federal and state powers are involved, a state law that conflicts with a federal law is prohibited. A federal action pursuant to a power specifically delegated to it by the Constitution always has the capacity to override a state law addressing the same action. Thus, when Congress chooses to act exclusively in a concurrent area, it is said that Congress has preempted this area. A federal regulatory scheme preempts a state law every time there is an outright conflict between the two or when the state regulation interferes with federal objectives.

The facts almost never lead to such a clear-cut result, however. Congress rarely makes obvious its intent to preempt an entire subject area against state regulation. It is the job of the courts to decide whether Congress intended to exercise exclusive dominion over the area in question. The Commerce Clause is a typical area where such conflict occurs.

More recently Congress enacted the Federal Telecommunications Act of 1996 (FTA) to open up competition within that industry. The FTA provided for the deregulation of the telephone industry and prohibited state and local governments from impeding the freedom to enter the rapidly expanding telecommunications industry. To achieve Congress's goals, the FTA prohibits any state or local law from "prohibit[ing] or having the effect of prohibiting the ability of any entity to provide any interstate or intrastate telecommunications service." (Section 253) Under the Supremacy Clause, the FTA preempts any state or local law that comes into conflict with it.

JUDICIAL REVIEW

Practically before the ink was dry on the Constitution, conflict developed as to how it should be interpreted and applied. The Supreme Court assumed the task of interpreting the Constitution in its 1803 decision of *Marbury v. Madison* (1 Cranch 137 (1803)). In that case, the Court reserved for itself the power to declare laws enacted by Congress to be unconstitutional. Known as the power of judicial review, it enables the Court to prevent the enforcement of laws or other governmental decisions that it determines to be repugnant to the Constitution.

In *Marbury*, Justice Marshall emphasized the fact that the Constitution was the expression of the popular will, and, therefore, properly controlled the exercise of all governmental power, including Congress. The Constitution is thus supreme over ordinary law and laws in defiance of the Constitution are null and void.

Judicial review is not limited solely to review of federal actions and laws. It extends as well as to state action. When the Supreme Court reviews the judgment of a state court, it is exercising its appellate, rather than its original, jurisdiction. Note, however, the Supreme Court's review of state court judgments is limited to questions of federal law; the Court may review state court decisions to determine whether they are in conformity with the Constitution, but it may not review state court decisions that merely adjudicate questions of state law.

CONGRESSIONAL REGULATORY AUTHORITY

Under Article I, Section 8, the Constitution lists several business-related fields in which Congress may legislate. The most important of these areas for our purpose are the powers to regulate commerce among and between the states, to lay and collect taxes, and to spend money for the general welfare. Accorded an ever-widening interpretation over many decades, these three powers have become the main constitutional avenues by which the federal government reaches its goal of regulating business. As discussed earlier, the Constitution, via the 10th Amendment gives the states a police power to legislate for the public health, safety, morals, and general welfare. However, today this power lacks much of the depth it once had because the federal government has continuously asserted and taken much of the ruling power for itself.

THE COMMERCE CLAUSE

The most important of the express domestic powers of Congress set forth in Article I, Section 8, is the commerce power. The Commerce Clause serves two distinct functions: (1) it acts as the source of

Congressional regulatory authority; and (2) it acts, implicitly, as an independent check on state regulation that unduly restricts interstate commerce.

Initially, during most of the 19th century, Congress's strength under the commerce power was not given much thought. Regulation was only occasional and fairly limited during that period. However, the latter part of the 19th century brought a rise in federal regulation and the Supreme Court increasingly concerned itself with defining the limits of the commerce power. By the late 1930s, the Court removed almost all federal limitations on regulating commerce and upheld what would once have been considered extremely extensive and intrusive laws regulating the economy. The Commerce Clause has become so pervasive that it is effectively an all-purpose police power allowing Congress to reach most activities, even those within a state's borders.

Under the present doctrines, the Court will uphold commerce-based laws if there is any rational basis upon which Congress can find some relation between its regulation and interstate commerce. The Court has achieved this result by recognizing three theories upon which a commerce-based regulation may be premised. The first major expansion of the Commerce Clause power is termed the "substantial economic effect" theory that provides that Congress may regulate all activities that have a "substantial economic effect" upon interstate commerce. The Court's 1937 decision in *NLRB v. Jones & Laughlin Steel Corp.* marks the loosening of the nexus required between the intrastate activity being regulated and the interstate commerce.

NLRB v. Jones & Laughlin Steel Corp.
301 U.S. 1 (1937)

In a proceeding under the National Labor Relations Act [the Act] of 1935, the National Labor Relations Board [NLRB] found that Jones & Laughlin Steel Corporation violated the Act by engaging in unfair labor practices affecting commerce. These practices included discrimination against union members with regard to hiring and tenure of employment and coercion and intimidation of its employees in order to interfere with their self-organization. The discriminatory and coercive action alleged was the discharge of certain employees.

The NLRB sustained the charge and ordered Jones & Laughlin to cease and desist from such discrimination and coercion, to offer reinstatement to ten employees, to provide restitution for their pay losses, and to post a notice for 30 days stating that the corporation would not discharge or discriminate against members, or those desiring to become members, of the labor union. Jones & Laughlin failed to comply; the Board petitioned to the Circuit Court of Appeals to enforce the order. The court denied the petition, holding that the order was beyond the range of federal power. The Supreme Court granted *certiorari*.

HUGHES, C.J....The scheme of the National Labor Relations Act...may be briefly stated. The first section sets forth findings with respect to the injury to commerce resulting from the denial by employers of the right of employees to organize and from the refusal of employers to accept the procedure of collective bargaining. There follows a declaration that it is the policy of the United States to eliminate these causes of obstruction to the free flow of commerce. The Act then defines the terms it uses, including the terms "commerce" and "affecting commerce." Section 2. It creates the National Labor Relations Board and prescribes its organization. Sections 3–6. It sets forth the right of employees to self-organization and to bargain collectively through representatives of their own choosing. Section 7. It defines "unfair labor practices." Section 8. It lays down rules as to the representation of employees for the purpose of collective bargaining. Section 9. The Board is empowered to prevent the described unfair labor practices affecting commerce and the Act prescribes the procedure to that end....

* * * * *

Contesting the ruling of the Board, the respondent [Jones & Laughlin] argues (1) that the Act is in reality a regulation of labor relations and not of interstate commerce;...

The facts as to the nature and scope of the business of the Jones & Laughlin Steel Corporation have been found by the Labor Board...

* * * * *

[Here, the Court detailed the structure of the company's multi-state organization.]

* * * * *

Summarizing these operations, the Labor Board concluded that the works in Pittsburgh and Aliquippa "might be likened to the heart of a self-contained, highly integrated body. They draw in the raw materials from Michigan, Minnesota, West Virginia, Pennsylvania in part through arteries and by means controlled by the respondent; they transform the materials and then pump them out to all parts of the nation through the vast mechanism which the respondent has elaborated."

* * * * *

First. The Scope of the Act.—The Act is challenged in its entirety as an attempt to regulate all industry, thus invading the reserved powers of the States over their local concerns...

* * * * *

...The grant of authority to the Board does not purport to extend to the relationship between all industrial employees and employers. Its terms do not impose collective bargaining upon all industry regardless of effects upon interstate or foreign commerce. It purports to reach only what may be deemed to burden or obstruct that commerce and, thus qualified, it must be construed as contemplating the exercise of control within constitutional bounds. It is a familiar principle that acts which directly burden or obstruct interstate or foreign commerce, or its free flow, are within the reach of the congressional power. Acts having that effect are not rendered immune because they grow out of labor disputes....It is the effect upon commerce, not the source of the injury, which is the criterion....Whether or not particular action does affect commerce in such a close and intimate fashion as to be subject to federal control, and hence to lie within the authority conferred upon the Board, is left by the statute to be determined as individual cases arise....

* * * * *

...Although activities may be intrastate in character when separately considered, if they have such a close and substantial relation to interstate commerce that their control is essential or appropriate to protect that commerce from burdens and obstructions, Congress cannot be denied the power to exercise that control.

* * * * *

...[T]he stoppage of [Jones & Laughlin's] operations by industrial strife would have a most serious effect upon interstate commerce. In view of respondent's far-flung activities, it is idle to say that the effect would be indirect or remote. It is obvious that it would be immediate and might be catastrophic. We are asked to shut our eyes to the plainest facts of our national life and to deal with the question of direct and indirect effects in an intellectual vacuum. Because there may be but indirect and remote effects upon interstate commerce in connection with a host of local enterprises throughout the country, it does not follow that other industrial activities do not have such a close and intimate relation to interstate commerce as to make the presence of industrial strife a matter of the most urgent national concern. When industries organize themselves on a national scale, making their relation to interstate commerce the dominant factor in their activities, how can it be maintained that their industrial labor relations constitute a forbidden field into which Congress may not enter when it is necessary to protect interstate commerce from the paralyzing consequences of industrial war? We have often said that interstate commerce itself is a practical conception. It is equally true that interferences with that commerce must be appraised by a judgment that does not ignore actual experience.

Experience has abundantly demonstrated that the recognition of the right of employees to self-organization and to have representatives of their own choosing for the purpose of collective bargaining is often an essential condition of industrial peace. Refusal to confer and negotiate has been one of the most prolific causes of strife....And of what avail is it to protect the facility of transportation, if interstate commerce is throttled with respect to the commodities to be transported!

* * * * *

...It is not necessary again to detail the facts as to respondent's enterprise....[I]t presents in a most striking way the close and intimate relation which a manufacturing industry may have to interstate commerce and we have no doubt that Congress had constitutional authority to safeguard the right of [Jones & Laughlin's] employees to self-organization and freedom in the choice of representatives for collective bargaining.

* * * * *

Our conclusion is that the order of the Board was within its competency and that the Act is valid as here applied....

Judgment reversed, in favor of the NLRB.

The second theory upon which the Court has expanded its Commerce Clause power is the "cumulative effect" theory. This principle provides that Congress may regulate not only acts which taken alone would have a substantial economic effect on interstate commerce, but also an entire class of acts, if the class has a substantial economic effect. The case which established this "cumulative effect" principle, was *Wickard v. Filburn* where the Court upheld federal legislation regulating the most local of all activities—production of wheat for personal consumption on the family farm.

Wickard v. Filburn
317 U.S. 111 (1942)

In 1938, Congress enacted the Agricultural Adjustment Act to stabilize agricultural production and so, give farmers reasonable minimum prices. The Act gave Claude Wickard, the Secretary of Agriculture, the power to pronounce a yearly national acreage allotment for the coming wheat crop. The allotment was apportioned among the states and their counties, and then among the farms within each county. Filburn was an Ohio farmer who raised a small portion of winter wheat. Some of it was sold but most of it was grown for personal use. Filburn's permitted allocation for 1941 was 11.1 acres. However, he planted and harvested 23 acres. He was assessed a penalty of $117.11 for violating the regulation.

JACKSON, J....It is urged that under the Commerce Clause,...Congress does not possess the power it has in this instance sought to exercise. The question would merit little consideration...except for the fact that this Act extends federal regulation to production not intended in any part for commerce but wholly for consumption on the farm....Such activities are, [Filburn] urges, beyond the reach of congressional power under the Commerce Clause, since they are local in character, and their effects upon interstate commerce are at most "indirect." In answer the Government argues that the statute regulates neither production nor consumption, but only marketing; and, in the alternative, that if the Act does go beyond the regulation of marketing it is sustainable as a "necessary and proper" implementation of the power of Congress over interstate commerce.

* * * * *

For nearly a century,...decisions of this Court dealt rarely with questions of what Congress might do in the exercise of its granted power under the Clause and almost entirely with the permissibility of state activity which it was claimed discriminated against or burdened interstate commerce. During this period there was perhaps little occasion for the affirmative exercise of the commerce power, and the influence of the Clause on American life and law was a negative one, resulting almost wholly from its operation as a restraint upon the powers of the states.

* * * * *

It was not until 1887, with the enactment of the Interstate Commerce Act, that the commerce power began to exert positive influence in American law and life. This...was followed in 1890 by the Sherman Anti-Trust Act and, thereafter, mainly after 1903, by many others....

When it first dealt with this new legislation, the Court adhered to its earlier pronouncements, and allowed but little scope to the power of Congress.......[H]owever, other cases called forth broader interpretations of the Commerce Clause destined to supersede the earlier ones, and to bring about a return to the principles first enunciated by Chief Justice Marshall[.]......It was soon demonstrated that the effects of many kinds of intrastate activity upon interstate commerce were such as to make them a proper subject of federal regulation.

[Thus,] even if [Filburn's] activity be local and though it may not be regarded as commerce, it may still, whatever its nature, be reached by Congress if it exerts a substantial economic effect on interstate commerce, and this irrespective of whether such effect is what might at some earlier time have been defined as "direct" or "indirect."

* * * * *

The effect of consumption of homegrown wheat on interstate commerce is due to the fact that it constitutes the most variable factor in the disappearance of the wheat crop. Consumption on the farm where grown appears to vary in an amount greater than 20 percent of average production.......That [Filburn's] own contribution to the demand for wheat may be trivial by itself is not enough to remove him from the scope of federal regulation where, as here, his contribution, taken together with that of many others similarly situated, is far from trivial....

It is well established by decisions of this Court that the power to regulate commerce includes the power to regulate the prices at which commodities in that commerce are dealt and practices affecting such prices. One of the primary purposes of the Act in question was to increase the market price of wheat, and to that end to limit the volume thereof that could affect the market. It can hardly be denied that a factor of such volume and variability as home-consumed wheat would have a substantial influence on price and market conditions. This may arise because being in marketable condition such wheat overhangs the market and if induced by rising prices tends to flow into the market and check price increases. But if we assume that it is never marketed, it supplies a need of the man who grew it which would otherwise be reflected by purchases in the open market....This record leaves us in no doubt Congress may properly have considered that wheat consumed on the farm where grown if wholly outside the scheme of regulation would have a substantial effect in defeating and obstructing its purpose to stimulate trade therein at increased prices.

* * * * *

Judgment for Wickard, reversing the decision of the lower court.

The third theory by which the Court expanded the Commerce Clause power is the "commerce-prohibiting" technique (police power regulations) which allows Congress to regulate intrastate police matters (public health, safety, morals, and welfare matters) that have some effect on interstate commerce. Thus, the Tenth Amendment no longer acts as an independent limitation on congressional authority over interstate commerce. As a result, Congress is completely free to impose whatever conditions it wishes upon the privilege of engaging in an activity that affects interstate commerce, so long as the conditions themselves violate no independent prohibition.

The era of the "commerce-prohibiting" technique was launched with the case of *Heart of Atlanta Motel v. United States* (1964), where the Court held that Congress has the power to prohibit racial discrimination in hotels and motels serving interstate travelers.

Heart of Atlanta Motel v. United States 379 U.S. 241 (1964)

The owner of a motel, who refused to rent rooms to blacks, despite the Civil Rights Act of 1964, brought an action to have the Civil Rights Act of 1964 declared unconstitutional. The motel owner alleged that Congress, in passing the act, had exceeded its power to regulate commerce.

CLARK, J....This is a declaratory judgment action...attacking the constitutionality of Title II of the Civil Rights Act of 1964....Appellant owns and operates the Heart of Atlanta Motel which has 216 rooms available to transient guests....It is readily accessible to interstate highways 75 and 85 and state highways 23 and 41. Appellant solicits patronage from outside the State of Georgia through various national advertising media, including magazines of national circulation; it maintains over 50 billboards and highway signs within the State, soliciting patronage for the motel; it accepts convention trade from outside Georgia and approximately 75 percent of its registered guests are from out of State. Prior to passage of the Act the motel had followed a practice of refusing to rent rooms to Negroes, and it alleged that it intended to continue to do so. In an effort to perpetuate that policy this suit was filed....

The sole question posed is, therefore, the constitutionality of the Civil Rights Act of 1964 as applied to these facts. The legislative history of the Act indicates that Congress based the Act on Section 5 and the Equal Protection Clause of the Fourteenth Amendment as well as its power to regulate interstate commerce under Art. I, Sec. 8, cl. 3 of the Constitution.

The Senate Commerce Committee made it quite clear that the fundamental object of Title II was to vindicate "the deprivation of personal dignity that surely accompanies denials of equal access to public establishments." At the same time, however, it noted that such an objective has been and could be readily achieved "by congressional action based on the commerce power of the Constitution." Our study of the legislative record, made in the light of prior cases, has brought us to the conclusion that Congress possessed ample power in this regard, and we have therefore not considered the other grounds relied upon....

While the Act as adopted carried no congressional findings, the record of its passage through each house is replete with evidence of the burdens that discrimination by race or color places upon interstate commerce....This testimony included the fact that our people have become increasingly mobile with millions of all races traveling from State to State; that Negroes in particular have been the subject of discrimination in transient accommodations, having to travel great distances to secure the same; that often they have been unable to obtain accommodations and have had to call upon friends to put them up overnight....These exclusionary practices were found to be nationwide, the Under Secretary of Commerce testifying that there is "no question that this discrimination in the North still exists to a large degree" and in the West and Midwest as well....This testimony indicated a qualitative as well as quantitative effect on interstate travel by Negroes. The former was the obvious impairment of the Negro traveler's pleasure and convenience that resulted when he continually was uncertain of finding lodging. As for the latter, there was evidence that this uncertainty stemming from racial discrimination had the effect of discouraging travel on the part of a substantial portion of the Negro community....We shall not burden this opinion with further details since the voluminous testimony presents overwhelming evidence that discrimination by hotels and motels impedes interstate travel....

The power of Congress to deal with these obstructions depends on the meaning of the Commerce Clause....[T]he determinative test of the exercise of power by the Congress under the Commerce Clause is simply whether the activity sought to be regulated is "commerce which concerns more States than one" and has a real and substantial relation to the national interest....

* * * * *

That Congress was legislating against moral wrongs in many of these areas rendered its enactment no less valid. In framing Title II of this Act Congress was also dealing with what it considered a moral problem. But that fact does not detract from the overwhelming evidence of the disruptive effect that racial discrimination has had on commercial intercourse....

It is said that the operation of the motel here is of a purely local character. But, assuming this to be true, "if it is interstate commerce that feels the pinch, it does not matter how local the operation that applies the squeeze." Thus the power of Congress to promote interstate commerce also includes the power to regulate the local incidents thereof, including local activities in both the States of origin and destination, which might have a substantial and harmful effect upon that commerce....

We, therefore, conclude that the action of the Congress in the adoption of the Act as applied here to a motel which concededly serves interstate travelers is within the power granted it by the Commerce Clause of the Constitution, as interpreted by this Court for 140 years....

Judgment in favor of the United States.

The federal power to regulate commerce acts to prevent states from interfering with federal regulation or burdening interstate commerce. Therefore, if the federal government imposes a requirement that interstate carriers must use a particular safety apparatus, a state is prohibited from requiring the use of a different device.

Without a doubt, the states hold a strong interest in regulating activities within their borders. Part of this inherent sovereignty includes the possession of police powers. The states may exercise police powers to regulate private activities to protect or promote the public safety, health, morals, or general welfare of their citizens. However, when that state regulation places some burden on interstate commerce, the courts will balance the state's interest in promulgating the law against the burden placed on interstate commerce.

It is difficult to determine the outcome when a court applies this balancing test. State laws that are enacted to create a public benefit for the local citizenry carry a strong presumption of validity. However, in two cases the Court invalidated state regulations limiting the length of trailer trucks traveling on interstate highways. In the first case, *Raymond Motor Transportation, Inc. v. Rice* (434 U.S. 429 (1978)), the Court determined that the statutes "place[d] a substantial burden on interstate commerce and they cannot be said to make more than the most speculative contribution to highway safety." (434 U.S. 429, 447.)

In *Kassel v. Consolidated Freightways Corp. of Delaware* (450 U.S. 662 (1981)), the Court went even further by concluding that an Iowa law prohibiting 65-foot double trailers from entering the state discriminated against interstate commerce and was, therefore, invalid.

When congressional intent relating to preemption is vague, courts apply a test. Before ruling that federal law preempts a state law, courts first decide whether Congress intended to supersede state law. Usually such intent is found if the federal law is so pervasive, comprehensive, or detailed that the states have no room to augment or add to it. Hence, the federal law "occupies the field." Obviously, even the test itself is subject to interpretation; the use of guiding words such as 'pervasive' and 'comprehensive' are open to a wide range of meaning as the following case illustrates.

City of Burbank v. Lockheed Air Terminal, Inc.
411 U.S. 624 (1973)

The owner-operator of the Hollywood-Burbank Airport brought suit against the City of Burbank to enjoin enforcement of a city ordinance forbidding any pure jet aircraft from taking off from the airport between 11 p.m. of one day and 7 a.m. of the next, and forbidding the airport operator from permitting any such takeoffs. The District Court enjoined enforcement of the ordinance, and the appellate court affirmed.

DOUGLAS, J. The Court in Cooley v. Board of Wardens, 12 How 299, first stated the rule of pre-emption which is the critical issue in the present case. Speaking through Mr. Justice Curtis, it said: "Now the power to regulate commerce, embraces a vast field, containing not only many, but exceedingly various subjects, quite unlike in their nature; some imperatively demanding a single uniform rule, operating equally on the commerce of the United States in every port; and some, like the subject now in question, as imperatively demanding that diversity, which alone can meet the local necessities of navigation.

"…Whatever subjects of this power are in their nature national, or admit only of one uniform system, or plan of regulation, may justly be said to be of such a nature as to require exclusive legislation by Congress."

* * * * *

Section 1508 provides in part, "The United States of America is declared to possess and exercise complete and exclusive national sovereignty in the airspace of the United States…" By Sec. 1348(a), (c) the Administrator of the Federal Aviation Administration (FAA) has been given broad authority to regulate the use of the navigable airspace, "in order to insure the safety of aircraft and the efficient utilization of such airspace…" and "for the protection of persons and property on the ground.…"

The Solicitor General, though arguing against pre-emption, concedes that as respects "airspace management" there is pre-emption. That, however, is a fatal concession, for as the District Court found: "The imposition of curfew ordinances on a nationwide basis would result in a bunching of flights in those hours immediately preceding the curfew. This bunching of flights during these hours would have the twofold effect of increasing an already serious congestion problem and actually increasing, rather than relieving, the noise problem by increasing flights in the period of greatest annoyance to surrounding communities. Such a result is totally inconsistent with the objectives of the federal statutory and regulatory scheme." It also found "[t]he imposition of curfew ordinances on a nationwide basis would cause a serious loss of efficiency in the use of the navigable airspace."

* * * * *

There is, to be sure, no express provision of pre-emption in the 1972 [Noise Control] Act. That, however, is not decisive. As we stated in Rice v. Santa Fe Elevator Corp., 331 U.S. 218, 230:

"Congress legislated here in a field which the States have traditionally occupied.…So we start with the assumption that the historic police powers of the States were not to be superseded by the Federal Act unless that was the clear and manifest purpose of Congress…Such a purpose may be evidenced in several ways. The scheme of federal regulation may be so pervasive as to make reasonable the inference that Congress left no room for the States to supplement it.…Or the Act of Congress may touch a field in which the federal interest is so dominant that the federal system will be assumed to preclude enforcement of state laws on the same subject.…Likewise, the object sought to be obtained by the federal law and the character of obligations imposed by it may reveal the same purpose.…Or the state policy may produce a result inconsistent with the objective of the federal statute."

It is the pervasive nature of the scheme of federal regulation of aircraft noise that leads us to conclude that this is pre-emption. As Mr. Justice Jackson stated, concurring in Northwest Airlines, Inc. v. Minnesota, 322 U.S. 292, 303: "Federal control is intensive and exclusive. Planes do not wander about in the sky like vagrant clouds. They move only by federal permission, subject to federal inspection, in the hands of federally certified personnel and under an intricate system of federal command. The moment a ship taxis onto a runway it is caught up in an elaborate and detailed system of controls."

Both the Senate and House Committees included in their Reports clear statements that the bills would not change the existing pre-emption rule. The House Report stated: "No provision of the bill is intended to alter in any way the relationship between the authority of the Federal Government and that of the State and local governments that existed with respect to matters covered by section 611 of the Federal Aviation Act of 1958 prior to the enactment of the bill." The Senate Report stated: "States and local governments are pre-empted from establishing or enforcing noise emission standards for aircraft unless such standards are identical to standards prescribed under this bill. This does not address responsibilities or powers of airport operators, and no provision of the bill is intended to alter in any way the relationship between the authority of the Federal government and that of State and local governments that existed with respect to matters covered by section 611 of the Federal Aviation Act of 1958 prior to the enactment of the bill."

These statements do not avail [City of Burbank]. Prior to the 1972 Act, section 611(a) provided that the Administrator "shall prescribe and amend such rules and regulations as he may find necessary to provide for the control and abatement of aircraft noise and sonic boom." Under section 611(b)(3) the Administrator was required to "consider whether any proposed standard, rule, or regulation is consistent with the highest degree of safety in air commerce or air transportation in the public interest." When the legislation which added this section to the Federal Aviation Act was considered [it was asked] whether the proposed legislation would "to any degree preempt State and local government regulation of aircraft noise and sonic boom." The Secretary [of Transportation] requested leave to submit a written opinion [in which] he stated:

"The courts have held that the Federal Government presently preempts the field of noise regulation insofar as it involves controlling the flight of aircraft....HR3400 would merely expand the Federal Government's role in a field already preempted. It would not change this preemption. State and local governments will remain unable to use their police powers to control aircraft noise by regulating the flight of aircraft."

According to the Senate Report, it was "not the intent of the committee in recommending this legislation to effect any change in the existing apportionment of powers between the Federal and State and local governments," and the Report concurred in the views set forth by the Secretary in his letter.

* * * * *

Our prior cases on preemption are not precise guide-lines in the present controversy, for each case turns on the peculiarities and special features of the federal regulatory scheme in question. Control of noise is of course deep seated in the police power of the States. Yet the pervasive control vested in EPA and in FAA under the 1972 Act seems to us to leave no room for local curfews or other local controls. What the ultimate remedy may be for aircraft noise which plagues many communities and tens of thousands of people is not known. The procedures under the 1972 Act are under way. In addition, the Administrator has imposed a variety of regulations relating to takeoff and landing procedures and runway preferences. The Federal Aviation Act requires a delicate balance between safety and efficiency, and the protection of persons on the ground. Any regulations adopted by the Administrator to control noise pollution must be consistent with the "highest degree of safety." The interdependence of these factors requires a uniform and exclusive system of federal regulation if the congressional objectives underlying the Federal Aviation Act are to be fulfilled.

If we were to uphold the Burbank ordinance and a significant number of municipalities followed suit, it is obvious that fractionalized control of the timing of take-offs and landings would severely limit the flexibility of the FAA in controlling air traffic flow. The difficulties of scheduling flights to avoid congestion and the concomitant decrease in safety would be compounded. In 1960 the FAA rejected a proposed restriction on jet operations at the Los Angeles airport between 10 p.m. and 7 a.m. because such restrictions could "create critically serious problems to all air transportation patterns....This decision, announced in 1960, remains peculiarly within the competence of the FAA, supplemented now by the input of the EPA. We are not at liberty to diffuse the powers given by Congress to FAA and EPA by letting the States or municipalities in on the planning. If that change is to be made, Congress alone must do it.

AFFIRMED.

A number of recent cases heard in the U.S. Supreme Court held that the federal government enacted laws beyond its powers to regulate interstate commerce. In *U.S. v. Lopez,* 115 S.Ct. 1624 (1995), the Court invalidated the Gun-Free School Zone Act. This statute made it a crime to knowingly possess a firearm in areas around schools. For the same reason, the Court held in *U.S. v. Morrison,* 120 S.Ct. 1740 (2000), that the Violence Against Women Act was unconstitutional.

State and local laws may not unduly burden interstate commerce. Doing so violates the Commerce Clause. If the federal government chooses not to regulate an area that it may constitutionally regulate (the so-called, dormant Commerce Clause), but a state regulates in that area, the statute it enacts may not unduly burden interstate commerce.

Huish Detergents, Inc. v. Warren County, Kentucky; Monarch Environmental, Inc.
214 F.3D 707 (2000)

Huish Detergents, Inc., challenges an ordinance enacted by Warren County, Kentucky, and a franchise agreement entered into by Warren County and Monarch Environmental, Inc., pursuant to which Monarch is the exclusive contractor for collecting and processing all the solid waste generated in the city of Bowling Green, Kentucky. Huish's claim is that the ordinance and companion agreement violate both the so-called "dormant" Commerce Clause of the United States Constitution and the Kentucky Constitution. The district court dismissed the suit under Fed.R.Civ.P. 12(b)(6) for failure to state a claim upon which relief may be granted. Because we hold that the district court erred in dismissing Huish's Commerce Clause claim, we reverse.

I.

Warren County, Kentucky, issued a Request for Proposal (RFP) and considered competitive bids from trash haulers interested in collecting and processing all municipal solid waste in Bowling Green, Kentucky. The County awarded the contract to Monarch and formalized the relationship in a written "franchise agreement." Under the franchise agreement, Monarch has the exclusive right for five years (1995–2000) to collect and process all municipal solid waste generated in Bowling Green. Monarch is obligated to operate the city's transfer station to process the waste it collects and must dispose of all waste at a landfill "approved and permitted by the State of Kentucky," effectively prohibiting the use of out-of-state disposal sites. The agreement can be renewed for three terms of five years each and will renew automatically for a five-year term absent prior notice by one of the parties.

The franchise agreement provides that all residential, commercial, and industrial entities that generate municipal solid in Bowling Green must employ Monarch to remove the waste; waste generators may not remove their own waste, and they are prohibited from using any company other than Monarch. Monarch bills its Bowling Green customers directly according to a fee schedule fixed by the franchise agreement; Monarch is solely responsible for collecting payment. The County receives a portion of the revenues Monarch generates servicing Bowling Green businesses and residents, and Monarch removes the waste generated at the County's own buildings at no charge.

On the same day that the franchise agreement became effective, the County passed an ordinance "executing" the franchise agreement and incorporating its provisions by reference. In essence, the ordinance transforms the franchise agreement provisions into law.

Huish operates a laundry detergent manufacturing facility in Bowling Green. Not surprisingly, this facility generates considerable solid waste. Under the ordinance and franchise agreement, Huish must use Monarch to remove this waste. Huish filed this lawsuit seeking to invalidate the County's ordinance/franchise scheme, claiming that the scheme violates the Commerce Clause, 42 U.S.C. §1983, and section 164 of the Kentucky Constitution.

The district court dismissed Huish's complaint pursuant to Fed.R.Civ.P. 12(b)(6). The court first concluded that the County is not entitled to Eleventh Amendment immunity and that Huish has the requisite standing to bring suit. With respect to the Commerce Clause claim, the court took the view that the County engaged in two separate challenged activities: (1) "taking over" the local waste collection, processing, and disposal markets; and (2) granting Monarch the exclusive right to collect, process, and dispose of waste generated in Bowling Green.

The court began its analysis of Huish's Commerce Clause claim by examining the County's decision to prohibit residents from independently purchasing waste collection, processing, or disposal services on the open market, which the court described as the County's "takeover" of the local waste collection market. The court held, as a preliminary matter, that the County was not acting as a market participant in taking this action and, therefore, its action was subject to Commerce Clause restrictions. Proceeding with a "dormant Commerce Clause" analysis, the district court concluded that the County's "takeover" of Bowling Green's waste collection, processing, and disposal market did not violate the dormant Commerce Clause. The court reasoned that the "takeover" did not discriminate against interstate commerce and that the burden imposed on interstate commerce was not excessive in relation to the benefits for the County.

The court then dismissed Huish's federal claims with prejudice and its pendent state law claim without prejudice. This appeal followed.

II.

A. STANDING

At the outset, we must address the defendants' contention that Huish lacks standing to bring this action. The defendants claim that, inasmuch as Huish is not a member of the solid waste industry, its injuries do not fall within the zone of interests protected under the Commerce Clause. The district court concluded that Huish has standing, and we agree.

In cases such as this involving a constitutional claim, the plaintiff must satisfy two tests for standing: first, it must meet basic Article III constitutional requirements; and second, the plaintiff's injury must fall within the "zone of interests" protected by the constitutional guarantee.

To establish Article III standing, Huish must demonstrate: (1) an injury in fact that is actual or threatened; (2) a causal connection between the defendants' conduct and the alleged injury; and (3) a substantial likelihood that the injury will be redressed by a favorable decision. Lujan v. Defenders of Wildlife, 504 U.S. 555, 560–561 (1992); Coyne v. American Tobacco Co., 183 F.3d 488, 494 (6th Cir. 1999). "At the pleading stage, general factual allegations of injury resulting from the defendant's conduct may suffice, for on a motion to dismiss we presum[e] that general allegations embrace those specific facts that are necessary to support the claim." Lujan, 504 U.S. at 561.

We find that Huish satisfies the requirements for standing under Article III, and, indeed, the defendants do not argue otherwise. Huish alleged an actual injury as a result of the County's ordinance and agreement with Monarch, in consequence of which Huish is forced to pay Monarch more to collect, process, and dispose of its waste than Huish would spend if it could purchase one or more of these services from a company operating out-of-state or perform the work itself. The fact that Huish is not a member of the waste industry does not undermine the causal connection between the challenged scheme and Huish's injury as a consumer.

* * * * * *

Huish must also satisfy a prudential limitation on our jurisdiction—a further standing requirement—by showing that the interest it seeks to protect "arguably fall[s] within the zone of interests protected or regulated by the statutory provision or constitutional guarantee invoked in the suit." Bennett v. Spear, 520 U.S. 154, 162 (1997); see also Association of Data Processing Serv. Orgs., Inc. v. Camp, 397 U.S. 150, 153 (1970). In this case, the constitutional guarantee arises under the Commerce Clause, which is designed to prevent economic protectionism and insure the free movement of goods between State borders, prohibiting "laws that would excite…jealousies and retaliatory measures" among the several States. C & A Carbone, Inc. v. Town of Clarkstown, New York, 511 U.S. 383, 390 (1994). Huish argues that it meets this additional standing requirement because it has pleaded an injury that falls within the zone of interests protected by the Commerce Clause, and we agree. Huish seeks to protect its right to contract with a company that can transport its waste for out-of-state processing and/or disposal. In making this claim, Huish is asserting its individual right as a consumer to purchase waste processing and disposal services across State boundaries, an interest that falls squarely within the zone of interests protected by the Commerce Clause. The Clause protects not only producers, but also consumers like Huish who " 'may look to the free competition from every producing area in the Nation to protect [it] from exploitation by any.' " Dennis v. Higgins, 498 U.S. 439 (1991) (quoting H.P. Hood & Sons, Inc. v. DuMond, 336 U.S. 525, 539 (1949)).

* * * * * *

For these reasons, we hold that Huish has standing. Because the County does not challenge the district court's holding on eleventh Amendment immunity, we do not consider that issue here.

* * * * * *

The "Dormant" Commerce Clause

The Commerce Clause grants Congress the power to regulate commerce among the States. It reads, with disarming simplicity: "[The congress shall have Power] [t]o regulate Commerce with foreign Nations, and among the several States, and with the Indian Tribes." U.S. Const., art. I, §8, cl. 3. As interpreted by the Supreme Court, the Clause, by negative implication, restricts the States' ability to regulate interstate commerce. See CTS Corp. v. Dynamics Corp. of Am., 481 U.S. 69, 87 (1987). There is, of course, no "dormant" clause to be found in the text of clause 3 of section 8 of article I. Clause 3 is the Commerce Clause; the judge-made notion that a negative implication is subsumed in the affirmative declaration of clause 3 that Congress has power "[t]o regulate Commerce…among the several States" should more properly be called the dormant aspect or component of the Commerce Clause. But it is too late in the day to rewrite the substantial case law that speaks, however inaccurately, of "the dormant Commerce Clause." Instead, we can only yield to this inaccurate but settled usage.

The Supreme Court has interpreted the Commerce Clause to "prohibit [ ] States from 'advanc[ing] their own commercial interests by curtailing the movement of articles of commerce, either into or out of the state.' " Fort Gratiot Sanitary Landfill, Inc. v. Michigan Dep't of Natural Resources, 504 U.S. 353, (1992) quoting H.P. Hood & Sons, 336 U.S. at 535. And this court, among others, has construed the Clause as limiting the regulatory activity of counties and cities as well as States. Waste Mgt., Inc. of Tennessee v. Metropolitan Gov't of Nashville and Davidson Cty., 130 F.3d 731, 735 (6th Cir.1997), cert. Denied, 523 U.S. 1094 (1998). Thus, where this opinion refers to "States," the defendant, Warren County, is included in this designation.

If an ordinance discriminates against interstate commerce by treating in-state and out-of-state interests differently, benefiting the former and burdening the latter, it is per se invalid unless the State has "no other means to advance a legitimate local interest." Carbone, 511 U.S. at 392; see also Waste Mgt., 130 F.3d at 735. On the other hand, if the law regulates evenhandedly, it will be upheld unless the burden it imposes on interstate commerce is

" 'clearly excessive in relation to the putative local benefits.' " Carbone, 511 U.S. at 390 (quoting Pike v. Bruce Church, Inc., 397 U.S. 137 (1970)).

As a preliminary matter, there is no question that a State law restricting the interstate travel of waste implicates the Commerce Clause, and, as we have indicated, this is equally so of a local ordinance. Any doubt about this fact was laid to rest by the Supreme Court in 1978. City of Philadelphia v. New Jersey, 437 U.S. 617, 621

(1978). Since then, the Court has reiterated that garbage is not valuable, in and of itself, but it is a "profitable business" because "its possessor must pay to get rid of it. In other words, the article of commerce is not so much the solid waste itself, but rather the service of [collecting], processing and disposing of it." Carbone, 511 U.S. at 390–91.

Whether the business arrangements between...generators of waste and the...operator of a waste [processing or] disposal site are viewed as sales of garbage or purchases of transportation and disposal services, the commercial transactions unquestionably have an interstate character. The Commerce Clause thus imposes some constraints on [a State's] ability to regulate these transactions. Fort Gratiot, 504 U.S. at 359 (internal quotation marks omitted).

* * * * * *

In Carbone, 511 U.S. 383, the Supreme Court held that a so-called flow control ordinance that required all solid waste in the town to be processed at a designated transfer station before leaving the town violated the dormant Commerce Clause. The town of Clarkstown, New York, had agreed to close its landfill and build a new solid waste transfer station. Id. at 387. A local private contractor constructed the transfer station and agreed to operate it for five years, at which time the town would buy the station for a nominal price. Id. To finance the transfer station, the town guaranteed a minimum waste flow to the station and permitted the contractor to charge a "tipping fee" to haulers depositing waste at the station. The town chose the flow control ordinance as the mechanism for ensuring the minimum waste flow.

Carbone operated a recycling center of its own in Clarkstown, performing functions equivalent to those performed at the new transfer station. Carbone challenged the flow control ordinance on dormant Commerce Clause grounds. In its defense, Clarkstown pointed to its need to finance the transfer station. Id. at 386. The Court sided with Carbone. The Court explained that by preventing any company "except the favored local operator" from processing waste generated in the town, the flow control ordinance deprived out-of-state businesses of access to the local market. Id. at 389. In other words, the offending ordinance "hoards solid waste, and the demand to get rid of it, for the benefit of the preferred processing facility." Id. at 392. The Court held that the ordinance's discrimination against out-of-state waste processors was per se invalid, rejecting Clarkstown's argument that it had no other means to advance its interest in ensuring the long-term viability of the transfer facility. Id. at 392–94.

* * * * * *

2. The Market Participation Exception

So-called dormant Commerce Clause principles are not implicated when the State's activity can be characterized as "market participa[tion]," rather than market regulation. White v. Massachusetts Council of Constr. Employers, Inc., 460 U.S. 204 (1983). "There is no indication of a constitutional plan to limit the ability of the States themselves to operate freely in the free market." Reeves, Inc. v. Stake, 447 U.S. 429 (1980). The market participation exception applies equally to States and municipalities. See White, 460 U.S. 204. Consequently, if we determine that Warren County was acting as a market participant with regard to any of its challenged actions, we need not proceed to consider whether the actions burdened interstate commerce in violation of the Commerce Clause. See id. at 210.

The market participation inquiry is limited to "whether the challenged program constitute[s] direct state participation in the market." Id. at 208. The Supreme Court has applied the market participation exception to the dormant component of the Commerce Clause only in cases where the State was spending "its own funds," see White, 460 U.S. at 214, Hughes v. Alexandria Scrap Corp., 426 U.S. 794 (1976), or selling a resource that it owned or produced, see Reeves, 447 U.S. 429. Of course, the State has no funds of "its own," only funds it has exacted from taxpayers and holds in trust for all of its citizens. The reference in these cases is to taxpayer funds in the hands of the State, or in this case, the County. White, Hughes, and Reeves stand for the proposition that, for purposes of analysis under the dormant Commerce Clause, a State acting in its proprietary capacity as a purchaser or seller may 'favor its own citizens over others.' " Camps Newfound/ Owatonna, Inc. v. Town of Harrison, Maine, 520 U.S. 564 (1997) (quoting Hughes, 426 U.S. at 810) (emphasis added).

The Supreme Court recently observed that the market participation exception makes sense because the evil addressed by [the Commerce Clause]—the prospect that States will use custom duties, exclusionary trade regulations, and other exercises of governmental power (as opposed to the expenditure of state resources) to favor their own citizens—is entirely absent where the States are buying and selling in the market. College Sav. Bank v. Florida Prepaid Postsecondary Educ. Expense Bd., 527 U.S. 666 (1999) (citation omitted).

3. Huish's Challenges to the Ordinance/Franchise Scheme

To address Huish's Commerce Clause claim, it is imperative that we properly characterize Huish's challenges into two categories: (1) the County's "takeover" of the private market for waste collection, processing, and disposal; and (2) the County's award of an exclusive franchise to Monarch for collecting, processing, and disposing of municipal waste. As to (1), the court held that the County was not a market participant and therefore not entitled to the market participation exception, but that its "takeover" of the waste-services market in Bowling Green did not violate the Commerce Clause. As to (2), the court held that the County was acting as a market participant in awarding an "exclusive franchise" to Monarch. Therefore, the court did not proceed to consider whether this "franchise" violated the Commerce Clause.

The district court correctly observed that it must evaluate each challenged activity separately, see USA Recycling, Inc. v. Town of Babylon, 66 F.3d 1272 (2d Cir.1995), but having said so, the court failed to do so. Specifically, by grouping several challenged activities together under the heading of a County "takeover," the court overlooked the unique aspects of two provisions of the ordinance/franchise scheme: (1) the requirement that Monarch process all waste at one location within Bowling Green; and (2) the prohibition on out-of-state disposal. We also note that, while we agree that Monarch acted as the County's "exclusive franchisee" for waste collection and processing in Bowling Green, the district court erred in characterizing Monarch as the County's "exclusive franchisee" for waste disposal. Monarch apparently was not involved in waste disposal at all, but rather purchased these services from a third party.

We identify Huish's three challenges to the ordinance/franchise scheme as follows: (1) the designation of a single in-state processing station for municipal waste; (2) the prohibition of out-of-state waste disposal; and (3) the award of an "exclusive franchise" to Monarch for waste collection and processing. At this stage of the proceedings, Huish's lawsuit can survive the Rule 12(b)(6) motion if any one of these three challenges states a valid Commerce Clause claim.

a. Designation of a Single In-State Processing Station

The defendants contend that the County acted as a market participant in requiring Monarch to process all municipal waste at a single Bowling Green transfer station. According to the defendants, the challenged restriction is not subject to Commerce Clause scrutiny because it appeared in an "agreement" with Monarch, rather than in an ordinance. We disagree with both the factual and legal premises of this argument and hold that the County was not acting as a market participant when it designated a single in-state processing site for all municipal waste.

First, as a factual matter, the defendants overlook the relationship between the ordinance and franchise agreement scheme. The ordinance did contain the challenged restriction because it incorporated the full franchise agreement by reference. More importantly the distinction that the defendants identify is legally irrelevant. The market participant exception does not come into play simply because a municipality labels its action as an "agreement." Rather, we must determine whether the municipality was acting in a proprietary capacity as a purchaser or seller with regard to the challenged action.

Here, it is clear that the County was not acting in a proprietary capacity in forcing all municipal waste to flow through the city's transfer station. The County was not "purchasing" the processing services with public funds, nor was it "selling" its own processing services. These factors routinely govern courts' analysis of the market participant exception in the waste context. See USA Recycling, 66 F.3d at 1288–89; SSC, 66 F.3d at 515–16; GSW, Inc. v. Long Cty., Georgia, 999 F.2d 1508 (11th Cir. 1993).

* * * * *

Thus, the market participation exception does not shield Warren County's action from scrutiny under the Commerce Clause.

Carbone controls the remainder of our analysis. To be sure, the essentially unitary ordinance/franchise scheme in this case was not identical to the flow control ordinance in Carbone. The county in Carbone required that all waste be processed at the town's transfer station. Here, on the other hand, the County "contracted" with Monarch to collect and then process all municipal waste. But the "contract" went further than that. Warren County dictated where Monarch must provide the processing services—at the city's transfer station and nowhere else. This explicit condition is the functional equivalent of the flow control ordinance in Carbone and discriminated against the interstate flow of waste for processing out-of-state.

Such discrimination constitutes a per se violation of the dormant aspect of the Commerce Clause, "absent the clearest showing that the unobstructed flow of interstate commerce itself is unable to solve the local problem." Carbone, 511 U.S. at 393.

* * * * * *

We hold, therefore, that for all these reasons, Huish's Commerce Clause claim survives the defendants' Rule 12(b)(6) motion. While this holding alone requires that we reverse the district court's judgment, we will proceed to consider Huish's remaining arguments, at lest to the extent that the district court purported to address them.

b. Prohibition on Out-of-State Disposal

The County did not act as a market participant in prohibiting out-of-state disposal of Bowling Green's municipal waste because the County neither bought nor sold disposal services with taxpayer funds. Indeed, even if the County's "agreement" with Monarch constituted market participation in either the waste collection or processing markets, the market participant exception would not insulate the County's regulation of the separate waste disposal market, which is downstream from the collection and processing markets. See South-Central Timber Dev., Inc. v. Wunnicke, 467 U.S. 82, 97–98 (1984) (plurality opinion); SSC, 66 F.3d at 515–16....The County's prohibition on out-of-state disposal, therefore, is subject to the restrictions of the Commerce Clause.

* * * * *

c. Award of "Exclusive Franchise" to a Single In-State Waste Collector and Processor

The district court declined to address the merits of Huish's challenge to Monarch's "exclusive franchise" for waste collection and processing on the grounds that the County was a market participant. The court reasoned that the County, through its franchise agreement, effectively "purchased" waste collection and processing services. We respectfully disagree.

The County used its regulatory power—not its proprietary purchasing power—to retain Monarch's services by requiring the County's residents to pay for those services. Stated another way, the County used its regulatory power to grant an exclusive right to collect and process Bowling Green waste, a result that no private party could accomplish on an open market.

* * * * *

Given our holdings in subsections (a) and (b) above, and our understanding that the district court did not specifically address whether the County violated the Commerce Clause by designating Monarch as the exclusive waste collector and process or for municipal waste, it is unnecessary for us to decide this issue here.

* * * * *

III.

The district court's dismissal of this action is REVERSED, and the case is REMANDED for further proceedings consistent with this opinion. Because we are reversing the dismissal of the Commerce Clause claim, we also REVERSE the dismissal of the section 1983 and state law claims. They too are REMANDED.

THE TAXING POWER

Congress can use taxation as a necessary and proper means for effectuating its delegated powers. Article I, section 8 of the Constitution states that "The Congress shall have Power To lay and collect Taxes, Duties, Imposts and Excises." At least in form, this is a fiscal power, not a regulatory power. Note, however, nearly any measure enacted in the form of a tax will have at least an incidental regulatory effect. For instance, if an excise tax on cigarettes is enacted, people may smoke fewer cigarettes. If the regulatory impact of the tax is one, which could be achieved directly, by use of one of the other enumerated powers (e.g. the Commerce Clause); the fact that the tax has a regulatory effect is not of constitutional significance. Conversely, if the regulatory effect is one that could not have been achieved directly, then the tax may be stricken as an invalid disguised regulation. This problem of distinguishing between taxes that are valid revenue raising measures, and taxes that have no real revenue purpose and that are therefore invalid disguised regulations, rarely surface in modern times. As long as the federal law is revenue producing on its face, the Court will not probe to discover hidden regulatory motives and will not be overly concerned with whether the effects of the law trespass on the traditional state police power domain.

THE SPENDING POWER

While Congress has no express power to legislate for the general welfare, Article I, section 8, gives Congress the power "to lay and collect Taxes...to pay the Debts and provide for the common Defense and general Welfare of the United States." One can view the federal taxing power as a stick and, in turn, the federal spending power as a reward. Congress's power to spend is very broad; it can be used to promote regulatory ends for the general welfare and sometimes for particular purposes.

Since the 1940s, congressional spending power regulation has been consistently upheld. However, the Supreme Court has viewed with a critical eye the use of the spending power for less than a general purpose. The exercise of the spending power must serve a general public purpose and not be directed at a specific interest. When Congress conditions the receipt of federal funds on specific requirements, it must do so unambiguously. Moreover, any condition must be reasonably related to the purpose for which the federal monies are spent. Arguably, federal spending power regulation is not as intrusive as other forms of federal regulation since a state has the option of not complying with a spending regulation and decide not to receive the federal funds.

EXAMPLE:

Congress, in order to prevent drivers under the age of 21 from drinking, withholds federal highway funds from states that permit individuals younger than 21 to purchase or possess in public any alcoholic beverage. South Dakota attacks the statute on the grounds that this condition interferes with its own exclusive power under the Tenth and Twenty-First Amendments.

Held, that the statute is valid. Even if, arguendo, direct congressional setting of the drinking age for the entire country would be unconstitutional, Congress's indirect use of its conditional spending power to achieve the same results is permissible. *South Dakota v. Dole*, 483 U.S. 203 (1987).

DUE PROCESS CLAUSE

The cardinal limitations against governmental interference are found in the first ten amendments of the Constitution commonly called the Bill of Rights. Their principal purpose is to protect individuals and businesses against various sorts of interference and restraints by the federal government. Today, virtually all the fundamental guarantees of the Bill of Rights have been incorporated into the Fourteenth Amendment thereby making them applicable to the states.

PROCEDURAL DUE PROCESS

Procedural due process focuses on the way the government acts and the enforcement mechanisms it uses. When the government deprives a person of an already acquired life, liberty or property interest, the Due Process Clauses of the Fifth and Fourteenth Amendments mandate procedural fairness. The requirements of procedural due process include the central premise that people must be given adequate notice of the government action to be instituted against them and some form of fair trial or hearing before that action can follow.

To set in motion the protections of due process, the government must deprive a person of life, liberty, or property. Within the concept of due process, the terms property and liberty encompass a broad and ill-defined range of freedoms. The key concept in defining property today is a legitimate claim of "entitlement" to a benefit, not simply some need, wish or presumption of it. When the government recognizes that an individual is legally entitled to a benefit, it thereby creates an expectancy that the benefit will not be arbitrarily terminated; thus, a property interest is created. "Property" can include interests in personal reputation or certain employment rights, e.g. termination of public employees only for good cause.

The concept of "liberty" embodies principles of freedom that lie at the roots of our legal system. Liberty interests generally fall under one of the following headings: (i) freedom from bodily restraint or "physical liberty"; (ii) substantive constitutional rights; and (iii) other fundamental freedoms.

When physical freedom is curtailed by commitment or imprisonment, liberty interests are burdened, thus, requiring extensive procedural protection. Similarly, "liberty" also includes incorporated rights such as freedom of expression and religion, as well as substantive rights including association and belief and privacy. Finally, due process "liberty" also encompasses a variety of fundamental interests relating to personal autonomy and choice.

In the following case, the Court's opinion focuses on the notice required by procedural due process when the government deprives a person of property.

Mennonite Board of Missions v. Adams
462 U.S. 791 (1983)

An Indiana Superior Court upheld the Indiana tax sale statute against constitutional challenge by the Mennonite Board of Missions (MBM), a mortgagee who contended that it had not received constitutionally adequate notice of the pending tax sale of and the opportunity to redeem the property following the tax sale since it was not informed of the pending sale either by the county auditor or by the mortgagor, who had been informed of the sale. The auditor, following the state law, had posted a notice of the sale in the county

courthouse and published a notice once each week for three consecutive weeks. The Indiana Court of Appeals affirmed.

On appeal, the U. S. Supreme Court reversed and remanded, holding that the manner of notice provided to the mortgagee did not meet the requirements of the due process clause of the Fourteenth Amendment.

MARSHALL, J....In Mullane v. Central Hanover Bank & Trust Co.,...this Court recognized that prior to an action which will affect an interest in life, liberty, or property protected by the Due Process Clause of the Fourteenth Amendment, a State must provide "notice reasonably calculated, under all circumstances, to apprise interested parties of the pendency of the action and afford them an opportunity to present their objections." Invoking this "elementary and fundamental requirement of due process," the Court held that published notice of an action to settle the accounts of a common trust fund was not sufficient to inform beneficiaries of the trust whose names and addresses were known. The Court explained that notice by publication was not reasonably calculated to provide actual notice of the pending proceeding and was therefore inadequate to inform those who could be notified by more effective means such as personal service or mailed notice[.]...

* * * * *

This case is controlled by the analysis in Mullane. To begin with, a mortgagee [MBM] possess (sic) a substantial property interest that is significantly affected by a tax sale....Ultimately, the tax sale may result in the complete nullification of the mortgagee's interest, since the purchaser acquires title free of all liens and other encumbrances at the conclusion of the redemption period.

Since a mortgagee clearly has a legally protected property interest, he is entitled to notice reasonably calculated to apprise him of a pending tax sale....When the mortgagee is identified in a mortgage that is publicly recorded, constructive notice by publication must be supplemented by notice mailed to the mortgagee's last known available address, or by personal service. However, unless the mortgagee is not reasonably identifiable, constructive notice alone does not satisfy the mandate of Mullane.

Neither notice by publication and posting, nor mailed notice to the property owner, are means "such as one desirous of actually informing the [mortgagee] might reasonably adopt to accomplish it."...Because they are designed primarily to attract prospective purchasers to the tax sale, publication and posting are unlikely to reach those who, although they have an interest in the property, do not make special efforts to keep abreast of such notices....Notice to the property owner, who is not in privity with his creditor and who has failed to take steps necessary to preserve his own property interest, also cannot be expected to lead to actual notice to the mortgagee....The county's use of these less reliable forms of notice is not reasonable where, as here, "an inexpensive and efficient mechanism such as mail service is available."...

Personal service or mailed notice is required even though sophisticated creditors have means at their disposal to discover whether property taxes have not been paid and whether tax sale proceedings are therefore likely to be initiated. In the first place, a mortgage need not involve a complex commercial transaction among knowledgeable parties, and it may well be the least sophisticated creditor whose security interest is threatened by a tax sale. More importantly, a party's ability to safeguard its interests does not relieve the State of its constitutional obligation.

...Notice by mail or other means as certain to ensure actual notice is a minimum constitutional precondition to a proceeding which will adversely affect the liberty or property interests of any party, whether unlettered or well versed in commercial practice, if its name and address are reasonably ascertainable.

We therefore conclude that the manner of notice provided to [MBM] did not meet the requirements of the Due Process Clause of the Fourteenth Amendment. Accordingly, the judgment of the Indiana Court of Appeals is reversed[.]

Judgment in favor of the Mennonite Board of Missions.

SUBSTANTIVE DUE PROCESS

Substantive due process focuses on the content or substance of a law, that is, the rules that establish standards of behavior for our society. Unless a law is compatible with the Constitution, it is a violation of substantive due process. Substantive due process requires that laws enacted by the government be clear and not overly broad.

In the context of economic regulations, it is very easy for state economic legislation to survive substantive due process attacks. The economic statute must be in furtherance of a legitimate state objective and there must be a minimally rational relation between the means chosen by the legislature and the state objective. In reality, virtually any health, safety or general welfare goal comes within the state's police power and is thus "legitimate." Further, the Court will presume that the statute is constitutional unless the legislation is completely arbitrary and irrational.

EXAMPLE:

The Court sustained against a due process attack on a federal prohibition on interstate shipment of "filled" milk, i.e., skimmed milk mixed with non-milk fat. The Court noted that Congress had acted upon findings of fact (e.g., committee reports) showing a public health danger from the filled milk. *U.S. v. Carolene Products Co.,* 304 U.S. 144 (1938).

TAKINGS CLAUSE

Another constitutional protection of a private economic interest is the ban on the taking of private property for the public use (i.e. a deprivation of an economic interest) without just compensation. Both the federal and state governments (via the Fifth and Fourteenth Amendments respectively) have the right to take private property for public use, provided it pays a fair price. This power is known as the right of "eminent domain."

Under the so-called Takings Clause, the government must pay for any property it "takes." On the other hand, if it merely "regulates" property under its police power, then it does not need to pay—even if the owner's use of the property or its value is substantially diminished. Thus, the crux of the majority of disputes involving the takings clause revolves around the whether the governmental action is a compensible "taking" or is it merely a non-compensible "regulation."

Generally, the problem of making this distinction arises in the context of land-use regulation. For a land use-regulation to avoid being a taking, it must "substantially advance legitimate state interests and it must not deny an owner economically viable use of his land. Examples of a legitimate state interests include maintaining a residential feeling through zoning, preserving landmarks, and protecting the environment. Few land use regulations are likely to be found to deny the owner all economically viable use of his land. However, regulations denying the owner the right to build any dwelling on the land would qualify.

When the government makes or authorizes a permanent physical occupation of the property, it automatically constitutes a taking, no matter how minor the interference with the owner's use and no matter how important the countervailing government interests.

EXAMPLE:

A state land use regulation prevented private property owners from rebuilding their house on their beach front property unless they first gave the public an easement across a sandy strip of their property adjacent to the ocean so that the public could get to and from the public beaches north and south of the owner's property (beaches which would be connected if the owner gave the public the required easement). Even though this easement would not have permitted the public to remain on the owners' land, the Court found that it constituted a physical occupation and thus a taking of the owners' property. *Nollan v. California Coastal Commission*, 483 U.S. 825 (1987).

Generally, the more drastic the reduction in value of the owner's property due to the government regulation, the more likely a taking is to be found. However, note that a very drastic diminution in value—almost certainly much more than 50%—is required.

The Takings Clause protects more than land and interests in land. Although the breadth of its scope is not clear, the clause has been applied to takings of personal property, liens, trade secrets, and contract rights.

THE CONTRACT CLAUSE

Under Article I, Section 10, "No State shall…pass any…Law impairing the Obligation of Contracts." This is another constitutional economic protection that effectively applies to both federal and state governments. The clause has different meaning depending on whether the government is impairing its own contract with a private party or contracts between private individuals.

If the state is trying to escape from its own financial obligations, then the court will strictly scrutinize this attempt and will only permit such an escape where a significant public need exists that cannot be reasonably handled any other way. However, when the state is re-writing contracts made between private parties, the judicial review is not so stringent. Here, even a substantial modification to contracts between private parties will be allowed so long as the state is acting reasonably in pursuit of a legitimate public purpose.

EXAMPLE:

If a state's economy is in turmoil causing widespread home mortgage foreclosures, the state probably may temporarily order a lower interest rate on home mortgages, or impose a moratorium on mortgage repayments, without violating the Contract Clause.

COMMERCIAL SPEECH AND THE FIRST AMENDMENT

The First Amendment provides, in part, that "Congress shall make no law…abridging the freedom of speech." For the purposes of this chapter, the First Amendment will be analyzed in the context of commercial speech only.

Communications that further the economic interests of the speaker are referred to as commercial speech. Commercial speech, such as advertising, gets First Amendment protection; however, this protection is more limited than the protections given to non-commercial speech, such as political speech. Commercial speech is not entitled to unfettered, absolute freedom, but rather the benefits of commercial speech are weighed against the benefits achieved by the government legislation that regulates that speech. In commercial speech cases, the court foregoes the ordinary strict scrutiny standard of review in favor of a less stringent balancing analysis. *Central Hudson Gas & Electric Co. v. Public Com'n* (1980) [total state ban on promotional advertising by utilities held unconstitutional], established that commercial speech may be restricted only to further a substantial government interest and only if the means used directly advances that interest. Even if these requirements are met, the regulation must not be more extensive than is necessary. This balancing test performed by the court can be summarized as follows:

Is there a substantial governmental interest that is furthered by the restriction of the commercial speech?

Does the restriction directly accomplish the government interest?

Is there any other way to achieve the government interest without regulating the commercial speech?

Under these standards, truthful commercial speech gets a fair degree of First Amendment protection. On the other hand, false or deceptive commercial speech may be forbidden by the government. Similarly, speech, which proposes an illegal transaction, may also be forbidden.

Given that commercial speech is subject to a less demanding standard of review than other protected speech, it might be expected that the Court would have fashioned a fairly clear definition of what constitutes "commercial speech." However, such is not the case.

In *Bolger v. Youngs Products Corp.*, the court considered the constitutionality of a federal law prohibiting the mailing of unsolicited advertisements for contraceptives as applied to certain promotional and informational material. Most of the mailings were held to fall "within the core notion of commercial speech—'speech which does not more than propose a commercial transaction.'" However, much of the material did more than offer to deal, thus presenting "a closer question." Clearly, the fact that the expression was embodied in an advertisement did not necessarily make it commercial speech. Neither the references to products nor the economic motivation for the mailings rendered the speech commercial. However, "[t]he combination of all these characteristics" provided a basis for invoking the *Central Hudson* test. The fact that the advertising sought to link the product to current public debate was deemed inadequate to elevate the expression to the fully protected category. Applying *Central Hudson,* neither the government interest in barring offensive material from unwilling recipients nor its interest in aiding parents of minor children justified the law's sweeping prohibition of the mailings at issue.

As seen in the *Bolger* case, the use of some products are so tightly tied in with the exercise of constitutional rights that the sale of the product can not constitutionally be banned. However, what about the advertising of products or services that are lawful, but believed by the legislature to be harmful? The Supreme Court has addressed this issue in *Packer Corp. v. Utah,* where it curtailed the advertising of cigarettes.

Packer Corporation v. Utah
285 U.S. 105 (1932)

PRIOR HISTORY: APPEAL FROM THE SUPREME COURT OF UTAH.

APPEAL from a judgment affirming a conviction for displaying a billboard poster advertising cigarettes.

OPINION BY: BRANDEIS

Section 2, of c. 145, Laws of Utah, 1921, as amended by c. 52, § 2, Laws of 1923, and c. 92, Laws of 1929, provides:

"It shall be a misdemeanor for any person, company, or corporation, to display on any bill board, street car sign, street car, placard, or on any other object or place of display, any advertisement of cigarettes, cigarette papers, cigars, chewing tobacco, or smoking tobacco, or any disguise or substitute of either, except that a dealer in cigarettes, cigarette papers, tobacco or cigars or their substitutes, may have a sign on the front of his place of business stating that he is a dealer in such articles, provided that nothing herein shall be construed to prohibit the advertising of cigarettes, cigarette papers, chewing tobacco, smoking tobacco, or any disguise or substitute of either in any newspaper, magazine, or periodical printed or circulating in the State of Utah."

The Packer Corporation, a Delaware corporation engaged in billboard advertising and authorized to do business in Utah, was prosecuted under this statute for displaying a large poster advertising Chesterfield cigarettes on a billboard owned by it and located in Salt Lake City. The poster was displayed pursuant to a general contract for advertising Chesterfield cigarettes, made by the defendant with an advertising agency in the State of Ohio. Both the poster and the cigarettes advertised were manufactured without the State of Utah and were shipped into it by Liggett & Myers Tobacco Company, a foreign corporation. The defendant claimed that the statute violates several provisions of the Federal Constitution; the objections were overruled; and the defendant was convicted and sentenced. On the authority of its recent decision in State v. Packer Corp., 297 Pac. 1013, the highest court of the State affirmed the judgment of the trial court. 2 P. 2d 114. The case is here on appeal under § 237 (a) of the Judicial Code, as amended by the Act of February 13, 1925, c. 229, 43 Stat. 937.

It is not denied that the State may, under the police power, regulate the business of selling tobacco products, compare Gundling v. Chicago, 177 U.S. 183, 188; Austin v. Tennessee, 179 U.S. 343, 348; and the advertising connected therewith, compare Rast v. Van Deman & Lewis Co., 240 U.S. 342, 364, 365; Tanner v. Little, 240 U.S. 369, 384, 385. The claim is that because of its peculiar provisions the statute violates the Federal Constitution.

First. The contention mainly urged is that the statute violates the equal protection clause of the Fourteenth Amendment; that in discriminating between the display by appellant of tobacco advertisements upon billboards and the display by others of such advertisements in newspapers, magazines or periodicals, it makes an arbitrary classification. The history of the legislation shows that the charge is unfounded. In Utah no one may sell cigarettes or cigarette papers without a license. Since 1890, it has been the persistent policy, first of the Territory and then of the State, to prevent the use of tobacco by minors, and to discourage its use by adults. Giving tobacco to a minor, as well as selling it, is a misdemeanor. So is permitting a minor to frequent any place of business while in the act of using tobacco in any form. Mere possession of tobacco by the minor is made a crime. And smoking by anyone in any enclosed public place (except a public smoking room designated as such by a conspicuous sign at or near the entrance) is a misdemeanor. In 1921, the legislature enacted a general prohibition of the sale or giving away of cigarettes or cigarette papers to any person, and of their advertisement in any form. Laws of Utah, 1921, c. 145, §§ 1, 2. After two years, however, the plan of absolute prohibition of sale was abandoned in favor of a license system. Laws of Utah, 1923, c. 52, § 1. But the provision against advertisements was retained, broadened to include tobacco in most other forms. In 1926, this statute was held void under the commerce clause, as applied to an advertisement of cigarettes manufactured in another State, inserted in a Utah newspaper which circulated in other States. State v. Salt Lake Tribune Publishing Co., 68 Utah 187; 249 Pac. 474. Thereupon the legislature, unwilling to abandon altogether its declared policy, amended the law by striking out the provision which prohibited advertising in newspapers and periodicals. The classification alleged to be arbitrary was made in order to comply with the requirement of the Federal Constitution as interpreted and applied by the highest court of the State. Action by a State taken to observe one prohibition of the Constitution does not entail the violation of another. J. E. Raley & Bros. v. Richardson, 264 U.S. 157, 160; Des Moines Nat. Bank v. Fairweather, 263 U.S. 103, 116, 117. Compare Dolley v. Abilene Nat. Bank, 179 Fed. 461, 463, 464. It is a reasonable ground of classification that the State has power to legislate with respect to persons in certain situations and not with respect to those in a different one. Compare Williams v. Walsh, 222 U.S. 415, 420.

Moreover, as the state court has shown, there is a difference which justifies the classification between display advertising and that in periodicals or newspapers: "Billboards, street car signs, and placards and such are in a class by themselves. They are wholly intrastate, and the restrictions apply without discrimination to all in the same class. Advertisements of this sort are constantly before the eyes of observers on the streets and in street cars to be seen without the exercise of choice or volition on their part. Other forms of advertising are ordinarily seen as a matter of choice on the part of the observer. The young people as well as the adults have the message of the billboard thrust upon them by all the arts and devices that skill can produce. In the case of newspapers and magazines, there must be some seeking by the one who is to see and read the advertisement. The radio can be turned off, but not so the billboard or street car placard. These distinctions clearly place this kind of advertisement in a position to be classified so that regulations or prohibitions may be imposed upon all within the class. This is impossible with respect to newspapers and magazines." 297 Pac. 1013, 1019. The legislature may recognize degrees of evil and adapt its legislation accordingly. Miller v. Wilson, 236 U.S. 373, 384; Truax v. Raich, 239 U.S. 33, 43.

Second. The defendant contends that to make it illegal to carry out the contract under which the advertisement was displayed takes its property without due process of law because it arbitrarily curtails liberty of contract. The contention is without merit. The law deals confessedly with a subject within the scope of the police power. No facts are brought to our attention which establish either that the evil aimed at does not exist or that the statutory remedy is inappropriate. O'Gorman & Young v. Hartford Fire Insurance Co., 282 U.S. 251, 257; Hardware Dealers Mutual Fire Insurance Co. v. Glidden Co., 284 U.S. 151.

Third. The defendant contends also that the statute imposes an unreasonable restraint upon interstate commerce because it prevents the display on billboards of posters shipped from another State. It does not appear from the record that the defendant is the owner of the posters. Its interest is merely in its billboards located in the State, upon which it displays advertisements for which it is paid. So far as the posters are concerned, assuming them to be articles of commerce, compare Charles A. Ramsay Co. v. Associated Bill Posters, 260 U.S. 501, 511, the statute is aimed, not at their importation, but at their use when affixed to billboards permanently located in the State. Compare Browning v. Waycross, 233 U.S. 16, 22, 23; General Railway Signal Co. v. Virginia, 246 U.S. 500, 510. The prohibition is non-discriminatory, applying regardless of the origin of the poster. Its operation is wholly intrastate, beginning after the interstate movement of the poster has ceased. Compare Hygrade Provision Co. v. Sherman, 266 U.S. 497, 503; Hebe Co. v. Shaw, 248 U.S. 297, 304. See also Corn Products Refining Co. v. Eddy, 249 U.S. 427, 433. To sustain the defendant's contention would be to hold that the posters, because of their origin, were entitled to permanent immunity from the exercise of state regulatory power. The Federal Constitution does not so require. Compare Mutual Film Corp. v. Industrial Commission, 236 U.S. 230, 240, 241. So far as the articles advertised are concerned, the solicitation of the advertisements, it may be assumed, is directed toward intrastate sales. Compare Di Santo v. Pennsylvania, 273 U.S. 34.

Whatever may be the limitations upon the power of the State to regulate solicitation and advertisement incident to an exclusively interstate business, the commerce clause interposes no barrier to its effective control of advertising essentially local. Compare Jell-O Co. v. Landes, 20 F.2d 120, 121; International Text-Book Co. v. District of Columbia, 35 App. D. C. 307, 311, 312.

Affirmed.

Despite the lack of a clearly fashioned definition of what constitutes "commercial speech," the *Central Hudson* test remains the dominant approach for resolution of commercial speech problems.

CORPORATE POLITICAL SPEECH

All corporate speech is not always commercial speech. Consider the case in which a corporation spends its funds to support a political candidate or enactment of a law. Previously, states restricted the amount of advertising that firms could produce. The states apprehended that corporations, with the huge sums of money at their disposal, could unduly influence election outcomes. In *First National Bank of Boston v. Bellotti,* 435 U.S. 765 (1978), the U.S. Supreme Court, nonetheless, struck down a Massachusetts law that prohibited certain corporations from making contributions or expenditures influencing voters on any issues that would not materially affect the corporate assets or their business. In its decision, the Court stated, "the concept that the government may restrict speech of some elements of our society in order to enhance the relative voice of others is wholly foreign to the First Amendment." Essentially, it ruled that corporate political speech is to be protected to the same extent and with the same zeal as is the political speech of ordinary citizens.

CHAPTER QUESTIONS

1. Explain and discuss how the U. S. Constitution protects the right to own private property.

2. Discuss the purpose for having judicial review.

3. How does the Supreme Court decide when a "taking" has occurred under the Fifth Amendment?

4. Differentiate between a physical taking and a regulatory taking.

5. Statement: Congress has absolute power over interstate commerce. Explain what this statement means.

6. Nowhere in the U. S. Constitution is found the power to establish a bank or create a corporation. Nevertheless, the Supreme Court declared a Maryland law imposing a tax on the Bank of the United States unconstitutional. By what means was the Court able to make such a decision? What clause in the Constitution was pivotal in reaching this decision? Explain.

7. Define the term *stare decisis*.

8. In *NLRB v. Jones & Laughlin Steel Corp.*, the Court acknowledged that certain manufacturing activities may be considered intrastate in character. How was the Court able to overcome this fact in deciding that the steel corporation violated its employees' rights to organize and determining that the National Labor Relations Act was valid?

9. By what means did the Supreme Court expand Congress's commerce power in deciding that the Heart of Atlanta Motel had to rent rooms to blacks? See *Heart of Atlanta Motel v. United States.*

10. Review: *NLRB v. Jones & Laughlin Steel Corp.*, decided in 1937; *Wickard v. Filburn*, decided in 1942; and *Heart of Atlanta Motel v. United States*, decided in 1964. These cases provide examples of the expansion of Congress's power to regulate commerce. Why do you think the Supreme Court ruled as it did in these cases? In forming your answer, consider the prevailing economic and social conditions of these times.

11. The U. S. Constitution requires that all direct taxes must be apportioned among the states according to the population as determined by the U. S. census. Provide examples of direct taxes. What indirect taxes may be imposed at the federal level?

12. Explain the difference between procedural due process and substantive due process.

13. What protections are afforded to commercial speech under the Constitution?

Chapter Four: International Perspectives

Introduction

Globalization is a term of art with which we are fully familiar. The past decade has seen a dramatic change in political, economic and business relationships across the world. Technology has provided an extraordinary acceleration of these trends. While globalization has many dramatic advantages, it also provides some significant challenges to the business community. The demands on the business community, as it operates in a variety of cultures and legal traditions, will only continue to insist that students of business have an understanding of international law and its impact.

This is an area of study that does not follow easily the other areas of the law that we will cover. Despite the fact that there are certain global, political and economic organizations, none of them has clear control over what we would consider the traditional aspects of the legislative process. For example, there is no single legislature, court, or executive that has jurisdiction over all aspects of international law. Unfortunately, this rich area of the law is sufficiently complex to prevent us from in-depth study in this venue. Fortunately, we will be able to examine some of the more interesting areas, especially those influencing contemporary business.

Sources of International Law

International law consists of those rules that have been accepted by the international community and include international agreements, the application of custom between nations, and the general principles of the major legal systems.

United States and International Law

In the United States, the U.S. Constitution grants most of the power over international relations to the federal government. The commerce clause (Article I, Section 8) specifically grants Congress the power to "regulate commerce with foreign nations." Article II, section 2 grants the president "the power, by and with the advice and consent of the Senate, to make treaties, provided two thirds of the senators present concur." Finally, the Supremacy Clause accords treaties the status of "law of the land." The status acknowledges that treaties enjoy the same standing as other federal laws.

The case of the *Paquete Habana* provides an early glimpse into the U.S. perspective on the incorporation of principles of international law into the broader development of American law.

The Paquete Habana; *The* Lola
175 U.S. 677 (1900)

GRAY, J.

These are two appeals from decrees of the District Court of the United States for the Southern District of Florida, condemning two fishing vessels and their cargoes as prizes of war.

Each vessel was a fishing smack, running in and out of Havana, and regularly engaged in fishing on the coast of Cuba; sailed under the Spanish flag; was owned by a Spanish subject of Cuban birth, living in the city of Havana; was commanded by a subject of Spain, also residing in Havana; and her master and crew had no interest in the vessel, but were entitled to shares, amounting in all to two-thirds, of her catch, the other third belonging to her owner. Her cargo consisted of fresh fish, caught by her crew from the sea, put on board as they were caught, and kept and sold alive. Until stopped by the blockading squadron, she had no knowledge of the existence of the war, or of any blockade. She had no arms or ammunition on board, and made no attempt to run the blockade after she knew of its existence, nor any resistance at the time of the capture.

The *Paquete Habana* was a sloop, 43 feet long on the keel, and of 25 tons burden, and had a crew of three Cubans, including the master, who had a fishing license from the Spanish Government, and no other commission or license. She left Havana March 25, 1898; sailed along the coast of Cuba to Cape San Antonio at the western end of the island, and there fished for twenty-five days, lying between the reefs off the cape, within the territorial waters of Spain; and then started back for Havana, with a cargo of about 40 quintals of live fish. On April 25, 1898, about two miles off Mariel, and eleven miles from Havana, she was captured by the United States gunboat *Castine*.

The *Lola* was a schooner, 51 feet long on the keel, and of 35 tons burden, and had a crew of six Cubans, including the master, and no commission or license. She left Havana April 11, 1898, and proceeded to Campeachy Sound off Yucatan, fished there eight days, and started back for Havana with a cargo of about 10,000 pounds of live fish. On April 26, 1898, near Havana, she was stopped by the United States steamship *Cincinnati*, and was warned not to go into Havana, but was told that she would be allowed to land at Bahia Honda. She then changed her course, and put for Bahia Honda, but on the next morning, when near that port, was captured by the United States steamship *Dolphin*.

Both the fishing vessels were brought by their captors into Key West. A libel for the condemnation of each vessel and her cargo as prize of war was there filed on April 27, 1898; a claim was interposed by her master, on behalf of himself and the other members of the crew, and of her owner; evidence was taken, showing the facts above stated; and on May 30, 1898, a final decree of condemnation and sale was entered, "the court not being satisfied that as a matter of law, without any ordinance, treaty or proclamation, fishing vessels of this class are exempt from seizure."

Each vessel was thereupon sold by auction; the *Paquete Habana* for the sum of $490; and the *Lola* for the sum of $800. There was no other evidence in the record of the value of either vessel or of her cargo.

* * * * *

We are of opinion that the act of 1891, upon its face, read in the light of settled rules of statutory construction, and of the decisions of this court, clearly manifests the intention of Congress to cover the whole subject of the appellate jurisdiction from the District and Circuit Courts of the United States, so far as regards in what cases, as well as to what courts, appeals may be taken, and to supersede and repeal, to this extent, all the provisions of earlier acts of Congress, including those that imposed pecuniary limits upon such jurisdiction; and, as part of the new scheme, to confer upon this court jurisdiction of appeals from all final sentences and decrees in prize causes, without regard to the amount in dispute, and without any certificate of the District Judge as to the importance of the particular case.

We are then brought to the consideration of the question whether, upon the facts appearing in these records, the fishing smacks were subject to capture by the armed vessels of the United States during the recent war with Spain.

By an ancient usage among civilized nations, beginning centuries ago, and gradually ripening into a rule of international law, coast fishing vessels, pursuing their vocation of catching and bringing in fresh fish, have been recognized as exempt, with their cargoes and crews, from capture as prize of war.

This doctrine, however, has been earnestly contested at the bar; and no complete collection of the instances illustrating it is to be found, so far as we are aware, in a single published work, although many are referred to and discussed by the writers on international law, * * * * * It is therefore worth the while to trace the history of the rule, from the earliest accessible sources, through the increasing recognition of it, with occasional setbacks, to what we may now justly consider as its final establishment in our own country and generally throughout the civilized world.

The earliest acts of any government on the subject, mentioned in the books, either emanated from, or were approved by, a King of England.

* * * * *

The doctrine which exempts coast fishermen with their vessels and cargoes from capture as prize of war has been familiar to the United States from the time of the War of Independence.

* * * * *

Since the United States became a nation, the only serious interruptions, so far as we are informed, of the general recognition of the exemption of coast fishing vessels from hostile capture, arose out of the mutual suspicions and recriminations of England and France during the wars of the French Revolution.

* * * * *

Wheaton, in his *Digest of the Law of Maritime Captures and Prizes,* published in 1815, wrote: "It has been usual in maritime wars to exempt from capture fishing boats and their cargoes, both from views of mutual accommodation between neighboring countries, and from tenderness to a poor and industrious order of people. This custom, so honorable to the humanity of civilized nations, has fallen into disuse; and it is remarkable that both France and England mutually reproach each other with that breach of good faith which has finally abolished it."

* * * * *

This statement clearly exhibits Wheaton's opinion that the custom had been a general one, as well as that it ought to remain so. His assumption that it had been abolished by the differences between France and England at the close of the last century was hardly justified by the state of things when he wrote, and has not since been borne out.

* * * * *

International law is part of our law, and must be ascertained and administered by the courts of justice of appropriate jurisdiction, as often as questions of right depending upon it are duly presented for their determination. For this purpose, where there is no treaty, and no controlling executive or legislative act or juridical decision, resort must be had to the customs and usages of civilized nations; and, as evidence of these, to the works of jurists and commentators, who by years of labor, research and experience, have made themselves peculiarly well acquainted with the subjects of which they treat. Such works are resorted to by judicial tribunals, not for the speculations of their authors concerning what the law ought to be, but for trustworthy evidence of what the law really is. Hilton v. Guyot, 159 U.S. 113, 163, 164, 214, 215.

* * * * *

This review of the precedents and authorities on the subject appears to us abundantly to demonstrate that at the present day, by the general consent of the civilized nations of the world, and independently of any express treaty or other public act, it is an established rule of international law, founded on considerations of humanity to a poor and industrious order of men, and of the mutual convenience of belligerent States, that coast fishing vessels, with their implements and supplies, cargoes and crews, unarmed, and honestly pursuing their peaceful calling of catching and bringing in fresh fish, are exempt from capture as prize of war.

The exemption, of course, does not apply to coast fishermen or their vessels, if employed for a warlike purpose, or in such a way as to give aid or information to the enemy; nor when military or naval operations create a necessity to which all private interests must give way.

Nor has the exemption been extended to ships or vessels employed on the high sea in taking whales or seals, or cod or other fish which are not brought fresh to market, but are salted or otherwise cured and made a regular article of commerce.

This rule of international law is one which prize courts, administering the law of nations, are bound to take judicial notice of, and to give effect to, in the absence of any treaty or other public act of their own government in relation to the matter.

* * * * *

In Brown v. United States, 8 Cranch, 110, there are expressions of Chief Justice Marshall which, taken by themselves, might seem inconsistent with the position above maintained of the duty of a prize court to take judicial notice of a rule of international law, established by the general usage of civilized nations, as to the kind of property subject to capture. But the actual decision in that case, and the leading reasons on which it was based, appear to us rather to confirm our position. The principal question there was whether personal property of a British subject, found on land in the United States at the beginning of the last war with Great Britain, could lawfully be condemned as enemy's property, on a libel filed by the attorney of the United States, without a positive act of Congress. The conclusion of the court was "that the power of confiscating enemy property is in the legislature, and that the legislature has not yet declared its will to confiscate property which was within our territory at the declaration of war." 8 Cranch, 129. In showing that the declaration of war did not, of itself, vest the executive with authority to order such property to be confiscated, the Chief Justice relied on the modern usages of nations, saying: "The universal practice of forbearing to seize and confiscate debts and credits, the principle universally received that the right to them revives on the restoration of peace, would seem to prove that war is not an absolute confiscation of this property, but simply confers the right of confiscation;" and again: "The modern rule then would seem to be that tangible property belonging to an enemy, and found in the country at the commencement of war, ought not to be immediately confiscated; and in almost every commercial treaty an article is inserted stipulating for the right to withdraw such property." 8 Cranch, 123, 125. The decision that enemy property on land, which by the modern usage of nations is not subject to capture as prize of war, cannot be condemned by a prize court, even by direction of the executive, without express authority from Congress, appears to us to repel any inference that coast fishing vessels, which are exempt by the general consent of civilized nations from capture, and which no act of Congress or order of the President has expressly authorized to be taken and confiscated, must be condemned by a prize court, for want of a distinct exemption in a treaty or other public act of the Government.

* * * * *

Upon the facts proved in either case, it is the duty of this court, sitting as the highest prize court of the United States, and administering the law of nations, to declare and adjudge that the capture was unlawful, and without probable cause; and it is therefore, in each case,

Ordered, that the decree of the District Court be reversed, and the proceeds of the sale of the vessel, together with the proceeds of any sale of her cargo, be restored to the claimant, with damages and costs.

INTERNATIONAL SYSTEMS—COMPARATIVE LAW

Comparative Law is an area of study that examines the similarities and differences between legal systems. There is a difference, however, between international law and comparative law. International law governs the relationships between or among nations. Comparative law is the study of legal systems of different nations. The above distinction will be an important one as we progress through this discussion.

There are three significant legal systems in use in the world today. They are the common law, civil law and Islamic law systems. We have discussed the common-law system at some length earlier in Chapter One.

CIVIL LAW SYSTEMS

Civil law systems find their origins in Roman law and were strongly influenced by the French and German Civil Codes of the nineteenth century. These civil codes were really the collected legal principles of those nations. The codes had a positive view of the protection of private property, individual freedom, and freedom of contract. The codes generally included areas of private law, typically encompassing the areas of tort, property, and tort law.

The separation of powers model supported by civil law systems is not directly comparable to the American model. Since civil law systems rely on a code, the legislature is the preeminent player. While the court systems interpret the code, they are not empowered to make new law as in the common-law system. Civil law systems include most Western European countries and Japan. In fact, the State of Louisiana is considered to have a mixed system, including both civil and common-law, that developed because of its French origins.

SOCIALIST LAW

A significant subset of civil law is socialist law. While the source of socialist law is a code, issues of property ownership, individual rights, and limits on governmental power are not viewed in the same way as they are in the broader civil law societies or for those based in common law.

Socialist law finds its underpinnings in the political and economic philosophy of a communist society. The countries that espoused those principles have experienced significant political and economic challenges as a result of the fall of the Berlin Wall in 1989. These challenges have had a dramatic impact on this legal system. Those countries whose legal systems are based on socialist law are presently attempting to reconcile these distinctions.

ISLAMIC LAW SYSTEMS

The Islamic legal system known as *Shari'a* (God's Rules) finds its roots in the Koran, the Sunna (the traditional teachings and practices of the Prophet Mohammed), the writings of Islamic scholars, and the consensus of the legal community. Islamic law is the primary source of law in Saudi Arabia and is followed, at some level, in most nations in the Middle East, North Africa, and southern Asia.

A significant challenge in Islamic law jurisdictions is the decision made in the 10th century by Islamic law scholars that the law had been sufficiently interpreted and that any need for independent reasoning or additional development was unnecessary. Given the reality of commercial developments since the 10th century, the reconciliation of the requirements of *Shari'a* and modern commerce can be a significant challenge.

PRINCIPLES OF INTERNATIONAL LAW
SOVEREIGN IMMUNITY

The doctrine of sovereign immunity requires that the domestic courts of a country must decline to hear cases against other nations (sovereigns) out of deference to their status as independent nation states. The historical significance of this doctrine looks to a time when a state's ruler personified the nation. The doctrine has survived the passing of those individual leaders and continues to apply despite the fact that the officers of its state now represent most nations. The practical application of this doctrine is that countries are granted immunity from suits in other countries. This effectively means that nations are granted absolute sovereign immunity from suit.

In 1976, however, the United States Congress passed the Foreign Sovereign Immunities Act effectively creating a narrower view of the absolute nature of sovereign immunity. This statute continues to support the theory that a nation state is immune from suits involving injuries resulting from governmental action. The significant change represented by the FSIA is that governments are not immune from suit when damages arise because of commercial or nongovernmental activity. For example, the "commercial activity" exception under the FSIA specifically excludes the state from the protection of sovereign immunity when the state is acting as a private party and enters into a commercial contract with a another private party.

The case of *The Schooner Exchange* provides insight into the fundamentals of sovereign immunity and an interesting look at how the new Supreme Court of the United States developed and applied principles of law.

The Schooner Exchange *v. M'Faddon, et al*
11 U.S. 116 (1812)

MARSHALL, Ch. J. Delivered the opinion of the Court as follows:

This case involves the very delicate and important inquiry, whether an American citizen can assert, in an American court, a title to an armed national vessel, found within the waters of the United States.

The question has been considered with an earnest solicitude, that the decision may conform to those principles of national and municipal law by which it ought to be regulated.

In exploring an unbeaten path, with few, if any, aids from precedents or written law, the court has found it necessary to rely much on general principles, and on a train of reasoning, founded on cases in some degree analogous to this.

The jurisdiction of courts is a branch of that which is possessed by the nation as an independent sovereign power.

The jurisdiction of the nation within its own territory is necessarily exclusive and absolute. It is susceptible of no limitation not imposed by itself. Any restriction upon it, deriving validity from an external source, would imply a diminution of its sovereignty to the extent of the restriction, and an investment of that sovereignty to the same extent in that power which could impose such restriction.

All exceptions, therefore, to the full and complete power of a nation within its own territories, must be traced up to the consent of the nation itself. They can flow from no other legitimate source.

This consent may be either express or implied. In the latter case, it is less determinate, exposed more to the uncertainties of construction; but, if understood, not less obligatory.

The world being composed of distinct sovereignties, possessing equal rights and equal independence, whose mutual benefit is promoted by intercourse with each other, and by an interchange of those good offices which humanity dictates and its wants require, all sovereigns have consented to a relaxation in practice, in cases under certain peculiar circumstances, of that absolute and complete jurisdiction within their respective territories which sovereignty confers.

This consent may, in some instances, be tested by common usage, and by common opinion, growing out of that usage.

A nation would justly be considered as violating its faith, although that faith might not be expressly plighted, which should suddenly and without previous notice, exercise its territorial powers in a manner not consonant to the usages and received obligations of the civilized world.

This full and absolute territorial jurisdiction being alike the attribute of every sovereign, and being incapable of conferring extra-territorial power, would not seem to contemplate foreign sovereigns nor their sovereign rights as its objects. One sovereign being in no respect amenable to another; and being bound by obligations of the highest character not to degrade the dignity of his nation, by placing himself or its sovereign rights within the jurisdiction of another, can be supposed to enter a foreign territory only under an express license, or in the confidence that the immunities belonging to his independent sovereign station, though not expressly stipulated, are reserved by implication, and will be extended to him.

This perfect equality and absolute independence of sovereigns, and this common interest impelling them to mutual intercourse, and an interchange of good offices with each other, have given rise to a class of cases in which every sovereign is understood to wave the exercise of a part of that complete exclusive territorial jurisdiction, which has been stated to be the attribute of every nation.

1st. One of these is admitted to be the exemption of the person of the sovereign from arrest or detention within a foreign territory.

If he enters that territory with the knowledge and license of its sovereign, that license, although containing no stipulation exempting his person from arrest, is universally understood to imply such stipulation.

Why has the whole civilized world concurred in this construction? The answer cannot be mistaken. A foreign sovereign is not understood as intending to subject himself to jurisdiction incompatible with his dignity, and the dignity of his nation, and it is to avoid this subjection that the license has been obtained. The character to whom it is given, and the object for which it is granted, equally require that it should be construed to impart full security to the person who has obtained it. This security, however need not be expressed; it is implied from the circumstances of the case.

Should one sovereign enter the territory of another, without the consent of that other, expressed or implied, it would present a question which does not appear to be perfectly settled, a decision of which, is not necessary to any conclusion to which the Court may come in the cause under consideration. If he did not thereby expose himself to the territorial jurisdiction of the sovereign, whose dominions he had entered, it would seem to be because all sovereigns impliedly engage not to avail themselves of a power over their equal, which a romantic confidence in their magnanimity has placed in their hands.

2d. A second case, standing on the same principles with the first, is the immunity which all civilized nations allow to foreign ministers.

Whatever may be the principle on which this immunity is established, whether we consider him as in the place of the sovereign he represents, or by a political fiction suppose him to be extra-territorial, and, therefore, in point of law, not within the jurisdiction of the sovereign at whose Court he resides; still the immunity itself is granted by the governing power of the nation to which the minister is deputed. This fiction of exterritoriality could not be erected and supported against the will of the sovereign of the territory. He is supposed to assent to it.

This consent is not expressed. It is true that in some countries, and in this among others, a special law is enacted for the case. But the law obviously proceeds on the idea of prescribing the punishment of an act previously unlawful, not of granting to a foreign minister a privilege which he would not otherwise possess.

The assent of the sovereign to the very important and extensive exemptions from territorial jurisdiction which are admitted to attach to foreign ministers, is implied from the considerations that, without such exemption, every sovereign would hazard his own dignity by employing a public minister abroad. His minister would owe temporary and local allegiance to a foreign prince, and would be less competent to the objects of his mission. A sovereign committing the interests of his nation with a foreign power, to the care of a person whom he has selected for that purpose, cannot intend to subject his minister in any degree to that power; and, therefore, a consent to receive him, implies a consent that he shall possess those privileges which his principal intended he should retain—privileges which are essential to the dignity of his sovereign, and to the duties he is bound to perform.

In what cases a minister, by infracting the laws of the country in which he resides, may subject himself to other punishment than will be inflicted by his own sovereign, is an inquiry foreign to the present purpose. If his crimes be such as to render him amenable to the local jurisdiction, it must be because they forfeit the privileges annexed to his character; and the minister, by violating the conditions under which he was received as the representative of a foreign sovereign, has surrendered the immunities granted on those conditions; or, according to the true meaning of the original assent, has ceased to be entitled to them.

3d. A third case in which a sovereign is understood to cede a portion of his territorial jurisdiction is, where he allows the troops of a foreign prince to pass through his dominions.

In such case, without any express declaration waving jurisdiction over the army to which this right of passage has been granted, the sovereign who should attempt to exercise it would certainly be considered as violating his faith. By exercising it, the purpose for which the free passage was granted would be defeated, and a portion of the military force of a foreign independent nation would be diverted from those national objects and duties to which it was applicable, and would be withdrawn from the control of the sovereign whose power and whose safety might greatly depend on retaining the exclusive command and disposition of this force. The grant of a free passage therefore implies a waver of all jurisdiction over the troops during their passage, and permits the foreign general to use that discipline, and to inflict those punishments which the government of his army may require.

But if, without such express permit, an army should be led through the territories of a foreign prince, might the jurisdiction of the territory be rightfully exercised over the individuals composing this army?

Without doubt, a military force can never gain immunities of any other description than those which war gives, by entering a foreign territory against the will of its sovereign. But if his consent, instead of being expressed by a particular license, be expressed by a general declaration that foreign troops may pass through a specified tract of country, a distinction between such general permit and a particular license is not perceived. It would seem reasonable that every immunity which would be conferred by a special license, would be in like manner conferred by such general permit.

We have seen that a license to pass through a territory implies immunities not expressed, and it is material to enquire why the license itself may not be presumed?

It is obvious that the passage of an army through a foreign territory will probably be at all times inconvenient and injurious, and would often be imminently dangerous to the sovereign through whose dominion it passed. Such a practice would break down some of the most decisive distinctions between peace and war, and would reduce a nation to the necessity of resisting by war an act not absolutely hostile in its character, or of exposing itself to the stratagems and frauds of a power whose integrity might be doubted, and who might enter the country under deceitful pretexts. It is for reasons like these that the general license to foreigners to enter the dominions of a friendly power, is never understood to extend to a military force; and an army marching into the dominions of another sovereign, may justly be considered as committing an act of hostility; and, if not opposed by force, acquires no privilege by its irregular and improper conduct. It may however well be questioned whether any other than the sovereign power of the state be capable of deciding that such military commander is without a license.

But the rule which is applicable to armies, does not appear to be equally applicable to ships of war entering the ports of a friendly power. The injury inseparable from the march of an army through an inhabited country, and the dangers often, indeed generally, attending it, do not ensue from admitting a ship of war, without special license, into a friendly port. A different rule therefore with respect to this species of military force has been generally adopted. If, for reasons of state, the ports of a nation generally, or any particular ports be closed against vessels of war generally, or the vessels of any particular nation, notice is usually given of such determination. If there be no prohibition, the ports of a friendly nation are considered as open to the public ships of all powers with whom it is at peace, and they are supposed to enter such ports and to remain in them while allowed to remain, under the protection of the government of the place.

In almost every instance, the treaties between civilized nations contain a stipulation to this effect in favor of vessels driven in by stress of weather or other urgent necessity. In such cases the sovereign is bound by compact to authorize foreign vessels to enter his ports. The treaty binds him to allow vessels in distress to find refuge and asylum in his ports, and this is a license which he is not at liberty to retract. It would be difficult to assign a reason for withholding from a license thus granted, any immunity from local jurisdiction which would be implied in a special license.

If there be no treaty applicable to the case, and the sovereign, from motives deemed adequate by himself, permits his ports to remain open to the public ships of foreign friendly powers, the conclusion seems irresistable, that they enter by his assent. And if they enter by his assent necessarily implied, no just reason is perceived by the Court for distinguishing their case from that of vessels which enter by express assent.

In all the cases of exemption which have been reviewed, much has been implied, but the obligation of what was implied has been found equal to the obligation of that which was expressed. Are there reasons for denying the application of this principle to ships of war?

In this part of the subject a difficulty is to be encountered, the seriousness of which is acknowledged, but which the Court will not attempt to evade.

Those treaties which provide for the admission and safe departure of public vessels entering a port from stress of weather, or other urgent cause, provide in like manner for the private vessels of the nation; and where public vessels enter a port under the general license which is implied merely from the absence of a prohibition, they are, it may be urged, in the same condition with merchant vessels entering the same port for the purposes of trade who cannot thereby claim any exemption from the jurisdiction of the country. It may be contended, certainly with much plausibility if not correctness, that the same rule, and same principle are applicable to public and private ships; and since it is admitted that private ships entering without special license become subject to the local jurisdiction, it is demanded on what authority an exception is made in favor or ships of war.

It is by no means conceded, that a private vessel really availing herself of an asylum provided by treaty, and not attempting to trade, would become amenable to the local jurisdiction, unless she committed some act forfeiting the protection she claims under compact. On the contrary, moteres may be assigned for stipulating, and according immunities to vessels in cases of distress, which would not be demanded for, or allowed to those which enter voluntarily and for ordinary purposes. On this part of the subject, however, the Court does not mean to indicate any opinion. The case itself may possibly occur, and ought not to be prejudged.

Without deciding how far such stipulations in favor of distressed vessels, as are usual in treaties, may exempt private ships from the jurisdiction of the place, it may safely be asserted, that the whole reasoning upon which such exemption has been implied in other cases, applies with full force to the exemption of ships of war in this.

"It is impossible to conceive," says Vattel, "that a Prince who sends an ambassador or any other minister can have any intention of subjecting him to the authority of a foreign power; and this consideration furnishes an additional argument, which completely establishes the independency of a public minister. If it cannot be reasonably presumed that his sovereign means to subject him to the authority of the prince to whom he is sent, the latter, in receiving the minister, consents to admit him on the footing of independency; and thus there exists between the two princes a tacit convention, which gives a new force to the natural obligation."

Equally impossible is it to conceive, whatever may be the construction as to private ships, that a prince who stipulates a passage for his troops, or an asylum for his ships of war in distress, should mean to subject his army or his navy to the jurisdiction of a foreign sovereign. And if this cannot be presumed, the sovereign of the port must be considered as having conceded the privilege to the extent in which it must have been understood to be asked.

To the Court, it appears, that where, without treaty, the ports of a nation are open to the private and public ships of a friendly power, whose subjects have also liberty without special license, to enter the country for business or amusement, a clear distinction is to be drawn between the rights accorded to private individuals or private trading vessels, and those accorded to public armed ships which constitute a part of the military force of the nation.

The preceding reasoning, has maintained the propositions that all exemptions from territorial jurisdiction, must be derived from the consent of the sovereign of the territory; that this consent may be implied or expressed; and that when implied, its extent must be regulated by the nature of the case, and the views under which the parties requiring and conceding it must be supposed to act.

When private individuals of one nation spread themselves through another as business or caprice may direct, mingling indiscriminately with the inhabitants of that other, or when merchant vessels enter for the purposes of trade, it would be obviously inconvenient and dangerous to society, and would subject the laws to continual infraction, and the government to degradation, if such individuals or merchants did not owe temporary and local allegiance, and were not amenable to the jurisdiction of the country. Nor can the foreign sovereign have any motive for wishing such exemption. His subjects thus passing into foreign countries, are not employed by him, nor are they engaged in national pursuits. Consequently there are powerful motives for not exempting persons of this description from the jurisdiction of the country in which they are found, and no one motive for requiring it. The implied license, therefore, under which they enter can never be construed to grant such exemption.

But in all respects different is the situation of a public armed ship. She constitutes a part of the military force of her nation; acts under the immediate and direct command of the sovereign; is employed by him in national objects. He has many and powerful motives for preventing those objects from being defeated by the interference of a foreign state. Such interference cannot take place without affecting his power and his dignity. The implied license therefore under which such vessel enters a friendly port, may reasonably be construed, and it seems to the Court, ought to be construed, as containing an exemption from the jurisdiction of the sovereign, within whose territory she claims the rites of hospitality.

Upon these principles, by the unanimous consent of nations, a foreigner is amenable to the laws of the place; but certainly in practice, nations have not yet asserted their jurisdiction over the public armed ships of a foreign sovereign entering a port open for their reception.

Bynkershoek, a jurist of great reputation, has indeed maintained that the property of a foreign sovereign is not distinguishable by any legal exemption from the property of an ordinary individual, and has quoted several cases in which courts have exercised jurisdiction over cases in which a foreign sovereign was made a party defendant.

Without indicating any opinion on this question, it may safely be airmed, that there is a manifest distinction between the private property of the person who happens to be a prince, and that military force which supports the sovereign power, and maintains the dignity and the independence of a nation. A prince, by acquiring private property in a foreign country, may possibly be considered as subjecting that property to the territorial jurisdiction; he may be considered as so far laying down the prince, and assuming the character of a private individual; but this he cannot be presumed to do with respect to any portion of that armed force, which upholds his crown, and the nation he is entrusted to govern.

The only applicable case cited by Bynkershoek, is that of the Spanish ships of war seized in Flushing for a debt due from the king of Spain. In that case, the states general interposed; and there is reason to believe, from the manner in which the transaction is stated, that, either by the interference of government, or the decision of the court, the vessels were released.

This case of the Spanish vessels is, it is believed, the only case furnished by the history of the world, of an attempt made by an individual to assert a claim against a foreign prince, by seizing the armed vessels of the nation. That this proceeding was at once arrested by the government, in a nation which appears to have asserted the power of proceeding in the same manner against the private property of the prince, would seem to furnish no feeble argument in support of the universality of the opinion in favor of the exemption claimed for ships of war. The distinction made in our own laws between public and private ships would appear to proceed from the same opinion.

It seems then to the Court, to be a principle of public law, that national ships of war, entering the port of a friendly power open for their reception, are to be considered as exempted by the consent of that power from its jurisdiction.

Without doubt, the sovereign of the place is capable of destroying this implication. He may claim and exercise jurisdiction either by employing force, or by subjecting such vessels to the ordinary tribunals. But until such power be exerted in a manner not to be misunderstood, the sovereign cannot be considered as having imparted to the ordinary tribunals a jurisdiction, which it would be a breach of faith to exercise. Those general statutory provisions therefore which are descriptive of the ordinary jurisdiction of the judicial tribunals, which give an individual whose property has been wrested from him, a right to claim that property in the courts of the country, in which it is found, ought not, in the opinion of this Court, to be so construed as to give them jurisdiction in a case, in which the sovereign power has impliedly consented to wave its jurisdiction.

The arguments in favor of this opinion which have been drawn from the general inability of the judicial power to enforce its decisions in cases of this description, from the consideration, that the sovereign power of the nation is alone competent to avenge wrongs committed by a sovereign, that the questions to which such wrongs give birth are rather questions of policy than of law, that they are for diplomatic, rather than legal discussion, are of great weight, and merit serious attention. But the argument has already been drawn to a length, which forbids a particular examination of these points.

The principles which have been stated, will now be applied to the case at bar.

In the present state of the evidence and proceedings, the *Exchange* must be considered as a vessel, which was the property of the Libellants, whose claim is repelled by the fact, that she is now a national armed vessel, commissioned by, and in the service of the emperor of France. The evidence of this fact is not controverted. But it is contended, that it constitutes no bar to an enquiry into the validity of the title, by which the emperor holds this vessel. Every person, it is alleged, who is entitled to property brought within the jurisdiction of our Courts, has a right to assert his title in those Courts, unless there be some law taking his case out of the general rule. It is therefore said to be the right, and if it be the right, it is the duty of the Court, to enquire whether this title has been extinguished by an act, the validity of which is recognized by national or municipal law.

If the preceding reasoning be correct, the *Exchange,* being a public armed ship, in the service of a foreign sovereign, with whom the government of the United States is at peace, and having entered an American port open for her reception, on the terms on which ships of war are generally permitted to enter the ports of a friendly power, must be considered as having come into the American territory, under an implied promise, that while necessarily within it, and demeaning herself in a friendly manner, she should be exempt from the jurisdiction of the country.

If this opinion be correct, there seems to be a necessity for admitting that the fact might be disclosed to the Court by the suggestion of the Attorney for the United States.

I am directed to deliver it, as the opinion of the Court, that the sentence of the Circuit Court, reversing the sentence of the District Court, in the case of the *Exchange* be reversed, and that of the District Court, dismissing the libel, be affirmed.

Act of State Doctrine

The nature of the sovereign extends to activities undertaken by the government within its own borders. The Act of State doctrine provides that the courts of one country cannot challenge the appropriateness or legitimacy of actions undertaken by another government within its own territory.

The *Kirkpatrick* case provides an interesting view into the underlying theory supporting this doctrine and its application in a modern case.

W.S. Kirkpatrick & Co., Inc. et al. v. Environmental Tectonics Corp., International
493 U.S. 400; 110 S. Ct. 701 (1990)

Scalia, J., delivered the opinion for a unanimous Court.

In this case we must decide whether the act of state doctrine bars a court in the United States from entertaining a cause of action that does not rest upon the asserted invalidity of an official act of a foreign sovereign, but that does require imputing to foreign officials an unlawful motivation (the obtaining of bribes) in the performance of such an official act.

I.

The facts as alleged in respondent's complaint are as follows: In 1981, Harry Carpenter, who was then Chairman of the Board and Chief Executive Officer of petitioner W. S. Kirkpatrick & Co., Inc. (Kirkpatrick), learned that the Republic of Nigeria was interested in contracting for the construction and equipment of an aeromedical center at Kaduna Air Force Base in Nigeria. He made arrangements with Benson "Tunde" Akindele, a Nigerian citizen, whereby Akindele would endeavor to secure the contract for Kirkpatrick. It was agreed that, in the event the contract was awarded to Kirkpatrick, Kirkpatrick would pay to two Panamanian entities controlled by Akindele a "commission" equal to 20% of the contract price, which would in turn be given as a bribe to officials of the Nigerian Government. In accordance with this plan, the contract was awarded to petitioner W. S. Kirkpatrick & Co., International (Kirkpatrick International), a wholly owned subsidiary of Kirkpatrick; Kirkpatrick paid the promised "commission" to the appointed Panamanian entities; and those funds were disbursed as bribes. All parties agree that Nigerian law prohibits both the payment and the receipt of bribes in connection with the award of a government contract.

Respondent Environmental Tectonics Corporation, International, an unsuccessful bidder for the Kaduna contract, learned of the 20% "commission" and brought the matter to the attention of the Nigerian Air Force and the United States Embassy in Lagos. Following an investigation by the Federal Bureau of Investigation, the United States Attorney for the District of New Jersey brought charges against both Kirkpatrick and Carpenter for violations of the Foreign Corrupt Practices Act of 1977, 91 Stat. 1495, as amended, 15 U.S.C. § 78dd-1 et seq., and both pleaded guilty.

Respondent then brought this civil action in the United States District Court for the District of New Jersey against Carpenter, Akindele, petitioners, and others, seeking damages under the Racketeer Influenced and Corrupt Organizations Act, 18 U.S.C. § 1961 et seq., the Robinson-Patman Act, 49 Stat. 1526, 15 U.S.C. § 13 et seq., and the New Jersey Anti-Racketeering Act, N. J. Stat. Ann. § 2C:41-2 et seq. (West 1982). The defendants moved to dismiss the complaint under Rule 12(b)(6) of the Federal Rules of Civil Procedure on the ground that the action was barred by the act of state doctrine.

* * * * *

II

This Court's description of the jurisprudential foundation for the act of state doctrine has undergone some evolution over the years. We once viewed the doctrine as an expression of international law, resting upon "the highest considerations of international comity and expediency," Oetjen v. Central Leather Co., 246 U.S. 297, 303–304 (1918). We have more recently described it, however, as a consequence of domestic separation of powers, reflecting "the strong sense of the Judicial Branch that its engagement in the task of passing on the validity of foreign acts of state may hinder" the conduct of foreign affairs, Banco Nacional de Cuba v. Sabbatino, 376 U.S. 398, 423 (1964).

Some Justices have suggested possible exceptions to application of the doctrine, where one or both of the foregoing policies would seemingly not be served: an exception, for example, for acts of state that consist of commercial transactions, since neither modern international comity nor the current position of our Executive Branch accorded sovereign immunity to such acts, see Alfred Dunhill of London, Inc. v. Republic of Cuba, 425 U.S. 682, 695–706 (1976) (opinion of WHITE, J.); or an exception for cases in which the Executive Branch has represented that it has no objection to denying validity to the foreign sovereign act, since then the courts would be impeding no foreign policy goals, see First National City Bank v. Banco Nacional de Cuba, 406 U.S. 759, 768–770 (1972) (opinion of REHNQUIST, J.).

The parties have argued at length about the applicability of these possible exceptions, and, more generally, about whether the purpose of the act of state doctrine would be furthered by its application in this case. We find it unnecessary, however, to pursue those inquiries, since the factual predicate for application of the act of state doctrine does not exist. Nothing in the present suit requires the Court to declare invalid, and thus ineffective as "a rule of decision for the courts of this country," Ricaud v. American Metal Co., 246 U.S. 304, 310 (1918), the official act of a foreign sovereign.

In every case in which we have held the act of state doctrine applicable, the relief sought or the defense interposed would have required a court in the United States to declare invalid the official act of a foreign sovereign performed within its own territory. In Underhill v. Hernandez, 168 U.S. 250, 254 (1897), holding the defendant's detention of the plaintiff to be tortious would have required denying legal effect to "acts of a military commander representing the authority of the revolutionary party as government, which afterwards succeeded and was recognized by the United States." In Oetjen v. Central Leather Co., supra, and in Ricaud v. American Metal Co., supra, denying title to the party who claimed through purchase from Mexico would have required declaring that government's prior seizure of the property, within its own territory, legally ineffective. See Oetjen, supra, at 304; Ricaud, supra, at 310. In Sabbatino, upholding the defendant's claim to the funds would have required a holding that Cuba's expropriation of goods located in Havana was null and void. In the present case, by contrast, neither the claim nor any asserted defense requires a determination that Nigeria's contract with Kirkpatrick International was, or was not, effective.

Petitioners point out, however, that the facts necessary to establish respondent's claim will also establish that the contract was unlawful. Specifically, they note that in order to prevail respondent must prove that petitioner Kirkpatrick made, and Nigerian officials received, payments that violate Nigerian law, which would, they assert, support a finding that the contract is invalid under Nigerian law. Assuming that to be true, it still does not suffice. The act of state doctrine is not some vague doctrine of abstention but a "principle of decision binding on federal and state courts alike." Sabbatino, supra, at 427. As we said in Ricaud, "the act within its own boundaries of one sovereign State...becomes...a rule of decision for the courts of this country." 246 U.S., at 310. Act of state issues only arise when a court must decide—that is, when the outcome of the case turns upon—the effect of official action by a foreign sovereign. When that question is not in the case, neither is the act of state doctrine. That is the situation here. Regardless of what the court's factual findings may suggest as to the legality of the Nigerian contract, its legality is simply not a question to be decided in the present suit, and there is thus no occasion to apply the rule of decision that the act of state doctrine requires. Cf. Sharon v. Time, Inc., 599 F.Supp. 538, 546 (SDNY 1984) ("The issue in this litigation is not whether [the alleged] acts are valid, but whether they occurred").

In support of their position that the act of state doctrine bars any factual findings that may cast doubt upon the validity of foreign sovereign acts, petitioners cite Justice Holmes' opinion for the Court in American Banana Co. v. United Fruit Co., 213 U.S. 347 (1909). That was a suit under the United States antitrust laws, alleging that Costa Rica's seizure of the plaintiff's property had been induced by an unlawful conspiracy. In the course of a lengthy opinion Justice Holmes observed, citing Underhill, that "a seizure by a state is not a thing that can be complained of elsewhere in the courts." 213 U.S., at 357–358. The statement is concededly puzzling. Underhill does indeed stand for the proposition that a seizure by a state cannot be complained of elsewhere—in the sense of being sought to be declared ineffective elsewhere. The plaintiff in American Banana, however, like the plaintiff here, was not trying to undo or disregard the governmental action, but only to obtain damages from private parties who had procured it. Arguably, then, the statement did imply that suit would not lie if a foreign state's actions would be, though not invalidated, impugned.

Whatever Justice Holmes may have had in mind, his statement lends inadequate support to petitioners' position here, for two reasons. First, it was a brief aside, entirely unnecessary to the decision. American Banana was squarely decided on the ground (later substantially overruled, see Continental Ore Co. v. Union Carbide & Carbon Corp., 370 U.S. 690, 704–705 (1962)) that the antitrust laws had no extraterritorial application, so that "what the defendant did in Panama or Costa Rica is not within the scope of the statute." 213 U.S., at 357. Second, whatever support the dictum might provide for petitioners' position is more than overcome by our later holding in United States v. Sisal Sales Corp., 274 U.S. 268 (1927). There we held that, American Banana notwithstanding, the defendant's actions in obtaining Mexico's enactment of "discriminating legislation" could form part of the basis for suit under the United States antitrust laws. 274 U.S., at 276. Simply put, American Banana was not an act of state case; and whatever it said by way of dictum that might be relevant to the present case has not survived Sisal Sales.

Petitioners insist, however, that the policies underlying our act of state cases—international comity, respect for the sovereignty of foreign nations on their own territory, and the avoidance of embarrassment to the Executive Branch in its conduct of foreign relations—are implicated in the present case because, as the District Court found, a determination that Nigerian officials demanded and accepted a bribe "would impugn or question the nobility of a foreign nation's motivations," and would "result in embarrassment to the sovereign or constitute interference in the conduct of foreign policy of the United States." 659 F.Supp., at 1392–1393. The United States, as amicus curiae, favors the same approach to the act of state doctrine, though disagreeing with petitioners as to the outcome it produces in the present case. We should not, the United States urges, "attach dispositive significance to the fact that this suit involves only the 'motivation' for, rather than the 'validity' of, a foreign sovereign act," Brief for United States as Amicus Curiae 37, and should eschew "any rigid formula for the resolution of act of state cases generally," id., at 9. In some future case, perhaps, "litigation…based on alleged corruption in the award of contracts or other commercially oriented activities of foreign governments could sufficiently touch on 'national nerves' that the act of state doctrine or related principles of abstention would appropriately be found to bar the suit," id., at 40 (quoting Sabbatino, 376 U.S., at 428), and we should therefore resolve this case on the narrowest possible ground, viz., that the letter from the legal adviser to the District Court gives sufficient indication that, "in the setting of this case," the act of state doctrine poses no bar to adjudication, ibid. * * * * *

These urgings are deceptively similar to what we said in Sabbatino, where we observed that sometimes, even though the validity of the act of a foreign sovereign within its own territory is called into question, the policies underlying the act of state doctrine may not justify its application. We suggested that a sort of balancing approach could be applied—the balance shifting against application of the doctrine, for example, if the government that committed the "challenged act of state" is no longer in existence. 376 U.S., at 428. But what is appropriate in order to avoid unquestioning judicial acceptance of the acts of foreign sovereigns is not similarly appropriate for the quite opposite purpose of expanding judicial incapacities where such acts are not directly (or even indirectly) involved. It is one thing to suggest, as we have, that the policies underlying the act of state doctrine should be considered in deciding whether, despite the doctrine's technical availability, it should nonetheless not be invoked; it is something quite different to suggest that those underlying policies are a doctrine unto themselves, justifying expansion of the act of state doctrine (or, as the United States puts it, unspecified "related principles of abstention") into new and uncharted fields.

The short of the matter is this: Courts in the United States have the power, and ordinarily the obligation, to decide cases and controversies properly presented to them. The act of state doctrine does not establish an exception for cases and controversies that may embarrass foreign governments, but merely requires that, in the process of deciding, the acts of foreign sovereigns taken within their own jurisdictions shall be deemed valid. That doctrine has no application to the present case because the validity of no foreign sovereign act is at issue.

The judgment of the Court of Appeals for the Third Circuit is affirmed.

It is so ordered.

INTERNATIONAL ECONOMIC AND POLITICAL ORGANIZATIONS

International organizations are either intergovernmental organizations (IGOs) or nongovernmental organizations (NGOs). NGOs are either nonprofit or for-profit organizations. Nonprofit NGOs serve private national groups that are involved in international relations. Prominent examples of nonprofit NGOs are the International Red Cross and Amnesty International. For-profit NGOs include multinational enterprises (MNEs) that are businesses functioning in two or more countries.

IGOs are sponsored by two or more nation states to coordinate activities of mutual interest. IGOs are becoming increasingly important mechanisms for states to work together to manage the complex interaction between them. Arguably the best known and most significant of the IGOs is the United Nations.

UNITED NATIONS

The United Nations was established in 1945 when its Charter was adopted by its member states. The Charter of the UN establishes its goals as maintenance of peace and security, promotion of economic and social cooperation, and protection of human rights. Each of the member states is a sovereign nation in its own right and is treated as an equal member of the organization.

The organs of the UN are the General Assembly, the Security Council, the Secretariat, the International Court of Justice, the Trusteeship Council, and the Economic and Social Council.

General Assembly

The General Assembly is a quasi-legislative body made up of representatives of all member states. The General Assembly is the main deliberative organ of the United Nations.

THE FUNCTIONS AND POWERS OF THE GENERAL ASSEMBLY INCLUDE:

- to consider and make recommendations on cooperation in the maintenance of international peace and security, including disarmament and arms regulation;

- to discuss any question relating to international peace and security and, except where a dispute or situation is being discussed by the Security Council, to make recommendations on it;

- to discuss and, with the same exception, make recommendations on any question within the scope of the Charter or affecting the powers and functions of any organ of the United Nations;

- to initiate studies and make recommendations to promote international political cooperation, the development and codification of international law; the realization of human rights and fundamental freedoms for all, and international collaboration in economic, social, cultural, educational and health fields;

- to make recommendations for the peaceful settlement of any situation, regardless of origin, which might impair friendly relations among nations;

- to receive and consider reports from the Security Council and other United Nations organs;

- to consider and approve the United Nations budget and to apportion the contributions among Members;

- to elect the non-permanent members of the Security Council, the members of the Economic and Social Council and those members of the Trusteeship Council that are elected;

- to elect jointly with the Security Council the Judges of the International Court of Justice; and, on the recommendation of the Security Council, to appoint the Secretary-General. (www.un.org)

Secretary-General

The Secretary-General is the "chief administrative officer" of the United Nations and is empowered to perform in that capacity "such other functions as are entrusted" to him or her by the Security Council, General Assembly, Economic and Social Council and other United Nations organs. The Charter also authorizes the Secretary-General to "bring to the attention of the Security Council any matter which in his opinion may threaten the maintenance of international peace and security." In many ways, the Secretary-General also represents the moral authority of the United Nations.

Security Council

The Security Council is made up of representatives of 15 member states, five of which are permanent member states. Since it is responsible for the maintenance of international peace and security, it is the only UN organ with the authority to use armed force.

THE FUNCTIONS AND POWERS OF THE SECURITY COUNCIL ARE:

- to maintain international peace and security in accordance with the principles and purposes of the United Nations;

- to investigate any dispute or situation which might lead to international friction;

- to recommend methods of adjusting such disputes or the terms of settlement;

- to formulate plans for the establishment of a system to regulate armaments;

- to determine the existence of a threat to the peace or act of aggression and to recommend what action should be taken;

- to call on Members to apply economic sanctions and other measures not involving the use of force to prevent or stop aggression;

- to take military action against an aggressor;

- to recommend the admission of new Members;

- to exercise the trusteeship functions of the United Nations in "strategic areas";

- to recommend to the General Assembly, the appointment of the Secretary-General and, together with the Assembly, to elect the Judges of the International Court of Justice. (www.un.org)

Secretariat

The Secretariat is the administrative arm of the UN. The Secretary General, elected by the General Assembly, is the leader of the Secretariat.

THE DUTIES CARRIED OUT BY THE SECRETARIAT INCLUDE:

- administering peacekeeping operations and mediating international disputes;

- surveying economic and social trends and problems;

- preparing studies on human rights and sustainable development

- inform the world's communications media about the work of the United Nations;

- organizing international conferences on issues of worldwide concern;

- interpreting speeches and translating documents into the Organization's official languages. (www.un.org)

International Court of Justice

The Court was established in 1945 under the Charter of the United Nations and acts as a world court. The principal judicial organ of the United Nations, it is based at The Hague, in the Netherlands. The Court decides disputes submitted to it by states through the application of international law in accordance with international treaties and conventions in force, international custom, general principles of law and, judicial decisions and teachings of the most highly qualified legal scholars.

The Court also issues advisory opinions when requested to do so by specific international organs and agencies. The only bodies at present authorized to request advisory opinions of the Court are the five organs of the United Nations and sixteen specialized agencies of the United Nations family.

INTERNATIONAL MONETARY FUND

The International Monetary Fund (IMF) is an IGO consisting of 184 member countries. It was established to promote international monetary cooperation, exchange stability, and orderly exchange arrangements; to foster economic growth and high levels of employment; and to provide temporary financial assistance to countries to help ease balance of payments adjustment.

The operations of the IMF involve surveillance, financial assistance, and technical assistance and have evolved to meet the needs of its member countries in an increasingly complex world economy.

Surveillance is a process of monitoring and consultation through the maintenance of an information flow with its member countries regarding the national and international consequences of their economic and financial policies.

Financial assistance provided by the IMF is a mechanism by which loans are made available to countries experiencing balance-of-payments problems. The restoration of conditions for sustainable economic growth enables countries to rebuild their international reserves, stabilize their currencies, and continue paying for imports without having to impose trade restrictions or capital controls.

Technical assistance supported by the IMF in its areas of expertise adds to the "development of the productive resources of member countries by enhancing the effectiveness of economic policy and financial policy." The IMF, by providing advice on fiscal policy, monetary policy, and macroeconomic and financial statistics, helps countries strengthen their human and institutional capacity giving advice on how to design and implement effective macroeconomic and structural policies.

THE PURPOSES OF THE IMF ARE:

- to promote international monetary cooperation through a permanent institution which provides the machinery for consultation and collaboration on international monetary problems;

- to facilitate the expansion and balanced growth of international trade, and to contribute thereby to the promotion and maintenance of high levels of employment and real income and to the development of the productive resources of all members as primary objectives of economic policy;

- to promote exchange stability, to maintain orderly exchange arrangements among members, and to avoid competitive exchange depreciation;

- to assist in the establishment of a multilateral system of payments in respect of current transactions between members and in the elimination of foreign exchange restrictions which hamper the growth of world trade;

- to give confidence to members by making the general resources of the Fund temporarily available to them under adequate safeguards, thus providing them with opportunity to correct maladjustments in their balance of payments without resorting to measures destructive of national or international prosperity;

- in accordance with the above, to shorten the duration and lessen the degree of disequilibrium in the international balances of payments of members. (www.imf.org)

WORLD BANK

The World Bank is the name that has come to be used for the International Bank for Reconstruction and Development (IBRD) and the International Development Association (IDA). The World Bank is one of the United Nations specialized agencies. Its members include the 184 member states of United Nations. It is not really a "bank" as we might identify one. This IGO is really a development bank; an organization that provides financing to national governments of members to support economic development. The member states are jointly responsible for both the financing of the Bank and the distribution of its resources.

WORLD TRADE ORGANIZATION

The World Trade Organization (WTO), established in 1995, is the only global international organization dealing with the rules of trade between nations. The WTO is located in Geneva, Switzerland and has 146 members, including both states and customs territories. The WTO agreements form the foundation of a global trading system. These agreements have been negotiated, signed and ratified by the majority of the world's trading nations. The WTO is an important part of the global system that provides trade stability to its member nations.

The system was developed through a series of trade negotiations, or rounds, held under the General Agreement on Tariffs and Trade (GATT). The GATT was initially adopted during the Geneva round in 1947 and since then eight additional rounds have been held. The first five rounds dealt mainly with tariff reductions. The last three rounds have included non-tariff issues in the negotiations. The last round, the 1986–94 Uruguay Round, led to the WTO's creation.

The WTO agreement is entirely institutional and procedural creating a framework that permits the various trade agreements negotiated since 1947 to be in effect "managed" structurally by the WTO. The WTO has five main organs: a Ministerial Conference, the General Council, a Council for Trade in Goods, a Council for Trade and Services, and a Council for Trade Related Aspects of Intellectual Property Rights.

THE PRIMARY GOAL OF THE WTO IS TO HELP PRODUCERS OF GOODS AND SERVICES, EXPORTERS, AND IMPORTERS CONDUCT THEIR BUSINESS BY:

- Administering trade agreements;
- Acting as a forum for trade negotiations ;
- Settling trade disputes;
- Reviewing national trade policies;
- Assisting developing countries in trade policy issues, through technical assistance and training programs;
- Cooperating with other international organizations. (www.wto.org)

CHAPTER QUESTIONS

1. The establishment of the WTO has led to controversy and concern across the world. What are the broader implications for the development global trading systems under the WTO?

2. Describe the sources of international law.

3. The U.S. Constitution grants most of the power for the conduct of international relations to the federal government. What are the specific areas of constitutional authority that address this issue?

4. What is the significance of the doctrine of sovereign immunity?

5. What is the impact of the Foreign Sovereign Immunities Act on the doctrine of sovereign immunity?

6. What is the difference between NGOs and IGOs?

7. What is the source of the authority of the United Nations? Discuss.

CHAPTER FIVE:
ETHICAL PERSPECTIVES

INTRODUCTION

The laws of the United States apply to all businesses organized within its borders. Businesses organized in the U.S. are also subject to the laws of the countries in which they do business. Businesspersons owe a duty to act ethically when conducting their business affairs and businesses are obligated to act in a socially responsible way, i.e., not to harm society. These are the very basic requirements, the Golden Rules, of business and businesspeople.

LAW AND BUSINESS ETHICS

Frequently, law, in its broadest sense, and ethics travel on parallel paths, moving toward the same goal. For example, the commission of a theft violates federal and state laws. If a person steals a car, he is violating a law. He is also breaking a code of ethics.

Simply stated, ethics is the study of good and bad behavior. Business ethics is the study of good and bad business behavior. Behavior includes how the business organization conducts its operation and affairs and how individual officers and managers come to decisions within the business organization. One has only to think of the recent court cases surrounding cigarette companies and their individual directors and managers to see how legal and ethical issues intertwine and diverge.

Ethics, or the lack thereof, can only be measured on a personal level. As such, it is very important to view business ethics not as one uniform system, but as a group of viewpoints obtained from the managers and directors of a business, corporations within a particular industry, and the industry as a whole. Each may judge the ethics of an event very differently.

The differences come from individual perspectives of what they consider ethical behavior. Ethical behavior is based on any number of theories or schools of ethical philosophy. Businesspersons, corporations and an entire industry may adhere to any one of these philosophies or part(s) of each philosophy.

SOCIAL RESPONSIBILITY

The concerns of business regarding its profit-making motives and non-profit making motives and their intended and unintended effects on individuals and groups not within the business encompass social responsibility. In other words, one may ask, "How do the various business-motivated acts impact on the consumer and environmental and political groups not directly involved in a business's operation?"

Prior to the rise of consumer awareness and consumer protection laws, businesses made many decisions based solely on a cost-benefit analysis and its impact on net profits. This method of doing business was often contrary to moral ethical values, and more specifically, ran up against the interests of consumers, the betterment of the environment and more. As a result, businesses today are being held to some degree of social responsibility for their conduct.

PROFIT-ORIENTED THEORY—THE MAXIMIZATION OF PROFITS

Traditionally, a business's social responsibility lay with its shareholders and maximizing their profits. Popular in the nineteenth century, this tenet adheres to the belief that the interests of other groups, local residents, employees, support services of the business, did not concern the business. The interests of these groups did not factor into the way a corporation conducted its business.

Advocates of this theory hold that in a free society such as that existing in the U.S., business has but one social responsibility. A company must use its resources and engage in activities that will increase its profits as long as the company engages in open and free competition without resorting to deception and fraud.

REGULATION THEORY

This theory holds that a company is socially responsible if it avoids harming society or corrects a social harm that it has caused. If a company operates under these minimal standards, it is acting in a socially responsible manner.

The legislative branch of government enacts laws to enforce this standard, for example, the Occupational Safety and Health Act, the Pure Food and Drug Act, and the Clean Air Act. Consumer protection laws establish safety standards for manufactured goods and provide recourse to persons injured by defective merchandise.

MANAGERIAL THEORY

This theory raises the moral minimum threshold by recognizing that others besides a company's shareholders are owed a duty of social responsibility. Employees, resource suppliers, customers, the residents of a community in which a company operates, etc., have relationships with that company and these stakeholders are affected by its actions.

Because various stakeholders' interests may be at odds with each other, it is difficult if not impossible to make business decisions that are socially responsible to all parties affected.

INSTITUTIONAL THEORY

The U.S. Constitution has created a legal fiction making corporations persons under certain circumstances and for specific purposes. The institutional theory holds that businesses have a responsibility to promote good works, even those not directly beneficial to it, just as individuals have. In this vein, companies should commit some of their profits to benefit the community in which it "lives," provide opportunities for its employees to contribute time to the betterment of that community—in other words, to be a good neighbor. Since corporations receive some social power from society, they have a duty to make the community a better place in which to live.

The problem with this theory is that corporations do not have unlimited resources to perform all the good works that may be required to improve the community. In addition, shareholders are generally more interested in profits—doing too much for the community will scare away potential investors.

PROFESSIONAL OBLIGATION THEORY

Under this theory, managers and officers of the board of directors of a corporation should be certified by meeting specific established standards of professionalism before they can assume their positions. All professional ethics codes define the particular profession. A professional must meet educational requirements, pass a licensing examination, abide by the code of conduct of that profession, obtain membership in a formal association, and demonstrate an independent commitment to advance the public good. Lawyers, accountants, doctors and architects fall within this group.

Believers of this theory hold that the occupations of business manager and board member should also be included in the definition of professional. Persons working in these occupations have an obligation that extends beyond their duty to shareholders; they should obtain formal education that provides knowledge in this field, they should be required to pass licensure examinations and they should be made to adhere to disciplinary codes and standards.

ETHICAL PHILOSOPHIES

ETHICAL FUNDAMENTALISM

This ethical theory encompasses the tenet that the individual finds his or her ethical beliefs in an outside source. A book, for example, the Bible, or a person, such as Kant (see below), may guide him or her. Some argue that ethical fundamentalism impedes people from determining right and wrong for themselves. For example, certain philosophies believe all killing of humans is immoral. In the Jewish faith, murder is immoral, but not everyone who is killed by another is murdered.

MORAL THEORIES

UTILITARIANISM—CONSEQUENTIAL THEORIES

Jeremy Bentham (1748–1832) and John Stuart Mill (1806–1873) first propounded this theory. Under its application, businesspeople judge acts as being good or bad based on whether the acts have achieved their desired results. People must choose those acts or follow those rules that provide the greatest good to society. However, this does not mean the result must benefit the greatest number of people.

An act is ethically correct (good) if, after adding up all of the benefits (good) and all of the risks (bad), the net result has a positive effect. For example, an airplane manufacturer fires a designer who for unknown reasons purposely misdesigns the structural supports of a new prototype of plane. The company has to spend hundreds of thousands of dollars to correct the errors, but in the process, it will avoid the loss of millions of dollars in lawsuits brought by survivors of those who die in its crashing airplanes. Under the utilitarian theory, the decision to fire the designer was correct because the outcome provided the greatest good to society.

KANTIAN ETHICS—DEONTOLOGICAL THEORIES

The term, deontology, is derived from the Greek word *deon,* meaning "duty." Adherents of this theory believe rules and principles determine whether or not actions are ethically good or bad. The "Golden Rule" is the main principle under this theory. The most famous proponent of deontology is Immanuel Kant (1724–1804). He believed that people owe moral duties based on universal principles. Therefore, even if a promise kept by the promissor turns out to be detrimental to himself, he is bound by this ethical theory to keep the promise anyway.

This is an example of absolute deontology. Actions may be judged as ethically good or bad based on absolute moral principles obtained by reasoning without regard to the consequences of those acts; that is, even if the result of the actions does not yield a net good.

Two precepts provide the basis of deontology: 1) consistency—all situations are treated in the same way without exception, and 2) reversibility—the actor must adhere to the rule he uses to judge the morality of another's conduct. Therefore, if it is acceptable for you to steal another's money, it is equally acceptable for others to steal your money. (The Golden Rule.)

ETHICAL RELATIVISM

This theory, based on each individual's interpretation of what is ethical behavior, is the one most criticized. It holds that individuals must decide for themselves what is ethical, based on their own personal perspective of what is right and wrong. An individual meeting his or her own personal ideal in making a decision may not be criticized for making that decision. Therefore, universal rules of ethics do not exist to guide each person's conduct. This theory does not promote societal order or ethical consistency.

SOCIAL CONTRACT OR SOCIAL JUSTICE THEORY

John Locke (1632–1704) and Jean Jacques Rousseau (1712–1778) were the developers of the social contract theory. This theory holds that each person presumptively enters into a social contract with every other member of society to obey moral rules that are required for people to live in peace and harmony. These moral rules are applied whenever conflicting interests need resolution.

John Rawls, a contemporary Harvard University philosopher, is the main modern day spokesperson for this theory. His distributive justice theory holds that fairness is the essence of justice. Going one step further, a tenet of this theory holds that principles of justice should be chosen by those who do not know their status in society—their "ignorance" permits the most equitable principles to be chosen. Therefore, those who did not yet know if they were in a favored class would support the principle of equal rights. Rawls provides a warning, though. He proposed that the least advantaged members of society must receive special treatment to allow them to become all that they can.

Criticism of this theory exists for two reasons: 1) In real society it is impossible to establish the "original position" for selecting moral principles; and 2) Many people would not choose to maximize the benefit of the most disadvantaged members of society.

HUMANIST THEORIES

This school of thought evaluates actions as ethically good or bad by considering what they contribute to the betterment of innate human qualities—intelligence, wisdom, self-control and kindness, for example. If one's acts do not contribute to the betterment of such qualities, they are ethically immoral. Natural law proponents believe that reason leads to a code of conduct derived from an ultimate source of conduct—a supreme being or nature, itself.

Review the following case and try to apply as many of the ethical theories to it you can.

Zivich v. Mentor Soccer Club, Inc.
696 N.E.2D 201 (1998)

We are asked to decide whether the exculpatory agreement executed by Mrs. Zivich on behalf of her minor son released the Club from liability for the minor child's claims and the parents' claims as a matter of law. We find that the exculpatory agreement is valid as to all claims. Summary judgment was appropriately entered in the Club['s] favor. The judgment of the court of appeals is affirmed.

Pursuant to Civ.R 56, summary judgment is appropriate when (1) there is no genuine issue of material fact, (2) the moving party is entitled to judgment as a matter of law, and (3) reasonable minds can come to but one conclusion and that conclusion is adverse to the nonmoving party, said party being entitled to have the evidence construed most strongly in his favor. The party moving for summary judgment bears the burden of showing that there is no genuine issue of material fact and that it is entitled to judgment as a matter of law.

Appellants argue that since practice had concluded, the injury occurred outside the scope of the exculpatory agreement. We find this contention meritless. We quote, with approval, Judge Nader's majority opinion rejecting this argument: "It should not come as any great surprise for a parent to learn that, during a period of inactivity at a soccer practice, his or her child fiddled with loose equipment, climbed on nearby bleachers, or scaled the goal. It should be equally clear that coaches supervising the practices will not be able to completely prevent such unauthorized activity, as some degree of bedlam is unavoidable, when children of tender years are brought together to play a game, and when their emotions are aroused. The risk of a seven[-]year[-]old child climbing on a goal shortly after winning an intrasquad scrimmage is, therefore, a natural incident of his participation in soccer practice. Thus, Bryan's injuries fall within the ambit of the release."

Appellants contend that the release is invalid on public policy grounds. In support of their argument, they refer to the general principle that contracts entered into by a minor, unless for "necessaries," are avoidable by the minor, once the age of majority is reached, or shortly thereafter. Appellants urge us to apply the seminal case * * * * * where the Washington Supreme Court relied upon * * * * * a six-part test to determine whether a particular release violates public policy. The Club, however, argues that the proper focus is not whether the release violates public policy but rather that public policy itself justifies the enforcement of this agreement. This is also the position advocated by Judge Ford in his concurring opinion. We agree with the Club and Judge Ford.

The General Assembly has enacted statutes designed to encourage landowners to open their land to pubic use for recreational activities without fear of liability. [T]hese statutes accord qualified immunity to unpaid athletic coaches and sponsors of athletic events. Hence, the General Assembly has articulated its intent of encouraging the sponsorship of sports activities and protecting volunteers. However, [the statutes] were enacted after this cause of action arose. Thus, our role is to render a decision that fills the gap left open before the effective date of the statutory enactments.

It cannot be disputed that volunteers in community recreational activities serve an important function. Organized recreational activities offer children the opportunity to learn valuable life skills. It is here that many children learn how to work as a team and how to operate within an organizational structure. Children also are given the chance to exercise and develop coordination skills. Due in great part to the assistance of volunteers, nonprofit organizations are able to offer these activities at minimal cost. In fact, the American Youth Soccer Organization pays only nineteen of its four hundred thousand staff members. The Little League pays only seventy of its 2.5 million members. Clearly, without the work of its volunteers, these nonprofit organizations could not exist, and scores of children would be without the benefit and enjoyment of organized sports. Yet the threat of liability strongly deters many individuals from volunteering for nonprofit organizations. Insurance for the organizations is not the answer, because individual volunteers may still find themselves potentially liable when an injury occurs. Thus, although volunteers offer their services without receiving any financial return, they place their personal assets at risk.

Therefore, faced with the very real threat of a lawsuit, and the potential for substantial damage awards, nonprofit organizations and their volunteers could very well decide that the risks are not worth the effort. Hence, invalidation of exculpatory agreements would reduce the number of activities made possible through the uncompensated services of volunteers and their sponsoring organizations. Therefore, we conclude that although Bryan, like many children before him, gave up his right to sue for the negligent acts of others, the public as a whole received the benefit of these exculpatory agreements. Because of this agreement, the Club was able to offer affordable recreation and to continue to do so without the risks and overwhelming costs of litigation. Bryan's parents agreed to shoulder the risk. Public policy does not forbid such an agreement. In fact, public policy supports it. Accordingly, we believe that public policy justifies giving parents authority to enter into these types of binding agreements on behalf of their minor children. We also believe that the enforcement of these agreements may well promote more active involvement by participants and their families, which, in turn, promotes the overall quality and safety of these activities.

Another related concern is the importance of parental authority. Judge Ford's concurring opinion also embraces this notion. Judge Ford found that the right of a parent to raise his or her child is a natural right subject to the protections of due process. Additionally, parents have a fundamental liberty interest in the care, custody, and management of their offspring. Further, the existence of a fundamental, privacy-oriented right of personal choice in family matters has been recognized under the Due Process Clause by the United States Supreme Court. Based upon these protections, Judge Ford believes that may decisions made by parents "fall within the penumbra of parental authority, e.g., the school that the child will attend, the religion that the child will practice, the medical care that the child will receive, and the manner in which the child will be disciplined." He found it notable that the law empowers a parent to consent to medical procedures for a minor child, gives a parent the general authority to decide to decline medical treatment for the child, and destroys the child's cause of action for battery when consent is given. Thus, Judge Ford believes that invalidating the release as to the minor's claim is inconsistent with conferring other powers on parents to make important life choices for their children. Nor is it appropriate to equate a preinjury release with a post injury release. As one commentator aptly explains:

"The concerns underlying the judiciary's reluctance to allow parents to dispose of a child's existing claim do not arise in the situation where a parent waives a child's future claim. A parent dealing with an existing claim is simultaneously coping with an injured child; such a situation creates a potential for parental action contrary to that child's ultimate best interests.

"A parent who signs a release before her child participates in a recreational activity, however, faces an entirely different situation. First, such a parent has no financial motivation to sign the release. To the contrary, because a parent must pay for medical care, she risks her financial interests by signing away the right to recover damages. Thus, the parent would better serve her financial interests by refusing to sign the release.

"A parent who dishonestly or maliciously signs a preinjury release in deliberate derogation of his child's best interests also seems unlikely. Presumably parents sign future releases to enable their children to participate in activities that the parents and children believe will be fun or educational. Common sense suggests that while a parent might misjudge or act carelessly in signing a release, he would have no reason to sign with malice aforethought.

Moreover, parents are less vulnerable to coercion and fraud in a preinjury setting. A parent who contemplates signing a release as a prerequisite to her child's participation in some activity faces none of the emotional trauma and financial pressures that may arise with an existing claim. That parent has time to examine the release, consider its terms, and explore possible alternatives. A parent signing a future release is thus more able to reasonably assess the possible consequences of waiving the right to sue."

* * * * * We agree with Judge Ford's concurring opinion[.]…When Mrs. Zivich signed the release she did so because she wanted Bryan to play soccer. She made an important family decision and she assumed the risk of physical injury on behalf of her child and the financial risk on behalf of the family as a whole. Thus, her decision to release a volunteer on behalf of her child simply shifted the cost of injury to the parents. Apparently, she made a decision that the benefits to her child outweighed the risk of physical injury. Mrs. Zivich did her best to protect Bryan's interests and we will not disturb her judgment. In fact, the situation is more analogous to Ohio's informed consent law that to the law governing children's property rights. In both

cases, the parent weighs the risks of physical injury to the child and the attendant costs to herself against the benefits of a particular activity.

Therefore we hold that parents have the authority to bind their minor children to exculpatory agreements in favor of volunteers and sponsors of nonprofit sport activities where the cause of action sounds in negligence. These agreements may not be disaffirmed by the child on whose behalf they were executed.

* * * * *

Judgment affirmed.

UNIT II
CONTRACTS

CHAPTER SIX:
CONTRACTS OVERVIEW

INTRODUCTION

A contract may best be defined as an enforceable promise. Professor Williston noted: "A contract is a promise, or a set of promises, for breach of which the law gives a remedy, or the performance of which the law in some way recognizes a duty." A promise is an undertaking that something either will or will not happen in the future. The term "contract" is also used by both laymen and lawyers to refer to a specific document in which the terms of a specific agreement are written. Who enforces promises? Generally, the parties themselves (i.e., the promisor, the person making the promise, and the promisee, the person to whom the promise is made) will carry out their promises; but in some cases, the legal system may be called upon to enforce promises where the parties fail to do so or where one of the parties commits a breach. We will discuss contract remedies in detail in Chapter Fourteen.

As noted by Professors Calamari and Perillo, "The law of contracts permeates every aspect of our society." Our legal system recognizes that almost everyone has the ability to enter freely into a contract or a contractual arrangement. This is called the principle of freedom of contract and is recognized and protected by the U.S. Constitution, in Article I, Section 10. However, freedom of contract is no longer completely unbridled or absolute. Today, courts will not enforce illegal bargains, certain contracts of employment, agreements that unreasonably restrain trade, unconscionable agreements, contracts entered into under duress or undue influence, contracts of "adhesion," and a whole range of agreements that are said to violate "public policy."

REQUIREMENTS OF A VALID CONTRACT

This discussion of contracts is not meant to be exhaustive. Rather, the text discusses contracts in the larger context of the legal, social, and regulatory environment of business.

The following are the four basic elements of a valid contract:

1. An agreement, consisting of an offer and an acceptance.

2. Consideration, which is defined as "something bargained for in return for a promise." (Today, courts focus especially on the concept of a bargain in deciding if a particular promise will be enforced.)

3. Legal capacity of the parties. Both the promisor and promisee must have the contractual capacity to enter into a contract. Contractual capacity involves issues such as age and mental state (e.g., persons suffering from senility or Alzheimer's disease), and may involve allied issues such as fraud, undue influence, or duress.

4. Legal purpose. A contract cannot be formed for an illegal or immoral purpose, violate a statute, or violate "public policy."

In addition, there are two "outside" factors that may make a contract unenforceable should one of the parties seek its enforcement in a court:

1. The Statute of Frauds, which requires that certain types of contracts must be in writing to be enforceable.

2. The Statute of Limitations, which prescribes the time period during which a party must sue for breach of contract.

All of these elements of a valid contract will be discussed in great detail in the chapters that follow.

CLASSIFICATION OF CONTRACTS

Whether by words or actions, or a combination of both, the parties must form or come to an agreement. An essential prerequisite to the formation of a contract is the mutual manifestation of assent (agreement) to the same terms. This is sometimes called the "meeting of the minds."

EXPRESS CONTRACT

An express contract is one in which all of the terms may be found in words, either orally or in writing. A brief word about oral contracts is appropriate. Strictly speaking, contracts are not required to be in writing, unless the Statute of Frauds applies. However, attempting to enforce an oral contract provides certain basic proof problems for the parties and for a court. Oral proof is valuable and probative, and in many cases, may be the only proof available. However, if parties' oral testimony conflicts, in the absence of written proof, a court may be required to decide a dispute on the basis of credibility, or believability of witnesses. The words of the humorist Will Rogers are quite appropriate: "An oral contract is not worth the paper it's printed on!"

IMPLIED CONTRACT (IMPLIED IN FACT)

An implied in fact contract is created by conduct, rather than words. An implied in fact contract exists where facts and circumstances indicate that a contract has been entered into. If Smith telephones an electrician to come to Smith's house to fix an electric socket, it may be inferred that Smith has agreed to pay the electrician a reasonable fee for his services although nothing has been expressly said about payment. An implied in fact contract may also arise where a person accepts a benefit from another party and that benefit was not intended to be a gift.

The following four steps generally establish an implied in fact contract:

1. Plaintiff furnished some service, goods, or property to the defendant;

2. Plaintiff expected to be paid for the service, goods, or property;

3. Defendant knew or should have known that payment was expected; and

4. Defendant had the opportunity to reject the service, property, or goods and did not do so.

EXAMPLE:

Every morning for a month, Freddy Glotz opens his front door and notices that the Ace Milk Company has delivered four bottles of milk. Freddy brings the full bottles into the kitchen, uses their contents, and leaves the empty bottles at the door. At the end of the one-month period, Freddy receives a bill for $120, representing $1 for each bottle of milk. Freddy refuses to pay the bill stating that "no contract was entered into because I had never promised to pay for the milk." Evaluate. Was there an express contract? Was there an implied contract? How could Glotz have rejected the benefit so that no implied contract would be found by a court?

The following case discusses the creation of an implied in fact contract and the obligation of the defendant, Caton, to pay for a service, despite the fact that he claimed he had no intention to do so. Pay close attention to why the court inferred Caton's promise to pay.

Day v. Caton
119 MASS. 513 (1876)

Background and Facts

Plaintiff Day owned a vacant lot that was next to defendant Caton's vacant lot. Day decided to build a brick wall between the adjoining lots. The evidence indicated that Caton knew the wall was being built. Caton claimed that there was no express agreement between him and Day to pay for a portion of the wall, and that his silence and subsequent "use" of the wall did not raise an implied promise to pay anything for it. In the trial court, the jury found for the plaintiff, Day. Caton appealed the decision of the trial court to the Supreme Judicial Court of Massachusetts in order to have the judgment overruled.

DEVENS, Judge

The ruling that a promise to pay for the wall would not be implied from the fact that the plaintiff, with the defendant's knowledge, built the wall, and that the defendant used it, was substantially in accordance with the request of the defendant, is conceded to have been correct.

The defendant, however, contends that the presiding judge incorrectly ruled that such promise might be inferred from the fact that the plaintiff undertook and completed the building of the wall with the expectation that the defendant would pay him for it, the defendant having reason to know that the plaintiff was acting with that expectation, and allowed him thus to act without objection.

The fact that the plaintiff expected to be paid for the work would certainly not be sufficient of itself to establish the existence of a contract, when the question between the parties was whether one was made. It must be shown that in some manner the party sought to be charged assented to it. If a party, however, voluntarily accepts and avails himself of valuable services rendered for his benefit, when he has the option whether to accept or reject them, even if there is no distinct proof that they were rendered by his authority or request, a promise to pay for them may be inferred. His knowledge that they were valuable, and his exercise of the option to avail himself of them, justify this inference. And when one stands by in silence, and sees valuable services rendered upon his real estate by the erection of a structure (of which he must necessarily avail himself afterwards in his proper use thereof), such silence, accompanied with the knowledge on his part that the party rendering services expects payment therefore, may fairly be treated as evidence of an acceptance of it, and as tending to show an agreement to pay for it.

* * * * *

(I)f silence may be interpreted as assent where a proposition is made to one which he is bound to deny or admit, so also it may be if he is silent in the face of facts which fairly call upon him to speak.

If a person saw day after day a laborer at work in his field doing services, which must of necessity insure to his benefit, knowing that the laborer expected pay for his work when it was perfectly easy to notify him if his services were not wanted, even if a request were not expressly proved, such a request, either previous to or contemporaneous with the performance of the services, might fairly be inferred. But if the fact was merely brought to his attention upon a single occasion and casually, if he had little opportunity to notify the other that he did not desire the work and should not pay for it, or could only do so at the expense of much time and trouble, the same inference might not be made. The circumstances of each case would necessarily determine whether silence with knowledge that another was doing valuable work for his benefit and with the expectation of payment indicated that consent which would give rise to the inference of a contract. The question would be one for the jury, and to them it was properly submitted in the case before us by the presiding judge.

IMPLIED IN LAW (ALSO CALLED QUASI-CONTRACT)

An implied in law contract is not a true contract created by the parties, but is an obligation imposed on the parties by law to "do justice" and to avoid unjust enrichment. A quasi-contract is based on the view that a person should not be allowed to profit or enrich himself inequitably at the expense of another. Thus, this doctrine is equitable rather than contractual in nature. It recognizes a social or moral obligation and not strictly a legal one. For example, if a physician gives a child necessary medical care in the face of parental neglect and inaction, the physician may recover from the parents the reasonable value of his services. (*Greenspan v. Slate,* 12 N.J. 426 (1953)).

A quasi-contract essentially is a legal fiction, based neither on any express promise by a party to pay for any benefit received nor on the conduct of a party which implies such a promise. Indeed, the defendant may not only have not solicited the benefit, but may be unaware that it has been conferred (as in the case where a person receives emergency medical treatment while unconscious), or may even object to the entire transaction.

It is sometimes helpful in distinguishing between an implied in law contract and an implied in fact contract to consider that an implied in fact contract usually arises over a longer, sustained period of time. Whereas, an implied in law contract may even arise in a single act or transaction.

EXAMPLE:

While Mr. and Mrs. Ferg are on week's vacation in Hoboken, the E-Z Roofing Company puts a new roof on the Ferg's home. When the Ferg's return home, they receive a bill for $2,500.00. When they refuse to pay the bill, the E-Z Roofing Company brings suit against the Ferg's based on a quasi-contract. Evaluate. Has there been unjust enrichment? What else would be required?

> Consider this example. Your neighbor notices that there is a hole in your fence and there is a danger that your chickens might escape. He repairs the fence, at a cost of $40. Would the court impose an obligation on you to reimburse your neighbor for this cost?

In determining a remedy in the case of a quasi-contract, the court will usually limit the plaintiff's recovery to the amount of the actual cost of the service, goods or property, usually excluding profit. This remedy is termed *quantum meruit*.

Bilateral and unilateral contracts: Every contract involves at least two contracting parties. In some cases, however, only one party has made a promise and therefore only that party is subject to a legal obligation. Such a contract is called a unilateral contract. A bilateral contract is one in which both parties, the promisor and promisee, have made promises and are bound to fulfill obligations towards each other. For example, in a typical sales contract, the seller is bound to deliver and the buyer is bound to pay the price. In a bilateral contract, each party is both the promisor and promisee, having made mutual promises.

EXAMPLE:

Heller says to Teston, "If you cut my lawn next Wednesday, I promise to pay you $10." Heller has made a promise but has not asked Teston for a return promise. Heller has requested Teston to perform an act, not to make a promise or commitment to do so. Heller has thus made an offer for a unilateral contract that arises when and if Teston performs the act called for. However, if Teston fails to cut the lawn, he is not in breach of contract since he made no promise to do so.

Suppose Heller had said to be, "I promise to pay you $10 if you promise to cut my lawn each week this summer." In this case, Heller's offer requests Teston to make a commitment or promise to cut the lawn. A bilateral contract arises when the requisite return promise is made by Teston.

Under the common law, a problem arose in a unilateral contract—where the promisor attempted to revoke an offer after the promisee had begun performance, but before the requested act was completed. ("I promise to pay you $10 if you climb the flag-pole." When you are about ten feet from the top, I yell to you, "I revoke.") Under the common law, acceptance could occur only upon full and complete performance. An offer was normally revocable until accepted. Under a more modern view, however, such an offer becomes irrevocable once the promisee begins performance. The promisee will thereafter be given a reasonable time to complete the act and thus to complete the contract.

Most business contracts contain mutual promises and are thus bilateral in nature, binding both the offeror and the offeree by their promises, to the terms of an agreement.

Executed and executory contracts: A contract that has been fully performed by both the promisor and promisee is termed an executed contract. A contract that has not yet been full performed by either party is said to be executory. You may also see the term "partially executed," which is used to designate a type of contract that is partially completed by one or both of the parties in a contract. [You should also be aware that the term "executed" may be used as a synonym for a party's signature on a contract, as "John executed a purchase agreement for Blackacre….".]

UNCONSCIONABILITY

Unconscionable contracts. Unconscionability is a word that defies a precise definition. The term itself is derived from moral philosophy and ethics. The closest we can get to a definition is "that which affronts the sense of decency." Under the early common law, courts would regularly enforce contracts entered into by parties, under the principle of freedom of contract—even contracts that appeared to be one-sided, unfair, oppressive, or burdensome. This principle was embodied in the concept of "*caveat emptor*," translated as "let the buyer beware." Around the turn of the 20th century, however, many courts began to adopt a more critical view and began to look to the essential nature of the bargain between the parties, any unusual bargaining power possessed by one of the parties, or to the process of formation of a contract. Indeed, Chief Justice Stone in 1912 described the concept of unconscionability as underlying "practically the whole content of the law of equity."

The modern basis for unconscionability appears in the Uniform Commercial Code § 2-302, which attempted to change the essential relationship between the parties from "*caveat emptor*" to "*caveat venditor*," or let the seller beware! The purpose of the doctrine of unconscionability is twofold: "prevention of oppression (sometimes called substantive unconscionability) and unfair surprise (procedural unconscionability)." It should be noted that in fashioning § 2-302, the writers of the Uniform Commercial Code intentionally failed to provide a precise definition of the term "unconscionable" in the belief that to do so might be to defeat the purposes of the rule.

Williams v. Walker-Thomas is the seminal case in the area of unconscionability. Judge Wright added much to the understanding of this difficult concept. Read the excerpt from brief *Williams v. Walker-Thomas,* and the case of *Jones v. Star Credit,* the following case, carefully. Note the reasons why the court ruled as it did in each case.

Williams v. Walker-Thomas Furniture Store 198 A. 2D 914 (D.C. APP. 1964)

Williams, a woman of limited education, was separated from her husband and living on welfare. She entered into a series of installment contracts with Walker-Thomas Furniture Company. During the period of 1957 to 1962, she purchased various items, including curtains, rugs, chairs, mattresses, a washing machine, and a stereo set. With each purchase, she paid part of the amount in cash and signed an installment agreement for the balance. Included in the installment agreement was a paragraph, in extremely fine print, that provided that payments, after the first purchase, were to be prorated on all purchases then outstanding. In other words, each time Williams made an additional purchase from Walker-Thomas under an installment agreement, her payments were credited against the total of all outstanding installment purchases from the company. This had the effect of keeping a balance due on every item until the total bill was paid. Prior to her final purchase, Williams had reduced her total balance outstanding to $164. The last purchase, a stereo, increased her balance to $678. After making several more payments, Williams defaulted. Walker-Thomas attempted to enforce the installment provision of the contract allowing it to repossess all the goods previously purchased by Williams. The contract was ruled "unconscionable."

Jones v. Star Credit Corporation
59 MISC. 2D 189, 298 N.Y.S. 2D 264 (1969)

Background and Facts

The purchasers of a freezer brought this action to reform the contract of sale. The purchasers alleged the contract was unconscionable.

WACHTLER, Justice.

On August 31, 1965 the plaintiffs, who are welfare recipients, agreed to purchase a home freezer unit for $900 as the result of a visit from a salesman representing Your Shop At Home Service, Inc. With the addition of the time credit charges, credit life insurance, credit property insurance, and sales tax, the purchase price totaled $1,234.80. Thus far the plaintiffs have paid $619.88 toward their purchase. The defendant claims that with various added credit charges paid for an extension of time there is a balance of $819.81 still due from the plaintiffs. The uncontroverted proof at the trial established that the freezer unit, when purchased, had a maximum retail value of approximately $300. The question is whether this transaction and the resulting contract could be considered unconscionable within the meaning of Section 2-302 of the Uniform Commercial Code which provides in part:

1) If the court as a matter of law finds the contract or any clause of the contract to have been unconscionable at the time it was made the court may refuse to enforce the contract, or it may enforce the remainder of the contract without the unconscionable clause, or it may so limit the application of any unconscionable clause as to avoid any unconscionable result.

2) When it is claimed or appears to the court that the contract or any clause thereof may be unconscionable the parties shall be afforded a reasonable opportunity to present evidence as to its commercial setting, purpose and effect to aid the court in making the determination.

There was a time when the shield of "caveat emptor" would protect the most unscrupulous in the marketplace—a time when the law, in granting parties unbridled latitude to make their own contracts, allowed exploitive and callous practices which shocked the conscience of both legislative bodies and the courts.

The effort to eliminate these practices has continued to pose a difficult problem. On the one hand it is necessary to recognize the importance of preserving the integrity of agreements and the fundamental right of parties to deal, trade, bargain, and contract. On the other hand there is the concern for the uneducated and often illiterate individual who is the victim of gross inequality of bargaining power, usually the poorest members of the community.

* * * * * The law is beginning to fight back against those who once took advantage of the poor and illiterate without risk of either exposure or interference. From the common law doctrine of intrinsic fraud we have over the years developed common and statutory law which tells not only the buyer but also the seller to beware. This body of laws recognizes the importance of a free enterprise system but at the same time will provide the legal armor to protect and safeguard the prospective victim from the harshness of an unconscionable contract.

Section 2-302 of the Uniform Commercial Code enacts the moral sense of the community into the law of commercial transactions. It authorizes the court to find, as a matter of law, that a contract or a clause of a contract was "unconscionable at the time it was made," and upon so finding the court may refuse to enforce the contract, excise the objectionable clause or limit the application of the clause to avoid an unconscionable result. "The principle," states the Official Comment to this section, "is one of the prevention of oppression and unfair surprise." It permits a court to accomplish directly what heretofore was often accomplished by construction of language, manipulations of fluid rules of contract law and determinations based upon a presumed public policy.

There is no reason to doubt, moreover, that this section is intended to encompass the price term of an agreement. In addition to the fact that it has already been so applied, the statutory language itself makes it clear that not only a clause of the contract, but the contract in toto, may be found unconscionable as a matter of law. Indeed, no other provision of an agreement more intimately touches upon the question of unconscionability than does the term regarding price.

* * * * * Fraud, in the instant case, is not present; nor is it necessary under the statute. The question which presents itself is whether or not, under the circumstances of this case, the sale of a freezer unit having a retail value of $300 for $900 ($1,439.69 including credit charges and $18 sales tax) is unconscionable as a matter of law. The court believes it is.

Concededly, deciding the issue is substantially easier than explaining it. No doubt, the mathematical disparity between $300, which presumably includes a reasonable profit margin, and $900, which is exorbitant on its face, carries the greatest weight. Credit charges alone exceed by more than $100 the retail value of the freezer. These alone, may be sufficient to sustain the decision. Yet, a caveat is warranted lest we reduce the import of Section 2-302 solely to a mathematical ratio formula. It may, at times, be that: yet it may also be much more. The very limited financial resources of the purchaser, known to the sellers at the time of the sale, is entitled to weight in the balance. Indeed, the value disparity itself leads inevitably to the felt conclusion that knowing advantage was taken of the plaintiffs. In addition, the meaningfulness of choice essential to the making of a contract, can be negated by a gross inequality of bargaining power.

There is no question about the necessity and even the desirability of installment sales and the extension of credit. Indeed, there are many, including welfare recipients, who would be deprived of even the most basic conveniences without the use of these devices. Similarly, the retail merchant selling on installment or extending credit is expected to establish a pricing factor which will afford a degree of protection commensurate with the risk of selling to those who might be default prone. However, neither of these accepted premises can clothe the sale of this freezer with respectability.

Support for the court's conclusion will be found in a number of other cases already decided. In American Home Improvement, Inc. v. MacIver, the Supreme Court of New Hampshire held that a contract to install windows, a door and paint, for the price of $2,568.60, of which $809.60 constituted interest and carrying charges and $800 was a salesman's commission was unconscionable as a matter of law. In State by Lefkowitz v. ITM, Inc., a deceptive and fraudulent scheme was involved, but standing alone, the court held that the sale of a vacuum cleaner, among other things, costing the defendant $140 and sold by it for $749 cash or $920.52 on time purchase was unconscionable as a matter of law. Finally, in Frostifresh Corp. v. Reynoso, the sale of a refrigerator costing the seller $348 for $900 plus credit charges of $245.88 was unconscionable as a matter of law.

Having already paid more than $600 toward the purchase of this $300 freezer unit, it is apparent that the defendant has already been amply compensated. In accordance with the statute, the application of the payment provision should be limited to amounts already paid by the plaintiffs and the contract be reformed and amended by changing the payments called for therein to equal the amount of payment actually so paid by the plaintiffs.

JUDGMENT AND REMEDY

Judgment was entered for the plaintiffs. The contract was reformed so that no further payments were required to be made. * * * * *

Generally, four major factors (conditions) appear in the cases that have dealt with the question of unconscionability:

1. The absence of meaningful choice (that is, a traditional "take it or leave it" or "boiler-plate" contract);

2. Great inequality of bargaining power (only one or a very few sellers in the marketplace);

3. The inclusion of terms that would cause unfair surprise, hardship, or oppression (e.g., penalty clauses, clauses which severely limit remedies, a "confession of judgment" clause); or

4. Circumstances where race, literacy, language, ethnicity, economic circumstances, or education are significant factors in determining the nature of the bargain, and the relationship between the parties.

Now, read *Wille v. Southwestern Bell*. Pay special attention to the expanded list of "unconscionable factors" noted by the court. Can you suggest any others for consideration? Do you agree with the inclusion of all of these factors?

Two important questions should be addressed at this point: Why was Mr. Wille unsuccessful? Is unconscionability for everyone?

Wille v. Southwestern Bell Telephone Company
219 KAN. 755 (1976)

Background and Facts

The plaintiff, an operator of a heating and air conditioning business, sued the telephone company to recover damages caused by the omission of his ad from the yellow pages of the telephone directory. The contract for the ad contained a provision limiting the liability of the telephone company to the cost of the ad. The plaintiff contended that this provision was unconscionable. The lower court found for the defendant the plaintiff appealed.

HARMAN, J.

Appellant asserts unconscionability of contract in two respects: the party's unequal bargaining power and the form of the contract and the circumstances of its execution.

American Courts have traditionally taken the view that competent adults may make contracts on their own terms, provided they are neither illegal nor contrary to public policy, and that in the absence of fraud, mistake, or duress, a party who has fairly and voluntarily entered into such a contract is bound thereby, notwithstanding it was unwise or disadvantageous to him. Gradually, however, this principle of "freedom of contract" has been qualified by the Courts as they were confronted by contracts so one-sided that no fair-minded person would view them as tolerable. An early definition of unconscionability was provided by Lord Chancellor Hardwicke, in the case of Chesterfield v. Jensen (1750).

* * * * * "A contract that such as no man in his senses and not under delusion would make on one hand, and as no honest and fair man would accept on the other; which are unequitable and unconscientious bargains; and of such even the Common Law has taken notice."

* * * * * This doctrine received its greatest impetus when it was enacted as a part of the Uniform Commercial Code but the writers did not define the limits or parameters of the doctrine. Perhaps this was the real intent

of the drafters of the code. To define is to limit its application and to limit its application is to defeat its purpose.

* * * * * The basic test is whether in the light of general commercial background and the commercial needs of the particular trade or case, the clauses involved are so one-sided as to be unconscionable under the circumstances existing at the time of the making of the contract. The principle is one of the prevention of oppression and unfair surprise, and not of disturbance of allocation of risks because of superior bargaining power.

* * * * * One type of situation is that involving unfair surprise: where there has naturally actually been no assent to the terms of the contract. Contracts involving unfair surprise are similar to contracts of adhesion. Most often these contracts involve a party whose circumstances, perhaps his inexperience or ignorance, when compared with the circumstances of the other party, make his knowing assent to the fine print terms fictional. Courts have often found an absence of a meaningful bargain. The other situation is that involving oppression: where, although there has been actual assent, the agreement, surrounding facts, and the relative bargaining positions of the parties indicate the possibility of gross overreaching on the part of the person with the superior bargaining power. The economic position of the parties is such that one becomes vulnerable to a grossly unequal bargain.

* * * * * These factors include: 1) the use of printed form or boilerplate contracts drawn skillfully by the party in the strongest economic position, which establish industry-wide standards offered on a take-it-or-leave-it basis to the party in a weaker economic position, 2) a significant cost-price disparity or excessive price, 3) a denial of basic rights and remedies to a buyer of consumer goods, 4) the inclusion of penalty clauses, 5) the circumstances surrounding the execution of the contract, including its commercial setting, its purposes and actual effect, 6) the hiding of clauses which are disadvantageous to one party in a mass of fine print trivia or in places which are inconspicuous to the party signing the contract, 7) phrasing clauses in language that is incomprehensible to a layman or that divert his attention from the problems raised by them or the rights given up through them, 8) an overall imbalance in the obligations and rights imposed by the bargain, 9) exploitation of the underprivileged, unsophisticated, uneducated and the illiterate, and 10) inequality of bargaining or economic power.

Important in this case is the concept of inequality of bargaining power. The UCC does not require that there be complete inequality of bargaining power or that the agreement be equally beneficial to both parties.

* * * * * At least some element of deception or substantive unfairness must presumably be shown.

The cases seem to support the view that there must be additional factors such as deceptive bargaining conduct as well as unequal bargaining power to render the contract unconscionable. In summary, the doctrine of unconscionability is used by the courts to police the excesses of certain parties who abuse their right to contract freely. It is directed against one-sided, oppressive and unfairly surprising contracts, and not against the consequences per se of uneven bargaining power or even a simple old-fashioned bad bargain.

Williston on Contracts states: Parties should be entitled to contract on their own terms without the indulgence of paternalism by courts in the alleviation of one side or another from the effects of a bad bargain. Also, they should be permitted to enter into contracts that actually may be unreasonable or which may lead to hardship on one side. It is only where it turns out that one side or the other is to be penalized by the enforcement of the contract so unconscionable that no decent, fair-minded person would view the ensuing result without being possessed of a profound sense of injustice, that equity will deny the use of its good offices in the enforcement of such unconscionability.

The inequality of bargaining power between the parties here is more apparent than real. There are many other modes of advertising to which the businessman may turn if the contract offered him by the telephone company is not attractive. We find in the record no basis for a conclusion that the application of the Limitation of Liability Clause could lead to a result so unreasonable as to shock the conscience. The language of the challenged paragraph is not couched in confusing terms designed to capitalize on carelessness but is clear and concise. Appellant was an experienced businessman and for at least thirteen years had used the yellow pages. In his business, it is reasonable to assume he as a seller and serviceman had become familiar with printed form contracts that are frequently used in connection with the sale and servicing of heating and air conditioning

equipment and their attendant warranties and limitations of liability. Each case of this type must necessarily rest upon its own facts but after examining the terms of the contract, the manner of its execution and the knowledge and experience of the appellant, we think the contract was neither unconscionable or inequitable so as to deny its enforcement.

AFFIRMED.

Should a court conclude that a contract is unconscionable (note that unconscionability is a matter of law to be decided by the judge), it may:

1. Refuse to enforce the contract;

2. Enforce the contract without the unconscionable clause; or

3. Limit the operation of the unconscionable clause (i.e., reform or rewrite the contract, as in *Jones v. Star Credit*).

A void contract is one that has no legal significance because it produces no legal obligation upon the part of a promisor. It generally cannot be enforced by a court. A contract to commit a crime or a tort or a contract that violates "public policy" is an example of a void contract. A voidable contract is a contract in which a party has the power to elect to avoid his or her legal duty established in the contract. In essence, one of the parties has the option or right to remove him or herself from the agreement with no negative legal consequences. If a party decides not to elect to remove him or herself from the contract, the contract will continue in full force. Examples of voidable contracts are those entered into by a minor, or a contract entered into because of fraud, mutual mistake, "legal duress," and undue influence. These topics will be discussed later in the text in Chapter Eight.

An unenforceable contract arises when a court is legally constrained from enforcing a contract because of some extrinsic factor not connected with the elements of a valid contract discussed above. For example, an otherwise valid contract may not be enforceable by the courts because of either the Statute of Frauds or the Statute of Limitations. Whether or not a contract is unenforceable is usually determined at a very early stage of a case, as a "threshold question," through a motion for a summary judgment, or through a motion to dismiss a lawsuit.

INTRODUCTION TO SALES CONTRACTS
THE SOURCES OF CONTRACT LAW

In general, the great bulk of law with which we will be dealing in a legal environment course will be the common law, embodied in court decisions. However, for the guidance of both courts and lawyers, the American Law Institute in 1932 published a "code-like document" called the *Restatement of Contracts*. While the *Restatement* was issued by a private organization, it was still highly persuasive. The principal drafter of the *Restatement* was Professional Samuel Williston, who taught contracts and other subjects at the Harvard Law School for forty-eight years. A second *Restatement* was circulated in 1964. The second *Restatement* reflected the views of Professor Arthur L. Corbin, author of a major treatise, *Corbin on Contracts,* of Yale Law School. The next major development occurred with the creation of the Uniform Commercial Code or UCC, a joint product of the American Law Institute and the National Conference of Commissioners on Uniform State Laws. A draft was approved in 1952. In 1953, Pennsylvania became the first state to enact the code. When the New York Law

Revision Committee's recommended against enactment unless extensive amendments were made, the Permanent Editorial Board made extensive revisions. As a result, the revised Code was eventually enacted by all states except Louisiana between 1957 and 1967. (Louisiana, whose legal system is based on the Code Napoleon, finally adopted the Code in its entirety in the late 1990s.)

The law of sales, found in Article 2 of the Uniform Commercial Code, deals with transactions (sales or leases) in goods. In general, Article 2 does not deal with contracts involving real property, services, or intangible property such as stocks and bonds. Goods are defined in UCC § 2-105 (1) as "all things" which are movable at the time of identification to the contract for sale and include growing crops and other things attached to realty. (A short-form definition may be: "goods are all things movable and tangible.") In addition, a court's evaluation of a contract dispute may depend on whether one of the parties to the transaction is a merchant, in which case special business standards of "good faith" and "honesty in fact" will be imposed. Section 2-104 delineates three ways that the status of merchant may occur:

1. A merchant is a person who deals regularly in goods of the kind involved in the sales contract. A merchant for one type of goods is not necessarily a merchant for any other type. For example, Charlie Ford, a Christmas tree retailer, is a merchant when buying or selling Christmas trees or perhaps even Christmas ornaments, but not necessarily when buying other general merchandise.

2. A merchant is a person who, by his occupation, holds himself out as having knowledge and skill peculiar to the practices or goods involved in the transaction (and thus, may be considered as an "expert").

3. A person who employs a merchant as a broker, agent, or other intermediary has the status of merchant in that transaction.

Examples of UCC provisions that apply especially to merchants include the memorandum substitute of the Statute of Frauds, firm offers, different and additional terms, confirmatory memoranda, warranties, and modifications of sales contracts. Some of these special provisions will be discussed in the chapter materials on contract law; others will be discussed later in the text in the chapter on sales.

CHAPTER CASE QUESTIONS

Day v. Caton

   a. What does it mean to have a judgment overruled?

   b. Why was the defendant's silence construed as an agreement to pay?

   c. Who normally decides questions of fact in contract cases? Who decides questions of law?

Williams v. Walker-Thomas

   a. What is an installment note? A revolving charge?

   b. What particular characteristics of Mrs. Williams were important to the court in determining if the contract was unconscionable??

   c. What remedies are available to a court in a case where it finds a contract to have been unconscionable?

Jones v. Star Credit

   a. Who decides the issue of unconscionability?

   b. What is *caveat emptor*? What do we mean by "freedom of contract"?

   c. For whom did the court show particular care and concern in its discussion of unconscionability?

   d. What remedy did the court apply? Was it fair to both parties?

   e. What cases did the court cite as precedents? How were they relevant?

   f. What contract term in particular was held to be unconscionable in this case?

Wille v. Southwestern Bell

   a. What early view of unconscionability was cited by Judge Harman?

   b. What test did the court apply?

   c. Of the circumstances cited in the case, which was most important to the court in arriving at its decision?

   d. Why did Mr. Wille lose and Mrs. Williams and Mr. and Mrs. Jones win?

   e. What is a "limitation of liability" clause?

CHAPTER SEVEN:
AGREEMENT: OFFER AND ACCEPTANCE

THE OFFER

An essential requirement in the formation of a contract is an agreement, defined as the mutual manifestation of assent to the same terms. The agreement is ordinarily reached through a process of offer and acceptance. An offer may be defined as a promise, made by the promisor, whereby the promisor asserts that without more, he/she will be bound. An offer is a commitment to do or to refrain from doing some specified thing in the future. Generally speaking, three elements are necessary for an offer to come into existence:

1. There must be serious intent on the part of the offeror to be bound by the terms of the offer;

2. The terms of the offer must be reasonably certain; and

3. The offer must be communicated to the offeree.

Let us look at the first element that requires a serious intention on the part of the offeror to be bound by the terms of the offer. This intention is measured by what is termed the "objective test," which is exemplified in a classic English common law case, *Carlill v. Carbolic Smoke Ball.* The objective test states that an offer will be judged by the objective or reasonable meaning of the words used whether a "reasonable man would conclude that an offer had been made." Under this theory, the subjective intention of the parties is ordinarily irrelevant. However, an offer that is made in obvious anger, jest, or as the result of excitement does not generally meet the requirement of a serious offer. Likewise, an offer must be distinguished from mere statements of intention, preliminary negotiations or discussions, inquiries, or invitations to make an offer.

Let us consider two cases that deal with the application of the "objective test." First, read *Lucy v. Zehmer,* and then read *Barnes v. Treece.* How did the "objective test" work in each of these cases?

Lucy v. Zehmer
196 VA. 493 (1954)

BUCHANAN, Justice.

* * * * * **The instrument sought to be enforced was written by A. H. Zehmer on December 20, 1952, in these words: "We hereby agree to sell to W. O. Lucy the Ferguson Farm complete for $50,000.00, title satisfactory to buyer," and signed by the defendants, A. H. Zehmer and Ida S. Zehmer.**

A. H. Zehmer admitted that* * * * * W. O. Lucy offered him $50,000 cash for the farm, but that he, Zehmer, considered that the offer was made in jest; that so thinking, and both he and Lucy having had several drinks,

he wrote out "the memorandum" quoted above and induced his wife to sign it; that he did not deliver the memorandum to Lucy, but that Lucy picked it up, read it, put it in his pocket, attempted to offer Zehmer $5 to bind the bargain, which Zehmer refused to accept, and realizing for the first time that Lucy was serious, Zehmer assured him that he had no intention of selling the farm and that the whole matter was a joke. Lucy left the premises insisting that he had purchased the farm.

The discussion leading to the signing of the agreement, said Lucy, lasted thirty or forty minutes, during which Zehmer seemed to doubt that Lucy could raise $50,000. Lucy suggested the provision for having the title examined and Zehmer made the suggestion that he would sell it "complete, everything there," and stated that all he had on the farm was three beefers.

Lucy took a partly filled bottle of whiskey into the restaurant with him for the purpose of giving Zehmer a drink if he wanted it. Zehmer did, and he and Lucy had one or two drinks together. Lucy said that while he felt the drinks he took he was not intoxicated, and from the way Zehmer handled the transaction he did not think he was either.

The defendants insist that* * * * * the writing sought to be enforced was prepared as a bluff or dare to force Lucy to admit that he did not have $50,000; that the whole matter was a joke; that the writing was not delivered to Lucy and no binding contract was ever made between the parties.

It is an unusual, if not bizarre, defense.* * * * *

In his testimony, Zehmer claimed that he "was high as a Georgia pine," and that the transaction "was just a bunch of two doggoned drunks bluffing to see who could talk the biggest and say the most." That claim is inconsistent with his attempt to testify in great detail as to what was said and what was done. * * * The record is convincing that Zehmer was not intoxicated to the extent of being unable to comprehend the nature and consequences of the instrument he executed, and hence that instrument is not to be invalidated on that ground.* * * * *

The appearance of the contract, the fact that it was under discussion for forty minutes or more before it was signed; Lucy's objection to the first draft because it was written in the singular, and he wanted Mrs. Zehmer to sign it also; the rewriting to meet that objection and the signing by Mrs. Zehmer; the discussion of what was to be included in the sale, the provision for the examination of the title, the completeness of the instrument that was executed, the taking possession of it by Lucy with no request or suggestion by either of the defendants that he give it back, are facts which furnish persuasive evidence that the execution of the contract was a serious business transaction rather than a casual, jesting matter as defendants now contend.

Not only did Lucy actually believe, but the evidence shows he was warranted in believing, that the contract represented a serious business transaction and good faith sale and purchase of the farm.

In the field of contracts, as generally elsewhere, "We must look to the outward expression of a person as manifesting his intention rather than to his secret and unexpressed intention. (Emphasis added.) The law imputes to a person an intention corresponding to the reasonable meaning of his words and acts."

Whether the writing signed by the defendants and now sought to be enforced by the complainants was the result of a serious offer by Lucy and a serious acceptance by the defendants, or was a serious offer by Lucy and an acceptance in secret jest by the defendants, in either event it constituted a binding contract of sale between the parties.

JUDGMENT AND REMEDY:

The Supreme Court of Virginia determined that the writing was an enforceable contract and reversed the decision of the lower court. Mr. and Mrs. Zehmer were required by court order to carry through with the sale of the Ferguson Farm to W.O. Lucy. What remedy would be appropriate in this case? Why?

Barnes v. Treece
549 P.2D 1152 (1976)

The defendant, Vend-A-Win, Inc., is a corporation engaged in the distribution of punch boards. Treece as vice president of the corporation, when speaking before the state gambling commission stated, "I'll put a $100,000 to anyone that finds a crooked punch board; if they find it, I'll pay it." The audience laughed. The next morning the plaintiff heard a television (news) report of Treece's statement; he also read about it in the newspaper.

A number of years earlier while employed as a bartender, plaintiff had bought two fraudulent punchboards. After locating his two punchboards, the plaintiff contacted the defendant and inquired if the statement about the $100,000 had been made seriously. The defendant informed the plaintiff that it had and asked him to bring the punchboards to the company office. The plaintiff took a board to the office and was given a receipt for it. Both Treece and the company refused to pay the $100,000 even though the board was admittedly fraudulent.

The trial court found a contract existed but only with Treece individually since he lacked authority to bind the corporation.

CALLOW, J.

The first issue is whether the statement of Treece was the manifestation of an offer which could be accepted to bind the offeror to performance of the promise. Treece contends that no contract was formed. He maintains that his statement was made in jest and lacks the necessary manifestation of a serious contractual intent.

When expressions are intended as a joke and are understood or would be understood by a reasonable person as being so intended, they cannot be construed as an offer and accepted to form a contract. However, if the jest is not apparent and a reasonable hearer would believe that an offer was being made, then the speaker risks the formation of a contract which was not intended. It is the objective manifestations of the offeror that count and not secret, unexpressed intentions.

If a party's words or acts, judged by a reasonable standard, manifest an intention to agree in regard to the matter in question, that agreement is established, and it is immaterial what may be the real but unexpressed state of the party's mind on the subject.

The trial court found that there was an objective manifestation of mutual assent to form a contract. This was a matter to be evaluated by the trier of fact. The record includes substantial evidence of the required mutual assent to support the finding of the trial court. Although the original statement of Treece drew laughter from the audience, the subsequent statements, conduct, and the circumstances show an intent to lead any hearer to believe the statements were made seriously. There was testimony, though contradicted, that Treece specifically restated the offer over the telephone in response to an inquiry concerning whether the offer was serious. Treece, when given the opportunity to state that an offer was not intended, not only reaffirmed the offer but also asserted that $100,000 had been placed in escrow and directed Barnes to bring the punchboard to Seattle for inspection. The parties met, Barnes was given a receipt for the board, and he was told that the board would be taken to Chicago for inspection. In present day society it is known that gambling generates a great deal of income and that large sums are spent on its advertising and promotion. In that prevailing atmosphere, it was a credible statement that $100,000 would be paid to promote punch-boards. The statements of the defendant and the surrounding circumstances reflect an objective manifestation of a contractual intent by Treece and support the finding of the trial court.

The trial court properly categorized Treece's promised $100,000 as a valid offer to make a unilateral contract. The offer made promised that a contract would result upon performance of the act requested. Performance of the act with the intent to accept the offer constituted acceptance.

The trial judge entered a specific finding that Barnes performed the requested act of acceptance when he produced a rigged and fraudulent punchboard. We concur with the trial court's holding that a binding unilateral contract was formed between Barnes and Treece and uphold the conclusions of the trial court in that regard.

AFFIRMED.

MEDIA OFFERS AND ADVERTISEMENTS

A shoe store advertised a well-known brand of sneakers in the following terms: "Nationally advertised at $85, today only $35 with coupon." Mickey Jordan comes into the store in response to the advertisement, selects a pair of shoes, and tenders his credit card. The sales clerk tells him that the price is $85. How much must Jordan pay? Is there a contract? At common law, an advertisement, a circular or flier, a radio or TV spot was not considered an offer; rather, they were considered as a statement of an intention to sell or a preliminary proposal inviting offers to purchase from customers. However, the case of *Lefkowitz v. Great Minneapolis Surplus Store* demonstrates a circumstance in which a "media offer," usually considered to be a mere "invitation," may be considered an offer, capable of being accepted by the offeree or customer, thus creating an enforceable contract.

What is the basis for the rule? A variation of the objective test indicated that advertisements would not be considered as offers because a seller normally does not have an unlimited supply of goods. If advertisements were offers, then everyone who "accepted" after the retailer's supply was exhausted could sue for breach of contract. Price lists are another form of invitation to negotiate or trade. The price list of the seller is not an offer to sell at that price. A price list merely invites the buyer to offer to buy at that price. As further evidence of the lack of intent to offer to sell at the listed prices, the words "prices subject to change" are usually printed somewhere on the price list.

Although most advertisements and the like are treated as invitations to negotiate, this does not mean that an advertisement can never be an offer. If the advertisement makes a promise so definite in character that it is apparent that the offeror is binding him or herself to the conditions stated, the advertisement will be treated as an offer. This is particularly true when the advertisement solicits performance—for example, by offering a reward for the capture of a criminal, or for the return of a lost article or where the ad contains a finite quantity (for example, an automobile VIN number). Suppose an advertisement stated, "To the first five persons in our store at 8:00 A.M. on May 1, we offer to sell Singer Sewing Machines, Model X, at $500." This statement invites an acceptance on terms stated rather than an invitation of an offer to buy. If you were one of the first five persons in the store at the time specified, your acceptance of the offer to sell creates a contract. Another example is a reward offered in a newspaper for the return of a lost dog. The finder's return of the dog in response to the advertisement creates a unilateral contract, as the reward obviously invited an acceptance, not an offer, from the offeree.

In the following case, the court had to decide whether a newspaper advertisement announcing a "special sale" in a department store should be construed as an offer, the acceptance of which would complete a contract. Take special note of the test enunciated in *Lefkowitz v. Great Minneapolis Surplus Store, Inc.* It can be applied more broadly to decide if a party has truly made an offer to sell or buy. This test will also be used to determine if a party has made an acceptance of an offer. It is an important formulation of the objective test.

> # *Lefkowitz v. Great Minneapolis Surplus Store, Inc.*
> # 251 MINN. 188, 86 N.W. 2D 689 (1957)

Background and Facts

Plaintiff Lefkowitz read a newspaper advertisement offering certain items of merchandise for sale on a first come–first served basis. Plaintiff went to the store twice and was the first person to demand the merchandise and indicate a readiness to pay the sale price. On both occasions, the defendant department store refused to sell the merchandise to the plaintiff, saying that the offer was intended for women only, even though the advertisement was directed to the general public. The plaintiff sued the store for breach of contract, and the trial court awarded him damages.

MURPHY, Justice

This case grows out of the alleged refusal of the defendant to sell to the plaintiff a certain fur piece which it had offered for sale in a newspaper advertisement. It appears from the record that on April 6, 1956, the defendant published the following advertisement in a Minneapolis newspaper:

> "Saturday 9 A.M. Sharp
>
> 3 Brand New
>
> Fur Coats
>
> Worth to $100.00
>
> First Come
>
> First Served
>
> $1 Each"

On April 13, the defendant again published an advertisement in the same newspaper as follows:

> "Saturday 9 A.M.—2 Brand New Pastel
>
> Mink 3-Skin Scarves
>
> Selling for $89.50. Out they go
>
> Saturday. Each...$1.00
>
> 1 Black Lapin Stole—Beautiful,
>
> worth $139.50...$1.00
>
> First Come – First Served"

The record supports the findings of the court that on each of the Saturdays following the publication of the above-described ads the plaintiff was the first to present himself at the appropriate counter in the defendant's store and on each occasion demanded the coat and the stole so advertised and indicated his readiness to pay the sale price of $1. On both occasions, the defendant refused to sell the merchandise to the plaintiff, stating on the first occasion that by a "house rule" the offer was intended for women only and sales would not be made to men, and on the second visit that plaintiff knew defendant's house rules.

* * * * * The defendant contends that a newspaper advertisement offering items of merchandise for sale at a named price is a "unilateral offer" which may be withdrawn without notice. He relies upon authorities which hold that, where an advertiser publishes in a newspaper that he has a certain quantity or quality of goods which he wants to dispose of at certain prices and on certain terms, such advertisements are not offers which become contracts as soon as any person to whose notice they may come signifies his acceptance by notifying the other that he will take a certain quantity of them. Such advertisements have been construed as an

invitation for an offer of sale on the terms stated, which offer, when received, may be accepted or rejected and which therefore does not become a contract of sale until accepted by the seller; and until a contract has been so made, the seller may modify or revoke such prices or terms.

* * * * * [However]* * * * * there are numerous authorities which hold that a particular advertisement in a newspaper or circular letter relating to a sale of articles may be construed by the court as constituting an offer, acceptance of which would complete a contract.

The test of whether a binding obligation may originate in advertisements addressed to the general public is "whether the facts show that some performance was promised in positive terms in return for something requested."

The authorities above cited emphasize that, where the offer is clear, definite, and explicit, and leaves nothing open for negotiation, it constitutes an offer, acceptance of which will complete the contract. * * * * *

Whether in any individual instance a newspaper advertisement is an offer rather than an invitation to make an offer depends on the legal intention of the parties and the surrounding circumstances. We are of the view on the facts before us that the offer by the defendant of the sale of the Lapin fur was clear, definite, and explicit, and left nothing open for negotiation. The plaintiff having successfully managed to be the first one to appear at the seller's place of business to be served, as requested by the advertisement, and having offered the stated purchase price of the article, he was entitled to performance on the part of the defendant. We think the trial court was correct in holding that there was in the conduct of the parties a sufficient mutuality of obligation to constitute a contract of sale.

The defendant contends that the offer was modified by a "house rule" to the effect that only women were qualified to receive the bargains advertised. The advertisement contained no such restriction. This objection may be disposed of briefly by stating that, while an advertiser has the right at any time before acceptance to modify his offer, he does not have the right, after acceptance, to impose new or arbitrary conditions not contained in the published offer.

JUDGMENT AND REMEDY

The Supreme Court affirmed the trial court's judgment, awarding the plaintiff the sum of $138.50 ($139.50 for the Lapin stole less the $1 purchase price) in damages for breach of contract against the defendant department store.

AUCTIONS

Whether placing an item "on the auction block" constitutes an offer to sell or merely an invitation to those bidders in attendance to come forward with an offer to purchase depends on what type of auction is involved.

An auction with reserve is not considered as an offer to sell. Rather, it is an invitation to the bidder to make an offer, which may be accepted or rejected by the auctioneer. The auctioneer may withdraw the goods until he announces his acceptance; the bidder may also withdraw his bid before that time. This rule, at least as it relates to the same of goods, is now incorporated in § 2-328 of the Uniform Commercial Code.

In an auction without reserve, once the item is placed "on the auction block," it has been offered for sale. It cannot be revoked if a responsive bid is made within a reasonable time. The auctioneer, however, may stipulate a minimum bid in the notice for the auction. In the sale of real property, an absolute auction (usually with a minimum price) is an example of an auction without reserve.

Under the second element, the terms of the offer must be reasonably certain, or definite, so that the parties or the court can determine the terms of the contract. Although the parties may have manifested an intention to make a contract, if the content of their agreement is "unduly uncertain and indefinite," no contract is formed. The *Restatement of the Law on Contracts,* § 32 noted: "An offer must be so definite in its material terms, or require such definite terms in the acceptance, that the promises and performances to be rendered by each party are reasonably certain." Material terms include, at a minimum, the subject matter of the contract, price, payment terms, quantity, quality, duration, and work to be done.

The 1916 case of *Varney v. Ditmars* (217 N.Y. 223) provides an excellent example of the rule of indefiniteness. There, an employer promised to pay the plaintiff $40 a week and "the first of January next year I will close my books and give you a fair share of my profits." The court stated:

> "The statement alleged to have been made by the defendant about giving the plaintiff and said designer a fair share of his profits is vague, indefinite, and uncertain, and the amount cannot be computed from anything that was said by the parties or by reference to any document, paper, or other transaction. The minds of the parties never met upon any particular share of the defendant's profits to be given the employees or upon any plan by which such share could be computed or determined. The contract so far as it related to the special promise or inducement was never consummated. It was left subject to the will of the defendant or for further negotiation. It is urged that the defendant by the use of the word fair, in referring to a share of his profits, was as certain and definite as people are in the purchase and sale of a chattel when the price is not expressly agreed upon, and that if the agreement in question is declared to be too indefinite and uncertain to be enforced, a similar conclusion must be reached in every case where a chattel is sold without expressly fixing the price therefore. The question whether the words "fair and reasonable" have a definite and enforceable meaning when used in business transactions is dependent upon the intention of the parties in the use of such words and upon the subject-matter to which they refer. In cases of merchandising and in the purchase and sale of chattels the parties may use the words "fair and reasonable value" as synonymous with "market value." * * * * * "

> "The contract in question, so far as it relates to a share of the defendant's profits, is not only uncertain, but it is necessarily affected by so many other facts that are in themselves indefinite and uncertain that the intention of the parties is pure conjecture. * * * * * The courts cannot aid parties in such a case when they are unable or unwilling to agree upon the terms of their own proposed contract."

Even under the common law, courts began to relax rigid standards of indefiniteness and would imply or insert reasonable terms in a contract wherever possible, especially where both parties had manifested a clear intention to enter into a contract.

Under UCC § 2-204, a contract will not fail for indefiniteness if the parties clearly intend to enter into a contract and if a "reasonably certain basis" exists for granting an appropriate remedy by a court.

There are many ways in which the UCC will attempt to fill in a missing term in a contract (assuming, of course, that the parties intended a contract to come into existence). These areas will be discussed at greater length in the chapter on sales.

   a.   Open price: If nothing is said as to price, or the price is left to be agreed by the parties and they fail to agree, or the price is to be fixed in terms of some agreed market or other standard as set or recorded by a third person or agency and is not so set or recorded, "the price is a reasonable price at the time for delivery" [§ 2-305].

b. If no place of delivery is specified, then delivery is to occur at the seller's place of business [§ 2-308 (a)], thus obligating the buyer to pay for freight, insurance, and delivery charges.

c. If the time for shipment or delivery is not stated, then the time shall be a reasonable time after the contract is formed [§ 2-309].

d. If the time for payment is not specified, then payment is due at the time and place of delivery [§ 2-310 (a)] and no credit arrangements are implied.

In addition, terms that are omitted or unclear may be supplied by custom and usage of trade or by prior or contemporaneous dealings between the parties, subject to the parol evidence rule discussed later in Chapter Ten.

Under the third element, the offer must be communicated to the offeree so that the offeree knows of the terms of the offer. An offer cannot be accepted by an offeree who is unaware of the offer or who has not become apprised of it. Special consideration must be given to reward cases. A reward is a unilateral contract that can be accepted only by the offeree performing the act called for. The following case is one of the classic cases found in the common law concerning rewards.

Glover v. Jewish War Veterans of the United States
68 A.2D 233 (1949)

Background and Facts

The Jewish War Veterans of the United States offered a reward of $500 in a newspaper "to the person or persons furnishing information resulting in the apprehension and conviction of the persons guilty of the murder of Maurice L. Bernstein." A day or so after the notice appeared, one of the men suspected in the crime was arrested and the police received information that the other murderer was the "boyfriend" of a daughter of Mary Glover, the plaintiff and claimant in the present case. That evening, the police visited Mary Glover. She provided names, addresses, and possible locations where her daughter and the suspect might be found. The suspect was arrested at one of the places suggested by Glover, and all suspects were subsequently convicted of the crime.

Glover claimed the $500 reward from the Jewish War Veterans, arguing that the information she gave to the police officers led to the arrest and conviction of the murderers. But there was some question as to whether she was entitled to the reward. At the time she gave the information to the police officers, she did not know that any reward had been offered for information leading to the arrest and conviction of the guilty persons. In fact, she did not learn about the reward until several days afterward. The trial court denied Glover the $500 reward. The appellate court reviewed the law of contracts concerning rewards.

CLAGETT, Associate Judge

The issue determinative of this appeal is whether a person giving information leading to the arrest of a murderer without any knowledge that a reward has been offered for such information by a nongovernmental organization is entitled to collect the reward. The trial court decided the question in the negative and instructed the jury to return a verdict for defendant.

We have concluded that the trial court correctly instructed the jury to return a verdict for defendant. While there is some conflict in the decided cases on the subject of rewards, most of such conflict has to do with rewards offered by governmental officers and agencies. So far as rewards offered by private individuals and organizations are concerned, there is little conflict on the rule that questions regarding such rewards are to be based upon the law of contracts.

Since it is clear that the question is one of contract law, it follows that, at least so far as private rewards are concerned, there can be no contract unless the claimant when giving the desired information knew of the offer of the reward and acted with the intention of accepting such offer; otherwise the claimant gives the information not in the expectation of receiving a reward but rather out of a sense of public duty or other motive unconnected with the reward. "In the nature of the case," according to Professor Williston, "it is impossible for an offeree actually to assent to an offer unless he knows of its existence." After stating that courts in some jurisdictions have decided to the contrary, Williston adds, "It is impossible, however, to find in such a case (that is, in a case holding to the contrary) the elements generally held in England and America necessary for the formation of a contract. If it is clear the offeror intended to pay for the services, it is equally certain that the person rendering the service performed it voluntarily and not in return for a promise to pay. If one person expects to buy, and the other to give, there can hardly be found mutual assent. These views are supported by the great weight of authority, and in most jurisdictions a plaintiff in the sort of case under discussion is denied recovery."

The American Law Institute in its Restatement of the Law of Contracts follows the same rule, thus: ("It is impossible that there should be an acceptance unless the offeree knows of the existence of the offer.") The Restatement gives the following illustration of the rule just stated: "A offers a reward for information leading to the arrest and conviction of a criminal. B, in ignorance of the offer, gives information leading to his arrest and later, with knowledge of the offer and intent to accept it, gives other information necessary for conviction. There is no contract."

We have considered the reasoning in state decisions following the contrary rule. Mostly, as we have said, they involve rewards offered by governmental bodies and in general are based upon the theory that the government is benefited equally whether or not the claimant gives the information with knowledge of the reward and that therefore the government should pay in any event. We believe that the rule adopted by Professor Williston and the Restatement and in the majority of the cases is the better reasoned rule and therefore we adopt it. We believe furthermore that this rule is particularly applicable in the present case since the claimant did not herself contact the authorities and volunteer information but gave information only upon questioning by the policy officers and did not claim any knowledge of the guilt or innocence of the criminal but only knew where he probably could be located.

AFFIRMED.

The rule established in *Glover* is not generally applied to offers made by public (governmental) bodies or certain charitable organizations, whose promises may be enforced even without prior knowledge of the reward on "public policy" grounds.

TERMINATION OF AN OFFER

It should be recognized that the communication of an offer creates a power or right in the offeree to transform the offer into a binding contract through an acceptance. However, an offer will not remain in existence indefinitely. The offer can be terminated through either operation of law, actions of the parties, the occurrence of a stated condition, or by its own terms, normally through the lapse of a period of time stipulated in the contract.

LAPSE OF TIME

Where the time specified in the contract has passed or an event or condition stipulated has occurred, the offer is terminated. For example, Freddy agrees to sell his stamp collection to Franky if Franky accepts by a certain date. Franky must accept this offer within the period stated. If he does not do so, the offer will have lapsed. (A leading case has held that in the absence of any clear statement to the contrary, the period of time during which an offer can be accepted should be measured from the day the offer is received. *Caldwell v. Cline,* 109 W.Va. 553 (1930)).

Should no time be specified in the offer itself, the offer will terminate at the end of a reasonable time, determined by such factors as the subject matter of the contract (an offer to buy or sell perishable goods would involve a relatively short period of time) and other relevant market and business conditions and circumstances.

Look at the case of a schoolteacher who failed to return his contract for employment within the time specified in the offer.

Corcoran v. Lyle School District No. 406 581 P.2D 185 (1978)

Background and Facts

Bradley T. Corcoran, plaintiff, appealed his dismissal from the Lyle School District for his failure to accept his employment contract for the 1976–1977 school year in a timely manner. Corcoran is a certified teacher. He received an unsigned copy of his proposed employment contract on June 4, 1976. It provided: "If this contract is not signed by said employee and returned to the Secretary of the school district on or before June 14, 1976, the Board reserves the right to withdraw this offer."

In addition, the superintendent of schools personally called Corcoran's attention to the time provision contained within the contract. At that time, Corcoran informed the superintendent that he was considering other employment. In any event, Corcoran did not return the contract with his signature on it until June 16. Two days later, he received a letter from the superintendent stating that the school board had decided not to accept any contracts returned after the June 14 deadline. Therefore, Corcoran would not be rehired for the forth-coming school year.

McINTURFF, Judge

Beyond the statutory rights contained in the continuing contract law, the relationship between the school district and its employees is a contractual one governed by general principles of law. It is well settled that an offeror may require acceptance within a specified reasonable time and that failure of the offeree to so accept constitutes a rejection of the offer. By his failure to timely return the contract in the face of express written and personal notice that such conduct could result in the school board's rejection of its offer, Mr. Corcoran effectively waived his continuing contract rights.

While certified teachers who have not been given notice of non-retention are entitled to contracts containing terms and conditions substantially identical to those of the previous year, they may not desire such employment. If they fail to accept or reject those contracts within a reasonable time, school districts should be released from their obligations to rehire them under their former contracts. Unless a reasonable contract-return deadline is established and enforced, school districts, as a practical matter, may not know until classes begin how many of their retained teachers will return to the classroom each fall.

Mr. Corcoran does not contend the 10-day contractual limit was unreasonable, nor has he alleged any circumstances which would have prevented him from returning his signed contract within the time established. Therefore, we need not determine the reasonableness of the 10-day return provision.

(B)y his own conduct Mr. Corcoran foreclosed the potential contractual relationship between himself and the school district.

Judgment of the lower court was affirmed. The school district was not required to rehire Corcoran.

OPERATION OF LAW

An offer may be terminated through operation of law. For example, destruction of the subject matter of the contract through no fault of the party (as where Faust offers to sell his champion breeding hog to Holtz, but the hog dies before Holtz can accept the offer) terminates an offer.

The death or incompetency of the offeror or offeree in a personal service contract also terminates an offer. Since an offer is considered personal to both the offeror and the offeree, an offer will be automatically terminated if the offeror or offeree dies, becomes incapacitated, or is ruled incompetent by a court of law.

Where a statute or court decision makes an offer illegal, the offer will be terminated. For example, the VFW orders 25 slot machines from the Bally Corporation. Before Bally can accept and deliver the machines, state law in N.J. changes, making the possession of such machines illegal. The offer to purchase is automatically terminated.

These circumstances: destruction of the subject matter of the contract, death or incompetency of a contracting party, or the operation of a statute are sometimes viewed under the doctrine of "objective impossibility" and may also be used as a defense to a claim of breach of contract or as an excuse for non-performance on the part of a party. This area of law will be further explored in the discussion of consideration.

ACTION OF THE PARTIES

An offer may also be terminated by actions of the parties. These actions may include:

REVOCATION OF THE OFFER BY THE OFFEROR

Revocation is a withdrawal of the offer by the offeror before the offeree accepts the offer. Generally speaking, an offer made to the general public or to a number of persons whose specific identity is unknown to the offeror, for example, in a newspaper advertisement or in a TV or radio ad, may be revoked only by using the same medium or at least by using "the best means of notice reasonably available under the circumstances" that would give equal publicity as the communication of the original offer.

> **Example:**
>
> Bo Bedosian had offered a $5,000 reward for the return of his pet camel in the local news-papers, the *Daily Gleaner* and the *Daily Herald*. In order to revoke the offer, Bo will have to publish the revocation in both papers or in some medium giving equal publicity to the rev-ocation. Should the offeror know of the identity of a person who is taking action upon the offer, the offer must specifically communicate the revocation to that person in order to have an effective revocation.

Irrevocable Offers

While most offers are revocable by the offeror, certain types of offers can be made irrevocable. Two types of offers fall within this category.

Option contracts, supported by consideration. Where the offeror promises to hold an offer open for a specified period of time and the offeree pays the offeror for the right (i.e., furnishes consideration), the option is irrevocable for the period of the option, or if no definite period is stated, for a reasonable period of time.

Jeremiah is driving in the country one morning and notices a house for sale. Because Jeremiah is not certain that his wife will like the house, he does not want to put a bid (a definite offer) on the house, but he is fearful that someone else might try to buy it. The seller agrees to "hold the house for a week" in order to let Jeremiah and his wife make up their minds. Jeremiah gives the seller $100 to hold the house for the seven-day period. The parties have created a binding option contract, which the seller cannot revoke during that seven-day period. [Whether or not the $100 will be credited towards the purchase price will depend on the wording of the option contract concerning this point.]

Firm offers under the Uniform Commercial Code. Under the common law, irrevocability was deter-mined by whether the option was "paid for" or "not paid for" (i.e., supported by consideration). An anomaly developed. A party could make a promise to hold an offer open and then could still revoke the offer before it was accepted because it had not been "paid for." The writers of the UCC intentionally changed the common law in UCC § 2-205.

The elements of a firm offer are:

1. The offer to buy or sell must be made by a merchant;

2. The object of the contract must be goods;

3. The offer must be in a writing and must be signed by the merchant;

4. The offer must give assurances that it will be held open (not revocable) for some peri-od of time.

In this case, and even in the absence of consideration, the offer will remain open for the period of time specified in the offer. If no time is specified, it will remain open for a reasonable period of time; but in no event will the period of irrevocability exceed three months. Of course, if the option is "paid for," the regular common law rule applies and the offer would be irrevocable for the period of time stated or for a reasonable period of time. How would UCC § 2-205 affect Jeremiah in the previous example?

Rejection by the offeree terminates an offer. Sometimes there is a very fine line between a rejection of an offer and an inquiry about trading on different terms. Suppose that Freddy were to respond to a friend's offer to buy his antique car: "That seems a bit low; I'll just bet that you can do a lot better than that." Is this communication a rejection of his friend's offer or a mere inquiry which will not terminate (destroy) his friend's offer?

A counteroffer by the offeree also terminates the original offer. Generally, a counter-offer is a rejection of the original offer and the making of a new offer by the offeree. Suppose that Berra offers to sell his new speedboat to Rizzuto for $10,000. Rizzuto responds, "$10,000 is too high; I'll give you $8,500." What is the legal effect of Rizzuto's communication? First, it is clearly not an acceptance. Secondly, it is a rejection of Berra's offer to sell the boat for $10,000 and a counteroffer by Rizzuto to buy the boat for $8,500. Now, if Berra agrees on $8,500, a contract will be formed based on this agreement. However, what happens if Berra rejects the offer to purchase the boat at $8,500 and the price of such speedboats skyrockets to $15,000. Can Rizzuto compel Berra to sell the boat to him at the original $10,000 price? The answer is no because Rizzuto's counteroffer legally terminated the original offer. Berra's offer is no longer "on the table."

ACCEPTANCE

An acceptance is an unconditional assent by either words or conduct by an offeree that manifests agreement to the terms of the offer. The acceptance must usually be made in the manner requested in the offer where the offeror has stipulated an express, authorized means of acceptance. The acceptance must be unequivocal—that is, it may not impose or add new terms or conditions or tamper with the terms of the offer or (as we have seen) a court might conclude that a rejection and a counter offer has taken place. (A different result might obtain under UCC § 2-207, the "different and additional terms" rule, discussed in the materials on sales.)

Generally speaking, silence is not considered as acceptance of an offer even if the offeror has stated "your silence indicates your acceptance of this offer." However, a different result might obtain if the same statement were made by the offeree. For example, Williams says to Megill: "I offer to sell you my tractor for $200. Megill replies, "If you do not hear from me by Wednesday, you may assume that I accept." Williams agrees. Here, Megill's silence will result in the creation of a contract even if he does not intend to accept.

There are other circumstances where an offeree's silence may constitute acceptance of an offer. Such situations arise where there is an affirmative "duty to speak" on the part of the offeree. A court would impose a duty to speak:

a. Where such a duty arises out of a contract itself (i.e., record or book club contracts frequently require that a member send back a card with a rejection of the month's selection or the selection will be automatically shipped). Igor Wells joins the "fruit of the month club." Because he is on vacation during the month of May, Igor neglects to return the card for May's fruit, the guava. Igor must now pay for the (spoiled) guava because his failure to return the card (silence) amounted to an acceptance of the offer to ship based on the express terms of the membership agreement.

b. Where prior dealings between the parties give the reasonable expectation of a reply. Berman, a retailer, has ordered snowshoes from Trotsky, the manufacturer, on numerous occasions and paid for them when they arrived. Trotsky then began to ship snowshoes on a recurring bases, simply sending Berman a "confirmatory invoice," promising to ship the snowshoes on the eighth of each month. Whenever Berman received a shipment of the goods from Trotsky, he would simply sell them at retail and send a check to Trotsky for the amount due. Trotsky would only hear from Berman if Berman did not wish to place an order for that month. The last shipment is the subject of controversy as Berman now refuses to pay for them, claiming that his "silence" on the matter cannot create a contract. Because of the prior dealings between the parties, Berman's silence (failure to notify Trotsky) will be construed as an acceptance of Trotsky's offer to ship. Berman will be bound by contract and must pay for the last shipment of snowshoes.

c. Where the offeree solicits an offer, many courts hold that the offeree is under a positive duty to reject the offer. Failure to reject the offer (silence) operates as an acceptance. Murdock is the baseball coach at St. Swithen's High School. Murdoch informs Messinger, a local sporting goods store owner, that he is interested in purchasing a complete set of uniforms and aluminum baseball bats for use by his high school baseball team. Murdoch invites Messinger to make an offer to fill the team's needs. Messenger replies that he has a great set of uniforms and has the perfect series of new aluminum bats at $25 each. He states that he will send the bats and uniforms to Murdock if he does not hear from him within ten days. When Murdock does not respond within the 10-day period, Messinger ships the equipment bill Murdock. Since Murdock solicited the offer, Murdock has a duty to reject Messenger's offer and his failure to reject (silence) will constitute an acceptance of Messenger's offer, resulting in a binding and enforceable contract.

d. The most common instance of acceptance by silence arises where the offeree avails himself of services, with a reasonable opportunity to reject them, and with reason to believe the services are offered with the expectation of compensation. Is this a formation of an implied in fact contract?

One final note of importance: Under the common law, if goods or other items (often books or magazines) were shipped to a party through the mails, the receiving party was under no duty to either reship or pay for the merchandise. However, if the party who received the merchandise used the item in question (i.e., opened the package and read the book or magazine), an acceptance of the sender's offer to sell might be established either based on an implied in fact or implied in law contract. The "receiving party" would now be obligated to pay the contract price or a reasonable price for the items. This common law rule was changed by the Postal Reorganization Act of 1970, which provided that if a party receives goods "totally unsolicited" in the mails, such goods may be kept, used, or disposed of without the individual incurring any obligation to pay for them. However, many states provide for an exception for unsolicited mailings made by charitable organizations. Would the rule apply to goods sent or received through UPS? Why or why not? Note that in many states, and under applicable state laws, the mailing of unordered merchandise, for which a payment is expected, also amounts to an "unfair trade practice." The Postal Reorganization Act may be found at 39 U.S.C. § 3009.

COMMUNICATION OF ACCEPTANCE

In a unilateral contract (one which involves the performance of some act), notification or communication to the offeror of the intent to accept is generally not required unless requested by the offeror, since acceptance will not be valid until the act has been fully performed. (Remember, however, that the offeror cannot revoke the offer once the offeree begins to perform the act in question. The offeree will be given a reasonable time to complete the act.)

An exception to this general rule might occur where the offeror has requested that notification be made or where the law requires such notice of acceptance. The *Restatement* notes that where the offeror has no adequate means of learning of the performance of the offeree with reasonable promptness and certitude, the offeree must exercise reasonable diligence in notifying the offeror of the intent to accept the offer. (Uncle Walter intends to have his summer house in Forked River painted. One local painting contractor indicates its interest in pursuing the project. Notification to Uncle Walter by the painter of his intention would seem reasonable here.)

Of course, in a bilateral contract, communication of acceptance is necessary, because acceptance of the offer is made when the mutual promises are made. Under UCC § 2-206 (1), an offer to buy goods may be accepted by the seller by either a promise to ship or by actual prompt shipment.

Harvey Manufacturing receives an order for 25 pontoon boats from Jones. Under the UCC, this offer to buy may be accepted by either Harvey's notice to the buyer that he will ship the boats or by Harvey's promptly shipping the boats. If it is expected that the shipment will take some time to accomplish, Harvey would be wise to send a notice to Jones that he has shipped the boats and that they are in transit.

METHOD AND TIMELINESS OF ACCEPTANCE IN BILATERAL CONTRACTS

When is an acceptance effective? Generally speaking, an acceptance must be made within the time period stated in the offer, or if no time period is stated, within a reasonable time. The offeree must also use an "authorized mode" of communication in accepting an offer that was not communicated face-to-face by the offeror. An anomaly or an accident of the common law concerned the so-called "acceptance upon dispatch" or "deposited acceptance rule" which held that an acceptance takes place at the moment the communication is placed in the mode of communication expressly or impliedly authorized by the offeror. The mail, telegram, etc., in effect becomes the agent of the offeror.

Read *Morrison v. Thoelke* and notice the application of the deposited acceptance or "mail box" rule. Notice also the judge's discussion of the role and importance of the common law and the rule of precedence in deciding a case.

Morrison v. Tholke
155 SO. 2D 889 (1963)

BACKGROUND AND FACTS

Defendants (Morrison) made an offer to buy real property owned by the plaintiffs, Thoelkes. They executed a contract for sale and purchase and mailed it to the plaintiffs for their acceptance and signature. The latter signed the contract and mailed it to the defendants. Before it was received by the defendants, the plaintiffs repudiated the contract by telephone. Nonetheless, when defendants received the contract they recorded it, thereby establishing their interest in the property as a matter of public record. Claiming that no contract existed, plaintiffs brought this suit to "quiet title" to the property—to remove the defendants' claim of an interest in it from the record. Defendants counterclaimed, seeking specific performance of the contract. The lower court entered a summary decree for the plaintiffs and defendants appealed.

Allen, J.

* * * * * The question is whether the contract is complete and binding when a letter of acceptance is mailed, thus barring repudiation prior to delivery to the offeror, or when the letter of acceptance is received, thus permitting repudiation prior to receipt. Appellants argue that posting the acceptance creates the contract; appellees contend that only receipt of the acceptance bars repudiation.

* * * * * In short, both advocates and critics muster persuasive arguments. As indicated, there must be a choice made (by the legal system) and such choice may, by the nature of things, seem unjust in some cases. Weighing arguments with reference not to specific cases but toward a rule of general application and recognizing the general and traditional acceptance of the rule as well as the modern changes in effective long-distance communication, it would seem that the balance tips towards accepting the notion that this case is controlled by the general rule that insofar as the mail is an acceptable medium of communication, a contract is complete and binding upon posting of the letter of acceptance.

The rule that a contract is complete upon mailing or the deposit of the acceptance in the mails, hereinbefore referred to as the "deposited acceptance rule" also known as the rule in Adams v. Lindsell * * * * * This rule, although not entirely compatible with ordered, consistent and sometime artificial principles of contract advanced by some theorists, is in our view, in accord with the practical considerations and essential concepts of contract law. Outmoded precedents may on occasion be discarded and the function of law should not be the perpetuation of error, but by the same token, traditional rules and concepts should not be abandoned save on compelling ground.

* * * * * We are constrained by factors hereinbefore discussed to hold that an acceptance is effective upon mailing and not upon receipt. Necessarily, this decision is limited to circumstances involving the mails and does not purport to determine the rule possibly applicable to cases involving other modern means of communication.

* * * * * However, adopting the view that the acceptance was effective when the letter of acceptance was deposited in the mails, the repudiation was equally invalid.

Summary decree is reversed and the case remanded for further proceedings.

An important issue in discussing acceptance is what is the authorized means or mode of acceptance. An authorized means either may be stated in the offer itself ("If you wish to accept, respond by telegram on or before June 15, 2004.") or may be impliedly authorized by facts, circumstances, or the law. However, remember that if the mail is authorized as a means of acceptance, the acceptance becomes valid and effective upon posting—whether or not the offeror receives it!

Section 30 of the *Restatement* provides that in the absence of a specified manner of acceptance, an offer invites an acceptance by "any medium reasonable in the circumstances." Under Section 65 of the *Restatement,* a medium is reasonable if it is one used by the offeror ("mirror image") or one customarily used in similar transactions. Note, however, that if the mails are used, Section 66 of the *Restatement* likewise requires that such mail must be properly addressed and that the offeree must take other reasonable precautions to insure safe and accurate transmission of the acceptance.

Since most offerors do not expressly stipulate the means by which an offeree may accept an offer, the common law designated three impliedly authorized means of acceptance:

a.   The means selected by the offeror implies that the offeree is authorized to use the same or a faster means of acceptance.

b.   When two parties are dealing with each other over a great distance, mailing is impliedly authorized, and the "mail box" rule comes into play.

c.   Note that under the UCC § 2-206 (1), acceptance of an offer for the sale of goods can be made by any medium that is reasonable under the circumstances.

The best way for an offeror to protect him or herself in order to avoid the implications of the "mail box" rule is to stipulate in the offer that the acceptance must be received and acknowledged by a certain date or it is not effective. Another strategy would restrict the acceptance to a single mode of communication.

One final "quirk." Unlike an acceptance that is valid when posted, a rejection is only valid upon its receipt.

CHAPTER QUESTIONS

1. On May 1, Freese makes an offer to sell Siebert a hot dog wagon for $900, stipulating that if Siebert wishes to accept, he should send his acceptance by telegram. On May 2, Freese sends a letter of revocation to Siebert that is received by Siebert at noon on May 4. However, on May 3, Siebert had a telegram delivered to Western Union notifying Freese of his intention to accept. The telegram, although properly addressed, is nevertheless missent and is not received by Freese until May 5. Is there a contract between Freese and Siebert? Analyze in a memorandum outlining the legal arguments.

2. On September 1, Vollmer offers to sell Zyski a motor scooter for $750. The offer, although contained in a letter, contained no express means of acceptance by Zyski. On September 2, Zyski mails a letter of acceptance. The letter, although properly addressed, is nevertheless lost in the mail and is not immediately received by Vollmer. Vollmer, believing that Zyski is not interested in selling his scooter, sells the scooter to Brown on September 20. The "lost" letter arrives on September 25. Decide whether there is or is not a contract. If you decide that a contract existed, what remedy would be appropriate?

3. Suppose that in problem 2, above, Zyski has posted a letter of rejection on September 2, but that letter was lost in the mail. On September 3, Zyski changes his mind and calls Vollmer in order to accept. When Vollmer receives the letter of rejection on September 4, he is confused. Advise Vollmer.

4. What are the implications of E-mail, a fax, or other new methods of communication?

CHAPTER CASE QUESTIONS

Lucy v. Zehmer

a. What remedy was Lucy seeking? Why?

b. What was the defense raised by the defendants? Was it credible?

c. When might the defense of intoxication be valid?

d. What test did the court apply? Why couldn't this court, or for that matter any court, apply the subjective test to contracts?

e. Explain the objective test. Which test do you support? Why?

Barnes v. Treece

a. When might a statement made in jest be considered as a true offer?

b. Did Treece's actions or words, when contacted by the plaintiff, help or hurt his case?

c.   What type of contract was involved here? When was it completed?

d.   Why was Vend-A-Win, Inc., not held liable? Why was Treece personally liable?

e.   What is an escrow account?

Lefkowitz v. Great Minneapolis Surplus Store

a.   What test did the court apply here to this "media offer"?

b.   How did the facts fit this test?

c.   What about the defendant's "house rule"? What was the legal effect of the "house rule"?

Morrison v. Thoelke

a.   What is recording? What is the effect of recording?

b.   What is the purpose of a suit to "quiet title"?

c.   What remedy did the plaintiffs seek? Why?

d.   What rule did the court cite?

e.   According to the court, what is the role of precedents? When can or should a precedent be changed?

f.   What is a summary decree?

g.   What case did the court cite in support of its decision?

CHAPTER EIGHT:
CONSIDERATION

INTRODUCTION

Parties may make all sorts of promises or agreements, but a contract has a special legal status. Courts will not necessarily enforce all promises; only those supported by valuable consideration are generally enforceable by a court.

Consideration may be defined as "something bargained for in return for a promise." Some promises have little or no legal significance because the element of bargain is missing. For example, if a party promises to give a gift to another party, a court would not generally impose an obligation to complete the gift because the bargain element is missing. Gifts are legally classified as donative transactions and are not enforceable because they are gratuitous and not supported by consideration.

Justice Cardozo has identified three elements that must be present before a promise is said to be supported by consideration.

1. The promisee must suffer legal detriment; that is, the promisee must do or promise to do what he or she is not legally obligated to do; or refrain from doing or promise to refrain from doing what he or she is legally permitted to do.

2. The detriment must induce the promise; that is, the promisor must have made the promise because he or she wishes to exchange it at least in part for the detriment to be suffered by the promisee.

3. The promise must induce the detriment; that is, the promisee must know of the offer and intend to accept it.

EXAMPLE:

Gert Rykowski owns a garage and automobile repair business in Newark that emits considerable air pollution in and around her property. (While the pollution may be highly offensive, it does not violate any applicable laws.) Gert's neighbors get together and offer Gert $15,000 if she will agree to close down the welding portion of the business that causes in the emission of pollution. Gert agrees. Even though her business was no longer very profitable and she had been contemplating closing down the welding shop, the consideration flowing from Gert to her neighbors is the promise by Gert to refrain from doing an act she had the legal right to perform. The consideration flowing to Gert from her neighbors is the promise to pay a sum of money that the neighbors are not otherwise legally required to pay.

Now, suppose that Gert's business had been ordered closed by the DEP, but her neighbors did not know of this fact when they made their offer. It may be argued that the promise lacked consideration since Gert no longer had the legal right to operate her business. She has suffered no legal detriment in return for her neighbor's promise.

Consideration may consist of the following:

a. In a bilateral contract, the consideration for the promisor's promise is a promise made by the promisee.

b. In a unilateral contract, the consideration for the promisor's promise is the act of the promisee.

c. A forbearance on the part of the promisee (which is defined as the giving up of a valid legal right).

d. The creation, modification, or destruction of a legal relationship. (Example: I promise to pay you $500 if you will agree to let me out of my apartment lease/revise my employment contract.)

Let us take a moment to discuss the interesting and unusual case of *Fiege v. Boehm,* 210 Md. 352 (1956). The plaintiff, Boehm, alleged that she and the defendant had consensual, premarital sex which resulted in the plaintiff becoming pregnant, and that the defendant had acknowledged both responsibility and paternity. Plaintiff gave birth to a female child and the defendant agreed to pay all her medical and miscellaneous expenses related to the birth. The defendant further agreed to compensate the plaintiff for the loss of salary and pay $10 per week for child support until his daughter reached 21 in exchange for plaintiff's abstaining from filing bastardy charges against the defendant. Plaintiff paid $480 but refused to pay the balance of $2,415.80. When plaintiff initiated bastardy charges against the defendant, blood tests revealed the child was not his. The defendant claimed that his promise was not enforceable because there was no consideration for it. The court nevertheless enforced the contract! Do you feel that the court was justified in requiring Mr. Fiege to pay the expenses of a child who could not have been his? How do we judge the sufficiency of forbearance? What test is appropriate? Courts routinely hold that even the surrender of an invalid claim (forbearance from suit) may serve as detriment if the claimant has asserted it in "good faith" and a "reasonable man" would believe that the claim is well founded. Was that the basis of the ruling in *Fiege v. Boehm?*

Let us now look at a classic 1891 case from New York that dealt with the issue of consideration and benefit and detriment. The case seems to indicate that the surrender of almost any legal right, privilege, or power will constitute legal detriment.

Hamer v. Sidway
124 N.Y. 538, 27 N.E. 256 (1891)

Background and Facts

William E. Story, Sr. was the uncle of William E. Story II. In the presence of family members and guests invited to a family gathering, Story, Sr., promised to pay his nephew $5,000 if he would refrain from drinking, using tobacco, swearing, and playing cards or billiards for money until he became 21. The nephew agreed and fully performed his part of the bargain. When he reached 21, he wrote and told his uncle that he had kept his part of the agreement and was thereby entitled to $5,000. The uncle replied that he was pleased with his nephew's performance, writing, "I have no doubt but you have, for which you shall have five thousand dollars, as I promised you. I had the money in the bank the day you were twenty-one years old that I intended for you, and you shall have the money certain. * * * * * P.S. You can consider this money on interest."

The nephew received his uncle's letter and thereafter consented that the money should remain with his uncle according to the terms and conditions of the letter. The uncle died about two years later without having paid his nephew any part of the $5,000 and interest. The executor of the uncle's estate (the defendant in this action) did not want to pay the $5,000 (with interest) to the nephew, claiming that there had been no valid consideration for the promise.

The court disagreed with the executor and reviewed the doctrine of detriment-benefit—as valid consideration under the law.

PARKER, Justice.

The defendant contends that the contract was without consideration to support it, and therefore invalid. He asserts that the promisee, by refraining from the use of liquor and tobacco, was not harmed, but benefited; that which he did was best for him to do, independently of his uncle's promise, and insists that it follows that, unless the promisor was benefited, the contract was without consideration, a contention which, if well founded, would seem to leave open for controversy in many cases whether that which the promisee did or omitted to do was in fact of such benefit to him as to leave no consideration to support the enforcement of the promisor's agreement. Such a rule could not be tolerated, and is without foundation in the law. The exchequer chamber in 1875 defined "consideration" as follows: "A valuable consideration, in the sense of the law, may consist either in some right, interest, profit, or benefit accruing to the one party, or some forbearance, detriment, loss, or responsibility given, suffered, or undertaken by the other." Courts "will not ask whether the thing which forms the consideration does in fact benefit the promisee or a third party, or is of any substantial value to any one. It is enough that something is promised, done, forborne, or suffered by the party to whom the promise is made as consideration for the promise made to him. In general, a waiver of any legal right at the request of another party is a sufficient consideration for a promise. Any damage, or suspension, or forbearance of a right will be sufficient to sustain a promise."* * * * * Now, applying this rule to the facts before us, the promisee used tobacco, occasionally drank liquor, and he had a legal right to do so. That right he abandoned for a period of years upon the strength of the promise of the testator that for such forbearance he would give him $5,000. We need not speculate on the effort that may have been required to give up the use of those stimulants. It is sufficient that he restricted his lawful freedom of action within certain prescribed limits upon the faith of his uncle's agreement, and now, having fully performed the conditions imposed, it is of no moment whether such performance actually proved a benefit to the promisor, and the court will not inquire into it, but were it a proper subject of inquiry, we see nothing in this record that would permit a determination that the uncle was not benefited in a legal sense.

JUDGMENT AND REMEDY

The court ruled that the nephew had provided legally sufficient consideration by giving up smoking, drinking, swearing, and playing cards or billiards for money, until he became twenty-one and was therefore entitled to the money.

MORAL OBLIGATIONS AND PAST CONSIDERATION

A promise based on moral obligation, or a moral duty, a sense of honor, or love or affection is generally not enforceable. Look at these examples:

Mackenzie Corry, Rachel's third husband, promises to pay her $5,000 "in consideration of the admiration and love I hold for you."

Richie Kasper, the proprietor of Westmarket Servicenter, promises Clee $3,000 "in consideration of your loyalty and dedication as an employee for the past fifteen years."

George Jones promises to take care of his parents should they ever become ill "in consideration of all of the love you've given me throughout my life." Are these promises enforceable?

While all of these promises were no doubt made on the expectation they would be kept, they are not legally enforceable in a court of law, because they were not supported by consideration. (In some states, however, a statute might intervene as in the case of a promise made to a charity, or to set up a pension system for long-time employees, or where a relative, usually a son or daughter, might be under a statutory duty to support a parent.)

Likewise, a promise based on past consideration is not enforceable, since any detriment had already been incurred. For example, "in consideration of the fact that you named your first son Stanislaus, I promise to pay you $10,000." Is this promise enforceable? If it were, any promise to make a gift could be made legally enforceable by searching out some past unbargained-for detriment and reciting it as consideration for the current promise to make a gift.

There are two important general rules that supply the basis for understanding consideration. First, a court of law will not usually question the adequacy of consideration, that is, simply stated, courts are not generally concerned if the transaction was a good bargain or a bad bargain in an economic sense only that there in fact was a bargain! This rule has one major exception: where a bargain is made by parties within a fiduciary or confidential relationship, courts may be concerned with the adequacy of the bargain and will carefully scrutinize it to assure that any consideration was adequate.

ADEQUACY

Economic inadequacy, except in unusual situations, does not prevent any bargained-for detriment from constituting consideration. The question of adequacy of consideration often arises when the items exchanged are not of equal value or where a party learns that he or she has simply made a bad bargain. Thus, while a promise to pay $1 for a $5,000 car might be legally sufficient, a court might conclude that the consideration was inadequate because there had not in fact been a bargain. The $1 may have been only a pro-forma token, or nominal amount. However, in general, a court will not remake a bargain for parties that turns out to be disadvantageous or just an "old-fashioned bad bargain." The question of adequacy, however, might be raised in a court of equity where a party is seeking the remedy of specific performance. For example, Nesbitt agreed to sell Botti a parcel of land worth $100,000 for $7,000. Nesbitt now refuses to deliver the deed and Botti sues for specific performance. A court of equity might look to the adequacy of the consideration in light of the circumstances and may refuse to award specific performance.

In the 1972 case of *Rose v. Lurvey*, 40 Mich. App. 230, the court concluded that while "mere inadequacy of consideration, unless it is so gross as to shock the conscience of the court, is not ground for rescission," the transfer of equity (ownership) in real property worth $12,000 for $1.05 exhibited "an inequality so strong as to amount to a gross inadequacy of consideration." The court stated:

"Inadequacy of price paid for real property is not sufficient alone to authorize a court of equity to set aside a deed of conveyance, unless it is so gross as to shock a conscientious person; but, if the inadequacy is so great as to shock a conscientious person, it alone may furnish sufficient ground for annulling the conveyance."

Some of the circumstances that a court might consider in deciding if consideration is adequate are fraud, unconscionability, duress, over-reaching, undue influence, or mistake. All of these topics (with the exception of unconscionability, discussed earlier) will be considered in detail later in our discussion of reality of assent.

PRE-EXISTING DUTY RULE

The second important rule concerning consideration is the pre-existing duty rule. The rule states that where a party does or promises to do what he is already legally bound to do or promises to refrain from doing or refrains from doing what he is not legally permitted to do, he has not incurred legally sufficient detriment. The pre-existing duty may arise out of a prior contract or may be imposed by a statute or law. Let's look at three examples of the import of the pre-existing duty rule.

Ray Ryker is an under-Sheriff in Bergen County. When a drunk driver kills Mrs. Gyros' husband, she posts a $5,000 reward for the capture of the driver. Later, when Ryker apprehends the driver in a drunk driving stop, he seeks the reward. Since Ryker was already under a pre-existing duty to perform the act in question by virtue of his job as an under-sheriff, he is not entitled to the reward because he has furnished no new or additional consideration to Mrs. Gyros for her promise.

A second situation merits close attention. Frederick agrees to hire Williams for a two-year period at $500 per week. After a six-month period, Frederick orally promises to increase Williams' wages to $600 per week. Later, when Williams notices that his pay has remained at $500, he contacts Frederick and Frederick refuses to increase the pay. Frederick's promise is unenforceable because it is essentially gratuitous and is not supported by consideration. Williams was already under a pre-existing legal duty (a contract) to work for a two-year period for $500 per week.

A third example might occur in a construction contract. In such a case, the pre-existing duty rule is a critical one because its application prevents a certain type of "contractual black-mail." Jacobs, a contractor, agrees to build a spec-home for the Martins. After completing about half of the job, Jacobs demands an additional $10,000 or he will "walk out on the job." Even if the Martins agree to the payment of the additional $10,000, their promise would not generally be enforceable because Jacobs was under a pre-existing legal duty to construct the home at the original contract price. Their promise to pay the additional amount of $10,000 is not supported by consideration and is barred by the pre-existing duty rule.

The pre-existing duty rule is a very hard and rigid rule. Consequently, courts frequently attempted to find some legal detriment or benefit, some additional obligation or duty, no matter how small or insignificant, so that the promise to pay the additional sum might be enforceable. For example, if Williams agrees to sign a contract for an additional two years of work, or, if Jacobs had agreed to several changes or additions to the construction design, both the promise by Frederick and the

Martins might be enforceable because Williams and Jacobs are now doing "more" than originally promised, thus supplying consideration for Frederick's and the Martins' promises.

Because of the harshness of the pre-existing duty rule, the courts have also developed exceptions. Some of these exceptions are termed as minority doctrines because not all courts them.

RESCISSION

It is entirely possible that two parties can mutually agree to terminate an existing agreement if the agreement is executory. The surrender of rights under the agreement by each party is the consideration for the mutual agreement of rescission. For example, Carr and Hanner enter into a contract whereby Carr will purchase Hanner's Honda. Carr later calls Hanner and informs him that he is no longer interested and "could he just back out." Hanner agrees. This may be termed a rescission of the original contract.

Problems frequently arise in applying this principle. For example, Molnar agrees to build an indoor soccer arena for Boris for a cost of $1,500,000. Five months later, Molnar contacts Boris and notifies him that unless Boris agrees to rescind the original contract and to make a new agreement for the sum of $1,700,000, he will be forced to stop working. Boris reluctantly agrees. Is Boris' promise enforceable? If we were to apply the pre-existing duty rule, Boris' promise is not enforceable because it is not supported by legally sufficient consideration. Molnar was under a pre-existing duty to perform at the original, agreed upon consideration.

Some courts, however, might decide that the new agreement is enforceable because the original contract was rescinded and replaced by the new agreement, applying the "rescission and new contract rule."

UNFORESEEN (UNFORESEEABLE) DIFFICULTIES

During the performance of a contract, a party might encounter unforeseen and substantial problems that could not have been anticipated at the time the contract was entered into. These problems must be of the type and character that are "entirely beyond the contemplation of the parties." Unforeseen difficulties would ordinarily not include occurrences such as strikes, labor shortages, inclement weather, or an increase in the price of components or goods. These difficulties indeed should have been foreseen and provided for in a contract as risks ordinarily and normally found and assumed in an "arms length" business relationship.

Suppose, for example, that Carmola agrees to supply Neely with all of her requirements of gas and oil at $1.25 per gallon and $.75 per quart, respectively. Almost overnight, a severe price increase occurs because of renewed fighting in the Persian Gulf. The price of gas and oil more than doubles. Neely reluctantly agrees to pay the additional amount requested by Carmola. A court might permit Carmola to rescind her contract or might enforce Neely's promise to pay any additional amounts on the theory of "unforeseen difficulties." (Note two additional considerations. First, while a plea to a court on such grounds might be successful on the first occasion where a severe price increase occurs, most analysts agree that such a plea would not be appropriate or successful on a subsequent occasion. Second, if the "unforeseen difficulty" involves a severe and unexpected increase in price, some courts will hold that the contract has been "frustrated" and will permit an increase in the price or will permit a party to remove him or herself from a contract. However, the increase in price or circumstances must be unusual, extreme, or severe. Moreover, as a minority doctrine, not all courts will accept such a theory or defense.) A second example merits attention.

Pittsburgh Testing Laboratory agreed to do the testing and inspection of materials required under a master contract between Farnsworth & Chambers and Douglas Aircraft Corporation. The contract was based upon an estimate for moving 600,000 tons of dirt and material. When Pittsburgh Testing Laboratory began the job, they discovered that the contract could not be completed within the estimated time, due principally to the necessity of moving 1,200,000 tons of dirt and material. Pittsburgh Testing Laboratory demanded additional compensation and Farnsworth & Chambers agreed. Later, Farnsworth & Chambers refused Pittsburgh Testing Laboratory's demand for payment. Pittsburgh Testing Laboratory sued based on Farnsworth & Chambers oral promise to pay the additional consideration. Will the court enforce the promise to pay the additional amount of money? If the court rigidly applied the pre-existing duty rule, the promise made to Pittsburgh Testing Laboratory might not be enforceable, since Pittsburgh Testing Laboratory "did no more than what it originally promised to do" in the contract. However, another court might enforce the promise to provide the additional compensation based on the theory of "unforeseen (unforeseeable) difficulties" —which is exactly what the court did in *Pittsburgh Testing Laboratories v. Farnsworth & Chambers*, 251 F.2d 77 (1958).

How do you feel about the unforeseen difficulties rule and about how it affects the sanctity of contracts and agreements?

MODIFICATION OF SALES CONTRACTS

Under the pre-existing duty rule, an agreement to modify a contract requires consideration. Uniform Commercial Code § 2-209 (1) deals with the question of the modification of sales contracts: "An agreement modifying a contract within this Article needs no consideration to be binding." But remember, the UCC places an important premium on fair dealings between parties. Thus, just as in the case of other promises or obligations, the Code (§ 1-203) requires "good faith" ("honesty in fact"), thus eliminating the possibility of blackmail or improper activity.

SPECIAL ASPECTS OF CONSIDERATION

Output and Requirement Contracts: UCC § 2-306. There are several special issues or aspects of consideration that impact the area of contract law. First, a contract may be attacked on the ground that the promises contained are indefinite or illusory because no specific quantity has been mentioned or stipulated. One such type of contract is a contract that measures the quantity either by the output of the seller or the requirements of the buyer. For example, Smith and Kearns entered into a two-year requirement contract under which Smith will supply Kearns with all of his requirements of tanning lotion. Alternatively, Kearns might agree to purchase the entire output of Smith's tanning oil factory. Under the common law, courts had a great deal of difficulty in dealing with, interpreting, and enforcing such requirement and output contracts. The difficulty at common law arose because of a lack of a stated quantity. The UCC deals with the question of "output and requirement" contracts in § 2-306 and states that a term which measures the quantity by the output of the seller or the requirements of the buyer means such "actual output or requirements as may occur in "good faith." In addition, the Code states that no quantity can either be demanded by the buyer or tendered by the seller that is "unreasonably disproportionate" to any stated estimate or if no stated estimate is given, no more than any "normal or otherwise comparable prior output or requirements" may be demanded or tendered.

A second special issue arises where a debtor realizes that he or she is in a relative position of strength with respect to the desire of a creditor to secure some amount of repayment. In this case, the debtor may hold the payment hostage to a demand that the creditor accept less than a contract requires. In contrast, there may be cases where the debtor has a genuine dispute with a creditor that the debtor wishes to resolve by making a final payment.

In the first case, generally speaking, even if the creditor agrees to accept the lesser amount, the promise is not enforceable. Even having received and accepted the payment, the creditor could commence an action for the balance, using the theory of "lack of consideration" to defeat the enforcement of a promise to accept the lesser amount in full satisfaction of the debt. In the second case, a debtor may attempt to discharge a disputed (termed unliquidated) amount through an accord and satisfaction.

ACCORD AND SATISFACTION

An accord and satisfaction is an attempt by a debtor to legally extinguish a debt by paying or tendering a lesser amount than that stipulated in the contract. The accord is defined as the agreement whereby one of the parties undertakes to give or perform, and the other to accept, in satisfaction of a claim, something other than that which was originally promised or agreed upon. Satisfaction takes place when the accord is executed (often when a party agrees to accept the lesser amount in satisfaction of the debt).

Read the following cases carefully.

A.G. King Tree Surgeons v. Deeb
356 A.2D 87 (1976)

DALTON, J.

This is a contract action brought by A.G. King Tree Surgeons for the contract price of $480, plus tax and interest, for tree pruning work performed at the home of defendant George Deeb on or about May 30, 1975.

Plaintiff alleges the work was performed pursuant to an oral contract made by telephone, after an estimate of $480 had been transmitted orally, also by phone, to defendant. The work agreed on and actually performed was, according to plaintiff, the pruning of 15 trees on defendant's property.

Defendant states by way of affirmative defense that * * * * * an accord and satisfaction was reached before the filing of this lawsuit. * * * * *

First, it is undisputed that defendant, upon receipt of the invoice for $504 (representing the $480 contract price plus $24 tax), protested to plaintiff by telephone that he had never entered into a contract for this amount and had only authorized an estimate from plaintiff, nor did he ever sign a contract or an acknowledgment of work performed. This is not, therefore, a case of a liquidated sum which is due and owing but rather a genuine dispute between the parties as to what liability, if any, defendant owes to plaintiff for the work performed.

Second, it is undisputed that shortly after this controversy arose defendant's attorney forwarded to plaintiff defendant's check in the amount of $100 with a notation typed on the reverse side (above the space for the endorser's signature) to the effect that this $100 was in full and final settlement of all claims of A.G. King against defendant for work performed in May 1975. Along with the check defendant's attorney sent a letter of transmittal which stated in no uncertain terms that although defendant denied that authorization was ever given to plaintiff to perform work for defendant, nevertheless the $100 check was submitted in good faith in an attempt to amicably settle the claim, and that if plaintiff wished to settle for this amount, he should deposit the check. Plaintiff corporation, through its president A. G. King, did deposit the check but only after he obliterated the notation placed on it by the drawer and substituted in its place a notation that the check was only in partial payment of the amount due. Based on this set of facts defendant argues that an accord and satisfaction was reached between the parties at the time the check was deposited, notwithstanding the fact that the president of plaintiff corporation altered the notation on the reverse side of the check. This court agrees.

The traditional elements of an accord and satisfaction are the following: (1) a dispute as to the amount of money owed; (2) a clear manifestation of intent to settle the dispute; (3) acceptance of satisfaction by the creditor.

The president of plaintiff corporation alleges, of course, that there could be no acceptance of any offer of settlement since he deliberately altered the check before depositing it, making it clear that he considered the $100 only a partial payment and not a full settlement of the matter. However, it is clear that plaintiff had no right to alter the check. If the check was unacceptable as a final settlement, plaintiff's remedy was to return the check to defendant and sue for the full amount claimed due. Plaintiff chose rather to alter the check, accept the $100 "in partial payment" and sue for the difference.

In this case, however, the check did not stand alone; it was accompanied by a letter from defendant's attorney which made it clear that (1) there was a genuine dispute between the parties as to what amount of money, if any, was due plaintiff; (2) defendant intended that the $100 check was to be in full satisfaction of the dispute between the parties; and (3) if, and only if, plaintiff agreed to settle the dispute for this amount, the check was to be deposited.

It is the opinion of this court that the check and letter can, and indeed must, be read together as constituting an offer to settle this dispute for $100, and that the depositing of the check constituted the acceptance of this offer. Once the check was deposited by plaintiff, no matter what alterations the corporation's president personally made on its reverse side, an accord and satisfaction was reached.* * * * *

The letter of transmittal * * * * * recites the basis of the genuine dispute between the parties and the intent of defendant to have the enclosed payment totally satisfy the dispute, and this satisfies the first two requirements of an accord and satisfaction. The third requirement of an accord and satisfaction is the acceptance of the offer and, in this case, the deposit of the check by plaintiff operated ipso facto as such an acceptance. * * * * *

Judgment for defendant.

Courts will only recognize the validity of an accord and satisfaction when the amount of the debt is in dispute; that is, the debt is unliquidated and reasonable persons may disagree over the amount owed (or, as in the case of A.G. King Tree Surgeons, if any amount is owed at all). An unliquidated debt is one that is not settled, fixed, or agreed upon. However, an agreement to accept a lesser amount for a liquidated debt (where the amount is ascertained, agreed-upon, or fixed) is not satisfaction, and the balance of the debt is still legally owed. The debtor has a clear pre-existing legal duty to pay the entire amount of the debt.

Suppose that Ervin purchases $500 of sporting goods from Sears. One month later, he receives a bill from Sears, sends back a check in the amount of $400, and marks "Paid in full" on the check. Under these circumstances, Sears could cash the check and still sue Ervin for the balance of $100. There was no genuine dispute as to the amount owed and thus there can be no accord and satisfaction.

Note that in A.G. King, the court stated that three elements are required to create an accord and satisfaction:

1. A genuine dispute;

2. A clear manifestation of an attempt to extinguish the debt (usually shown by words such as "Paid in full");

3. Acceptance by the creditor.

Review the *King* case and point out the factual basis of the accord and satisfaction that was present.

Unlike A.G. King Tree Surgeons, neither party in the following case denied the existence of a contract. The court found a lack of a bona fide dispute between the parties. Therefore, there could not be an accord and satisfaction without the addition of new consideration. Study the case and see if you can distinguish it from *A.G. King Surgeons*.

Loizeaux Builders Supply Co. v. Ludwig
144 N.J. SUPER. 556 (1976)

Dreier, J. C. C.

On or about February 13, 1973 plaintiff, a concrete supplier, contracted with defendant for the sale and delivery of concrete for use by defendant, a general contractor, at the "Smith Transport job" in Woodbridge, N.J. The initial contract terms were agreed to over the telephone. Mr. Krause, plaintiff's vice-president in charge of production, testified that he notified defendant's president, Donald B. Ludwig, of the price defendant would be charged per cubic yard of concrete, and further alerted defendant to the additional "usual" charges that would be imposed if warranted. With regard to these unspecified "usual" additional charges, plaintiff agreed that defendant would not be charged for "waiting time" if the time was not excessive. As to the price terms of the contract, both parties testified that it was agreed that prices for concrete given by plaintiff would be adhered to for the year.

The testimony of the parties also indicates that the deliveries ran through March 1974. The routine procedure was for defendant to call plaintiff and order a specified number of cubic yards of concrete and (after an initial strike period not now in dispute) such orders would then be delivered to defendant's job site in plaintiff's trucks. Defendant was billed on the tenth, twentieth and thirtieth of each month by invoices, many of which were introduced at trial. Payments on account were made by defendant up to June 30, 1974, and thereafter by a single check dated July 22, 1974 in the amount of $1,943.84 on which was noted that plaintiff was "Paid in Full." Plaintiff claims that the sum of $1,368.61 is still due. The sales tax, in the reduced amount of $139.50, was conceded by defendant to be due, and the amount was so stipulated by the parties. The court will deal with the remaining items in order.

At the outset it should be noted that the contractual dealings between the parties extended for a period in excess of one year from the initial telephone conversation. This was not a requirements contract under N.J.S.A. 12A:-306. Donald Ludwig testified that he did not consider himself bound in any way to order his supplies from plaintiff. He felt no obligation to deal exclusively with plaintiff but rather stated that if a supplier at a lower price had come to his attention, he could have dealt with it instead of plaintiff. Krause agreed that defendant could have bought its supply of concrete elsewhere. Accordingly, the relationship between the parties is best characterized as a series of separate contracts, with the added element that several of the contract terms related back to the parties' original agreement.

The parties both agree that the price term for concrete originally agreed to was fixed for "the year." Defendant claims that the year should be measured from the first order of concrete placed with plaintiff, thus contemplating a "contract" year directly related to defendant's estimated time on the job. Plaintiff, however, states that its offer to hold the price for the year meant the calendar year, i.e., 1973.

The fundamental rule of construction of contracts calls for the ascertainment of intent of the parties in light of the general purpose of the contract. The subsequent conduct of the parties is also relevant in revealing their original understanding. Michael v. Brookchester, Inc., 26 N. J. 379, 388 (1958); American Exp. Co. v. Rona Travel Service, Inc., 77 N. J. Super. 566 (Ch. Div. 1962).

In this case there are no circumstances surrounding the general purposes of this contract or the subsequent conduct of the parties that would lead this court to lend to the term "the year" (as opposed to "a year") anything other than its usual and natural meaning. Also, defendant was under no obligation to deal with plaintiff after having received notice at the end of 1973 of price increases effective January 1, 1974. Having chosen to re-order concrete from the plaintiff notwithstanding knowledge of the price increases, defendant is not now in a position to assert its nonacquiescence.

With respect to the remaining disputed charges, defendant, while acknowledging these charges to be customary, maintains that they were not specifically agreed to at the outset, and therefore were not a part of the contract. This was strenuously denied by plaintiff.

Defendant's position is untenable for two reasons. First, it assumes the existence of a single requirements contract which, as noted above, did not exist, even under defendant's own characterization of the relationship. But even if defendant's version of the original conversation were accepted by this court, defendant was alerted to these additional charges at the time he received his first invoice from plaintiff, which contained an itemization of these additional charges. If defendant disagreed with these charges, it was free to cease ordering its supplies from plaintiff. Cf. N.J.S.A. 12A:2-208(1).

In addition, the disputed charges were established by plaintiff to be subject of an industry-wide pricing policy, which may be recognized by the court as relevant in determining the meaning of the agreements between the parties. N.J.S.A. 12A:2-208(2); Public Service Mut. Ins. Co. v. White, 4 N. J. Super. 523, 526 (App. Div. 1949); Leitner v. Braen, 51 N. J. Super. 31 (App. Div. 1958). These charges being customary in the trade strongly corroborates plaintiff's version of the initial negotiation between the parties. The court is mindful that it should not undertake to write a contract for the parties. Where, however, it is evident that the parties intended to contract, it is within the province of the court to construe the terms of their contract consistent with a result that is fair and just. Paley v. Barton S. & L. Ass'n, 82 N. J. Super. 75 (App. Div. 1964); N.J.S.A. 12:2-204. The construction including recognized additional charges accomplishes that end. The "less than truckload" charge falls within the category of usual charges for which defendant is responsible.

There was an express agreement between the parties that the usual waiting time charges would be waived by plaintiff, if not found to be excessive. This court finds that the waiting time experienced by plaintiff's trucks and drivers was not excessive, even applying the standards testified to by plaintiff's witnesses (although that testimony was somewhat ambiguous). Accordingly, plaintiff will now be held to its original agreement not to charge defendant for waiting time where such time was not excessive.

The only item in dispute, which the court finds not to have been a part of the terms of any of the agreements between the parties, is the so-called service charges by plaintiff. As noted earlier, defendant billed every ten days for deliveries that took place in the previous ten-day period, and it was agreed by the parties that defendant would pay upon receipt of invoice. Defendant did so until June 30, 1974, when it ceased making payments on account. But nowhere did the addition of any service charge appear on an invoice mailed to defendant. Defendant's only notices of such charges were notations in fine print on the bottom of monthly summary statements mailed by plaintiff to defendant. The court finds these charges to have been an unwarranted unilateral action by plaintiff.

Having thus established defendant's initial liability for the less than truckload charges and the price increase, the final issue to be dealt with is defendant's claim that its obligations to plaintiff were discharged through an accord and satisfaction represented by a check dated July 22, 1974 in the amount of $1,943.84 and marked "Paid in Full" after the payee's name. The check was sent in response to demands by plaintiff for payment on its account which indicated a balance of $3,312.45. Defendant tendered its check for $1,943.84 after deducting the specific charges for price increase, less than truckload charge, waiting time and sales tax from the total amount due.

The check was received by plaintiff and was deposited on July 25, 1974. Plaintiff immediately attempted to contact defendant, but failed to reach him. On July 29, 1974 plaintiff, through its attorney, notified defendant that it considered its deductions invalid and demanded payment in full.

Ludwig testified that prior to sending the check he conferred with Krause (or Mr. Dickerson) and stated his disagreement with the additional charges. At that time he advised plaintiff that he was tendering his check in full satisfaction of the matter. Defendant further testified that plaintiff's representative agreed to accept that amount in settlement. Plaintiff, denying any such conversation, points to defendant's responding letter of August 7, 1974 in which no mention was made of any prior agreement by plaintiff to accept defendant's check in settlement. Defendant's letter merely argues the merits of its deduction from the balance. This court finds that no prior agreement was entered into by plaintiff that it would accept the check in settlement.

Nevertheless, the question remains as to whether plaintiff's act of accepting and depositing the check, notwithstanding its protest, constitutes an accord and satisfaction in law.

The general rule is that where a check bearing a notation that it is offered in full settlement of a disputed claim is delivered to a creditor, who then retains the check and makes use thereof, an accord and satisfaction may be found. Eckert v. Wallace, 75 N. J. L. 171 (Sup. Ct. 1907); Rose v. American Paper Co., 83 N. J. L. 707 (Sup. Ct. 1912); Decker v. Smith & Co., 88 N. J. L. 630 (E. & A. 1916), and, most recently, A. G. King Tree Surgeons v. Deeb, 140 N. J. Super. 346 (Cty. D. Ct. 1976). This is so notwithstanding the fact that the creditor may protest accepting the check in full payment. The tender having been made upon the condition that it be accepted in full satisfaction or not at all, the creditor is deemed to have accepted the condition by depositing the check for collection. U.S. for Use of Glickfeld v. Krendel, 136 F. Supp. 276 (D.C.N.J. 1955); 15 Williston Contracts 3 ed. 1972), 1854. See also, Brady, Bank Checks (1972), .19.

The above is clearly the majority view and supported by the greater weight of authority. On principle, however, it appears that where, as here, the debtor has merely paid the amount of the claim, acknowledged by it to be due, and no more, it is difficult to justify a rule that places a creditor in the dubious position of surrendering part of that which he claims to be due in return for an amount which neither party claims to be in dispute. See also, 6 Corbin, Contracts (1950), 289. While this court acknowledges that it is bound by the above-cited authority, it finds that a crucial element of accord and satisfaction is not present in this case.

As stated in U.S. for Use of Glickfeld v. Krendel, supra, the three essential elements of accord and satisfaction may be crystallized as follows: (a) a bona fide dispute as to the amount owed; (b) a clear manifestation of intent by the debtor to the creditor that payment is in satisfaction of the disputed amount, and (c) acceptance of satisfaction by the creditor. 136 F. Supp. at 282. The court need go no further than the first element, for it is fundamental that where there is no bona fide dispute between the parties, there can be no accord and satisfaction without the added element of new consideration. Defendant was informed at the outset that it would be charged the usual additional charges and that defendant was aware of what these charges encompassed. This is not a case where one party denies the existence of any contract at all, A. G. King Tree Surgeons v. Deeb, supra, or where it is claimed that the creditor has improperly carried out its obligations under the contract. The facts in this case necessitate a finding that no accord and satisfaction took place when defendant's check for $1,943.84 was cashed by plaintiff. Eckert v. Wallace, supra.

As stated in Decker v. Smith & Co., 88 N. J. L. 630 (E. & A. 1916):

While it is not necessary that the dispute or controversy should be well-founded, it is necessary that it should be in good faith. Without an honest dispute, an agreement to take a lesser amount in payment of a liquidated claim is without consideration and void. An arbitrary refusal to pay, based upon the mere pretense of the debtor, made for the obvious purpose of exacting terms which are inequitable and oppressive, is not such a dispute as will satisfy the requirements of the rule. [at 634]

Accordingly, judgment will be entered for plaintiff in the amount of $608.26. No costs to either party.

SUBSTITUTES FOR VALUABLE CONSIDERATION

Some promises may be enforced without consideration, either on grounds of public policy or in the exercise of a court's equitable jurisdiction.

1. A composition of creditors' agreement is an agreement between an insolvent debtor and his/her creditors under which the creditors will accept either a specified amount or a percentage of the amount owed. Such an agreement is fully enforceable without consideration. These agreements frequently are substitutes for a filing of a petition in bankruptcy and are favored by courts.

2. The doctrine of promissory estoppel: This equitable doctrine is usually applied where a promisor makes a gratuitous promise, often involving a promise to make a gift. The parties are not bargaining for anything in a true commercial sense. For example, Aunt Edna tells her godson, Richard: "I promise to pay you $500 per week so you won't have to work any longer." Later, Richard quits his job, but Aunt Edna now refuses to pay. The doctrine of promissory estoppel may permit the court to enforce Aunt Edna's promise under certain circumstances if Richard has relied on the promise and changed his position.

The essence of promissory estoppel is based on the requirement of reliance on the part of the promisee and is found in Section 90 of the *Restatement of the Law of Contracts*, quoted in *Hoffman v. Red Owl Stores, Inc.*:

"A promise which the promisor should reasonably expect to induce action or forbearance of a definite and substantial character on the part of the promisee and which does induce such action or forbearance is binding if injustice can be avoided only by enforcement of the promise."

In short form, the four elements of promissory estoppel are:

1. A promise must be made;

2. Justifiable reliance on the part of the promisee must be found;

3. The promisee must suffer some detriment (that is, the promisee must have undertaken some act that he or she ordinarily would not have undertaken);

4. The promisee would suffer damage if the promise was not enforced.

In recent years, courts have tended to expand the application of the doctrine of promissory estoppel to situations beyond "gratuitous promises" to make a gift. Such a case is the *Red Owl Stores* case.

Hoffman v. Red Owl Stores, Inc.
26 WIS. 2D 683, 133 N.W. 2D 267 (1965)

BACKGROUND AND FACTS

Red Owl Stores, Inc. (defendant) induced the Hoffmans (plaintiffs) to give up their current business and run a Red Owl franchise. The Hoffmans relied on the representations of Red Owl, and when the deal ultimately fell through because of Red Owl's failure to keep its promise concerning the operation of the franchise agency store, the Hoffmans brought this suit to recover their losses. It appeared that at no time had Red Owl Stores ever actually promised a franchise to Hoffman—the matter was still the subject of intense and protracted negotiations.

CURRIE, Chief Justice.

Recognition of a Cause of Action Grounded on Promissory Estoppel. Section 90 of Restatement, 1 Contracts, provides (at p. 110):

"A promise which the promisor should reasonably expect to induce action or forbearance (of a definite and substantial character) on the part of the promisee and which does induce such action or forbearance is binding if injustice can be avoided only by enforcement of the promise."

Because we deem the doctrine of promissory estoppel, as stated in Section 90 of Restatement, 1 Contracts, as one which supplies a needed tool which courts may employ in a proper case to prevent injustice, we endorse and adopt it.

Applicability of Doctrine to Facts of this Case.

The record here discloses a number of promises and assurances given to Hoffman by Lukowitz in behalf of Red Owl upon which plaintiffs relied and acted upon to their detriment.

Foremost were the promises that for the sum of $18,000 Red Owl would establish Hoffman in a store. After Hoffman had sold his grocery store and paid the $1,000 on the Chilton lot, the $18,000 figure was changed to $24,100. Then in November, 1961, Hoffman was assured that if the $24,100 figure were increased by $2,000 the deal would go through. Hoffman was induced to sell his grocery store fixtures and inventory in June, 1961, on the promise that he would be in his new store by Fall. In November, plaintiffs sold their bakery building on the urging of defendants and on the assurance that this was the last step necessary to have the deal with Red Owl go through.

We determine that there was ample evidence to sustain the answers of the jury to the questions of the verdict with respect to the promissory representations made by Red Owl, Hoffman's reliance thereon in the exercise of ordinary care, and his fulfillment of the conditions required of him by the terms of the negotiations he had with Red Owl.

There remains for consideration the question of law raised by defendants that agreement was never reached on essential factors necessary to establish a contract between Hoffman and Red Owl. Among these were the size, cost, design, and layout of the store building; and the terms of the lease with respect to rent, maintenance, renewal, and purchase options. This poses the question of whether the promise necessary to sustain a cause of action for promissory estoppel must embrace all essential details of a proposed transaction between promisor and promisee so as to be the equivalent of an offer that would result in a binding contract between the parties if the promisee were to accept the same.

Originally the doctrine of promissory estoppel was invoked as a substitute for consideration rendering a gratuitous promise enforceable as a contract. In other words, the acts of reliance by the promisee to his detriment provided a substitute for consideration. If promissory estoppel were to be limited to only those situations where the promise giving rise to the cause of action must be so definite with respect to all details that a contract would result were the promise supported by consideration, then the defendants' instant promises to Hoffman would not meet this test. However, Section 90 of Restatement, 1 Contracts, does not impose the requirement that the promise giving rise to the cause of action must be so comprehensive in scope as to meet the requirements of an offer that would ripen into a contract if accepted by the promisee. Rather the conditions imposed are:

1) Was the promise one which the promisor should reasonably expect to induce action or forbearance of a definite and substantial character on the part of the promisee?

2) Did the promise induce such action or forbearance?

3) Can injustice be avoided only by enforcement of the promise?

We deem it would be a mistake to regard an action grounded on promissory estoppel as the equivalent of a breach of contract action. As Dean Boyer points out, it is desirable that fluidity in the application of the concept be maintained. While the first two of the above listed three requirements of promissory estoppel present issues of fact which ordinarily will be resolved by a jury, the third requirement, that the remedy can only be invoked where necessary to avoid injustice, is one that involves a policy decision by the court. Such a policy decision necessarily embraces an element of discretion.

We conclude that injustice would result here if plaintiffs were not granted some relief because of the failure of defendants to keep their promises which induced plaintiffs to act to their detriment.

The trial court's judgment was affirmed. Hoffman was entitled to damages, the exact amount to be determined when the case was returned to the trial court.

The acceptance of promissory estoppel as a substitute for consideration does not mean that every gratuitous promise will be enforced on equitable grounds merely because the promisee has changed position. Liability is created only when there is "justifiable reliance on the promise." The promisor must have known or had reason to believe that the promisee would likely be induced to change position as a result of the promise.

It is recognized that promises (subscriptions) to a religious, educational, or charitable institution or organizations are, in essence, promises to make a gift. As such, they are not enforceable as a contract promise because such promises are not supported by legally sufficient consideration. However, public policy considerations may dictate that such promises ought to be enforced by the courts (in many cases, an institution may have changed its position, i.e., purchased land or equipment, hired an engineer or architect to prepare for a project, made a commitment for the use of funds). As such, a court may enforce such a promise based on promissory estoppel to the extent "justice requires."

One final point. In enforcing a promise based on promissory estoppel, a court may only enforce the promise to the extent of the reasonable reliance damages of the promisee. For example, suppose Jerry Lynch promises to donate $50,000 to St. Rose Church for the Athletic Fund and its drive to build an athletics complex. Based on Lynch's pledge, St. Rose hires an engineer and clears two fields of underbrush. Later, Lynch reneges on his promise. If Lynch were sued on his promise under a contract theory, a court would probably dismiss the suit because, as we know, a promise to make a gift is generally not enforceable because it is not supported by consideration. However, if a court were to apply the doctrine of promissory estoppel, St. Rose might be able to enforce the promise to the extent of its reasonable reliance damages the monies actually expended by St. Rose in reliance on Lynch's promise. Remember, promissory estoppel is not consideration; it is a substitute for consideration.

Chapter Case Questions

A.G. King Tree Surgeons v. Deeb

a.   What did King do when he received Deeb's check?

b.   What are the elements of an "accord and satisfaction"? Were they present here?

Hoffman v. Red Owl Stores

a.   Where do we find the rule of promissory estoppel?

b.   What are the elements of the rule?

c.   Is the court enforcing the contractual promise made by Red Owl?

d.   What is a franchise?

CHAPTER NINE:
CAPACITY

Courts will frequently afford special protection to a party who may enter into an agreement "with the inexperience of youth" or to a party who might lack the required mental capacity to enter into a contract.

Contractual capacity is one of the major elements of a valid contract. A contract entered into by a party who lacks the requisite capacity may be either void or voidable. If one of the parties to a contract has been adjudged incompetent or insane by a court after a competency hearing, or a contract is entered into by a person who has been committed to an asylum or other institution (and a guardian of his or her property has been appointed prior to entering into the agreement), that contract will normally be judged "void" by the court. Otherwise, a party may allege and will have to prove that he or she lacked the ability to enter into a contract for one or more of the following reasons: the contract was entered into under the influence of drugs or alcohol; mental incompetence (perhaps senility or Alzheimer's disease); mental retardation; intoxication; the side effects of medication; temporary delirium deriving from physical injuries sustained in an accident; confusion; etc.

Generally, unless there has been an adjudication of incompetency, contractual capacity is a question of fact for a jury. In order to set aside a contract on grounds of lack of capacity, it is necessary to show that a party did not "understand the nature or consequences of the transaction" or that "by reason of mental illness or defect... [a party] is unable to act in a reasonable manner in relation to the transaction and the other party has reason to know of this condition." Thus, upon such a showing, a party may exercise its option to disaffirm or remove him or herself from a contract. The contract is voidable.

Suppose that Groucho's family, concerned about his growing senility, goes to court in order to seek a declaration that Groucho is incompetent to take care of his own affairs. Zeppo is appointed as guardian over Groucho's property. Should Groucho enter into any contracts during this period of incompetency, any such contract would be absolutely void. However, if a court action had not yet taken place, Groucho (or his relatives/heirs) might still allege that Groucho lacked the capacity to enter into a contract; that is, he did not understand the nature of the transaction. Such an issue, of course, would be one of fact for the jury to decide. Look back to *Lucy v. Zehmer;* recall how difficult it was to prove the allegation that Zehmer "lacked the capacity to enter into a contract," i.e., that he was as "high as a Georgia pine"!

MINORS' CONTRACTS

Some preliminary considerations are in order. A minor is any person who has not yet attained the required "age of majority" in a given state. This age (usually 18, but in some states the age may still be 21) may or may not be the same age as is the age for voting, getting married, or purchasing or consuming alcoholic beverages. Each state by statute determines its own "age of majority" for entering into a contract.

The word "minor" may be synonymous with the word "infant." In some states, if a minor becomes emancipated (that is, the minor is considered to be "on his own") that minor will be treated legally as an adult for the purposes of entering into contract. Examples of minors who may be considered emancipated are those who are married, who are serving in the armed forces, who make significant incomes (i.e., child stars, like Gary Coleman or Shirley Temple), or who live on their own. Emancipation is likewise a question of fact for a jury.

An adult who enters into a contract with a minor has no right to terminate the contract. Only the minor enjoys the right to disaffirm the contract. If both parties to a contract are minors, then each of the parties will have the right to disaffirm the contract.

A contract entered into by a minor is an example of a voidable contract.

There are three rules that generally apply to minors' contracts.

MAJORITY RULE

A minor may, at any time prior to reaching his/her age of majority, and for a reasonable time thereafter (usually no more than 30 days), disaffirm a contract, return the consideration in his/her possession or under his/her custody control at the time of disaffirmance in whatever form it is currently in, and receive back his/her full consideration. This rule has been termed the "shoe box" rule (as will be seen in an example following).

MINORITY RULE

This is also called the "New York Rule." A minor may disaffirm the contract, but is responsible in either quasi-contract or under a theory of restitution for the depreciation, wear and tear, damage, fair use, or reasonable rental value of the items under his/her care, custody, or control.

THIRD RULE

A minor may only disaffirm a contract if he/she can return the consideration in its exact original form. This third rule will apply especially to so-called "lay away" contracts, where goods remain with the seller until they have been fully paid for. No particular form of language or conduct is required to effectuate a disaffirmance as long as the minor makes his or her intention clear.

EXAMPLE:

Mark Hughes (age 15) purchases an auto from E-Z Autos. On the way home from the dealer, Mark is so excited that he negligently ignores a railroad crossing gate. He begins to proceed across the tracks where a locomotive obliterates the car, carrying it 500 feet down the tracks, smashing it into a stone bridge. Mark, however, is miraculously thrown to safety by the force of the crash. Groggy, Mark awakes and notices an empty shoebox next to the now compacted car. Mark places the car in the shoebox and staggers back to the E-Z Auto showroom where he announces: "I have some good news and some bad news." "The bad news is that I'm a minor and I'm going to disaffirm the contract I entered into with you. The good news is that you're going to get your car back." Whereupon E-Z's manager, Fred Sleeze, looks out at the street but does not notice the car. Mark hands Fred the shoebox with the compacted car placed neatly inside.

Analyze this fact pattern in light of the three minors' contract rules.

Read the following case, *Harvey v. Hatfield,* carefully. Note especially the reasoning cited behind the minors' contract rules discussed in this case. How do you know which rule a given state will apply?

Harvey v. Hatfield

Plaintiff, a minor, sues by his guardian ad litem to recover $1000 he had advanced under a proposed contract to buy a house trailer. He appeals from an adverse judgment.

Plaintiff, a student attending college turned 19 on October 13, 1959. A few days after his birthday, he quit school and got a job. In the latter part of October, he went to the defendant's lot and selected a trailer he liked. He told the defendant of the above facts, of his plans to be married and of his desire to buy the trailer. The defendant advised him that he would have to get his father's signature to get financing through the defendant.

Plaintiff responded that he thought he could arrange financing and that he could arrange to raise a thousand dollars as a down payment. He paid $500 on November 13 after having paid $500 on November 6 and applied to the bank for financing. The bank refused to accept his application for a loan because of his minority and because his father would not sign with him.

After the plaintiff's plans failed to materialize, he asked the defendant to return his money. Defendant refused but finally did agree to a statement which the plaintiff typed up and which both signed. It released the trailer in question for sale and granted plaintiff $1000 (plus interest) credit on a trailer of his choice next Spring. About February 1, 1960, plaintiff's attorney sent a letter to the defendant disaffirming the contract and demanding the return of his money. Upon refusal, this suit was commenced.

Since time immemorial, Courts have quite generally recognized the justice and propriety of refusing to grant enforcement to contracts against minors except for necessities. It is fair to assume that because of their immaturity, they may lack the judgment, experience and will power which they should have to bind themselves to what may turn out to be burdensome and long lasting obligations. Consequently, courts are properly solicitous of their rights and afford them protection from being taken advantage of by designing persons, and from their own imprudent acts, by allowing them to disaffirm contracts entered into during minority which upon more mature reflection, they conclude are undesirable. * * * * *

Accordingly, adults dealing with minors must be deemed to do so in an awareness of the privilege the law affords the minor of disaffirming his contracts. * * * * *

* * * * * A minor is bound not only for the reasonable value of necessaries but also for his contracts, unless he disaffirms them before or within a reasonable time after he attains his majority and restores to the other party all money or property received by him by virtue of said contracts and remaining in his control at any time after attaining majority.

Defendant advances the following proposition. * * * * * That even if the contract is disaffirmed, he is entitled to an offset of the actual damages he has sustained from the loss of sale of the trailer from the $1000.

Defendant urges that from the fact that plaintiff was "on his own," working and contemplating marriage, he could reasonably regard him as "engaged in business as an adult" and that he was therefore capable of entering into a binding contract.

The defendant's position is not sound. * * * * *

Our statute cannot be construed to support the defendant's contention that the disaffirming party must compensate him for damages he may have incurred.

The code only requires that the minor restore "to the other party all money or property received by him by virtue of said contracts and remaining within his control at any time after attaining his majority." The trailer was left in the possession of the defendant. That fulfills the requirement of the statute.

The plaintiff minor having disaffirmed the contract is entitled to the return of his money.

REVERSED.

THE NECESSARIES DOCTRINE

It is now well settled that a minor is liable for necessaries furnished him or her under the theory of quasi-contract. Thus, a minor is liable for the reasonable value of necessaries furnished that cannot be returned in their original condition. While there is no one universally accepted definition, necessaries generally include those items furnished to a minor for his/her life, health, or safety. A list might include such items as food, clothing, shelter, medical, and educational expenses.

Two special aspects of the necessaries doctrine must be understood. First, there has been a tendency by courts to expand and increase the category of items that would be considered as necessaries (i.e., items such as life or health insurance; automobiles; sporting goods; audio equipment; a college loan; etc.). Second, the court will often look to both the value of the item in question and the station or status in life of the minor to determine if a contract is for necessaries. Thus, a $25 cloth coat may be a necessary item for all minors; but a $5,000 mink jacket would only be a necessary for someone of unusual means.

Finally, most courts will apply the New York rule to contracts where the minor has been furnished a personal service (i.e., dance or karate lessons; babysitting jobs; employment assistance), on the theory that the minor cannot return the service already rendered to him or her.

Let's look at a contract entered into by a minor to obtain employment. Note especially the formulation of necessaries by the court.

Gastonia Personnel Corp. v. Rogers
276 N.C. 279, 172 S.E. 2D 19 (1970)

BACKGROUND AND FACTS

Bobby L. Rogers, defendant, was nineteen years old, married, and nearing completion of his associate of arts degree when he went to the office of plaintiff, an employment agency, and signed a contract for assistance in obtaining suitable employment. The contract contained the following provision:

"If I ACCEPT employment offered me by an employer as a result of a lead (verbal or otherwise) from you within twelve (12) months of such lead even though it may not be the position originally discussed with you, I will be obligated to pay you as per the terms of the contract."

Under the contract, the defendant was otherwise free to continue his own quest for employment. He became obligated to the plaintiff only if he accepted a job to which the plaintiff agency had referred him.

After several telephone calls to prospective employers, the employment agency arranged an interview with an employer who ultimately hired the defendant. The service charge to defendant of $295 was never paid. Plaintiff attempted to collect its fee. Defendant attempted to disaffirm the contract on the theory that services of a professional employment agency are not "necessaries" and hence can be disaffirmed. The trial court agreed with the defendant.

BOBBITT, Chief Justice

* * * * *

Under the common law, persons, whether male or female, are classified and referred to as infants until they attain the age of twenty-one years. (Under modern law, the age is lowered to eighteen years.)

An early commentary on the common law, after the general statement that contracts made by persons (infants) before attaining the age of twenty-one "may be avoided," sets forth "some exceptions out of this generality," to wit: "An infant may bind himself to pay for his necessary meat, drink, apparel, necessary physic, and such other necessaries, and likewise for his good teaching or instruction, whereby he may profit himself afterwards." Coke on Littleton, 13th ed. (1788), p. 172. If the infant married, "necessaries" included necessary food and clothing for his wife and child.

In accordance with this ancient rule of the common law, this Court has held an infant's contract, unless for "necessaries" or unless authorized by statute, is voidable by the infant, at his election, and may be disaffirmed during infancy or upon attaining the age of twenty-one.

The nature of the common law requires that each time a rule of law is applied it be carefully scrutinized to make sure that the conditions and needs of the times have not so changed as to make further application of it the instrument of injustice.

In general, our prior decisions are to the effect that the "necessaries" of an infant, his wife and child, include only such necessities of life as food, clothing, shelter, medical attention, etc. In our view, the concept of "necessaries" should be enlarged to include such articles of property and such services as are reasonably necessary to enable the infant to earn the money required to provide the necessities of life for himself and those who are legally dependent upon him.

The evidence before us tends to show that defendant, when he contracted with plaintiff, was nineteen years of age, emancipated, married, a high school graduate, within "a quarter or 22 hours" of obtaining his degree in applied science, and capable of holding a job at a starting annual salary of $4,784.00. To hold, as a matter of law, that such a person cannot obligate himself to pay for services rendered him in obtaining employment suitable to his ability, education and specialized training, enabling him to provide the necessities of life for himself, his wife and his expected child, would place him and others similarly situated under a serious economic handicap.

In the effort to protect "older minors" from improvident or unfair contracts, the law should not deny to them the opportunity and right to obligate themselves for articles of property or services which are reasonably necessary to enable them to provide for the proper support of themselves and their dependents. The minor should be held liable for the reasonable value of articles of property or services received pursuant to such contract.

The services of a professional employment agency were construed to be a "necessary." The case was remanded to the lower court for a new trial. The defendant would be expected to pay the reasonable value of the services rendered to him pursuant to the employment contract.

RATIFICATION

Ratification is an act or an expression in words by which a minor, after he reaches his age of majority, indicates an intention to be bound by the contract entered into during minority. Obviously, an effective ratification cannot take place prior to the attainment of majority.

Ratification may be express, that is, a minor may give actual notice that he or she will be bound. The notice may come in the form of a letter, a telegram, or a phone call. Ratification may also be implied from conduct, such as making a payment on account after reaching the age of majority, retaining, or continuing to use property after attaining majority. Ratification might also result from a minor literally doing nothing after reaching his/her age of majority. Courts, however, remain divided on the issue of silence.

A MINOR'S MISREPRESENTATION OF AGE

Suppose a minor is asked about his/her age. The minor lies (misrepresents) and states that he/she is over the age of majority. According to the majority rule, a minor may still disaffirm the contract; even though he/she has misrepresented his/her age. There are several other rules that jurisdictions may follow:

If a minor misrepresents, he/she may not disaffirm. This represents the extreme view on the matter.

If a minor misrepresents, he/she will be prohibited (estopped) from using minority as a defense, unless he/she can return the consideration "as delivered."

Some courts will permit a minor who has misrepresented his/her age to disaffirm, but will allow the minor to be sued in tort for fraud, resulting in a "set-off" of any amount of disaffirmance.

It is important to ascertain the precise view of a state's courts on this issue, as well as the necessaries doctrine, and which rule the state has adopted concerning the issue of disaffirmance.

CHAPTER CASE QUESTIONS

Harvey v. Hatfield

a. What is a guardian *ad litem*? When might one be used?

b. Why do courts refuse to grant enforcement to minors' contracts?

c. What happens if an adult claims that he did not know a party was a minor?

d. When and under what circumstances is a minor liable for a contract?

e. What rule did the defendant propose? Was it accepted by the courts?

f. Why did the defendant urge that the court adopt the view that the plaintiff was "on his own"?

g. What does it mean to be emancipated?

Gastonia Personnel v. Rogers

a. What term did the court use for a minor?

b. How did Judge Coke describe necessaries?

c. How did the court "enlarge" the concept of necessaries?

CHAPTER TEN:
GENUINENESS OF ASSENT

In this chapter, we shall consider four areas of contract law that deal with the issue of evaluating the nature of consent given by a party to a contract. These questions are usually raised after a contract has been entered into, either as a defense to a breach of contract or in an attempt to rescind a contract because some problem existed at the beginning of a contract that allegedly precluded genuine assent. The four areas we shall consider are: 1) Unilateral and bilateral mistake; 2) Misrepresentation and fraud; 3) Duress; and 4) Undue influence.

MISTAKE

In a case where one of the parties claims that a mistake has been made, it is alleged that the words of a contract do not convey the subjective intent of the parties.

There are two types of mistake. A unilateral mistake is a mistake made by one party in a contract; a bilateral mistake (mutual mistake) is made by both parties in the contract. A mistake may be made as to facts or may be made as to the identity of the subject matter, a matter of judgment of the value of an item, or the quality of an item. Generally speaking, only a mistake as to a matter of fact, and not a mistake in judgment, will permit a party to rescind a contract.

The most frequently cited fact pattern for which relief for a unilateral mistake is sought involves a mistake in a bid made by a construction contractor, usually caused by a computational or mathematical error or a misunderstanding of the terms of the invitation to bid. In general, a unilateral mistake does not afford a party any right to rescind the contract unless the other party knows or has reason to know the mistake; unless enforcement of the contract against the mistaken party would be oppressive; or unless enforcement might result in an unconscionable result and rescission of the contract would impose no substantial hardship on the other party.

A classic case from 1898 exemplifies the harsh rule found in the common law. Odell Construction Co. made a bid to install plumbing in an apartment building. When the president of the company, Herbert Odell, added up the costs on the job, he and his secretary apparently forgot to include figures for the pipe fittings. Because of this omission, Odell's bid was $6,500 below those of the other bidders and, of course, it was accepted by the prime contractor, Sunspan, Inc. Since Odell had made a unilateral mistake, the court would not afford a remedy to Odell in these circumstances.

Under a more modern view, however, exceptions to the general rule in the common law have been recognized. Reflecting our earlier discussion, many courts will not apply the unilateral mistake rule when the other party to the contract knows or should have known that a mistake was made, or where the mistake was the result of an inadvertent computational or mathematical error, without gross negligence, thus permitting the "blundering party" to assert a personal defense against enforcement of the contract. Note, however, that the mistake must be palpable; that is, the mistake must be known or obvious to the party receiving the bid.

Take this example. A construction company bids on a golf course addition. In marking up its bid, the president fails to take into account a major component. The bid it submitted was fully 20% below what it should have been. In such a case, a court might conclude that since the bid received was "far below" that which was expected, the receiving party should have known that a mistake was made and it is incumbent on that party to check to see if the bid was correct or serious (*Santucci v. City of Chicago*). Contrast this decision to Odell.

Where both parties to a contract share a common assumption about an important fact upon which they have based their bargain and that assumption turns out to be false, the bargain may be avoided. The classic case of a mutual mistake of fact involved a ship named "Peerless" that was scheduled to leave Bombay with a shipment of Surat cotton goods. The case of *Raffles v. Wichelhaus* discusses the question of a mutual mistake of fact. Notice also the unusual form of the case, stated under English common law.

Raffles v. Wichelhaus and Another
906, 159 ENG. REP. 375 (1864)

BACKGROUND AND FACTS

The defendant purchased a shipment of Surat cotton from the plaintiff "to arrive ex Peerless' from Bombay." The defendant expected the goods to be shipped on the *Peerless* sailing from Bombay in October. The plaintiff expected to ship the goods on another *Peerless*, which sailed from Bombay in December. By the time the goods arrived and the plaintiff tried to deliver them, the defendant was no longer willing to accept them.

Declaration. For that it was agreed between the plaintiff and the defendants, to wit, at Liverpool, that the plaintiff should sell to the defendants, and the defendants buy of the plaintiff, certain goods, to wit. 125 bales of Surat cotton, guaranteed middling fair merchant's Dhollorah, to arrive ex "Peerless" from Bombay; and that the cotton should be taken from the quay, and that the defendants would pay the plaintiff for the same at a certain rate, to wit, at the rate of 17d. per pound, within a certain time then agreed upon after the arrival of the said goods in England. Averments: that the said goods did arrive by the said ship from Bombay in England, to wit, at Liverpool, and the plaintiff was then and there ready, and willing and offered to deliver the said goods to the defendants. Breach: that the defendants refused to accept the said goods or pay the plaintiff for them.

Plea. That the said ship mentioned in the said agreement was meant and intended by the defendants to be the ship called the "Peerless," which sailed from Bombay, to wit, in October; and that the plaintiff was not ready and willing and did not offer to deliver to the defendants any bales of cotton which arrived by the last mentioned ship, but instead thereof was only ready and willing and offered to deliver to the defendants 125 bales of Surat cotton which arrived by another and different ship, which was also called the "Peerless," and which sailed from Bombay, to wit, in December.

There is nothing on the face of the contract to show that any particular ship called the "Peerless was meant; but the moment it appears that two ships called the "Peerless" were about to sail from Bombay there is a latent ambiguity, and parol evidence may be given for the purpose of showing that the defendant meant one "Peerless," and the plaintiff another. That being so, there was no consensus ad idem, and therefore no binding contract.

The judgment was for the defendants.

In order to address the question of mutual mistake, courts employ a variant of the objective test: While persons are bound by the reasonable impressions they create in the mind of the other party, regardless of whether that impression is the same as their subjective intentions, courts will nevertheless try to find whether or not a true "meeting of the minds" took place. Consider these examples.

Minerva placed an ad in the *Daily Gleaner* which offered a "Chevy for sale" (no description) for $2,500. Greene knew that Minerva had a nice '95 Chevy that would certainly be worth at least $2,500. However, Minerva meant her '82 Chevy (worth about $200—at most). Clearly, this situation involves a mutual or bilateral mistake of fact. Greene could rescind the contract, based on this mutual mistake of fact.

Winston buys Manion's stamp collection for $2,000. Later, Manion learns that included in the collection is a unique "Bermuda purple," worth approximately $50,000. Neither party knew that the stamp was so valuable. Both parties knew what the subject matter of the contract was—the stamp collection. Both Winston and Manion simply made a mistake about the value of the collection. Therefore, the contract probably cannot be rescinded. Suppose that the case had reached a court of equity where Winston is seeking specific performance of his contract with Manion. Would that change the result? What is the difference between this case and the prior case? Both involved mutual mistakes. Do you recall the case of the thirteen-year-old boy from Milwaukee who bought a baseball card for $1.00, only later to find out that the card was worth $10,000? Should he be required to return the card based on a mistake?

Note that in the *Peerless* case, the court focused on the requirement of a "meeting of the minds" (*consensus ad idem*) and determined that because of the mutual mistake of fact, no true contract was ever entered into by the parties.

MISREPRESENTATION AND FRAUD

An action for fraud is technically an action in tort (deceit) and not in contract. However, fraud affects the issue of the genuineness of a party's consent or assent to the contract and thus fraud is, at least, an important contract consideration. It is often said that the issues of fraud and misrepresentation represent a "curious mixture" of contract and tort law. Cases can normally be divided into two main categories: (1) the defrauded party obtains what he bargained for, but because of a misrepresentation, the item is worth less than he had reason to expect; (2) the defrauded party obtains something substantially different from what he was led to expect. In these cases, the defrauded party has been deprived of the "benefit of his or her bargain" and this will ordinarily be sufficient to permit a disaffirmance of the contract.

There are three types of fraud under the common law. Fraud in execution is a real defense rendering a contract void. It consists of a deception that has the consequence of preventing a party from realizing that a contract is even contemplated. A second type of fraud occurs when an oral contract is reduced to a writing. Here, the victim of fraud trusts that the fraudulent party will reduce the oral agreement to a written expression. Acting on the assurance that this has been done faithfully, the victim signs the writing without reading it. Depending on the jurisdiction, the innocent party may be permitted to assert the personal defense of fraud, ignoring the fact that the fraud could have been uncovered had the victim taken the step to read the document before signing it.

The third type of fraud, fraud in the inducement, occurs where consent to a bargain is induced by lies, misstatements, or half-truths. Fraud in the inducement is a personal defense, which renders the contract voidable at the option of the innocent victim. We shall refer to this type of fraud as contract fraud. (The distinction between a real or universal defense and a personal defense is especially critical in the area of commercial paper under Article 3 of the UCC.)

The basic distinction between fraud and misrepresentation lies in the presence or absence of scienter, which is defined as the intent to deceive. Scienter arises either from the knowledge of falsity by a party or the reckless disregard of the truth of a statement. Sometimes we see the term "innocent misrepresentation" used to describe the situation where a party has misrepresented but has not done so with "scienter." The misrepresentation is innocent only in the sense that it was not done with scienter or intent. It is still actionable.

If a court finds that fraud or misrepresentation was committed, the innocent party may be permitted to rescind the contract and will be restored to the original, pre-contract condition. Alternatively, the innocent party may enforce the contract and seek compensatory damages for the difference between the value of the item as promised in the contract and the value of the item received by the innocent party. In addition, in some circumstances, an innocent party may seek punitive damages to punish the party who committed fraud for their bad behavior. Depending on the jurisdiction, if an innocent misrepresentation has occurred, the innocent party can rescind the contract, but may not be able to seek damages for the innocent misrepresentation.

Four elements are necessary to prove contract fraud. We shall be discussing each of these requirements in great detail. Contract fraud involves: 1) A false representation of a material fact; 2) Scienter; 3) Justifiable Reliance; and 4) Damages.

A material fact is defined as any fact that is important in inducing a party to enter into a contract. According to the *Restatement,* §470(2), materiality exists whenever "the misrepresentation would be likely to affect the conduct of a reasonable man." There are four special aspects or rules concerning this first element of proving fraud.

MISREPRESENTATION OF FACT

Relief is granted for misrepresentation of fact, and not for erroneous statements of opinion. However, the distinction between fact and opinion is sometimes rather tenuous. Statements or representations of a future fact, a prediction, or a statement of an opinion are generally not actionable as fraud. It is recognized that a seller may be permitted to employ a certain amount of "sales puffing" or "trade talk" without incurring liability for fraud. However, a statement of opinion given by an expert (a disinterested professional) to an unsophisticated purchaser may give rise to a cause of action for fraud. This opinion may become one of fact, depending on the circumstances of the case.

> **EXAMPLE:**
>
> Margot takes her watch to a jeweler for an appraisal. The jeweler tells Margot that the watch is "not a very good" one and that "in my opinion, it is worth about $75." Based upon this opinion, Margot sells the watch to Babcock. It is an interesting question whether Margot might be able to rescind her contract with Babcock on a theory of bilateral or mutual mistake; however, if such an action were not possible, Margot might sue the jeweler for fraud. Even though the jeweler has stated an opinion, that opinion would be actionable because the jeweler is an expert and clearly Margot has relied on the jeweler's advice when selling the watch to Babcock.

The case of *Vokes v. Arthur Murray* illustrates how a dance instructor, who made various statements concerning Vokes's dance potential, committed fraud. It will be one of the most memorable and interesting cases from your study of contract law. Note especially the use of the English language by the judge. Before you read *Vokes,* it might be a good idea to have a thesaurus close by! Do you believe that the statements were mere opinions? Do you think that Mrs. Vokes bears any personal responsibility here?

Vokes v. Arthur Murray, Inc.
212 SO. 2D 906 (1968)

BACKGROUND AND FACTS

The defendant, Arthur Murray, Inc., operated dancing schools throughout the nation through local franchised operators, one of whom was the defendant. The plaintiff, Audrey E. Vokes, a widow without family, wished to become "an accomplished dancer" to find "a new interest in life." In 1961 she was invited to attend a "dance party" at J. P. Davenport's "School of Dancing." Vokes went to the school and received elaborate praise from her instructor for her grace, poise, and potential as "an excellent dancer." The instructor sold her eight half-hour dance lessons for $14.50 each, to be utilized within one calendar month.

Subsequently, over a period of less than sixteen months, Vokes bought a total of fourteen dance courses, which amounted to 2,302 hours of dancing lessons for a total cash outlay of $31,090.45, all at Davenport's school.

PIERCE, Judge

These dance lesson contracts and the monetary consideration therefore of over $31,000 were procured from her by means and methods of Davenport and his associates which went beyond the unsavory, yet legally permissible, parameter of "sales puffing" and intruded well into the forbidden area of undue influence, the suggestion of falsehood, the suppression of truth, and the free exercise of rational judgment, if what plaintiff alleged in her complaint was true. From the time of her first contact with the dancing school in February, 1961, she was influenced unwittingly by a constant and continuous barrage of flattery, false praise, excessive compliments, and panegyric encomiums, to such extent that it would be not only inequitable, but unconscionable, for a Court exercising inherent chancery power to allow such contracts to stand.

She was incessantly subjected to overreaching blandishment and cajolery. She was assured she had "grace and poise"; that she was "rapidly improving and developing in her dancing skill"; that the additional lessons

She was induced at another point to purchase an additional 126 hours of lessons in order to be not only eligible for the Miami trip but also to become "a life member of the Arthur Murray Studio," carrying with it certain dubious emoluments, at a further cost of $1,752.-30.

At another point, while she still had over 1,000 unused hours of instruction she was induced to buy 151 additional hours at a cost of $2,049.00 to be eligible for a "Student Trip to Trinidad," at her own expense as she later learned.

Also, when she still had 1100 unused hours to her credit, she was prevailed upon to purchase an additional 347 hours at a cost of $4,235.74, to qualify her to receive a "Gold Medal" for achievement, indicating she had advanced to "the Gold Standard."

On another occasion, while she still had over 1200 unused hours, she was induced to buy an additional 175 hours of instruction at a cost of $2,472.75 to be eligible "to take a trip to Mexico."

Finally, sandwiched in between other lesser sales promotions, she was influenced to buy an additional 481 hours of instruction at a cost of $6,523.81 in order to "be classified as a Gold Bar Member, the ultimate achievement of the dancing studio."

All the foregoing sales promotions, illustrative of the entire fourteen separate contracts, were procured by defendant Davenport and Arthur Murray, Inc., by false representations to her that she was improving in her dancing ability, that she had excellent potential, that she was responding to instructions in dancing grace, and that they were developing her into a beautiful dancer, whereas in truth and in fact she did not develop in her dancing ability, she had no "dance aptitude," and in fact had difficulty in "hearing the musical beat." The complaint alleged that such representations to her "were in fact false and known by the defendant to be false and contrary to the plaintiff's true ability, the truth of plaintiff's ability being fully known to the defendants, but withheld from the plaintiff for the sole and specific intent to deceive and defraud the plaintiff and to induce her in the purchasing of additional hours of dance lessons." It was averred that the lessons were sold to her "in total disregard to the true physical, rhythm, and mental ability of the plaintiff." In other words, while she first exulted that she was entering the "spring of her life," she finally was awakened to the fact there was "spring" neither in her life nor in her feet.

It is true that "generally a misrepresentation, to be actionable, must be one of fact rather than of opinion." But this rule has significant qualifications, applicable here. It does not apply where there is a fiduciary relationship between the parties, or where there has been some artifice or trick employed by the representor, or where the parties do not in general deal at "arm's length" as we understand the phrase, or where the representee does not have equal opportunity to become apprised of the truth or falsity of the fact represented.

" * * * * * A statement of a party having * * * * * superior knowledge may be regarded as a statement of fact although it would be considered as opinion if the parties were dealing on equal terms."

It could be reasonably supposed here that defendants had "superior knowledge" as to whether plaintiff had "dance potential" and as to whether she was noticeably improving in the art of terpsichore. And it would be a reasonable inference from the untended averments of the complaint that the flowery eulogists heaped upon her by defendants as a prelude to her contracting for 1944 additional hours of instruction in order to attain the rank of the Bronze Standard, thence to the bracket of the Silver Standard, thence to the class of the Gold Bar Standard, and finally to the crowning plateau of a Life Member of the Studio, proceeded as much or more from the urge to "ring the cash register" as from any honest or realistic appraisal of her dancing prowess or a factual representation of her progress.

" * * * * * (W)hat is plainly injurious to good faith ought to be considered as a fraud sufficient to impeach a contract," and that an improvident agreement may be avoided " * * * * * because of surprise, or mistake, want of freedom, undue influence, the suggestion of falsehood, or the suppression of truth."

Judgment and Remedy.

Vokes's complaint, which had originally been dismissed from the trial court, was reinstated, and the case was returned to the trial court to allow Vokes to prove her case.

STATEMENTS OF QUALITY

Statements of quality or value or commendations, using such adjectival phrases as "good," "adequate," "great," "successful," "the best," "the finest quality," etc., are generally not actionable. However, there may be circumstances where such statements may be actionable, as where the parties are not acting on equal footing or where one party has superior knowledge about the true facts of a situation. In such a case, a court may find that the "opinion line has crossed into the law of fact." (*Wat Henry Pontiac v. Bradley*, 202 Okl. 82 (1949)).

The case of *Sellers v. Looper* concerns the phrase "a good well." Note the use of the JNOV after the jury returned its verdict. What is a JNOV? How and why is it used?

Sellers v. Looper
264 ORE. 13; 503 P.2D 692 (1972)

BACKGROUND AND FACTS

This is an action for damages based upon fraudulent misrepresentation pertaining to a well on property the plaintiffs purchased from defendants. The trial court found for plaintiffs. On motion, the trial court found JNOV and plaintiffs appealed.

Defendants argue here that the plaintiff had not submitted evidence sufficient to establish fraudulent representations to induce plaintiffs to enter into the contract to purchase the property.

The plaintiffs contend: Statements regarding quality, value or the like may be considered misrepresentations of fact where the parties are not on equal footing and do not have equal knowledge or means of knowledge "and the decision of whether a representation is of fact or of opinion is always left to the jury" and therefore the order setting aside the jury's verdict should not have been entered.

* * * * * Defendant's argue that the representation of a "good well" was a mere inclusion of adjectival words of commendation or opinion and therefore, not actionable.

In Holland v. Lentz, we held:

* * * * * It is recognized that statements of opinion regarding quality, value or the like, may be considered as misrepresentations of fact, that is, of the speaker's state of mind, if a fiduciary relationship exists between the parties, as for example, representations of value of a real estate broker to his principal; or where the parties are not on equal footing and do not have equal knowledge or means of knowledge.

Prosser stated: * * * * * misrepresentation will not lie for misstatements of opinion as distinguished from those of fact * * * * *

The evidence discloses that defendants owned a house and acreage located in Illinois Valley near the city of Cave Junction, Oregon. In May of 1969, defendants executed a listing agreement to sell the property with Mrs. McLean, a real estate broker. This agreement included information given by the defendants to Mrs. McLean. Mrs. McLean testified:

I asked the Loopers: Do you have a good well * * * * * and the comment came back, "Yes, we have a good well * * * * *."

On May 28, 1969, plaintiffs contacted Mrs. McLean.

Q: At the time you told them that there was a good well on the property, did you tell them that for the purpose of inducing them to buy the Looper's property?

A: A good well on any property is a tremendous inducement. If you have a good well, that's a selling point...

Q: At the time you told them that there was quote, a good well on the property, what did you mean to convey by that, what meaning did you mean to get across to the prospective buyers?

A: * * * * * that it was an adequate well, there was plenty of water * * * * *

Q: Plenty of water for what?

A: Adequate for household, and usually that includes a modest garden.

In the early evening of July 28, 1969, the parties met and inspected the house and "looked at the well and pumphouse." No specifications as to the depth of the well or how many gallons it would pump per hour were given the plaintiffs and the realtor did not have this information. The sale was later consummated.

On August 15, 1969, plaintiffs moved onto the property and on August 22, 1969, the well went dry. Plaintiffs drilled two additional wells but found no water.

We conclude that there was sufficient evidence to submit the case to the jury. A reasonable person could believe that a "good well" meant a well with adequate water for family household use and the plaintiffs relied on this representation.

The evidence shows that defendants knew the water in the well got low in the Fall of the year and they had to be careful in flushing the indoor toilet or the well would probably go dry. The plaintiffs were not on equal footing with the defendants and did not have equal knowledge of the adequacy or lack of adequacy of the water in the well. The jury returned a verdict for the plaintiffs and "These matters are ordinarily for the determination of the jury * * * * *"

Reversed With Instructions to Reinstate the Jury's Verdict.

CONCEALMENT

Active concealment occurs where a party, through conduct, conceals the true nature of a situation. Actions such as turning back the odometer of a car, adding oil to the crankcase of a car where the oil would have otherwise run out and the engine would have seized, painting over cracks in the ceiling or wall, and gluing together pieces of a set of china all amount to active concealment. This is often termed the "half-truths" rule since a party to a contract will often disguise the true and complete nature of a transaction. Consider these two examples.

EXAMPLE:

Capone agrees to purchase a collie puppy from Spindell. The puppy is blind in one eye but when Spindell shows the puppy to Capone, he skillfully keeps the puppy's head turned so that Capone does not notice the defect. Spindell has committed fraud through concealing the true nature of the puppy's eye condition.

Paul Hemmeter purchased a home in South Bend, Indiana. When Paul notices that water is pooling in his basement, he calls his neighbor to help in the bailing-out operation. His neighbor tells Paul: "Gee, that's funny. There used to be a big crack in the basement floor. Mrs. Lovejoy (the former owner) must have painted over it." Has Mrs. Lovejoy committed fraud? What theory? Evaluate.

MISREPRESENTATION OF LAW

Under the common law, a statement made by a person concerning a matter of law was not actionable as fraud because of a curious rule that "everyone was presumed to know the law." The rule established was that a statement of the law governing a given set of facts is merely the expression of opinion: no lawyer or layperson ought to rely on such opinion without further research.

The case of *Puckett Paving v. Carrier Leasing* exemplifies the common law rule concerning statements as to a matter of law. Note that in this case, the court stated that a different result might have been obtained had there been a fiduciary relationship (a special relationship of trust and confidence) between the parties.

Puckett Paving v. Carrier Leasing Corp.
236 GA. 891; 225 S.E. 2D 910 (1976)

BACKGROUND AND FACTS

Carrier brought an action to recover four heavy-duty trucks from Puckett. The pleadings and the evidence show that Puckett was in possession of the vehicles under the terms of two certain leases providing for monthly payments in stated sums for 44 months.

Puckett had an option to purchase same for a stated price after all monthly payments had been made; that Puckett had made all monthly payments but refused to purchase the vehicles or to return them. Carrier elected to recover the vehicles rather than damages.

Puckett filed an answer and cross claim alleging that the contracts were induced by fraud in that an agent of Carrier "assured defendant that the lease agreements entered into would be considered a lease by the IRS" but that the IRS considered the same to be a sale and not a lease, resulting in damage to Puckett. The trial Court ordered Puckett to return the vehicles.

We affirm. Assuming such statements were made by an agent of Carrier to Puckett, they could only have been expressions of an opinion as to how the IRS had treated such agreements or would treat them in the future.

"Where no fiduciary relationship exists, misrepresentations as to a question of law will not constitute remedial fraud, since everyone is presumed to know the law and therefore cannot in legal contemplation be deceived by erroneous statements of law, and such representations are ordinarily regarded as mere expressions of opinion."

Affirmed.

As times change, a new rule has developed. A professional who gives an opinion as to a matter of law in a professional setting, would be responsible for the truth of the statement made. Professionals such as lawyers, accountants, architects, financial planners, real estate brokers, tax professionals those professions which require a greater or more substantial knowledge of the law than possessed by a layperson would fall within the rule of law found in the case of *Yorke v. Taylor*, 356 Mass. 42 (1969). Would the application of the rule in *Yorke v. Taylor* have changed the result in *Puckett Paving?*

Do you think that the H&R Block Corporation ("the Tax People") would be liable for fraud or misrepresentation if one of their tax preparers makes a mistake in preparing an individual's income taxes by asserting that a family dog may be claimed as a dependant on mom and dad's income tax return? Would the case be one of fraud or innocent misrepresentation? What might be the damages?

SCIENTER

The second element of a cause of action for fraud is that of scienter: either knowledge of falsity or reckless disregard of the truth. Scienter implies an intent to deceive, a "guilty mind," and is required to prove fraud. Without proof of scienter a plaintiff will only be able to prove misrepresentation.

Eddie Roper offered a "1993 VW" for sale at the stated price of $10,000. Eddie believed that the VW was in fact a 1993. After purchasing the car, Lars Daly takes it to a local garage for servicing and learns that it is a 1990 model. One big problem now is that the 1990 model will not pass state inspection because of its outdated emission system. Lars sues Eddie, seeking the return of his $10,000. What theory? What basis?

Suppose that in the above example Eddie had been asked about the model year and answered either:

a. "It is a 1993" and he knew it was a "1990."

b. "It is a 1993" but he did not know what model year it really was. Is there fraud now in either case? What basis?

In most cases, scienter will be found in the words or actions of a party. When might silence constitute fraud?

Under the common law, in a typical contract negotiation, neither party had the positive duty to come forward with facts and disclose them to the opposite party in a typical contract negotiation. It was said that the parties were operating "at arms length" and thus, no "duty to speak" existed. Parties were expected to protect their own interests.

This common law rule has been supplanted in many cases by decisions that have established a "duty to speak." Some of the circumstances establishing a "duty to speak" include:

a. In the sale of a home or other real property, the seller must disclose material "latent defects," that is, any defect that would not be readily discovered upon an inspection and which is known by the seller. The application of this rule depends on state law.

b. If a serious defect or serious potential problem is known to the seller (i.e., a crack in the engine block that might cause a serious steering problem), but could not reasonably be discovered by the buyer, the court may impose a "duty to speak."

c. Where a fiduciary relationship exists. A fiduciary relationship is a special relationship of "trust and confidence" between parties. Examples of a fiduciary relationship include lawyers and their clients, partners in a partnership, a broker and a client, directors of a corporation and their shareholders, and a guardian and his or her ward.

Would you find that fraud existed in the following fact pattern? What basis?

Fidelity Brokerage House contacts its clients using a phone bank or "boiler room" operation. To its potential customers in New Jersey, it has recommended the purchase of shares in the Fibex Corporation. To potential clients in California who already own Fibex stock, it has recommended that they sell their shares. Is there a duty of full disclosure? Has Fidelity committed fraud?

d. To correct a prior statement which, although true when made, has now become false or untrue due to a change in facts or circumstances.

Read *Bergeron v. Dupont.* How did the court formulate the rule? Who or what is a Master?

Bergeron v. Dupont
359 A.2D 627 (1976)

BACKGROUND AND FACTS

The plaintiff purchased a mobile home park from the defendant. Subsequent to the transfer of title, plaintiff brought this action to recover damages allegedly sustained as a result of fraudulent misrepresentations by the defendant, Lawrence Dupont, Jr., through his agent.

On January 25, 1973, the plaintiff and defendant executed a purchase and sale agreement which specified a sale price of $89,999. In the course of negotiations, the agent represented that the septic system in the park was satisfactory, requiring only an occasional pumping out for proper functioning.

Subsequent to the signing of the agreement but prior to the closing, complaints were lodged by park residents in February, 1973, with the water supply and pollution control commission to the effect that effluent from some of the systems was emerging above ground. Tests by the State in February were inconclusive because of weather conditions, but on March 13 and 14, tests disclosed that three of the systems had failed. The Defendant was informed by a sanitary engineer from Concord sometime during this period that they were testing the system because of the emergence of the effluent.

The title was transferred on March 14, 1973, and shortly thereafter the plaintiffs were informed that three of the septic systems had failed. The plaintiff replaced them and the cost of replacement was the basis for the verdict.

The master found on the issue of defendant's fraud as follows: At no time did the defendant reveal to the plaintiff that the state was investigating a complaint from tenants. The defendant's representations to the plaintiff regarding the conditions of the septic tank and systems were a material factor in persuading the plaintiff to buy the mobile home park. When the defendant acquired new knowledge regarding the conditions of the septic systems, he came under the duty to disclose this additional information to the plaintiff since it was at variance with the representations previously made.

The Master correctly ruled that a representation which was true when made could be fraudulent if the maker failed to disclose subsequent information which made the original representation false. While it is true that one who makes a representation believing it to be true and does not disclose its falsity until after the transaction has been consummated has committed no fraud, both parties herein treat March 14, the date of the closing, as the time at which the rights of the parties became fixed.

AFFIRMED.

JUSTIFIABLE RELIANCE

The third element of proving fraud is that of "justifiable reliance," that is, the party claiming that he or she has been defrauded must prove reasonable or justifiable reliance upon the misrepresentation in entering into the contract. This is very similar to a finding of causation in the area of tort law. The question of reliance is preeminently a question of fact. The plaintiff need not prove that the false statement was the sole factor in entering into the contract; rather, that it was an important element in inducing him or her to enter into a contract.

It is recognized that a certain amount of "sales puffing" or "trade talk" may be expected in a sales contract. The common law noted that it was the duty of every person "to take notice of obvious facts and to investigate the truth of representations." Thus, if a statement was obviously or patently false, a plaintiff could not say that he justifiably relied upon it. For example, while a statement by a car salesman that a car might get "45 miles to a gallon of gas" when in reality, it will get only 30 miles to a gallon, might form the basis for a cause of action for fraud, a statement that the car might get "400 miles to a gallon" probably would not. Sometimes, then, the more outrageous a statement, the less likely an action for fraud could be maintained, although, it must also be recognized that "the law will afford relief even to the simple and credulous who have been duped by art and falsehood." (*Kendall v. Wilson*, 41 Vt. 567 (1869).

Similarly, if a party knows the truth of a statement, he or she may not later claim justifiable reliance. So, if a salesperson were to falsely assure a businessperson that a copy machine will produce 75 full copies per minute, and the businessperson knows that the machine will in fact only produce 35, there can be no action for fraud since no "justifiable reliance" can be shown on the part of the businessperson.

Is there a requirement of investigation or of inspection of goods or property by a purchaser? Generally, yes, especially if an inspection or investigation would not require the services of an expert, the expenditure of considerable time or money, or any special training or expertise. However, if a defect in property is latent (not readily seen) or hidden, the buyer would be justified in relying on statements or representations of the seller, and no inspection would be required.

DAMAGES

Finally, the innocent party must suffer some pecuniary or monetary injury or damage because of the fraud or misrepresentation. If the plaintiff is only attempting to rescind or cancel the contract, the court will not require other proof of monetary damages. However, if the plaintiff is seeking damages in the form of money, proof of an injury is required.

Review the materials presented earlier paying close attention to both benefit of the bargain and punitive damages for fraud.

As a final look at the area of fraud, we will read the case of *Miller v. Plains Insurance Co.*

The court permitted an insurance company to deny coverage because of a material misstatement of fact made by a party in filing an application for insurance. It ruled that no contract had even come into existence.

Miller v. Plains Insurance Co.
409 S.W. 2D 770 (1966)

BACKGROUND AND FACTS

The plaintiff in this action, D.C. Miller, is suing the insurance company of the owner and driver of the automobile in which his wife was killed. The owner and operator of the automobile, Hazel Gales, also perished in the crash. She was insured by Plains Insurance Company, the defendant. The policy provided, among other

things, $500 medical expense coverage and up to $10,000 uninsured motorists coverage. This coverage provides for payment to the insured in case the insured is involved in an accident where someone else is at fault and does not have any insurance.

At the trial, Miller was awarded both $500 in medical expenses and $10,000 under the uninsured motorists provision. On appeal, the defendant argued that had it known certain representations were untrue, it would not have undertaken the risk in insuring Gales, who had a record for moving traffic violations and, in particular, for hazardous driving and did not disclose it when applying for the policy.

TITUS, Judge

What is a material misrepresentation? A misrepresentation that would likely affect the conduct of a reasonable man in respect to his transaction with another is material. Materiality, however, is not determined by the actual influence the representation exerts, but rather by the possibility of its so doing. A representation made to an insurer that is material to its determination as to what premium to fix or whether it will accept the risk, relates to a fact actually material to the risk which the insurer is asked to assume. The word "risk" does not relate to an actual increase in danger but to a danger determined by the insurer's classification of the various circumstances affecting rates and insurability. That the fact misrepresented has no actual subsequent relation to the manner in which the event insured against occurred, does not make it any the less material to the risk. Thus, whether a misrepresentation is material in an application for an automobile insurance policy, is determined by whether the fact, if stated truthfully, might reasonably have influenced the insurance company to accept or reject the risk or to have charged a different premium, and not whether the insurer was actually influenced.

It is a well-known fact insurance companies rely on expense, loss, and other statistical data to measure differences among risks and thus ascertain rates to be charged for individual risks in accordance with standards for measuring variations in hazards. This is recognized and, to some extent, controlled by our statutes. Questions as to traffic violations of prospective insured and as to previous accidents in which they have been involved are legitimate fields of research for insurance companies, for these are not only rate-determining facts but may also determine if the risk will even be insured. In consideration of the authorities previously cited, * * * * * we are of the opinion the misrepresentations involved in this case might reasonably be expected to have influenced the insurance company to have accepted or rejected Mrs. Gales as an insured or to have charged her a different premium for issuing her a policy. As the only evidence in this case is that if defendant had known the truth it would have declined the risk, we are drawn to the conclusion the misrepresentations were material and should permit defendant to avoid its liability under the policy.

Judgment and Remedy

The trial court was reversed. The defendant, Plains Life Insurance Company, did not have to pay the $10,000 uninsured motorists claim or the $500 medical expense coverage because of the material misrepresentation of fact made by Hazel Gales when she filled out the application on which her insurance policy was issued. In essence, the court decided there was no true assent by the insurance company to insure Gales under that premium for that policy. No insurance contract ever came into existence.

Do you believe that a fair result was reached in this case? How did Miller participate in the fraud committed? Do you agree with the definition of materiality found here?

DURESS

Duress is the use of coercive force or a threat of force against a party to induce apparent consent. Under the common law, any wrongful act or threat that overcomes the free will of a party constitutes actionable or "legal" duress.

There are two types of duress recognized under the common law: physical duress and economic duress. The common law termed economic duress as "duress of goods." Duress may be used either as a defense to an action for breach of contract or as grounds for rescission of a contract.

In determining duress, a court will evaluate the nature of the threat against a party to a contract or against someone "near or dear" to a party in a contract. Under the common law, the law evolved to permit relief for duress in a variety of situations. These included a threat of physical violence or force ("I'm going to make you an offer you can't refuse"); a threat to initiate a criminal suit or a threat of arrest, criminal prosecution or criminal imprisonment; wrongful seizing or withholding property, or threats wrongfully to seize or to withhold goods or land; or "other wrongful acts." Generally, however, the threat to file a civil suit where there are "good grounds" for the suit (e.g., where a breach has actually occurred or where a required or timely payment has not been made), would not constitute actionable duress.

Economic duress will not generally be found where one of the parties is in desperate need of the subject matter of the contract or is being economically pressured into "making a deal," and the other party takes advantage of that need or desire in order to drive a very hard, even one-sided bargain.

However, the abusive or oppressive threat to deploy pressure has been recognized by some courts as constituting economic duress if the parties were truly "mismatched" and the victim's will was "overmatched." [Does this sound like an application of the rule of unconscionability?]

Under the category of "other wrongful acts," in order to rescind a contract or to be successful in defending a suit for breach based upon economic duress, a party must prove that the duress was in some way improper, illegal, immoral, or unconscionable.

EXAMPLE:

Crotty and Schneeman are involved in an automobile accident on South Orange Avenue. Crotty agrees to settle the case for $5,000, but Schneeman balks. Crotty's attorney sends Schneeman a letter demanding the payment of $5,000 or he will immediately file a negligence suit and seek damages in the amount of $100,000. Schneeman agrees but later backs out of the deal, claiming that he entered the contract under duress. Is he correct? Suppose that Crotty had threatened Schneeman with a criminal prosecution for driving without insurance? Would that change the result?

The "Flamingo Kid" notices Bert cheating in a game of gin-rummy. He approaches Bert and says that unless Bert agrees to hire him as a salesperson in his car dealership, he will expose his cheating to the Club Board of Directors. In fear of imminent exposure, Bert signs the employment contract. Can Bert claim duress and void the contract of employment?

Sabitus falls six months behind on his home mortgage note. The bank contacts him and states that unless he agrees to refinance the mortgage at a higher rate (14% as opposed to 6%); they will "pull the mortgage" and will foreclose on it. Sabitus agrees to refinance, but later seeks to avoid the refinanced mortgage on the ground that he entered the agreement under duress. Is Sabitus correct?

UNDUE INFLUENCE

Closely related to the concept of duress is that of undue influence. Undue influence originated in a court of equity as a ground for setting aside a transaction that was imposed by a dominant party over a subservient party. Undue influence involves the deployment of over-persuasive bargaining strategies designed to overcome the will of a party. There are two broad classes of undue influence. In the first instance, the *Restatement*, Section 497 notes that one party uses a dominant psychological position in an unfair manner to induce the subservient party to consent to an agreement to which he or she would not otherwise have consented. In the second instance, a party uses a position of trust and confidence to unfairly persuade the other party into a transaction. The party being taken advantage of does not, in reality, exercise free will in entering into a contract. Many allegations of undue influence arise after the death of the person alleged to have been unduly influenced. Typically, relatives of the deceased seek to set aside a will or an *inter vivos* transfer or gift of property.

Generally speaking, two conditions must be present in order to prove undue influence:

Susceptibility (that is, the person allegedly being influenced must be open to the influence caused by old age, infirmity, mental or physically weakness, handicap, psychological dependency);

Opportunity (that is, a special relationship of trust and confidence exists between the parties.) This relationship may encompass a number of traditional or non-traditional fiduciary or confidential relationships: attorney-client, parent-child, trustee-beneficiary, guardian-ward, administrator-legatee, husband-wife, physician-patient, nurse-patient, pastor-parishioner, or even a good friend-aged or confused individual. The following elements, found in *Odorizzi v. Bloomfield School District*, 246 Cal. App. 2d 123 (1966) are common to a finding of undue influence:

1. Discussing the bargain at an unusual or inappropriate time;

2. Consummation of the transaction at an unusual place;

3. Insistence that the transaction be concluded at once, with extreme emphasis on the risks or disadvantages of delay;

4. The use of multiple persuaders;

5. The absence of any independent third party advice;

6. Statements discouraging a weaker party to consult an independent advisor.

According to a rule enunciated in the seminal case of *Wenger v. Rosinsky*, once the *prima facie* elements of susceptibility and opportunity are shown, the burden of proof is shifted to the dominant party to prove, by clear and convincing proof, that:

1. There was no abuse of confidence;

2. The transaction was done in "good faith";

3. The gift or will was made in a manner that was free, independent, and voluntary.

Undue influence may be raised as a defense if the transaction sought to be enforced was the product of unfair persuasion. In equity, the usual remedy was cancellation of any instrument procured by undue influence, avoidance of the transaction, and "restoration of the status quo ante."

CHAPTER CASE QUESTIONS

Raffles v. Wichelhaus

a. Why did the dispute arise?

b. What was the nature of the "mutual mistake" made by the parties?

c. What is a latent ambiguity?

d. What do the words "*consensus ad idem*" mean?

Vokes v. Arthur Murray, Inc.

a. What is "sales puffing"?

b. When will an opinion be actionable as fraud?

c. What does it mean to deal "at arm's length"?

d. Does Mrs. Vokes bear any responsibility for her loss?

Sellers v. Looper

a. What is a JNOV? How and when is it used?

b. What were the parties' opposing views on the question of a commendation?

c. What were the precise words used by Mrs. McLean regarding the condition of the well? What do they signify to you? What did they mean to the court?

d. Who decides the issue of whether a statement is one of fact or opinion?

e. Whose testimony was most important in this case? Why?

f. What is a fiduciary relationship?

g. When will parties to a contract not be acting on "equal footing"?

Puckett Paving v. Carrier Leasing Corporation

a. Why did Puckett Paving sue Carrier?

b. Why do opinions as to law generally not constitute remedial fraud?

c. Are there any exceptions?

d. Is the rule in this case currently in use? What is the modern view?

Bergeron v. Dupont

a. Who is a "Master"? Why do courts use a Master to decide a case?

b. When did the defendant learn about the deteriorating condition in the septic tank?

c. What was the measure of plaintiff's damages?

d. When did the rights of the parties become fixed?

e. How did the master rule in the case?

f. What is a "closing"? What events take place at a closing?

Miller v. Plains Insurance Co.

a. What is "uninsured motorist" coverage?

b. When would a representation found in an insurance application be considered material?

c. What was the effect of the court finding that a misrepresentation had taken place?

d. Was the result in this case a fair one?

CHAPTER ELEVEN:
WRITING AND FORM

THE STATUTE OF FRAUDS

In 1677, the English Parliament enacted an Act for the Prevention of Fraud and Perjuries. The Act required certain types of contracts to be evidenced by a writing and signed by the party against whom enforcement is sought (the party to be charged). The writing requirement was designed to promote clarity, lessen the possibility of false testimony, and promote "deliberation, seriousness…and show[s] that the act was a genuine act of volition." The Statute of Frauds is entirely based on the subject matter of the contract. If the subject matter of the contract falls within one of the categories of the Statute, the ability to collect monetary damages, enforce the contract, or to seek specific performance is conditioned on proof that a signed writing exists. Professors Calamari and Perillo note that the terms "within the Statute of Frauds" or "falls within the Statute of Frauds" mean that if the contract or promise is covered by the Statute, it is not enforceable "unless it is in a satisfactory writing or unless it is enforceable for some other reason despite the absence of such a writing." Interestingly, the Statute of Frauds has nothing to do with the concept of contract fraud, previously discussed; rather, the Statute of Frauds denies enforceability to certain contracts that do not comply with its requirements.

In general, four types of business contracts "fall within" the Statute of Frauds:

1. Contracts involving the sale of land, an interest in land, or a lease which extends for more than a certain period of time (usually one year);

2. Contracts that by their terms cannot be performed within one year of their formation;

3. The promise to answer for the debt, miscarriage, or default of another (so-called secondary or collateral promises);

4. Under the Uniform Commercial Code, contracts for the sale of goods for $500 or more.

In this chapter, we shall look carefully at the Statute of Frauds, its application, and some important exceptions.

At its essence, the Statute of Frauds requires a writing or a memorandum. The memorandum or writing may be in any form. It may be a receipt, a telegram, a letter, an exchange of correspondence, the records of a business, an acknowledgment, or even a letter that purports to repudiate a contract. The writing or memorandum must state with reasonable certainty: (1) the identity of both contracting parties; (2) the subject matter of the contract so that it can be identified either from the writing, or if the writing is unclear, by the aid of extrinsic or parol evidence; (3) the essential "terms and conditions of all the promises constituting the contract and by whom and to whom the promises are made." The signature requirement includes any mark or sign, "written, printed, stamped, photographed, engraved, or otherwise placed upon any writing, memorandum, or instrument with the intent to execute or authenticate it." The memorandum need not be signed by both parties. However, it must be signed by the party to be charged (normally the defendant, but in the case of a counterclaim, it must be signed by the plaintiff), or by the authorized agent of a party.

Contracts Involving the Sale of Land or an Interest in Land

Generally, a contract that involves the sale of land is not enforceable unless it is in writing or is at least evidenced by a written "memorandum of agreement" between the parties to the transaction. The Statute of Frauds operates as a defense to a suit based on an oral contract for the sale of land and would bar the enforcement or specific performance of the oral contract.

A contract for the sale of land, of course, involves the sale of the land or real property itself (called real estate), and includes all physical objects that are permanently attached to the land, such as buildings, plants, trees, and other objects. A fixture (an item of personal property that has become so attached to the land or which is used to become a part of the real property) is also treated as a part of real property for the purpose of determining the applicability of the Statute of Frauds.

Example:

Manny orally promises to sell Ronnie his elk farm in Sussex County. Later, Manny refuses to turn over the property. If Manny is sued, Ronnie will not be able to enforce the contract. Likewise, if Ronnie refuses to "close" on the deal, Manny cannot force Ronnie to pay for the land. Enforcement of the contract in both cases would be barred by the Statute of Frauds. Would the contract cover the two barns found on Manny's property? How about the pig troughs and the three storage sheds?

The above type of contract involves the transfer of complete and full ownership of property. Such an estate is termed a fee simple. The Statute of Frauds also requires a writing for the transfer of other interests in land, including a life estate, a mortgage, an easement, and a lease. Let's take a closer look at these "interests in land."

A life estate is an ownership of an interest in land that lasts for the lifetime of a person. A life estate may be measured by the life of the grantor ("I, Freddy Glotz, give my farm to Homer Sneaker for so long as I live"); the life of the grantee ("I, Freddy Glotz, give my farm to Homer Sneaker for so long as he lives"); or the life of a third party, called an *estate pur autre vie* ("I, Freddy Glotz, give my farm to Homer Sneaker for so long as Bon Jovi lives").

A real estate mortgage is a conveyance of an interest in land as security for the repayment of a loan. (In some states, called "title" states, the owner of the property, called the mortgagor, is required to actually convey title to the mortgagee, the bank, individual, or financial institution granting the mortgage. In other states, called "lien" states, the mortgagee will only acquire a lien against the property.) A real estate mortgage is required to be in writing under the Statute of Frauds.

An easement is a legal right to use land without acquiring ownership of the land. Easements are of two general types. An express easement arises when the grantor (owner) expressly agrees to permit another person to use the land. An express easement must be in writing to be enforceable. Implied easements are created either through conduct or through necessity. As such, an implied easement need not be (and probably would not be) in writing. An example of an implied easement might be where a fruit grower uses a dirt road owned by a neighbor to reach the back portion of his own property for a period of over twenty-five years. The fruit grower has acquired an implied easement to use his neighbor's property. An easement by implication comes into being where one property is landlocked and there is no means of ingress or egress except through a part or portion of another person's property.

A lease is the transfer of possession and enjoyment of real property for a specified purpose and a period of time. In most states, leases for a period less than one year are exempted from the Statute of Frauds. In New Jersey, the Statute of Frauds applies to leases entered into for more than two years.

Under the common law, a contract involving the sale of land or an interest in land will be judged strenuously. The writing or memorandum must state the essential terms of the agreement so that the agreement can be determined from the writing itself, without reference to any outside sources. In most jurisdictions, the writing must contain the same elements as a deed, including the legal description of the property. In New Jersey, a legal description will contain the lot and block numbers. There are many other ways used to describe property, depending on the jurisdiction: street address; common designation; metes and bounds; historic designation ("the Ferguson Farm," "the King Ranch").

There is a major exception to this application of the Statute of Frauds. The "part performance" exception may be applicable when an oral contract for the sale of land has been partially performed. If the court finds sufficient part performance, the oral contract will be enforced and the court may grant specific performance of the oral contract. Courts are especially prone to find part performance where the parties cannot be returned to the status quo.

The case of *Louron Industries v. Holman* exemplifies the part performance doctrine. Be careful to note the nature of proof required. If proof by conduct or certain acts is introduced to prove the existence of an oral contract, such proof must point clearly and unmistakably to the existence of the oral contract. The three categories of part performance are: (1) Where the buyer pays a part of the purchase price and has taken actual and exclusive possession of the property; (2) Where the buyer has made permanent, valuable, and substantial improvements to the property with the consent of the seller; and (3) Where the buyer has given consideration to the seller and the amount represents a greater amount than that usually paid by a lessee under the terms of a lease. Point number two is especially critical and will be found in most applications of the part performance doctrine.

Louron Industries, Inc. v. Holman
502 P.2D 1216 (1972)

Plaintiffs sued defendants for specific performance of an oral contract to sell land. Plaintiffs had originally leased the land from defendants and had signed a written contract of purchase. Believing that defendants had also signed the agreement, plaintiffs made substantial improvements to the land beyond those permitted by

the lease. Defendants asserted the statute of frauds as a defense, but the lower court found sufficient part performance and held for plaintiffs. Defendants appealed.

EDGERTON, J.

* * * * * Appellants * * * * * contend there was not a sufficient writing or part performance to take this case out of the statute of frauds * * * * * (W)e disagree.

In Miller v. McCamish, * * * * * the court stated:

(This Court has long held that an agreement to convey an estate in real property, though required ... to be in writing with the formal requisites specified for a deed, may be proved without a writing, given sufficient part performance; and that specific performance will be granted where the acts allegedly constituting the part performance point unmistakably and exclusively to the existence of the claimed agreement.)

And in Richardson v. Taylor Land & Livestock Co., * * * * * the Supreme Court pointed out what are evidences of part performance, saying:

The principal elements or circumstances involved in determining whether there has been sufficient part performance by a purchaser of real estate under an oral contract otherwise within the statute of frauds, are (1) delivery and assumption of actual and exclusive possession of the land; (2) payment or tender of the consideration, whether in money, other property, or services; and (3) the making of permanent, substantial, and valuable improvements, referable to the contract.

In considering these factors of part performance in relation to the facts of this case, respondent's possession of the real property in and of itself would not be sufficient to take the case out of the statute of frauds because possession had been gained under the terms of the lease rather than by the contract to purchase. That possession alone would not point unequivocally to the existence of a seller-buyer relationship but would be equally consistent with the relationship of landlord and tenant. However, the payment of the $1,000 earnest money to appellants' agent, when the terms of the lease called for $65 per month rental, was consistent with the sale and pointed toward a vendor-vendee relationship and was inconsistent with continuation of the lease. Moreover, the evidence shows that respondent made very substantial permanent improvements to the real property. These were in excess of those allowed by the terms of the lease and so they, too, were consistent with a sale rather than a lease. These factors bring the case within the rule announced above and constitute sufficient evidence of part performance to take the case out of the statute of frauds. * * * * *

Affirmed.

PERFORMANCE BEYOND ONE YEAR

The original Statute of Frauds provided that a writing was required for "an agreement that is not to be performed within the space of one year from the making thereof." Probably no section of the Statute of Frauds is least favored by courts and has been subject to more interpretation. In order for a particular contract to fall within the Statute of Frauds, the performance of the contract must be objectively impossible to perform within a year from the date of the formation of the contract. The one-year period begins to run the day after the contract is made. The issue is one of possibility, not probability, or even likelihood that the promise can be performed within a year.

EXAMPLE:

Johnny Vollmer will graduate from Seton Hall University on May 23. The Ajax Finance Co. orally agrees to hire Johnny immediately (May 23) for one year at $3,000 per month. Is this contract subject to the Statute of Frauds? Since the one-year period begins on May 24 and will conclude on May 23 of the succeeding year, full performance of the contract is possible within one year of its making. The promise is not within the Statute of Frauds; no writing is required.

Elvis Pretzel orally hires Fred to be his agent "for three years." This oral contract falls within the Statute of Frauds. Three years is certainly greater than a year! Both of these promises are example of a "straight time" contract. Let's change the example to one of a "task" contract. Elvis agrees to perform a series of thirty-six concerts. Even though it is unlikely that Elvis would perform thirty-six concerts in a one-year period (after all, "the King" regularly performs only one concert per month), the legal issue is one of possibility and not probability or likelihood of performance. Thus, since performance of thirty-six concerts within one year is not logically impossible, this promise falls outside of the Statute of Frauds and is not required to be in writing.

Elvis hires "the Colonel" for a period of three years, during which time the Colonel is to procure thirty-six concert bookings for him. This is an example of a "time-task" contract. Again, the issue is one of possibility of performance of the task within the one-year period. As long as it is possible to perform the task of procuring thirty-six concert bookings within one year, the promise falls outside of the Statute of Frauds and is not required to be in writing. (In the area of employment law, indefinite period contracts are also termed as an "employment at will" contract.)

A final type of contract is a contract entered into for an indefinite period of time. *Hardin Associates, Inc. v. Brummett* discusses an indefinite term employment contract, which by definition, falls outside the Statute of Frauds.

Hardin Associates, Inc. v. Brummett
613 S.W. 2D 4 (1981)

Hardin Associates was in the business of developing shopping centers, and it hired Brummett to head a new division called the development division. Brummett was hired on an oral contract of employment for an indefinite time. In February 1978, Hardin eliminated the development division, and Brummett went to work for another company. When Hardin refused to pay Brummett certain fees earned under the terms of the employment contract, Brummett sued. Hardin claims that the oral indefinite employment contract is unenforceable because it was within the statute of frauds. The trial court found for Brummett.

CORNELIUS, J.

* * * * * Hardin asserts that Brummett's contract was in violation of our Statute of Frauds, which provides that an agreement which is not to be performed within one year is unenforceable unless it is in writing. We disagree. Indefinite term employment contracts are considered performable within one year and do not come within the purview of the Statute of Frauds. Even if it be considered that the contract was for the definite time needed to complete the Commerce Square project, the rule is that, where the time for performance is indefinite in that the agreement merely provides for the performance of a particular act or acts which can conceivably be performed within one year, the Statute of Frauds is inapplicable, however improbable performance within one year might be.

The judgment of the trial court is affirmed.

PROMISES TO ANSWER FOR THE DEBT OF ANOTHER

A promise to answer for the debt, miscarriage, or default of another is an example of a secondary or collateral promise. A contract or promise of guaranty or suretyship is such a promise. A secondary promise is also called a "triggered promise," since its performance only comes into existence when triggered by the failure of the primary party to pay or perform. The Statute of Frauds generally applies to a secondary or collateral promise.

It is important to clearly distinguish between primary and secondary promises. Let's look at two promises made by John Kinder:

1. "If Mom can't make the payments on her car, then I will."

2. "Send Mom the VCR and send me the bill."

In example one, John has made a promise to pay for Mom's car, but his obligation to pay only arises only upon the condition that Mom defaults or fails to make the required payments. In example two, John has made a primary or original promise to pay for the VCR. In fact, Mom has made no promise at all.

The Statute of Frauds will apply if the guarantor or surety's obligation is contingent upon (triggered by) the primary party's inability or refusal to pay and is therefore secondary or collateral. The Statute of Frauds would apply to example one, above, but not to example two.

Read *Howard, Weil v. Abercrombie*. Notice the method of analysis to determine the nature of the promise made. In order for the Statute of Frauds to apply, three conditions must be present.

1. Three parties are involved;

2. Two promises are involved;

3. The secondary or collateral promise is to pay the debt of the primary promisor or fulfill some sort of a contractual duty or obligation of the primary promisor, but only if the primary promisor fails to do so.

Howard, Weil, Labouisse v. Abercrombie
140 GA. APP. 436; 231 S.E. 2D 451 (1976)

BACKGROUND AND FACTS

Plaintiff, a customer of the defendant brokerage firm, sued to recover an amount charged against his account. The amount was due from another customer (Waters) but the plaintiff had orally agreed to "stand behind Waters account * * * * *"

While it is obvious that the brokerage firm had psychological reasons to believe that any deficit accumulated by Waters in his personal account would be covered by Abercrombie, and that Abercrombie had "backed" Waters by lending him money and covering his deficits, we agree that there was no legal obligation to continue to do so. It is not contended that the oral "guarantee," if made, was for any particular amount.

* * * * * Had the Defendant wanted an unconditional guaranty to this effect, it should of course have had this matter committed to writing. Such a writing would doubtless state the ceiling amount of the funds pledged, the time limit and other general conditions.

A promise to answer for the debt, default, or miscarriage of another must be in writing. There are various exceptions. If the agreement of the third party guarantor is an original undertaking; that is, one furthering his own interests rather than underwriting the debt of another, it is not within the Statute of Frauds. * * * * * There is no scintilla of evidence that the extension of credit was of benefit to Abercrombie or that he in any way attempted to substitute himself for Waters as a potential debtor to the brokerage firm. * * * * *

The case is more nearly controlled by Southern Coal and Coke v. Randall: There the debtor company was behind in its payments for shipments of coal. It desired to enter new orders, which the creditor was unwilling to fill. The president of the debtor corporation then orally stated that if they would continue shipping, "he would guarantee they were paid." The Court held that the promise of future payments was collateral and not an original undertaking, thus within the Statute of Frauds.

* * * * * Professor Williston: "If as between them, the original debtor still ought to pay, the debt cannot be the promisor's own, and he is undertaking to answer for the debt of another."

"When one person tells another to let a third person have goods and that he will see that the debt is paid, in order for the promisor to be bound in the absence of a writing, it is requisite that credit be given exclusively to the promisor."

Even reliance on the oral promise will not remove it from the statute.

The "main purpose" doctrine exception applies to certain types or categories of secondary or collateral promises. The main purpose doctrine exception provides that while the promise to answer for the debt of another generally must be in writing under the Statute of Frauds, where the secondary promisor has "some purpose of his own" (generally to secure some personal monetary or pecuniary gain or some personal benefit), the Statute of Frauds does not apply and no writing is required.

EXAMPLE:

Mark Greene is a major stockholder in a corporation that operates a fast food restaurant. When the restaurant falls behind in making payments on its account, Greene calls the supply house, Mickey's Meat Market, and states: "This is the biggest weekend of the year coming up. If the business can't pay its bills, don't worry, I will pay them personally!" Later, when the restaurant fails to make its required payment, Mickey's contacts Greene who now refuses to pay, asserting the Statue of Frauds as defense. A lawsuit is commenced by Mickey's. Is Greene correct? Ordinarily, Greene's promise would fall within the Statute of Frauds. It is clearly secondary or collateral. However, the "main purpose" doctrine would be applied since Greene (with his personal financial stake in the business) had a "purpose of his own" in making this secondary promise. No writing is required.

In applying the main purpose doctrine exception, it will be necessary to analyze the reason why the secondary promisor made the promise. If the reason for the promise was "strictly business," such as a promise normally made by a bank, a financial institution, or some other type of commercial guarantor or lender, the promise must be in writing. However, if the reason for the promise was "purely personal," based on some familial or personal relationship, or a "mixed business and personal reason," the promise will fall outside of the Statute of Frauds and is not required to be in writing. If we return to our original example ("If Mom can't make payments on her car, I will"), most courts would apply the "main purpose" doctrine to this situation and would not require John's promise to be in writing because John had a "personal" rather than a "business" reason for making the promise.

Consider the following case of *Wilson Floors Co. v. Sciota Park, Ltd.,* in which the court addressed the "main purpose" doctrine exception. [In this case, the court termed the exception "the leading object" rule.]

Wilson Floors Co. v. Sciota Park, Ltd.
54 OHIO ST. 2D 451, 377 N.E. 2D 514 (1978)

BACKGROUND AND FACTS

Wilson Floors contracted to provide flooring materials for a residential and commercial development known as "The Cliffs," which was owned by the defendant. When Unit, the general contractor for Sciota, fell behind in payments to Wilson, Wilson stopped work on the project. The bank financing the development orally assured Wilson that he would be paid if he returned to work. After Wilson's final bill was not paid by Unit, he proceeded with this action against the bank.

DECISION AND RATIONALE

Judgment was entered in favor of Wilson. The court held, "So long as the promisor undertakes to pay the subcontractor whatever his services are worth irrespective of what he may owe the general contractor, and so long as the main purpose of the promisor is to further his own business or pecuniary interest, the promise is

enforceable." The bank's main purpose in making the guaranty was to derive a benefit for itself by retaining the subcontractors already working on the project to keep costs down. Therefore, the oral promise to pay Unit's debts was enforceable.

CONTRACTS FOR THE SALE OF GOODS—U.C.C. § 2-201

The Statute of Frauds generally applies to a contract for the sale of goods if the price is $500 or more. The Statute of Frauds provision, found in Section 2-302, relates to a contract for:

a. The sale of goods (all things movable and tangible);

b. For the price of $500 or more.

This is a cumulative requirement, that is, the "sale" is a total purchase concept. Even though no one item may meet the $500 requirement, if the total or cumulative purchase meets or exceeds $500, the entire transaction falls within the Statute of Frauds.

Having met these threshold requirements, the Statute then requires:

a. Some writing sufficient to show an agreement ("that a contract for sale has been made between the parties");

b. Signed by the party against whom enforcement is sought ("the party to be charged") or by his authored agent or broker.

Under the UCC, a writing is not insufficient because it omits or incorrectly states a term agreed upon, but the contract is not enforceable beyond the quantity of goods shown in such writing. Thus, the UCC is much more lenient on the question of the sufficiency of the writing than was the common law, which required all of the "important terms" of a contract to be contained in the writing (i.e., price, quantity, parties, time for performance, etc.). Under the UCC, there are only three "definite and invariable" requirements as to the writing. First, it must evidence an intention to enter into a contract; second, it must be "signed," which includes any authentication that identifies the party to be charged; and third, it must specify a quantity.

The UCC requires either a written contract or a written memorandum (discussed later in this chapter). However, the emphasis under the UCC is clearly on "some writing"—that is, a confirmation, sales slip, check, note, order slip, telegram, letter, etc. The signature or "signing" is not required to be at the end of a document and can be placed anywhere on the writing. A signature can even consist of a stamped name, a symbol, or a party's initials, if a party so intends.

The Code requires that a quantity be stated, and even the quantity need not be stated "accurately," as long as the writing reflects the intention of the parties. However, the contract is not enforceable beyond the quantity stated in the contract.

EXCEPTIONS TO THE U.C.C.

There are three main exceptions to the UCC Statute of Frauds provision. An oral contract will be enforceable to the extent that a seller accepts payment or to the extent that a buyer accepts delivery of the goods contracted for ("goods paid for/accepted" also called the "partial performance" doctrine.)

Where goods are to be specially manufactured or custom made for a buyer and are of the type not "ordinarily sold in the regular course of the seller's business," if the seller has either begun their manufacture or incurred obligations for their manufacture, no writing is required.

Finally, if there is no writing, but the defendant admits in his pleadings, testimony or otherwise that a contract for sale was made, the Statute of Frauds will not apply.

The UCC also provides for an effective substitute for the writing and signature requirements of the Statute of Frauds. When merchants have concluded an oral contract, it is common for one party to send to the other a letter of confirmation, a purchase order, or perhaps a printed form of the contract for their review and perhaps "counter-signature." Why can't this memorandum satisfy the Statute of Frauds? Generally, because it is not signed "by the party to be charged" but by the potential plaintiff in a lawsuit!

However, between merchants (that is, if both parties are merchants), an oral contract for the sale of goods is enforceable if one of the parties within a reasonable time of the making of the oral agreement sends a written confirmation of the essential terms of an oral contract to the other party, and the party receiving has reason to know its contents and does not provide written notice of objection to the confirmatory memorandum within 10 days.

Note that the memorandum substitute is the proper method to provide protection to a merchant whenever an oral contract or order is made for goods over $500. It would also be wise to send the memorandum by registered or certified mail in order to later prove that the other party "had reason to know its contents." Why does the memorandum substitute require that both parties are merchants?

EXAMPLE:

Freddy Glotz orally orders an $8,000 mink jacket for his wife, which is tailored to his wife's exact measurements. Later, Freddy backs out of the deal and is sued. The tailor will be unable to resell the jacket because of its "special sizing." When sued, Freddy asserts the Statute of Frauds as a defense. How would the tailor counter? Suppose that the tailor had sent Freddy the following memorandum (to which Freddy had never responded):

"Thank you for your order of a brand new mink jacket at a purchase price of $8,000. I'm sure you and your lovely wife will be pleased with it." Will this memo satisfy the Statute of Frauds? Why or why not?

Finally, you should be aware that there is a split of authority concerning the issue of whether a farmer is or is not a merchant. A few courts have held that farmers are merchants; others have concluded just the opposite. It is important to ascertain your state's position on this and other provisions of the UCC that are applicable to only to merchants.

INTERPRETATION OF CONTRACTS

Professor Thayer insightfully commented that there is no "Lawyer's Paradise where all words have a fixed, precisely ascertained meaning." (Thayer, *A Preliminary Treatise on Evidence at Common Law* 390 (1898)). Section 226 of the *Restatement* notes: "Interpretations of words and of other manifestations of intention forming an agreement is the ascertainment of the meaning to be given to such words and manifestations." Whenever parties to a contract cannot agree on the terms of their contract and go to court to litigate the issue, the court will apply certain basic principles of construction and interpretation of the agreement.

The purpose of interpreting contracts is to determine and then give the proper effect to the intention of the parties. Generally speaking, courts will give a reasonable meaning to the words used in a contract. In applying this principle, courts will utilize the "plain meaning rule," that is, if a writing appears to be plain and unambiguous on its face, its meaning must be determined from the "four corners" of the instrument itself without resort to extrinsic evidence of any nature. In pursuit of "plain meaning," courts will use an objective standard, the expressed intention of the parties, rather than any secret or hidden intention in interpreting a contract. In doing so, courts will read and interpret a contract in its entirety so as to give effect to all of its parts. This is yet another application of the objective test of *Lucy v. Zehmer.*

Certain problems may arise which may result in intervention and interpretation by the courts:

When a contract is partly written and partly printed, the written part will prevail if there should be a conflict. If an amount is expressed in conflicting words and figures, the words will prevail. Example: "three thousand dollars" ($300)—the correct sum will be three thousand dollars.

Usage of trade and customs of a community can be used to explain the meaning of unclear or ambiguous language found in a contract. This is especially true under the UCC.

Actions of parties occurring after executing a contract but prior to a controversy may be used by a court to demonstrate the real intention of the parties to an agreement.

Language in a contract that is either unclear or ambiguous will be interpreted most strongly against the party who prepared the contract or the party who caused the confusion. An example exists in a provision of an insurance contract, which may be capable of more than one interpretation. Such a contract provision will be construed against the insurance company that, of course, prepared the contract. For example, "exception clauses" are strictly construed in insurance contracts. If an insurance company wishes to exclude any coverage, the exclusion must be clearly and unambiguously stated. This rule also applies to so-called "boiler plate" contracts, often offered to the buyer on a "take it or leave it" basis.

THE PAROL (ORAL) EVIDENCE RULE

When a contract is reduced to a writing, it is logical to assume that the written contract contains all the terms agreed to by the parties. Professor Corbin states "When two parties have made a contract and have expressed it in a writing to which they have both assented as the complete and accurate integration of that contract, evidence whether parol or otherwise, of antecedent [prior] understandings and negotiations will not be admitted for the purpose of varying or contradicting the writing." The parol evidence rule states that oral testimony is generally not admissible to vary the terms of a written contract when such oral testimony relates to statements made prior to the signing of the contract or to statements made at the same time [contemporaneous] the contract was made, if the parties intended as the final expression of their agreement. There are several important exceptions to the parol evidence rule:

a. Where the words used in a contract are ambiguous, that is, where words are capable of more than one meaning, oral or parol evidence may be offered to explain the ambiguity in the contract.

b. When a written contract is obviously incomplete (as where a detail is omitted or a blank is not filled in), oral or parol testimony is admissible to supply the missing term. Example: A promise (or covenant) not to compete contained a provision describing the area of non-competition as being "within a ten mile radius of the city of _____," and the name of the city was not filled in. The court permitted oral testimony to fill in the missing name of the city.

c. The failure of a condition precedent. If parties to a written contract orally agree that a contract will not to be effective unless or until a certain event or condition takes place, the court will permit oral testimony to show that the condition precedent was not fulfilled. In this case, the party offering the oral proof is not trying to vary the terms of the written agreement; rather, the introduction of the oral proof is essential to show that the agreement never came into existence.

EXAMPLE:

Fred signs a written contract in which he agrees to "close" on the purchase of a farm "on or about December 15, 2004." However, it was clearly understood that Fred would only be required to complete the purchase if he could arrange a suitable mortgage. The ability to arrange for a mortgage is an example of a "condition precedent." Oral or parol evidence would be permitted to prove the existence and failure of this condition. (A conditional clause, however, should be clearly stated in the contract.)

---

d. Changes, modifications, or additions to a contract are not covered by the parol evidence rule, since the parol evidence rule only applies to oral proof of provisions made before or at the time of the signing of the written agreement. (Note, however, that other provisions, such as the Statute of Frauds or the rules concerning consideration might apply to keep oral proof from being introduced.)

It is also settled that the parol evidence rule does not prevent a party from using contemporaneous or prior negotiations or expressions to indicate that the writing was never intended to be a final expression of their agreement.

ORAL PROOF AND THE UCC

The UCC contains several provisions concerning the interpretation of contracts. Unless there is a confirmatory memorandum or a writing intended by the parties as a final expression of their agreement, Section 2-202 of the Code generally permits the introduction of oral proof of a prior agreement or contemporaneous oral agreement that would explain or supplement but not contradict the terms of a written contract. Contracts may be explained or supplemented by: (1) prior course of dealings between the buyer and the seller; 2) trade usage; or 3) course of performance between the parties to a contract. Such proof may be helpful in showing the intention of the parties and in assisting a court in interpreting contracts where confusion or ambiguity exists.

In addition, under UCC § 2-202, consistent (meaning non-contradictory) additional terms to a contract may be considered in interpreting a contract and in determining the intention of the parties.

The clearer the parties to a contract are in creating agreements, the less likely that a court will need to apply these special "rules of construction" at a later date.

Chapter Case Questions

Louron Industries v. Holman

a. What was the basis for plaintiff's suit? Why?

b. Had the defendants signed the contract? Why did the plaintiff's expect a court to enforce the contract even though there was no writing?

c. What must proof point toward in cases of the application of the "part performance" doctrine?

d. What are the circumstances that will bring the case under the "part performance" doctrine?

e. What particular facts here were most important for the plaintiff's case?

f. What is "earnest money"?

Hardin v. Brummett

a. What is an "employment at will" contract?

b. What is an "indefinite period" contract?

c. What is the rule employed in these types of contracts?

Howard, Weil, Labouisse v. Abercrombie

a. Who was suing at the trial level? Why?

b. Why had the broker charged Abercrombie's account?

c. What type of promise had Abercrombie made?

d. Had the defendant wished to protect itself, and assure that Abercrombie's promise would be enforced, what should it have done?

e. What case was used as a precedent here?

Wilson Floors Co. v. Sciota Park, Ltd.

a. What is the "main purpose" doctrine?

b. Why did the bank make its promise to Wilson?

c. What is the alternate name for this doctrine?

CHAPTER TWELVE:
LEGALITY

Generally speaking, a contract which involves the violation of a law, a statute, or which is against public policy is not enforceable by a court of law. We sometimes say that such a contract is void or is a nullity. Likewise, should the subject matter of a contract involve some form of criminal activity or the commission of a tort, the contract is also void and unenforceable.

Clara Bow agrees to write a completely false account of the military career of Senator Herman in return for a $10,000 payment by Herman's primary election opponent. Later, when the opponent fails to compensate her, Ms. Bow sues for breach of contract. The court will be unable to enforce the contract because it is void and unenforceable. The contract involved the commission of the tort of libel. The contract may also violate public policy.

There are several special aspects or rules concerning the question of illegality:

    a. When only a part of a contract is illegal, and the illegal provision or portion does not involve serious moral turpitude, the illegal portion of the agreement may be disregarded and the legal part of the contract may be enforced. The contract is said to be divisible or severable. However, if the entire contract is so completely integrated that the parts cannot be separated, the entire agreement may be void and unenforceable.

Tina signs a lease for a beautiful Manhattan loft apartment. However, in order to be moved ahead in the waiting list, Tina agrees to pay the rental agent an improper $1,000 "gratuity." Here, the agreement to pay the gratuity may be severed from the basic rental agreement, which is still enforceable.

    b. If an agreement is executory, one of the parties may be able to rescind the agreement before the illegal act is committed or performed and may recover any consideration previously given (i.e., obtain restitution) for the commission of the illegal act. This doctrine is also known as the doctrine of *locus poenitentiae*. However, this is a minority doctrine and a majority of courts will simply refuse to recognize the terms of an illegal agreement in any way.

AN AGREEMENT CONTRARY TO PUBLIC POLICY

Public policy has been the stated rationale for striking down or refusing to enforce contracts or clauses of contracts on grounds of immorality, unconscionability, economic policy, unprofessional conduct, and other criteria. At the outset, it must be recognized that "public policy" is a very vague area of the law. Even though a contract or an agreement does not violate some formal statute or law, a contract may still be unenforceable if it violates public policy. Public policy is determined by viewing and assessing a wide variety of statutes, court and administrative decisions, and public attitudes and perceptions about the nature of law and society. It is essentially a "legal value judgment" concerning the nature and type of contractual relationships a society will recognize and enforce.

Public policy is closely associated with the area of a government's police power, which may give a legislature the right to pass laws for the "public health, safety, or morality." (For example, zoning laws are enacted pursuant to the "police power.") The area of public policy is broad and general. Read the case of *Laos v. Soble,* which turned on the application of public policy to a contract in which Laos was promised a fee contingent upon the nature of his testimony in a matter before the court. What aspect of public policy was involved? *Laos v. Soble* also involves an inherent government power to "take" private property for a public use, termed the right of eminent domain.

Laos v. Soble
503 P.2D 978 (1972)

HOWARD, J.

This is an appeal from a judgment in favor of defendants in a lawsuit to recover from them a fee purportedly due and owing to the plaintiff.

The plaintiff's claim was predicated upon the following document, written in longhand and signed by attorney Soble:

"7–24–70

Paul Laos

Your fee is 1500.00 for appraisal fees for 200,000 or below & 2500.00 for anything over $200,000.

Joseph H. Soble"

The case was tried to the court, both Laos and Soble testifying as to the circumstances which gave rise to this writing. The trial court, in ruling in defendants' favor, apparently believed Sobel's version, i.e., that the agreed-upon compensation was for Laos' services as an appraisal witness in an impending condemnation trial. Since, according to him, he did not avail himself of such services, the obligation to pay Laos did not arise.

On appeal, Laos contends that the document upon which he relied reflects that he was entitled to judgment as a matter of law. We believe that the document reflects the contrary—that, as a matter of public policy, the contract is illegal and therefore void. Although illegality was neither asserted in the trial court nor on appeal, we have a duty to raise such questions sua sponte when the face of the record reflects illegality.

An agreement to pay a witness a fee contingent on the success of the litigation is against public policy and void.

Professor Corbin points out that the use of "expert" testimony has been subject to grave abuses and that bargains for obtaining same should be under close supervision by the court. A similar concern was expressed in Belfonte v. Miller:

* * * * * The difficulties and dangers which surround so-called expert testimony are well understood by the profession and it is the manifest duty of our courts to carefully scan all special compensation in addition to the witness fees allowed by the law * * * * * The rule applied to such contracts is not to be affected by proof that the behavior of the parties was in fact exemplary, for it is the tendency of such contracts which serves to generate their undesirability. Improper conduct or bias can be predicted easily when the compensation of the witness is directly related to the absolute amount of an award which may in turn be dependent to a great degree on the testimony of that same witness. * * * * *

We are of the opinion, and so hold, that a contract providing for compensation of a witness contingent on the success of the litigation is subversive of public justice for the reason that his evidence may be improperly influenced. Public policy considerations brand such contract illegal.

Although the trial court's denial of plaintiff's claim was correct, but for a different reason, we affirm.

In class, we shall discuss the now famous *Baby "M"* case from New Jersey and see how the decision of the appellate court turned at least in part on the analysis of the public policy aspect of a surrogate mother's contract entered into between Mrs. Whitehead and Mr. & Mrs. Stern. Try to find this case on the Internet before class. What is your opinion?

There are two other areas where public policy considerations may militate against the enforcement of an otherwise legal contract:

a. Even where gambling is legal (as is casino gambling in Atlantic City or Nevada), it is usually against "public policy" to use the courts for the enforcement of a promise to repay an otherwise legal gambling debt.

b. An agreement that restrains the ability to marry or remarry is generally void as against "public policy."

LICENSING STATUTES

Every state has adopted certain so-called vocational and professional licensing statutes that regulate the professional and business conduct of certain groups in society.

TYPES OF LICENSES

A regulatory license regulates the standards of conduct of certain professionals. In order to procure a regulatory-type license, certain baseline qualifications must be met. Qualifications may include possessing special skill, special knowledge, special training, or meeting a minimum educational level. In addition, the party seeking a regulatory license may be required to demonstrate that he or she has passed a professional certification or licensure examination.

Think of at least five professions that would be covered by the rule.

A revenue license is often no more than an occupational tax. The purpose of revenue license is merely to raise revenue necessary to generally monitor the underlying activity. Any applicant will be granted the license upon the payment of the proper fee. A revenue license is also called a ministerial license. In deciding whether a particular license is regulatory or revenue in nature, it is important to assess the legislative intent and legislative history of the underlying statute.

If a court concludes that a regulatory license is required, a party seeking enforcement of any underlying contract must prove that the proper license was in force at the time the contract came into existence. Failure to possess a regulatory license at the time any consideration is furnished prevents a court from enforcing an agreement or contract concerning that professional activity or conduct. Where the purpose of the licensing statute is merely to raise revenue, an underlying contract may still be enforced, even though the required license had not been obtained. The individual, however, may be required to procure the proper license before judgment is entered by the court.

Read the case of *Markus and Nocka v. Julian Goodrich Architects.* Do you agree that the contract should not have been enforced? In refusing to enforce the contract, was the Vermont court upholding an important element of public policy (i.e., protecting the citizens of Vermont from "untrained, unqualified, and unauthorized practitioners") or, was it protecting business within its own borders? One of the earliest formulations of the basis for the rule stated that a statute enacted under the police power is one that is "for the protection of the public welfare, health and morality against fraud and incompetence...." (*Cope v. Rowlands,* 150 Eng. Rep. 707 (1836).

Markus & Nocka v. Julian Goodrich Architects, Inc.
230 A.2D 739 (1969)

BARNABY, J.

The defendant was the principal architect on a project involving an addition to the DeGoesbriand Hospital in Burlington, Vermont. The hospital directed the defendant to engage the services of the plaintiff firm as consulting architects. The plaintiff is a Massachusetts architectural firm specializing in hospital design. The arrangement was accomplished and evidenced in an exchange of letters between the parties. The project with which the plaintiff was connected involved the development of an outpatient department, emergency department, laboratory and x-ray departments. The duties of the plaintiff included a study of the medical needs to be incorporated into the addition, inspection of the premises, consultation with hospital staff, preparation of construction and equipment estimates, detail drawings of specialized rooms, participation in revision of preliminary sketches, and provision of specifications for cost and bid purposes. The plaintiff's staff made numerous trips to Burlington, consulting with hospital personnel and medical staff, and prepared plans and detailed drawings. As the matter finally wound up, the design recommendations of the plaintiff were not accepted by the hospital staff, and the new expansion was finally put out to bid and constructed on the basis of plans and working drawings of the defendant. The compensation of the plaintiff was to be 1 percent of construction cost plus travel expenses, and this 1 percent figure was the basis of the judgment in favor of the plaintiff awarded below.

It is unquestioned that these activities were carried on in connection with construction to be under-taken within Vermont. The facts show that the plans and sketches were developed based on information obtained from visits to the Vermont site and consultation with the Vermont hospital personnel. Indeed, the acts evidencing performance under the contract, sufficient at law or not, have no other relevance than to this Vermont project on its Vermont site. Thus they are within the ambit of the Vermont architectural registration statute. * * * * *

Architectural contracts entered into in violation of such registration statutes are held to be illegal, and the provisions for payment of commissions under them are unenforceable. The underlying policy is one of protecting the citizens of the state from untrained, unqualified, and unauthorized practitioners. It has been applied to many professions and special occupations for similar protective purposes. * * * * *

26 V.S.A. 121 specifically mentions consultation as one of the activities prescribed for one not registered. This is not to say that any kind of consultation between architects of different states can be contractually valid only with registration. It does mean that when the nonresident architect presumes to consult, advise, and service, in some direct measure, a Vermont client relative to Vermont construction he is putting himself within the scope of the Vermont architectural registration law. Nothing in that law suggests that the services must be somehow repetitive to be prohibited. No basis for excusing this plaintiff from its express provisions appears here. * * * * *

Judgment reversed and judgment for the defendants to recover their costs.

COVENANTS (PROMISES) NOT TO COMPETE

A covenant not to compete may be found in two general types of business contracts:

1. A promise made by the seller of a business or of an enterprise to a buyer;

2. A clause which is part of an employment contract which restricts an employee from discussing or divulging so-called "trade secrets" (special or limited insider information) or which restricts or completely forbids the employee from engaging in competition or going to work with a competitor when an employment contract is terminated.

An agreement by a person to refrain from exercising his or her trade or profession, standing alone, is generally viewed as being illegal and contrary to public policy because it is "inimical to the interests of society in a free and competitive market and to the interests of the person restrained in earning a livelihood." (See *United States v. Addyston Pipe & Steel Co.*, 85 F. 271 (1898)). Such a promise or covenant is often termed a "naked covenant." A promise made by the seller of a business will be enforced if it is reasonable in both time and area. When the area is too broad or extensive or the time is too long for the reasonable protection for the buyer (especially where the intangible element of "good will" is involved), a covenant not to compete will generally not be enforced.

Under a strict common law rule, if such a covenant "failed" in any respect (i.e., the court concluded that a covenant was unreasonable as to either time or area), the court could not enforce any part of the covenant. Nor would a court re-write (reform) any of the provisions of a contract to make a provision reasonable. Why? First, courts do not really like such covenants and consider them to be in "restraint of trade." Second, to re-write a covenant to make it reasonable (i.e., twenty-five miles unreasonable for a restaurant—ten miles is reasonable; 5 years unreasonable for a barber—6 months is reasonable) would put the court in a position of actually writing a contract for the parties, subjecting them to an agreement they had not actually made.

In recent years, however, courts have in fact become more proactive in this area. Some courts now follow the "blue pencil" or "reasonableness" rule, which permits the court to "strike out" any unreasonable provisions from an agreement and to modify the time or area to provide reasonable protection to the parties. The "blue pencil" rule has its origins in the doctrine of severability as applied to illegal contracts.

A clause in a contract of employment is likewise closely scrutinized by courts and will be strictly construed when enforcement is sought. The burden of proof is placed on the party seeking to enforce the covenant. Some of the criteria used by the courts in determining whether such a clause in a contract of employment will be enforceable are:

1. Is the restraint reasonable in the sense that it is no greater than necessary to protect the legitimate business interests of the employer in such areas as protection of trade secrets or other confidential information?

2. Is the restraint unreasonable and unduly harsh on the employee in terms of time or area?

3. Would the employee's work for a competitor irreparably injure or harm the employer's business or threaten such irreparable injury (especially with regard to an intangible such as "good will")?

4. Is the employment of a unique, extraordinary, or unusual type?

Courts are sometimes reluctant to enforce a covenant where the public will be denied a necessary or essential service. In this case, the court might in fact prefer to award monetary damages for the breach of the covenant instead of issuing an injunction or a restraining order. An example might be where a veterinarian signs a covenant not to compete in which he agrees not to compete against his former associates for a period of three years. In the small farming community where the vet lives, there are no other vets. In these circumstances, a court might be reluctant to enforce the covenant because the public might be denied an important service. The court might instead award money damages against the vet for breach of the covenant, the amount to be determined as a matter of proof during a trial.

It should be noted that in a few states (most notably, California), an employer cannot restrict a regular employee, not in possession of any specialized information or "trade secrets," from engaging in employment, when the term of a contract ends, holding that such restrictions are void and a violation of public policy. In general, however, properly drawn covenants are enforceable and provide important protections in business relationships. One other exception occurs in the case of a covenant not to compete applicable to attorneys. In most states, such covenants are per se illegal.

Read *Frederick v. P.B.M.* and consider the application of the rules discussed to the facts of the case. Did it surprise you that the lower court granted the injunction?

Frederick v. Professional Bldg. Main. Indus., Inc. 168 IND. APP. 647; 344 N.E.2D 299 (1975)

Garrard, J.

In 1967, appellee (PBM) employed Frederick as a management trainee in PBM's contract cleaning and maintenance business. In 1972, Frederick resigned. When he then sought to engage in the contract maintenance business on a part time basis, PBM brought this action to enforce a covenant against competition. The trial court enjoined Frederick and he appeals. The issue is whether the covenant given by Frederick is enforceable.

It reads as follows:

James Frederick hereby covenants that he will not engage in contract maintenance business, including, but not limited to, janitorial services, window cleaning, floor cleaning, commercial or residential cleaning, either as a sole proprietor, partner, or agent or employee of a corporation or other business organization in the following localities:

The counties of Lake, Porter, La Porte and St. Joseph in Indiana; of Will and Cook, in Illinois, except Chicago; and the counties of Berrien and Van Buren in Michigan.

This covenant shall extend for a period of ten years from the date of termination of this contract.

Such covenants are in restraint of trade and are not favored by the law. However, they will be enforced if they are reasonable. * * * * * This determination must be made upon the basis of the facts and circumstances surrounding each case. It depends upon a consideration of the legitimate interests of the covenantee which might be protected, and the protection granted by the covenant in terms of time, space and the type of conduct or activity protected.

While the burden of proving the facts and circumstances rests with the party seeking to enforce the covenant, the ultimate determination of whether the covenant is reasonable is a question of law for the courts.

In addition, if the covenant as written is not reasonable, the Courts may not enforce a reasonable restriction under the guise of interpretation, since this would amount to the court subjecting the parties to an agreement they had not made.

In the case before us, the evidence discloses that Frederick was employed by PBM at a management level. Through his employment, Frederick acquired skills related to the performance of janitorial services provided by PBM and to the technique of surveying a proposed job and computing a competitive and profitable bid. However, the potential use by a former employee of merely skill and ability he has acquired will not justify a restraint.

Frederick was also privy to bidding and cost analysis which PBM considered confidential. While there was no evidence that this information was novel or unique, so as to construe it as a trade secret, it is apparent that it might be used in an effort to undercut PBM's bids. * * * * *

The evidence disclosed that PBM conducted its operations in the eight counties enumerated in the covenant. However, it was not established that Frederick worked in all eight counties. * * * * * The covenant restraining him from engaging in the contract maintenance business was unreasonable in prohibiting activity in counties where he had not worked. * * * * *

No evidence was introduced bearing directly on the reasonableness of the covenant's ten year term. * * * * *

Bringing these factors together, it appears that Frederick was to be restrained from acting not only as a proprietor but also as an employee in furnishing janitorial services by contract. The geographic area of the restriction was more broad than the area in which he worked. He was not in possession of any trade secrets, but did have pricing information which in the immediate short term, might enable him to undercut PBM. On this basis, he was to be restrained for ten years. Such a restraint is unreasonable, and the covenant is therefore void.

REVERSED.

USURY

Usury involves a contract that carries an excessive and illegal rate of interest. Most states regulate the rate of interest by a specific statute. Such statutes typically provide for a "legal rate" where no rate has been stated in a loan, and a maximum rate that is the most that can be legally charged under law.

If a court determines that an agreement is usurious, a number of remedies are available. The majority of states today will deny recovery of any and all interest on usurious loans. Some states require the forfeiture of both principal and interest; other states permit the borrower to recover double or triple the interest previously paid. Still other states may permit the charging of a "legal rate" where the interest rate charged "inadvertently" surpassed the legal rate. There are several statutory exceptions to usury laws:

1. Installment sales. A seller may legitimately charge one price for a credit sale and another for a cash sale. The difference between the cash and credit price is not considered interest. Consider the different price paid for gas at the retail pump—even when the credit price will result in a higher basis for any finance charge assessed. A current controversy surrounds the "rent-to-own" industry. See if you can find any information on this practice.

2. Fees for services and certain expenses incidental to a loan may be charged in addition to the maximum rate of interest (consider the addition of "points" on a loan to secure the purchase of a home).

3. Most states permit the charging of advance interest, the compounding of interest, and accelerating maturity on a note when payments are missed without considering these higher charges as usurious, so long as the total interest does not exceed the maximum rate permitted for the full period of the loan.

It has been stated that with so many exceptions, the original purpose of protecting borrowers from excessive interest rates may no longer be accomplished through the application of laws against usury. Thus, separate consumer protection statutes have been enacted in order to serve important consumer protection interests.

EXCULPATORY CLAUSES

An exculpatory clause is a provision of a contract that relieves a party of liability for its own ordinary negligence. Exculpatory clauses are not favored by the courts and will be strictly construed against the party writing them.

At common law, however, courts would regularly enforce exculpatory clauses on the ground of "freedom of contract," especially where a contract was entered into by two private parties, and no gross negligence, fraud, willful injury, or violation of a law was involved. Later, courts modified their views and began to refuse to enforce or uphold exculpatory clauses in an employment relationship, so that an employer would be liable to employees for any negligence, despite the existence of any exculpatory clause.

However, where there is a public interest involved, an exculpatory clause will generally be held to be void and against public policy. A public interest is established where one of the parties is a public institution (that is, one owned or operated by the government or some subsidiary or branch of the government, i.e., a public hospital, a public school, or a municipally owned parking facility). In recent years, courts have significantly narrowed the scope of parties who may exculpate themselves from liability and have created a new category, termed a "quasi-public" institution, which can not exculpate itself from liability based on negligence. A quasi-public institution may be defined as a private party or business entity that:

1. Deals with a large number of people;

2. Solicits the public business;

3. Deals in a necessary and/or vital service (i.e., transportation, education, banking, etc.).

Such an institution cannot exculpate itself from liability. What types, organizations, or businesses might fall within the definition of a quasi-public institution? The *U-Haul* case, which was instrumental in establishing the concept of a quasi-public institution, will be discussed in class. What type of service was U-Haul involved in providing?

Read the case of *Hy-Grade Oil v. New Jersey Bank.* How did the court reach its conclusion that Hy-Grade Oil could not absolve itself from liability based on its own negligence? Do you agree with this view or do you subscribe to the notion of absolute "freedom of contract"?

Hy-Grade Oil Co. v. New Jersey Bank
350 A.2D 279 (1975)

Hy-Grade Oil Company (plaintiff) brought this action against New Jersey Bank (defendant), which refused to credit Hy-Grade's account with an amount assertedly deposited by Hy-Grade in the bank's night depository box.

BISCHOFF, Judge.

The resolution of this appeal requires us to determine whether a clause in a "night depository agreement" between a bank and a customer, providing that "the use of the night depository facilities shall be at the sole risk of the customer," is valid and enforceable.

In February, 1974, in order to protect the increasing cash supply generated by operations of its fuel business, plaintiff's manager, Flaster, signed a night depository agreement with defendant bank. This agreement (in printed form and apparently used by other banks in the area) contained the following provision:

* * * * * it is hereby expressly understood and agreed that the use of the night depository facilities is a gratuitous privilege extended by the bank to the undersigned for the convenience of the undersigned, and the use of the night depository facilities shall be at the sole risk of the undersigned.

It is clear that where a party to the agreement is under a public duty entailing the exercise of care he may not relieve himself of liability for negligence, and unequal bargaining power or the existence of a public interest may call for the rejection of such clauses.

The Uniform Commercial Code contains many provisions protecting banks in their daily operations. We find it significant that the Legislature provided in the same statute, that a bank may not, by agreement, disclaim responsibility for "its own lack of good faith or failure to exercise ordinary care" in the discharge of the duty imposed upon it by that statute.

A review of the cases in other states considering the validity of similar exculpatory clauses in night depository contracts indicates that the majority rule is to give full force and effect to the clauses.

The basic theory underlying these and other similar cases is that the absence of an agent of the bank when the night depository facilities are used creates the possibility of dishonest claims being presented by customers. In New Jersey we have rejected such a thesis in other situations and have held that the possibility of fraudulent or collusive litigation does not justify immunity from liability for negligence.

Other courts have refused to recognize the validity of such clauses. In holding such a clause inimical to the public interest, the court in Phillips Home Furnishings, Inc. v. Continental Bank (1974) said:

We find the public need for professional and competent banking services too great and the legitimate and justifiable reliance upon the integrity and safety of financial institutions too strong to permit a bank to contract away its liability for its failure to provide the service and protections its customers justifiably expect, that is, for its failure to exercise due care and good faith. * * * * *

We therefore hold that a bank cannot, by contract, exculpate itself from liability or responsibility for negligence in the performance of its functions as they concern the night depository service.

Judgment for New Jersey Bank reversed.

CHAPTER CASE QUESTIONS

Laos v. Soble

   a. What defense did Soble raise at the trial?

   b. What standard did the court apply on appeal? How was this issue raised?

   c. What was Professor Corbin's view of such circumstances?

   d. Why did the court affirm the lower court's decision?

   e. What is "public policy"?

   f. What is "expert testimony"? What type of testimony can expert witnesses offer that other witnesses cannot offer?

Marcus and Nocka v. Julian Goodrich Architects

   a. What service was the plaintiff to perform?

   b. Where were the services to be performed? Why was that fact critical?

   c. What was the basis of the judgment of the lower court?

   d. What is the policy behind registration statutes?

   e. The defendants were able to recover their costs. What are such "costs"?

Frederick v. Professional Building Maintenance Industries, Inc.

   a. What was the time period and area provided in the covenant?

   b. What is such a covenant called?

   c. What view does the court take of such covenants? Why?

   d. When might such a covenant be enforced by a court?

   e. Where will we usually find such covenants?

   f. What is the usual remedy sought in such cases?

   g. Why doesn't the court simply rewrite a covenant to make it reasonable?

   h. What is the "blue pencil" rule?

   i. Who bears the burden of proof concerning such covenants?

   j. What are "trade secrets"? What is "good will"?

Hy-Grade Oil v. New Jersey Bank

   a. Why did Hy-Grade Oil sue its bank?

   b. How did the bank defend? What was the basis of its defense?

c. How did the court arrive at its decision?

d. What was the decision? Did that mean that Hy-Grade Oil will have its account properly credited?

e. What is a public institution?

f. What is a quasi-public institution?

g. What is an exculpatory clause?

h. How can a party legally limit liability?

CHAPTER THIRTEEN:
PERFORMANCE AND DISCHARGE

Most contracts will be terminated according to the provisions of the agreement, i.e., by performance of the parties. However, some contracts will be terminated or ended by certain acts of the parties, by operation of law, by impossibility of performance (an issue discussed previously in the chapter on consideration), mutual rescission, or through some legally recognized excuse or agreement.

When payment is called for in a contract, the contract is completed by the payment of money. If a check is tendered by a debtor or by a purchaser, the payment by the check is a conditional payment and the underlying obligation is not discharged until the check is actually "paid" by the bank. Unless the agreement stipulates otherwise, a creditor can refuse to accept a check because technically a check is not legal tender. Rather, a check is a substitute for money. (See UCC § 2-511.) If payment is only to be accepted in cash or in some other form (for example, a barter transaction), this should be clearly stated in the contract.

A tender is defined as an "unconditional offer of a debtor to pay to the creditor the exact amount due on the date due."

If a creditor refuses to accept a tender by the debtor, the debt is not discharged, but the refusal to accept the tender stops the running of any interest charges, may lift any liens filed against property held by the debtor, and may also prevent charging court costs and attorney's fees to the debtor in the event a suit is filed.

TIME FOR PERFORMANCE

Where a time of performance is stated in the contract and the time is clear and unambiguous, performance must be made on or before that date.

When no time is specified in the contract, a party has a reasonable time to perform. Where the nature of the contract is such that time is not an important factor, reasonable delay may be permitted by a court.

Where a clause in a contract expressly states "time is of the essence" or the nature of the contract itself is such that time is obviously an important factor (construction contracts or contracts for purchase or sale of perishable goods), the failure to perform on time may be actionable and may under certain circumstances permit a party to rescind a contract, seek a substitute performance, seek the remedy of cover or resale, or seek monetary damages.

THE DOCTRINES OF MATERIAL BREACH AND SUBSTANTIAL PERFORMANCE

When a party fails to perform a promise according to its terms, it is important to determine if the breach is material. If the breach is material, the aggrieved party may sue for "total breach" and the aggrieved party may have the power to cancel the contract. If the breach is not material, the aggrieved party may sue for "partial breach," but may not cancel the contract. While the rules may seem clear, there is no simple test to determine whether the breach is material. Materiality is ordinarily a question of fact for a jury. Among the factors to be considered are:

1. To what extent, if any, the contract has been performed at the time of the breach. "A breach which occurs at the very beginning [of a contract] is more likely to be deemed material even if it is relatively small." (Note, 21 Colum. L. Rev. 358 (1921)).

2. A willful breach is more likely to be considered as material than a breach caused by negligence or other circumstances.

3. A quantitatively serious breach is more likely to be considered material.

It is recognized that actual and full performance is required in most cases to discharge a contractual obligation. It is also recognized that some agreements (for example, certain construction contracts) are quite complex. In such cases, a court may apply the doctrine of substantial performance to determine if a breach has occurred. This doctrine permits recovery where there has been substantial performance, subject to an offset (deduction) for a nominal, trifling, or technical breach, or a departure from the strict letter of the contract. In order to apply the substantial performance doctrine, the part of the contract that is unperformed must not destroy the value or the purpose of the contract and the doctrine does not apply where the breach is willful.

PERFORMANCE SUBJECT TO THE STANDARD OF SATISFACTION

When one party to an agreement contracts to "personally satisfy" the promisee, courts will apply one of two tests, depending on the nature of the contract:

When a contract involves personal taste, skill or fancy, the promisee has, in effect, the final word and may reject a performance, even if it is alleged that such a rejection is subjectively arbitrary or capricious. However, most courts will require at least "good faith" in the rejection; that is, a court will require an "honest reason" for the rejection. The interesting case of former Secretary of State Henry Kissinger and his rejection of an official portrait on grounds that he "just didn't like it" provides an application of this rule.

Where the subject matter of the contract concerns matters that are not purely personal in nature, the courts will apply an objective standard; that is, if a reasonable person would be satisfied with the performance, the promisor may be permitted to recover under the terms of the contract.

EXAMPLE:

A manufacturer of pre-fabricated housing offers the following statement: "All windows, doors, and other parts of the home all made to your satisfaction."

In this case, most courts would apply the objective or reasonable person standard to judge a rejection of the items described in the contract.

Contracts may also contain a provision that completion of the contract "depends upon the satisfaction of a third party" (an architect, a building inspector, an appraiser, etc.). In such a case, the court would apply an objective test and might permit recovery by a builder of amounts due under the contract if the court determines that the certificate of approval is unnecessary, or was withheld due to "bad faith," fraud, mistake, or gross error on the part of the third party.

Read the *Plante* case. What standard did the court apply? Note especially the measure of damages.

Plante v. Jacobs
10 WIS. 2D 567, 103 N.W. 2D 296 (1960)

BACKGROUND AND FACTS

The Jacobs' entered into a written contract with the plaintiff, Plante, to furnish the materials and to construct a house on their lot, in accordance with plans and specifications, for a sum of $26,756. During the course of construction, the plaintiff was paid $20,000. Disputes arose between the parties concerning the work being done. The Jacobs refused to continue paying. The plaintiff did not complete the house. The trial court found that the contract was substantially performed. The Jacobs were told to pay $4,152.90 plus interest and court costs.

DECISION AND RATIONALE

The appellate court upheld the trial court's judgment. Although there were some twenty items of incomplete or faulty performance by the builder, none of these was made the essence of the contract. Therefore the court held that substantial performance was evident. The court held, however, that the correct rule for determining damages due to faulty construction amounting to incomplete performance "is the difference between the value of the house as it stands with faulty and incomplete construction, and the value of the house if it had been constructed in strict accordance with the plans and specifications. This is the diminished-value rule."

DISCHARGE BY ACTS OF THE PARTIES (CONDITIONS)

The legal distinction between a covenant and a condition is very important. A covenant is a promise and determines what must be performed in order to discharge a contractual duty. Conditions determine when and if a duty defined must be performed at peril of breach of contract. The failure of a promisor to perform a covenant may be a breach of contract. If circumstances arise which leave a condition unsatisfied, the legal consequence is that the dependent promise does not become a matter of any contractual duty.

Many contracts contain conditions either express or implied that control performance. A condition is traditionally defined as an act or an event, other than a lapse of time, which affects a duty to render a promised performance. These conditions are termed concurrent, precedent, or subsequent.

Concurrent conditions are those conditions that require that the performance of both parties take place at the same time. Thus, neither party can demand that the other party perform first. Most bilateral contracts contain concurrent conditions (i.e., the sale of goods, which requires both payment and delivery to occur simultaneously; a real estate transaction where the buyer tenders the money and the seller tenders the deed).

A condition precedent is an act, an event, circumstance, or contingency that must occur according to the express or implied terms of the agreement or be satisfied or excused before a duty of performance is required under a contract. A non-technical formulation of a condition precedent might be: "I am not liable to perform this promise unless_____." In the case of a unilateral contract, Smith's performance is a condition precedent to Jones' duty of payment. As an example, an insurance policy may require that an insured driver must give notice of a loss within a certain specified period after the occurrence of the loss. Failure to provide the insurance carrier with the required notice may permit the insurer to deny liability or coverage. A second example occurs in many real estate contracts: "This contract is contingent upon the buyer securing a suitable mortgage...."

A condition subsequent is any fact, the existence or occurrence of which by agreement of the parties, operates to discharge or terminate an existing duty of performance. For example, a contract may provide that a party will be released from "any and all obligations" upon the happening of a certain event (for example, "if interest rates raise to 10% or more by June 1, 2004, the borrower may withdraw from this transaction"). A simple test can be found in the following: "I am liable to perform this promise until or unless _____ [a factual circumstance will be inserted]."

Parties to a contract may mutually agree to terminate or rescind an agreement and place each other in their original positions. The surrender of rights under the original agreement by each party is the consideration for the mutual agreement of rescission. It should be noted that the mutual rescission of a contract to sell or buy land would be required to be in writing under the Statute of Frauds.

OTHER ACTS OF TERMINATION

NOVATION

The abandoning of a prior contract and substituting a new contract in its place. A novation is accomplished by an agreement to discharge immediately a previous contractual duty or to release the party who was originally bound to a contract and substitute a new party who agrees to undertake performance and to be bound by the contract. A novation may never be presumed (even from the passage of a significant amount of time) and must always be affirmatively proven by the party who is claiming a release from a prior contract. If the original contract was required to be in writing under the Statute of Frauds, so too must the novation be in writing.

ACCORD AND SATISFACTION

An accord is an agreement to substitute performance in satisfaction of an original debt or obligation. When the agreement is executed and satisfaction has been made, it is called an accord and satisfaction (discussed earlier in the case of *A.G. King Tree Surgeons v. Deeb*).

ANTICIPATORY BREACH

At common law, a breach of contract could not occur until the time for performance had arrived. However, since the English case of *Hochester v. DeLaTour* (1853), courts have recognized that a total breach of a contract may occur if a party unequivocally repudiates the contract. A repudiation is a "positive statement to the promisee or other person having a right under the contract, indicating that the promisor will not or cannot substantially perform his contractual duties." (*Martin v. Kavanewsky*, 157 Conn. 514 (1969)). In April of 1852, the plaintiff and defendant entered into a contract under which the plaintiff was to work for a fixed period of time commencing on June 1, 1852. On May 11,

1852, the defendant stated he would not perform. The defendant contended that no breach could occur until the time for performance (June 1, 1852) had arrived. The court disagreed and created the doctrine of anticipatory breach.

Under the common law, when an anticipatory breach occurs, the aggrieved party has the right to elect between two remedies. An aggrieved party may:

a.   Wait until the time for performance and sue for the actual breach; or

b.   Treat the repudiation as an anticipatory breach and sue immediately.

The UCC incorporated the common law rule concerning anticipatory repudiation in UCC § 2-610. The UCC notes that the aggrieved party may "for a commercially reasonable time await performance by the repudiating party" or "may immediately resort to any remedy for breach." As we will see in the discussion on sales, the Code also provides that when reasonable grounds for insecurity arise, a party may demand "adequate assurances of performance," and in the interim, may suspend his performance until he receives such assurances. (UCC § 2-609). The Code further provides that, "After receipt of a justified demand, failure to provide within a reasonable time not exceeding thirty days such assurance of due performance as is adequate under the circumstances of the particular case is a repudiation of the contract." Grounds for insecurity will be judged according to "reasonable commercial standards" of "good faith" and "honesty in fact."

OPERATION OF LAW

A contract may be discharged by operation of law when a statute has made the subject matter of the agreement unlawful, a violation of public policy, unenforceable, or where a statute may excuse performance. Chapter Twelve discusses the area of the legality of the subject matter of a contract.

For example, a discharge in bankruptcy is the result of a bankruptcy proceeding in which the debtor is released from an obligation to pay a debt.

IMPOSSIBILITY

Review the material presented earlier on the termination of offers concerning the issue of impossibility. Here is another "dance lesson" case. It is less dramatic than the *Vokes* case.

Parker v. Arthur Murray, Inc.
10 ILL. APP. 3D 1000, 295 N.E. 2D 487 (1973)

BACKGROUND AND FACTS

Plaintiff Parker, a thirty-seven-year-old college-educated bachelor who lived alone, contracted over two years for a total of 2,734 hours of dance lessons for which he had paid $24,812.80. Each contract, and each extension, contained the same boldface words, "NON-CANCELABLE CONTRACT," and some included a statement that no refunds would be made. Parker was seriously injured in an automobile accident and rendered incapable of continuing his dance lessons. Parker sued Arthur Murray to recover money paid for unused lessons.

DECISION AND RATIONALE

The trial court's ruling that impossibility of performance was grounds for rescission was upheld, and despite the contract provisions Parker was allowed to recover the prepaid sums of money for unused lessons. The appellate court held that the plaintiff never contemplated waiving the right to invoke the doctrine of impossibility of performance. "Although neither party to a contract should be relieved from performance on the ground that good business judgment was lacking, a court will not place upon language a ridiculous construction. We conclude that plaintiff did not waive his right to assert the doctrine of impossibility."

The modern doctrine of impossibility can be traced to the 1863 case of Taylor v. Caldwell (122 Eng. Rep. 309 (K.B. 1863). In this case, the defendant had promised to allow the plaintiff to use his music hall for giving concerts. Prior to the time of performance, a fire destroyed the music hall. The English court held that the defendant was excused from performance and that his failure to perform did not constitute a breach of contract. Since this case, American courts have held that objective impossibility is an excuse for non-performance of a contract where there has been a destruction, material deterioration, or unavailability of the subject matter or means of performance of the contract through no fault of a party seeking the excuse. In some cases, a court will require the parties to have contemplated a particular source of supply or the condition when the parties entered into an agreement.

It is interesting to note that the principle of impossibility is well illustrated by a number of cases involving the closing of the Suez Canal in 1956 and in 1967. (See 23 Rutgers L. Rev. 41 (1969). Because a substitute route around Africa was available, the court held that canal closings neither excused performance nor were grounds for the recovery of additional compensation under the theory of unforeseen difficulties.

Finally, the Restatement, Section 281, basically mirrors Section 2-615 of the Uniform Commercial Code and has introduced the concept of "commercial impracticability" into the discussion. It suggests that increases in costs "well beyond the normal range" that create "extreme and unreasonable difficulty" or "expense" could trigger the application of the doctrine of commercial impracticability, thus excusing performance or permitting a party to seek additional consideration.

CHAPTER QUESTIONS

1. Explain the doctrine of substantial performance.

2. How do courts address performance subject to the satisfaction of one of the parties?

3. Many contracts contain conditions. Explain conditions concurrent, precedent or subsequent.

4. What are the requirements for a novation?

5. What is required for accord and satisfaction (refer *A.G. King Tree Surgeons v. Deeb*)?

6. In the case of anticipatory breach of contract an aggrieved party may do what two things?

7. Explain how the doctrine of impossibility was applied in *Parker v. Arthur Murray, Inc.*

CHAPTER FOURTEEN:
REMEDIES FOR BREACH OF CONTRACT

A breach of contract occurs when a promisor fails, without any legal excuse, to perform any of the obligations or undertakings of a contract. In such a case, the non-breaching party, also called the aggrieved party, is entitled to seek a remedy against the breaching party. In most cases, this involves a suit for money damages.

DAMAGES
COMPENSATORY DAMAGES

Damages that are awarded to compensate the non-breaching party for the loss of the bargain are compensatory damages, also known as "general" or "benefit of the bargain" damages. For a breach of contract, "the law of damages seeks to place the aggrieved party in the same economic position he would have been in had the contract been [fully] performed." In a contract for the sale of goods, at least two possibilities exist. If the seller commits a breach and fails to deliver the goods called for in the contract, one possible measure of damages is the difference between the contract price and the market price of the goods at the time of the breach.

> **EXAMPLE:**
>
> Suppose that Seton Hall University contracts to buy 10 IBM PCs from Computers R-Us at $4,000 each. If Computers R-Us fails to deliver the PCs as called for in the contract, and the current price of the computers is $4,500, Seton Hall's measure of damages in this case is $5,000 (ten times $500).

In other cases, the buyer may avail himself of the remedy of "cover"; that is, the buyer may go into the marketplace and make "in good faith and without any unreasonable delay any reasonable purchase or a contract to purchase" goods in substitution for those due from the seller. In this case, the buyer may recover from the seller the difference between the cost of cover and the contract price, plus any incidental or consequential damages, less any expenses saved. The remedy of cover is found in UCC § 2-712, and is the preferred action for a buyer under the Code.

Incidental damages [UCC § 2-715] are any reasonable expenses incurred in effecting cover (i.e., transportation charges, freight charges, phone calls, etc.) or in the resale of the goods [UCC § 2-710].

> **EXAMPLE:**
>
> In our PC example, if Seton Hall absolutely needed the PCs for an important conference, they might go to a local computer dealer and effect cover. Suppose the cover price was $4,650. Under the UCC, Seton Hall would be entitled to recover the difference between the cover price ($4,650) and the contract price ($4,000), equaling $650 per unit, plus any incidental damages, minus any expenses saved, provided, of course, that this purchase had been made in "good faith."

On the other side of the equation, under UCC § 2-706, a seller may elect to resell the goods which a buyer has wrongfully rejected or where the buyer has refused to take delivery. Here, the seller may recover the difference between the resale price and the contract price (together with any incidental damages under UCC § 2-710, but less any expenses saved). All of the elements of the resale must be reasonable, and in some cases, notice of the resale must be given to the breaching party.

Interestingly, prior to 1854, there were almost no rules of contract damages. Assessment of damages was generally left to the discretion of the jury. In 1854, the important case of *Hadley v. Baxendale* was decided. The court laid down two important rules, applicable generally to the area of contract damages. First, the aggrieved party may recover those damages "as may fairly and reasonably be considered…arising naturally, i.e., according to the usual course of things, from such breach of contract itself." Second, the aggrieved party may recover damages "such as may reasonably be supposed to have been in the contemplation of both parties, at the time they made the contract, as the probable result of the breach of it." Under the first rule, for example, cover or resale damages under UCC § 2-712 or UCC § 2-706 will naturally and obviously flow from the breach so everyone will be deemed to contemplate them. Under the second rule, "special" or "consequential" damages may be deemed to be within the contemplation of the parties, but only under well-defined "special circumstances."

Consequential damages are caused by special circumstances occurring beyond the contract itself. Such damage, loss, or injury does not flow directly and immediately from the act of the breaching party, but from some of the consequences or results of such an act. In order for the courts to award consequential damages (often in the form of lost profits), the breaching party must know that special circumstances will cause the non-breaching party to suffer this additional loss. In practical terms, the non-breaching party may have to give the breaching party "notice" of the special circumstances. For example, the ice shipment for the Fubarski Meat Market is not delivered as required by contract. Consequently, Fubarski's entire freezer of fresh kielbasa is ruined. Fubarski goes to the local 7-Eleven and purchases ice, at an additional cost of $100 over the contract price. The ice company would be liable for the additional $100. In addition, the ice company might also be held liable for the meat spoilage as consequential damages. A second type of special or consequential damages occurs in cases where a defective product causes personal injury. Compensation for personal injury would be consequential damages. These issues are discussed in great detail in the materials in products liability.

Let's look at the classic common law case of *Hadley v. Baxendale*.

Hadley v. Baxendale
156 ENG. REP. 145 (1845)

BACKGROUND AND FACTS

The plaintiffs ran a flour and gristmill in Gloucester, England. The crankshaft attached to the steam engine broke, causing the mill to shut down. The shaft had to be sent to a foundry located in Greenwich so that the new shaft could be made to fit the other parts of the engine. The defendants were common carriers, who transported the shaft from Gloucester to Greenwich. The plaintiffs claimed that they had informed the defendants that the mill was stopped and that the shaft must be sent immediately. The freight charges were collected in advance, and the defendants promised to deliver the shaft the following day. They did not do so, however. Consequently, the mill was closed for several days. The plaintiffs sued to recover their lost profits during that time. The defendants contended that the loss of profits was "too remote." The court held for the plaintiffs, and the jury was allowed to take into consideration the lost profits. The high court reversed.

OPINION

We think that there ought to be a new trial in this case; but, in so doing, we deem it to be expedient and necessary to state explicitly the rule which the Judge, at the next trial, ought, in our opinion, to direct the jury to be governed by when they estimate the damages.

* * * * * Now we think the proper rule in such a case as the present is this:—Where two parties have made a contract which one of them has broken, the damages which the other party ought to receive in respect of such breach of contract should be such as may fairly and reasonably be considered either arising naturally, i.e., according to the usual course of things, from such breach of contract itself, or such as may reasonably be supposed to have been in the contemplation of both parties, at the time they made the contract, as the probable result of the breach of it. Now, if the special circumstances under which the contract was actually made were communicated by the plaintiffs to the defendants, and thus known to both parties, the damages resulting from the breach of such a contract, which they would reasonably contemplate, would be the amount of injury which would ordinarily follow from a breach of contract under these special circumstances so known and communicated. But, on the other hand, if these special circumstances were wholly unknown to the party breaking the contract, he, at the most, could only be supposed to have had in his contemplation the amount of injury which would arise generally, and in the great multitude of cases not affected by any special circumstances, from such a breach of contract. For, had the special circumstances been known, the parties might have specially provided for the breach of contract by special terms as to the damages in that case; and of this advantage it would be very unjust to deprive them. Now the above principles are those by which we think the jury ought to be guided in estimating the damages arising out of any breach of contract.

* * * * * Now, in the present case, if we are to apply the principles above laid down, we find that the only circumstances here communicated by the plaintiffs to the defendants at the time the contract was made, were, that the article to be carried was the broken shaft of a mill, and that the plaintiffs were the millers of that mill. But how do these circumstances show reasonably that the profits of the mill must be stopped by an unreasonable delay in the delivery of the broken shaft by the carrier to the third person? Suppose the plaintiffs had another shaft in their possession put up or putting up at the time, and that they only wished to send back the broken shaft to the engineer who made it; it is clear that this would be quite consistent with the above circumstances, and yet the unreasonable delay in the delivery would have no effect upon the intermediate profits of the mill. On the other hand, again, suppose that, at the time of the delivery to the carrier, the machinery of the mill had been in other respects defective, then, also, the same results would follow. Here it is true that the shaft was actually sent back to serve as a model for a new one, and that the want of a new one was the only cause of the stoppage of the mill, and that the loss of profits really arose from not sending down the new shaft in proper time, and that this arose from the delay in delivering the broken one to serve as a model. But it is obvious that, in the great multitude of cases of millers sending off broken shafts to third persons by a carrier under ordinary circumstances, such consequences would not, in all probability, have

occurred; and these special circumstances were here never communicated by the plaintiffs to the defendants. It follows, therefore, that the loss of profits here cannot reasonably be considered such a consequence of the breach of contract as could have been fairly and reasonably contemplated by both the parties when they made this contract. * * * * *

The English court ordered a new trial, holding that the special circumstances that caused the loss of profits had not been sufficiently communicated by the plaintiffs to the defendants. The plaintiff would be required to give "express notice" of these circumstances in order to collect special damages.

PUNITIVE DAMAGES

These damages are also called exemplary damages. They are designed to punish a "guilty" party for intentional, malicious, willful, or wanton wrongdoing and to make an example of the breaching party. The purpose of awarding punitive damages is to deter the wrongdoer from similar conduct in the future, as well as to deter others from engaging in similar conduct. Generally, punitive damages will not be awarded in cases of simple breach of contract, except for a category of cases involving contract fraud (due to the presence of "scienter," or the intent to deceive) discussed later in Chapter Ten. The court may add an additional amount (in some cases, three times the actual damages, called treble damages) in order to punish the breaching party for this wrongful conduct. The United States Supreme Court entered the debate concerning punitive damages in 1996 and held in *BMW of North America, Inc. v. Gore* (517 U.S. 559) that under the Due Process Clause of the Fourteenth Amendment the amount of punitive damages awarded by a jury cannot be "grossly excessive" and must bear some reasonable relationship to the actual damages sustained. There have also been attempts by several state legislatures to limit or even abolish punitive damages in a wide variety of tort cases.

NOMINAL DAMAGES

Where a party has suffered no true or provable damage, a court may choose to award only nominal damages. In the PC case, if the cost of the PCs had declined, and Seton Hall could not demonstrate any incidental damages, Seton Hall would only be entitled to the award of nominal damages for this "technical breach," because no actual monetary loss had been sustained.

LIQUIDATED DAMAGES

While parties are not generally empowered to provide for penalties in the event of a breach of contract, frequently, a contract will specify an exact dollar amount that is to be paid in the case of a default or a breach. Such a clause is called a liquidated damage clause. Under the common law, a court would enforce a liquidated damage clause if three criteria were met:

1. The injury caused by the breach must be difficult or impossible to accurately estimate;

2. The amount set as liquidated damages in the contract a reasonable preestimate of the probable loss; and

3. The parties must intend to provide for damages rather than a penalty.

If the court concludes that a liquidated damage clause is a penalty, it will not be enforced by the court. Liquidated damage clauses are frequently found in construction contracts or in lease agreements.

Suppose that you had attempted to rent an apartment and had filed a rental application. As part of the application process, you had to put down one-month's rent (approximately $800) that the contract stated you would forfeit if you failed to rent the apartment. When you change your mind, you are informed that your deposit will be retained as liquidated damages. Can the landlord keep the deposit? What standards should the court apply? Evaluate.

Under Uniform Commercial Code § 2-718(1), liquidated damages may be awarded, "but only at an amount which is reasonable in light of the anticipated or actual harm caused by the breach, the difficulties of proof of loss, and the inconvenience or non-feasibility of otherwise obtaining an adequate remedy. A term fixing unreasonably large liquidated damages is void as a penalty." What do you think happens when a court refuses to enforce a liquidated damage clause?

ATTORNEYS' FEES

In the United States (as opposed to Great Britain), an award of damages will not ordinarily include reimbursement of the successful party's attorney's fees. Attorney's fees should be viewed in light of the prior discussion of consequential damages. However, it has become common practice for commercial and residential leases, notes, and contracts for sale of real estate to contain a clause providing for the collection or awarding of "reasonable attorney's fees." A majority of courts uphold such agreements, permitting recovery of a stipulated amount in excess of the damages that would accrue, provided that the amount demanded is reasonable.

THE REMEDY OF SPECIFIC PERFORMANCE

The remedy of specific performance is an extraordinary remedy developed in Courts of Equity to provide relief when the legal remedies of damages were inadequate. It is most appropriate when the non-breaching party is not seeking monetary damages; rather, the non-breaching party wants the court to issue a decree ordering a party affirmatively to carry out contractual duties, or desires performance of the promises in the contract.

Generally, courts will award specific performance if monetary damages are inadequate to put the non-breaching party in as good a position as if the contract had been performed. In the case of most goods, monetary damages will be deemed adequate, since substitute goods may be readily available in the marketplace through the remedy of cover, or the goods can be sold in the marketplace through the remedy of resale. However, under the common law, if the goods were considered unique, a court of equity may issue a decree of specific performance. Such "unique" items included antiques, objects of art, racehorses, stock in a closely held corporation, and all land.

Courts are very reluctant to grant specific performance in personal service contracts because public policy considerations discourage what would amount to involuntary servitude. In addition, courts do not generally desire to monitor a continuing personal service contract to assure that it is carried out.

Read *Tower City Grain v. Richman* for a discussion of specific performance under the UCC. Although the UCC liberalizes the availability of the remedy of specific performance, such relief remains the extraordinary rather than the ordinary remedy. Thus, the Code permits a buyer to replevy goods as a remedy for breach—but in rather limited circumstances.

Tower City Grain Co. v. Richman
232 N.W. 2D, 61 N.D. (19757)

Plaintiff sued the defendant for specific performance of an oral contract for the sale of wheat. The lower court ordered specific performance and the defendant appealed. The defendant contended that specific performance was not a proper remedy in this case.

PEDERSON, J.

* * * * * The Uniform Commercial Code is controlling in the instant case and states in part:

1. Specific performance may be decreed where the goods are unique or in other proper circumstances.

2. The decree for specific performance may include such terms and conditions as to payment of the price, damages, or other relief as the court may deem just. (Emphasis added.)

While the Richmans' contention that fungible goods were not a proper subject for the remedy of specific relief under prior law is correct, the adoption of the Uniform Commercial Code in 1966 liberalized the discretion of the trial court to grant specific performance in a greater number of situations. The Official Comment to § 2-716, UCC, provides in pertinent part:

1. The present section continues in general prior policy as to specific performance and injunction against breach. However, without intending to impair in any way the exercise of the court's sound discretion in the matter, this Article seeks to further a more liberal attitude than some courts have shown in connection with the specific performance of contracts of sale.

2. In view of this Article's emphasis on the commercial feasibility of replacement, a new concept of what are "unique" goods is introduced under this section. Specific performance is no longer limited to goods which are already specific or ascertained at the time of contracting. The test of uniqueness under this section must be made in terms of the total situation which characterizes the contract.

In addition, (the Code) states that "the remedies provided by this title shall be liberally administered to the end that the aggrieved party may be put in as good a position as if the other party had fully performed." We cannot presume that an award of damages fails to put an aggrieved party in as good a position as if the other party had fully performed. There was no finding or conclusion to that effect by the trial court in this case.

A complaint which prays for the equitable remedy of specific performance must clearly show that the legal remedy of damages is inadequate. A defendant should not be deprived of a jury trial, to which he would be entitled in an action at law, unless the plaintiff is clearly entitled to the equitable remedy he seeks.

Historically, specific performance, which is an equitable remedy, was applied primarily to contracts relating to goods which were "unique." All real estate was deemed to be unique, and so were goods which had sentimental as distinguished from market value. Another basis for invoking specific performance was the inadequacy of the remedy at law.

A factual basis for a conclusion that the remedy of specific performance is available should be found by the trier of facts in order, that this court, on appeal may know the basis upon which it arrived at such a conclusion.

There is no finding by the trial court in this case that indicates what it believes to be the proper circumstances. Our examination of the record indicates no evidence upon which such finding could be based. The fact that the complaint prayed for specific performance and that the Richmans have in their possession the type and quantity of wheat called for in the contract are not adequate to support such a finding.

The buyer may obtain specific performance of the contract for the sale when the goods are unique or other proper circumstances are shown. Because the purpose of this section is to liberalize the right to specific performance, it would appear that it is not to be of great significance whether a given circumstance is regarded as involving "unique goods" or "proper circumstances"; ordinarily, circumstances which are proper will impart uniqueness to the goods. "Uniqueness in a reasonable commercial setting is the significant point."

Without holding that specific performance can never be invoked to enforce a contract for grain or other fungible goods, we conclude that it was a manifest abuse of discretion and an error as a matter of law for the trial court to grant such a remedy under the circumstances of this case.

Judgment reversed and remanded with leave to amend.

As can be seen, the writers of the UCC attempted to broaden the scope of specific performance by adding a section [§2-716(1)] which states that specific performance may be decreed where the goods are "unique" or "in other proper circumstances." Yet, many courts are reluctant to go beyond the conventional notion of unique goods found in the common law. Under the code, what is the precondition to filing a suit for specific performance? What are "proper circumstances"? Why are some courts so reluctant to impose this remedy?

One case in which the court expressed a view that specific performance would be appropriate is *Campbell Soup Co. v. Wentz.* (However, note that the court ultimately refused to issue the decree for specific performance because it ruled that the contract was unconscionable. What did the court find unconscionable about the contract between the parties?)

Campbell Soup Co. v. Wentz
172 F.2D 80 (1948)

BACKGROUND AND FACTS

Campbell Soup Company, the plaintiff, entered into a contract for the sale of carrots with farmers who grew and produced the particular variety of carrots used in the company's canned goods. Under the terms of the contract, a farmer was required to cut, clean, and bag the produce. When the carrots were delivered, the company determined if they conformed to company specifications. Another provision in the contract excused the company from accepting carrots under certain circumstances but retained the right to prohibit the sale of those carrots elsewhere unless the company agreed. The carrots involved in this case were Chantenay red carrots.

Campbell Soup made a written contract with the defendant, Wentz, a Pennsylvania farmer. Wentz was to deliver all the Chantenay red carrots he grew on his fifteen-acre farm that year for $30 per ton. During the year, the market price of the carrots rose sharply to about $90 per ton, and Chantenay red carrots became virtually unobtainable. The defendant told a Campbell representative that he would not deliver his carrots at the contract price. Then, he sold the rest of his carrots to a neighboring farmer. Campbell bought about half the shipment from the neighboring farmer and then realized that it was purchasing its own "contract carrots." Campbell refused to purchase any more and sought an injunction against both the defendant and the neighboring farmer to prohibit them from selling any more of the contract carrots to others. In addition, Campbell sought to compel specific performance of the contract against Wentz. The trial court denied the equitable relief requested by Campbell.

GOODRICH, Circuit Judge

* * * * *

The trial court denied equitable relief. We agree with the result reached, but on a different ground from that relied upon by the District Court.

* * * * *

We think that on the question of adequacy of the legal remedy the case is one appropriate for specific performance. It was expressly found that at the time of the trial it was "virtually impossible to obtain Chantenay carrots in the open market." This Chantenay carrot is one which the plaintiff uses in large quantities, furnishing the seed to the growers with whom it makes contracts. It was not claimed that in nutritive value it is any better than other types of carrots. Its blunt shape makes it easier to handle in processing. And its color and texture differ from other varieties. The color is brighter than other carrots. The trial court found that the plaintiff failed to establish what proportion of its carrots is used for the production of soup stock and what proportion is used as identifiable physical ingredients in its soups. We do not think lack of proof on that point is material. It did appear that the plaintiff uses carrots in fifteen of its twenty-one soups. It also appeared that it uses Chantenay carrots diced in some of them and that the appearance is uniform. The preservation of uniformity in appearance in a food article marketed throughout the country and sold under the manufacturer's name is a matter of considerable commercial significance and one which is properly considered in determining whether a substitute ingredient is just as good as the original.

* * * * *

Judged by the general standards applicable to determining the adequacy of the legal remedy we think that on this point the case is a proper one for equitable relief. There is considerable authority, old and new, showing liberality in the granting of an equitable remedy. We see no reason why a court should be reluctant to grant specific relief when it can be given without supervision of the court or other time-consuming processes against one who has deliberately broken his agreement. Here the goods of the special type contracted for were unavailable on the open market, the plaintiff had contracted for them long ahead in anticipation of its needs, and had built up a general reputation for its products as part of which reputation uniform appearance was important. We think if this were all that was involved in the case specific performance should have been granted.

We are not suggesting that the contract is illegal. Nor are we suggesting any excuse for the grower in this case who has deliberately broken an agreement entered into with Campbell. We do think, however, that a party who has offered and succeeded in getting an agreement as tough as this one is, should not come to a chancellor and ask court help in the enforcement of its terms. That equity does not enforce unconscionable bargains is too well established to require elaborate citation.

Campbell Soup Company's petition for an injunction and for specific performance was denied by both the trial court and the Court of Appeals. The appellate court recognized that if the contract had not been unconscionable, specific performance would have been available to the company. The unique nature of the product involved meant that there was no adequate legal remedy. However, since specific performance is an equitable remedy, the petitioner must come to court "with clean hands." It has often been said: "He who seeks equity must do equity." What specifically does this mean?

THE REQUIREMENT OF MITIGATION

In situations where a breach of contract has occurred, the non-breaching party may be required to lessen or mitigate damages. A party who has suffered a wrong by a breach may not unreasonably sit by and allow damages to accumulate or worsen. The law will not permit the aggrieved party to recover from the breaching party those damages that he "should have foreseen and could have avoided by reasonable effort without undue risk, expense, or humiliation." (Restatement, Contracts § 336(1)).

The doctrine requires reasonable efforts to mitigate damages. However, the wronged party is not required to act if the cost of avoidance would involve unreasonable expense. The case of *Parker v. Twentieth Century Fox* demonstrates the operation of the mitigation principle in a case of employment.

Parker v. Twentieth Century Fox Film Corp. 474 P.2D 689 (1970)

BURKE, Judge.

Shirley McLain Parker signed a contract to play the female lead in Twentieth Century Fox's projected motion picture Bloomer Girl. Before production began, the corporation decided not to produce the picture and notified the actress of its decision. With the professed purpose of avoiding damage to the actress, the corporation offered her the leading role in another film entitled Big Country, Big Man. She rejected the alternate role and sued for damages. The corporation claimed the actress had unreasonably refused to mitigate harm to her career by refusing to accept the substitute role. Parker won the case.

The trial court pointed out that although the contract for the substituted role offered identical compensation and terms as the prior contract, Bloomer Girl was to have been a musical, and Big Country was to be a dramatic western movie. Furthermore, the musical was to be filmed in California, the western in Australia. The original contract also specified that the actress could approve the director for the musical, and if that person failed to direct the picture, she was to have the right to approve any substitute director. The actress also had the right to approve of the musical's dance director and the screenplay. The western offer eliminated or impaired each of those rights. Twentieth Century Fox's sole defense is that the actress unreasonably refused to mitigate damages by rejecting the substitute offer of employment.

In this case, the offer to star in the western was for employment both different from and inferior to that of making the musical, and no factual dispute exists on that issue. The female lead as a dramatic actress in a western style motion picture can by no stretch of the imagination be the equivalent of or substantially similar to the lead in a song-and-dance production. In addition, the western offer proposed to eliminate or impair the approvals the actress had under the original musical contract, and thereby constituted an offer of inferior employment.

There is a split of authority in real estate leasing cases, although a modern view would indicate that the lessor must at least attempt to mitigate damages in case of a breach by a lessee.

EXAMPLE:

Two Seton Hall University students are renting an apartment in South Orange. For no good reason, the students decide to move out, causing a breach of the lease agreement. Under these circumstances, most states would require that the landlord use reasonable means to secure a new tenant. If such a tenant becomes available, the landlord will be required to mitigate the damages that are recoverable from the former tenant. Of course, the breaching party is liable for the difference between the amount of the original rent and the rent received from the new tenant. The landlord would also be entitled to recover any costs reasonably incurred in the mitigation effort. Now suppose the landlord did absolutely nothing and refused to take steps to rent the apartment. The court might reduce the amount of damages awarded by the amount the landlord could have received had reasonable steps in mitigation been taken.

In case of employment contracts, the burden of proof is on an employer who improperly terminated an employee to prove the existence of an alternate job and to prove that the employee could have been hired—that is, that the employee had failed to mitigate.

CHAPTER QUESTIONS

1. Explain the relationship between compensatory and incidental damages

2. What are consequential or special damages? How is this type of remedy addressed in *Hadley v. Baxendale?*

3. When will the court enforce a liquidated damages clause?

4. How is the remedy of specific performance applied in *Tower City Grain?*

5. Why did the court refuse to issue a decree for this remedy in *Campbell Soup Co. v. Wentz?*

6. Explain the requirement of mitigation.

CHAPTER FIFTEEN:
THIRD PARTY RIGHTS

When does a third party, not an original party to a contract, acquire rights or obligations under the contract? When can a third party enforce a contract to which he or she was not a party? In strict legal terms, the issue is one of standing; that is, does a party have a legal right to sue on a contract to which he or she is not a party? The doctrine of standing is often used to prohibit remote parties from prosecuting suits. If a party lacks standing, he or she will be denied the opportunity to sue in a court of law. In this chapter, two separate issues will be discussed: assignments/delegations and third party beneficiary contracts.

ASSIGNMENT AND DELEGATION

An assignment involves the transfer of rights. A delegation involves the appointment of another to perform one's duties or obligations. Assignments under the common law were ordinarily ineffective and not favored. The common law held that contractual relations were too personal to permit the interjection of a third party into the relationship without the consent of the obligor, the person to whom a contractual duty was owed. This view was supplanted by the development of a body of law concerning assignment and delegation of contracts.

TERMINOLOGY

The person who makes the assignment is called the assignor. The person to whom the assignment is made is the assignee. If the third party to the arrangement is owed duties under the contract by the assignor, the third party is called the obligor. If the third party owes a duty in the contract (most often, the obligation of payment), the third party is called an obligee.

Technically speaking, we assign rights and delegate duties. [For the sake of clarity in this chapter, we shall use the terminology of an assignment throughout.]

EXAMPLE:

1. The Smith Manufacturing Corporation has entered into a bilateral contract with C.P. Jones to provide Jones, a local appliance retailer, with 300 washing machines at $300.00 each. Jones is obligated to pay the Smith Corporation for the washing machines and the Smith Corporation has promised to provide the washing machines to Jones on a certain date. The Smith Corporation now delegates its duty to Harris Brothers, also a local manufacturer. In this case, the Smith Corporation is the assignor and Harris Brothers is the assignee. Jones is the obligor because he is owed a duty now by Harris Brothers, through the assignment of the contract by the Smith Corporation.

---

2. The Smith Manufacturing Corporation has a contract to provide C.P. Jones with 300 washing machines at $300.00 each. Jones is obligated to pay the Smith Corporation for the machines. The Smith Corporation now assigns the right to receive the payment due to it from Jones to Robert Sutton. Jones is now required to pay Sutton upon receiving notice from the Smith Corporation to do so. In this case, the Smith Corporation is the assignor and Robert Sutton is the assignee. Jones is the third party obligor. Jones is also an obligee, since it now has an obligation to pay Sutton.

3. The Smith Corporation has a contract to provide Jones with 300 washing machines. Jones now assigns the right to receive the performance (the delivery of the 300 washing machines) to Glotz, also a local appliance dealer. In this case, Jones is the assignor and Glotz is the assignee. The Smith Corporation is the obligee.

THE SIMPLE RULES OF ASSIGNMENTS

We will discuss the area of assignments in terms of some simple and understandable rules.

SPECIFIC DUTIES

A person who has specific duties under a contract cannot relieve himself of those duties by delegating them to another party. The original party (the assignor) is still liable if the assignee does not perform. Failure of the assignee to perform after the contract has been assigned gives rise to a cause of action against both the assignor and the assignee. In Example 1, above, even if the Smith Corporation had delegated the duty to provide the washing machines to Harris Brothers, the Smith Corporation still continues to bear a contractual duty to perform. If Harris Brothers fails to perform, as required in the contract between the Smith Corporation and Jones, the Smith Corporation is legally responsible for the breach committed by Harris Brothers. Of course, the Smith Corporation can sue Harris Brothers for failure to carry out its duties under the assignment, if Harris Brothers had promised to tender the performance.

COURTS' PERSPECTIVE

Courts today generally favor an assignment or a delegation. Why? The assignment or delegation of a duty in a contractual relationship might keep a suit for breach of contract from reaching court. For example, in Example 1, if the Smith Corporation is unable to provide Jones with the washing machines, but is able to bring in Harris Brothers who can perform, a breach of contract can be avoided and a potential suit may never reach a court.

LACK OF THIRD PARTY CONSENT

Generally, contract rights may be assigned without the consent of the third party obligor. It is generally recognized that in practically every case, a right to receive payment of money is fully assignable. In Example 2, where the Smith Corporation assigned his right to receive money to Robert Sutton, the Smith Corporation is generally not required to obtain the consent of Jones in order to make this assignment.

SPECIFIC STIPULATION

Should a contract specifically stipulate that contract rights cannot be assigned without consent of the third party obligor, such a provision for "non-assignment without consent" will generally be enforced. However, several courts have recently ruled that a provision for "non-assignment without consent" may violate public policy and have ruled such a provision illegal and non-enforceable. A number of other courts have ruled that such a provision must be construed to impose upon the third party the standard of "reasonable refusal." An example of a contract that will frequently contain a "non-assignment" clause is a lease. Where there is an attempted assignment of a commercial lease (usually termed a subletting), courts may be more sympathetic to the application of the "reasonable refusal" or objective standard. However, in a residential lease, courts are prone to adopt a more subjective determination on the part of the lessor, so long as no law or statute is violated.

RIGHTS NOT ASSIGNABLE

There are certain contracts that are not assignable without consent of the third party obligor. These include a contract involving personal rights and duties; a contract involving artistic skills; a contract to produce entertainment; a contract involving a fiduciary relationship (i.e., lawyer, accountant, doctor); a contract involving "special skill, special knowledge or special experience"; a personal service contract; or where an assignment might substantially change or alter the duty of performance of the third party, as might be the case in a "requirement or output contract." (See UCC § 2-306.) These contracts can only be assigned with the consent of the third party. Without the consent of the third party, the assignment is invalid and void and will give rise to a suit for breach of contract against the party attempting to make the assignment.

At this point, read *Nolan* and *Macke*, which deal with this issue of assignments.

Nolan v. Williamson Music, Inc.
300 F. SUPP. 1311 (1969)

BACKGROUND AND FACTS

Robert Nolan, the composer of "Tumbling Tumbleweed," entered into an agreement with the Sam Fox Publishing Company (Sam Fox) whereby Nolan conveyed "all rights of every kind nature and description" in his song to Fox, "his successors and assigns." In consideration, Sam Fox agreed to pay Nolan certain royalties. Several years later, without formally ever notifying Nolan, Sam Fox assigned all of its rights and interest in the song to Williamson Music, Inc. In return, Williamson agreed to take on the duty of paying royalties. Nolan filed a suit to rescind the contract, arguing that the contract was breached when Fox did not obtain Nolan's agreement to the assignment.

Decision and Rationale

The court held that the assignment was not a breach of contract. Contracts that are personal in nature cannot be assigned without the consent of both parties, but Nolan could not show that his contract with Sam Fox involved such personal elements of trust and confidence as not to be assignable. The court found that "it was not a breach of contract for Sam Fox to assign the copyright to Williamson. The 1934 transfer from plaintiff (Nolan) to Sam Fox of all rights of every kind, nature and description' which plaintiff had in the copyright was clearly absolute on its face."

Macke Co. v. Pizza of Gaithersburg, Inc.
259 MD. 479, 270 A 2D 645 (1970)

Background and Facts

Pizza Shop contracted with Virginia Coffee Services, Inc., for installation of vending machines. Thereafter, the Macke Company bought out Virginia Coffee Service.

The purchase agreement included Virginia's assignment of its vending machine contracts to Macke. Later, Pizza Shop tried to rescind the contracts on the ground that the assignment was such a "material change" in the performance of obligations that it resulted in breach of contract.

Decision and Rationale

The contract between Virginia Coffee, Service and Pizza Shop could validly be assigned. While one cannot delegate the obligation to provide personal services, the contract at issue here did not specify or involve personal services. Even if Pizza Shop had claimed that it contracted with Virginia Coffee Service on the basis of that company's "skill and reputation," this would not prevent assignment of the contract unless there was a material change in the service Macke provided. According to the Restatement of Contracts: "Performance or offer of performance by a person delegated has the same legal effect as performance or offer of performance by the person named in the contract, unless, performance by the person delegated varies or would vary materially from performance by the person named in the contract as the one to perform, and there has been no assent to the delegation."

RIGHTS AND OBLIGATIONS

The assignee "Steps into the Shoes of the Assignor." The assignee takes the contract subject to all the defenses and rights that could have been asserted against the assignor by the third party. In turn, the assignee acquires and assumes all of the rights of the assignor against the third party.

The Smith Corporation agrees to sell 300 washing machines to Jones, delivery date on December 1. On November 1, the Smith Corporation delegates (assigns) the duty of supplying the washing machines to Harris Brothers because the Smith Corporation is too busy or is otherwise unable to perform. On December 1, Harris Brothers fails to make delivery.

What rights has Jones?

i.   Jones can sue the Smith Corporation because the Smith Corporation is an original party to the contract. The Smith Corporation is not relieved of liability after the assignment.

ii. Jones can also sue Harris Brothers because as the assignee, Harris Brothers is liable for its breach of contract if it fails to perform.

iii. If Jones decides to sue Harris Brothers, Jones will be required to prove that Harris Brothers was legally obligated to perform a contractual duty as the assignee of the contract from the Smith Corporation.

iv. Jones can decide to join both the Smith Corporation and Harris Brothers in a suit, but Jones can only collect damages once. It is more probable that Jones will choose to sue the Smith Corporation and will leave it to the Smith Corporation to implead or "bring in" Harris Brothers for its failure to deliver the washing machines.

v.   Suppose that Jones does not pay for the machines or refuses to accept the washing machines when they are delivered? Who has rights against Jones? In this instance, there are two potential plaintiffs: the Smith Corporation and Harris Brothers. The Smith Corporation can sue Jones because the Smith Corporation is the original party to the contract. Harris Brothers can also sue Jones, because Harris Brothers is owed payment for their delivery of the washing machines. Obviously, however, a court will require Jones to pay only one judgment. However, in this instance, it would be most logical for Harris Brothers to sue Jones because Harris Brothers has performed the duties in the contract. Remember, that Harris Brothers would be required to prove that it is the assignee of the contract or a court might rule that Harris Brothers lacked standing to sue.

vi.   Now, suppose that the washing machines, which are delivered by Harris Brothers, are defective and Jones decides to sue for breach of contract. Whom can Jones sue? Jones can sue the Smith Corporation with whom it had a contract. Jones can also sue Harris Brothers because Harris Brothers has committed a breach by delivering defective merchandise. However, in such cases, Jones would probably sue the Smith Corporation, the party with whom it had a contract. Then, as above, it would be the responsibility of the Smith Corporation to bring in (or implead) Harris Brothers because of the failure of Harris Brothers to perform.

vii.   Let's introduce one more complication. Suppose the Smith Corporation owes a debt to Harris Brothers. The Smith Corporation assigns Harris Brothers the "right to the proceeds" of its contract with Jones. However, the machines delivered by the Smith Corporation to Jones are defective. Harris Brothers now attempts to enforce its right to collect against Jones. Must Jones pay Harris Brothers, despite the breach committed by Smith? Harris Brothers asserts to Jones: "Hey, I only received the right to collect. Any problems with the machines, you'll have to see the Smith Corporation...." Is Harris Brothers correct? Generally speaking, the courts will apply the "Rights and Duties Doctrine" to this situation. The "rights and duties doctrine" holds that a party cannot split its right to collect from the duty to perform in a contract. Thus, while Harris Brothers, as the assignee, has the right to enforce the contract against Jones, Harris Brothers is also legally responsible if the Smith Corporation has committed a breach and has failed to perform on the contract. Harris Brothers has taken this contract subject to all the rights and defenses that Jones could have asserted against Smith.

viii.   There is a procedure whereby an assignor like the Smith Corporation can relieve itself of the obligations under a contract; that is, where the Smith Corporation will no longer be obligated to perform under the original contract. This procedure is called a novation. As discussed previously, a **novation** is never assumed or presumed, even after years and years. A novation must be affirmatively proven.

As previously discussed, there are three elements necessary to prove a novation:

1.   Harris Brothers must agree to be bound by the contract as a primary party;

2.   Jones must agree to accept Harris Brothers as a primary party, no longer looking to the Smith Corporation for performance;

3.   The Smith Corporation must be released of its obligation under the contract by Jones.

It is usually easy to demonstrate the existence of the first two elements of a novation. The third element, the release, is usually a "sticking point" in determining if a novation has been created. For example:

Harry rents a retail store at the Livingston Mall. After three months of bad business, Harry decides to close his business and assigns the lease of the store to Glotz, who agrees to pay the monthly rent for the remaining 54 months of the lease. After five months, Glotz fails to make any further payments on the lease. The Livingston Mall sues Harry. Harry claims that a novation had been entered into. Is he correct? Evaluate.

    ix.   If the original contract between the Smith Corporation and Jones was required to be in writing under the Statute of Frauds, the assignment must also be in writing. This is an application of the "equal dignity doctrine." The emphasis of the "equal dignity doctrine" is on the phrase "required to be in writing." Review the requirements of the Statute of Frauds under both the common law and the UCC. In the area of assignments, there are two aspects of the Statute of Frauds most applicable to the "equal dignity doctrine": a contract for the sale of goods for a purchase price of $500 or more (UCC § 2-201) and a contract for the sale of land or a lease extending for more than one year (two years in New Jersey).

    x.   Suppose that an assignor makes two or more assignments of the same contract right, i.e., to receive money from the third party. Two rules apply under these circumstances:

        a.   The English Rule, which states that the first of the assignees to give notice of the assignment to the third party will win. This is a traditional notice rule.

        b.   The American Rule, which states that the first party to whom an assignment is made is legally entitled to the proceeds. The basis for the American Rule is that once the assignor makes the first assignment, there is nothing left to assign to any other party. This rule is sometimes known as "First in time, first in right." (*Superior Brassiere v. Zimetbaum,* 214 App. Div. 525 (1925)).

Thus, as in Example 2, where the Smith Corporation had assigned the right to receive a payment from Jones to Harris Brothers, suppose that the Smith Corporation had also assigned these same proceeds to Manny, Moe, and Jack. Apply the American and English rules to these situations.

The Uniform Commercial Code incorporates the common law rules discussed above concerning the assignment of a right to receive money or some other "contract right," but provides for the non-assignment without consent in three circumstances: if the assignment would materially change the duty of the other party to a contract; increase materially the burden or risk imposed on a party by his contract; or impair materially his chance of obtaining return performance (UCC § 2-210). The UCC rule may be seen as a logical expansion of the common law rule concerning consent of the third party in personal service type contracts. The Uniform Commercial Code rule would apply to Example 3, above.

THIRD PARTY BENEFICIARY CONTRACTS

The common law established that a person "not in privity" of contract could not sue on a contract. Privity of contract was held to apply only to those who exchanged mutual promises. However, the law of contracts also determined that a contract made for the benefit of a third person could be enforced by that third person. Thus, at the formation of a contract, one of the parties can make a promise, the performance of which will benefit a designated third person, and the promisee likewise intends to benefit the third person. The designated person is termed a third party beneficiary. The status of a third party beneficiary must be established at the formation of the contract or some other appropriate time (i.e., where a beneficiary of an insurance policy is changed), otherwise it will not be recognized.

A third party beneficiary may be contrasted to an assignee, a status discussed previously in this chapter. An assignee is a party who acquires a status subsequent to the formation of a contract owing to the decision of one of the parties to either delegate a duty or assign the right to receive all or a designated portion of the performance owing from the other party. Under the common law, courts recognized four types of beneficiaries: creditor beneficiaries, donee beneficiaries, parties "intended to benefit," and incidental beneficiaries.

If the purpose of a promisee is to discharge an obligation or debt that the promisee owes, the third party is said to be a creditor beneficiary. An example of a creditor beneficiary contract is as follows: Ted Kaczinski made a loan to Fred Tarkanian of $25,000 in June 2002, in order to assist Tarkanian in financing various equipment purchases. Tarkanian promised to repay Kaczinski in January 2003. In November 2002, Tarkanian entered into a separate contract with Bob Knight. Tarkanian and Knight agreed that the money due Tarkanian from this contract would be paid to Kaczinski in order to satisfy the original debt owed to Kaczinski by Tarkanian. Kaczinski is the creditor beneficiary of the contract between Tarkanian and Knight. In order to determine whether Kaczinski has enforceable rights concerning the contract between Tarkanian and Knight, the intent of the parties is critical; that is, did Tarkanian and Knight intend to benefit Kaczinski by their contract? Kaczinski now acquires standing as a creditor beneficiary and may sue Knight for breach should he fail to pay as stipulated in the agreement.

Sometimes a party's main purpose in making a contract is to confer a gift upon a third party. The third party is termed a donee beneficiary. A donee beneficiary can enforce a contract promise, just as a creditor beneficiary can.

A common example of a donee beneficiary situation occurs in a typical life insurance or annuity contract. For example, a designated beneficiary can enforce payment against the insurance company upon the death of the insured.

The classic example of a donee beneficiary contract occurred in the case of *Lucas v. Hamm* (1961). In this case, a lawyer promised to draft a will for a promisee. Under the will, the plaintiffs were to be beneficiaries. Because the will was improperly drawn, the plaintiffs received $75,000 less from the testator's estate than the testator had intended. The court held that the plaintiffs were the intended beneficiary of the testator's contract with the lawyer because it was clear that the ultimate beneficiaries of a will are the parties named in a will. The plaintiffs had standing to sue.

In some jurisdictions, a third party might also be permitted to sue for a breach of contract based on a category of beneficiaries termed "those clearly intended to benefit." This category of beneficiaries is relevant in the host of contracts made by governmental units for the benefit of its taxpayers or residents. Suppose that the City of Newark entered into a contract with Grabowski Brothers Paving to repave a portion of Central Avenue. If Grabowski Brothers committed a breach of contract could a third party, whose car was damaged because of a breach, sue Grabowski Brothers for breach of the contract between Newark and Grabowski Brothers? Was the third party "clearly intended to benefit" from the contract? According to § 133 of the *Restatement,* the intent to benefit is ascertained by whether "the beneficiary would be reasonable in relying upon the promise as manifesting an intention to confer a right on him." Under the common law no individual citizen had the right to enforce a contract on its own behalf. (*Restatement, Second* § 145). However, three classes of cases developed in which members of the public would be classified as beneficiaries under the rule. First, if Grabowski agreed to perform services that the City of Newark was under a legal duty to perform for individual members of the public, individual citizens may have the right to file suit directly against Grabowski. The primary application of this rule has been in cases where a contractor has assumed the city's duty to repair or otherwise maintain a public street or highway. The second situation involves the exaction of a promise by the government from a contractor to compensate (indemnify) members of the public for an injury done to them in situations where the city owes no independent duty to the public. A third category of cases involves contracts entered into by the government in order to secure certain advantages for the public in contracts with water, gas and other utility companies, as well as common carriers. The possible application of this doctrine shows the expansion of the third party beneficiary rule beyond the common law.

An incidental beneficiary is a party that receives a general, non-specific benefit from a contract between two parties, but that benefit is not direct or intended. Generally, an incidental beneficiary cannot enforce a contract to which he or she is not a party. The incidental beneficiary often rests his or her case on a moral rather than a legal claim. There are several factors which would indicate that a benefit was intended to be conferred on a third party and that the party was not just an incidental beneficiary: (1) if performance is rendered directly to the third party; (2) if the third party has the right to control the details of the performance; (3) if a third party has been expressly designated as a beneficiary.

EXAMPLE:

The Glotz Corporation contracts with the city of Milford to build a community center and gym for the city of Milford. If Glotz subsequently refuses to build the community center or if Glotz breaches the contract, Jim MacDonald, a resident of Milford, cannot enforce the contract against Glotz because MacDonald is only an incidental beneficiary of the contract.

Jeremy is given an "incentive scholarship" by the Livingston Town Council to study medicine at Rutgers College. Jeremy promises to return to Livingston to serve in the town medical clinic for a period of two years after graduation Should Jeremy fail to keep his side of the bargain, a local taxpayer will not have standing to sue for breach of contract because the taxpayer is only an incidental beneficiary of the contract between Jeremy and the town council.

There has been an expansion of the rights of third parties in recent years, even under the theory of "intended beneficiary." Both in contract actions and in actions based upon tort (where the issue is one of duty to a third party), courts are less reticent to recognize the rights of injured third parties. This trend has been especially pronounced in warranty cases, where the UCC permits a person in the family or household of the buyer, or a guest in the home of a buyer to bring a warranty action. (UCC § 2-318, Alternative A).

CHAPTER QUESTIONS

1. What is standing?

2. What is an assignment? A delegation?

3. Why do courts today favor assignment of contracts?

4. How do courts address "non-assignment without consent" clauses?

5. How did the court address assignment in *Nolan v. Williamson Music, Inc.?* In *Macke Co.v. Pizza of Gaithersburg, Inc.?*

6. What is meant by the following statement: The assignee "steps into the shoes of the assignor"?

7. If an assignor makes two or more assignments of the same contract, what two rules apply? How do these rules differ?

8. What is a third party beneficiary? A donor third party beneficiary? An incidental third party beneficiary?

UNIT III
BUSINESS ASSOCIATIONS

CHAPTER SIXTEEN:
AGENCY

INTRODUCTION

Agency is an important legal concept in business today and involves a relationship between a principal and an agent. In the *Restatement of Agency*, agency is defined as the fiduciary relationship resulting from the manifestation of consent by one person to another that the other shall act on behalf of the first party subject to his control; the other consenting to so act.

The **agent** is the individual authorized to act for and on behalf of a principal. The **principal** is the one who hires an agent. A **fiduciary** is one who has a duty to act primarily for the principal's benefit.

Example: A fiduciary relationship exists between an attorney (the agent) and the client (the principal).

Each state enacts its own laws of agency, which are similar in scope. However, differences do exist. The application of agency law is especially important for U.S. concerns doing business in other countries. Numerous American businesses are entering international markets. To avoid problems that arise from language differences and unfamiliarity with foreign laws and customs, many U.S. companies hire agents who are knowledgeable in these matters. Their use results in smoother operation of the affairs of an American company in these foreign markets.

CREATING THE AGENCY RELATIONSHIP

An agency relationship may be formed by oral agreement or written contract. Either way, such a relationship exists only if and when the principal acts to ask another to act on the principal's behalf.

Like a contractual relationship, an agency can only be created for a legal purpose. Further, the formation of an agency must meet two requirements: 1) The principal must not be a minor or incompetent (a minor or incompetent cannot hire an agent to make contracts on his behalf), and 2) The agent cannot be a minor or incompetent (a contract made by an agent and a third party is deemed to be made between the principal and the third party).

If these basic requirements are met, an agency relationship may be created in any of four ways: 1) by agreement; 2) by implied authority; 3) by estoppel (apparent agency); or 4) by ratification.

AGENCY BY AGREEMENT

Parties that form an agency relationship by making a written or oral agreement are making an agency by agreement. This may also be called an express agency. The principal gives the agent the authority to contract on behalf of the principal. If the principal does not hire another agent for a specified length of time or until a specific duty is completed, the principal and agent have formed an exclusive agency contract.

A power of attorney gives an agent the power to sign legal documents on behalf of the principal. This can create an agency relationship. A power of attorney may be general or specific. A general power of attorney is very broad in the authority it gives to the agent. A specific power of attorney gives an agent limited powers to act in specific ways for specific purposes as enumerated in the document.

Powers of attorney are commonly used for health care matters. If the principal is unable to make health related decisions, the agent will have the legal power to act on his behalf.

AGENCY BY IMPLIED AUTHORITY

A legal agency relationship can also be created by the conduct of the parties to the agreement even though not expressly stated. The specific circumstances surrounding the situation determine the extent to which an agent may conduct business on behalf of the principal. But, an agency by implied authority may not conflict with an agency by agreement.

Helene A. Gordon et al, v. Andrew Tobias
262 CONN. 844; 817 A.2D 683 (2003)

The dispositive issue in this appeal is whether the trial court properly concluded that a now defunct mortgage loan brokerage corporation, Mutual Mortgage Services, Inc. (Mutual), had acted as an agent for the defendant, Andrew Tobias, for the purpose of receiving payments of the balance due on a mortgage held by the defendant on property owned by the plaintiffs, Helene A. Gordon and William J. Gordon. The defendant appeals from the judgment of the trial court settling title on the property in the plaintiffs. The defendant claims that there was no evidence to support the trial court's finding that Mutual had acted as his agent when it received payment on the mortgage at the time title to the property transferred to the plaintiffs. The plaintiffs claim in response that the evidence produced at trial supports the trial court's finding of an agency relationship. We agree with the plaintiffs and, accordingly, we affirm the judgment of the trial court.

The record reveals the following undisputed facts. Elixir Limited Partnership (Elixir), which is not a party to this appeal, was a condominium developer engaged in the development of a number of condominium units in Madison. In order to finance construction on various condominium units, Elixir borrowed money from Mutual, which, in turn, secured its loan by taking mortgages on the individual condominium units. Mutual used the defendant's money to fund the mortgage at issue in the present case. On February 16, 1994, Mutual assigned the mortgage at issue in the present case from Elixir to the defendant. Both the mortgage on the condominium and the assignment to the defendant were recorded in the Madison land records. Thereafter, payments on the mortgage were made by Elixir to Mutual, which then remitted the payments to the defendant. Early in 1995, the plaintiffs became interested in buying one of the condominium units constructed by Elixir and encumbered by the mortgage that had been assigned to the defendant. The plaintiffs hired a real estate attorney who completed a title search that revealed the mortgage on the property. After counsel for the plaintiffs contacted Elixir regarding the purchase of the property, Elixir agreed that, at the closing, it would pay off the amount due under the mortgage, $125,046.66, to Mutual. Subsequently, on February 2, 1995, the plaintiffs closed on the condominium purchased from Elixir, which then gave Mutual a check for the amount due and conveyed the property to the plaintiffs by warranty deed.

Although Mutual received full payment on the mortgage at the closing, it neither remitted this sum to the defendant, nor informed him of the closing. Rather, Mutual continued to send periodic payments to the defendant until July, 1997, when the president of Mutual died and Mutual's scheme was revealed. After the defendant refused to release the mortgage, the plaintiffs filed an action, pursuant to General Statutes § 47–31, in order to quiet title in the property in favor of themselves. After trial, the trial court concluded, inter alia, that Mutual was an agent of the defendant for the purposes of receiving payment of the outstanding amount due on the mortgage that was paid at the February, 1995, closing. Thus, the trial court concluded that payment to Mutual, as agent for the defendant, constituted payment to the defendant and, consequently, discharged the plaintiffs' obligation under the mortgage. Accordingly, pursuant to § 47–31, the trial court quieted title in the property in favor of the plaintiffs. This appeal followed.

The defendant claims that there was insufficient evidence in the record to support the trial court's finding that Mutual was an agent of the defendant for the purposes of collecting payments on the mortgage that he held on the plaintiffs' property. We disagree.

It is well settled that, "[t]he nature and extent of an agent's authority is a question of fact for the trier where the evidence is conflicting or where there are several reasonable inferences which can be drawn." (Internal quotation marks omitted.) Maharishi School of Vedic Sciences, Inc. (Connecticut) v. Connecticut Constitution Associates Ltd. Partnership, 260 Conn. 598, 606, 799 A.2d 1027 (2002). "To the extent that the trial court has made findings of fact, our review is limited to deciding whether such findings were clearly erroneous." Id., at 605, 799 A.2d 1027. "A finding of fact is clearly erroneous when there is no evidence in the record to support it...or when although there is evidence to support it, the reviewing court on the entire evidence is left with the definite and firm conviction that a mistake has been committed....In making this determination, every reasonable presumption must be given in favor of the trial court's ruling." Id.

Turning to the merits of the defendant's claim, "[a]gency is defined as the fiduciary relationship which results from manifestation of consent by one person to another that the other shall act on his behalf and subject to his control, and consent by the other so to act....Restatement (Second), 1 Agency § 1 [1958]....Thus, the three elements required to show the existence of an agency relationship include: (1) a manifestation by the principal that the agent will act for him; (2) acceptance by the agent of the undertaking; and (3) an understanding between the parties that the principal will be in control of the undertaking." Beckenstein v. Potter & Carrier, Inc., 191 Conn. 120, 132–33, 464 A.2d 6 (1983).

Moreover, "it is a general rule of agency law that the principal in an agency relationship is bound by, and liable for, the acts in which his agent engages with authority from the principal, and within the scope of the [agency relationship]." Maharishi School of Vedic Sciences, Inc. (Connecticut) v. Connecticut Constitution Associates Ltd. Partnership, supra, 260 Conn. at 606, 799 A.2d 1027. An agent's authority may be actual or apparent. Id., at 606–607, 799 A.2d 1027. "Actual authority may be express or implied." Id., at 607, 799 A.2d 1027. Because the plaintiffs do not claim that Mutual had express actual authority, we must review whether the trial court properly found implied actual authority. "Implied authority is actual authority circumstantially proved. It is the authority which the principal intended his agent to possess....Implied authority is a fact to be proven by deductions or inferences from the manifestations of consent of the principal and from the acts of the principal and [the] agent." Connecticut National Bank v. Giacomi, 242 Conn. 17, 70, 699 A.2d 101 (1997).

As the trial court's memorandum of decision reveals, the court found that the defendant had authorized Mutual to collect monthly payments on the note secured by the mortgage on the plaintiffs' property and remit those payments to him. This conclusion was based on the trial court's findings that the defendant was "an investor living in Florida and had no interests in managing such details for himself." Moreover, the trial court concluded, "the entity designated to collect payments on the note secured by the mortgage was plainly authorized to receive payment of the outstanding amount of the mortgage when the property was sold." On the basis of the trial court's well reasoned decision, we conclude that the court's determination that Mutual had actual implied authority to collect the amount due under the mortgage was not clearly erroneous.

The trial court also concluded that Mutual had apparent authority to collect the amounts due under the mortgage held by the defendant. "Apparent authority is that semblance of authority which a principal, through his own acts or inadvertences, causes or allows third persons to believe his agent possesses....Consequently, apparent authority is to be determined, not by the agent's own acts, but by the acts of the agent's principal....The issue of apparent authority is one of fact to be determined based on two criteria....First, it must appear from the principal's conduct that the principal held the agent out as possessing sufficient authority to embrace the act in question, or knowingly permitted [the agent] to act as having such authority....Second, the party dealing with the agent must have, acting in good faith, reasonably believed, under all the circumstances, that the agent had the necessary authority to bind the principal to the agent's action." Tomlinson v. Board of Education, 226 Conn. 704, 734–35, 629 A.2d 333 (1993).

We conclude that the trial court also properly found that Mutual had apparent authority to collect the mortgage payment due on the mortgage held by the defendant. The defendant collected mortgage payments from Mutual for more than two years knowing that the loan on the property had matured, yet he neither objected to nor demanded full payment of the amount due. Rather, the defendant demanded that Mutual invoke a higher interest rate in order to provide incentive for the borrowers to pay off the loan. Similarly, the defendant testified at trial that Mutual had serviced the mortgage loans for him, which included collecting the checks, arranging payment of the amount due under the mortgage, and obtaining mortgage releases. We conclude that the trial court properly concluded that Mutual had apparent authority to collect the amount due under the mortgage held by the defendant. Payment to an agent constitutes payment to the principal. Manchester v. Sullivan, 112 Conn. 223, 225 152 A. 134 (1930). Thus, the trial court's conclusion that Elixir's payment to Mutual in 1995, of the total amount due discharged any obligation under the mortgage was not clearly erroneous.

Judgment is affirmed.

Courts will usually allow agents to receive payments owed to the principal, hire and discharge employees, buy equipment and supplies, and enter into contracts. Case law demonstrates how far various courts allow implied authority to stretch.

AGENCY BY ESTOPPEL (APPARENT AUTHORITY)

The writing, speaking and/or acting of a principal may lead a third party to reasonably believe that an individual is acting as the principal's agent. If so, the principal is estopped from denying that the individual is an agent.

Robert M. Bailey v. Richard Worton d/b/a Worton Asphalt & Paving 752 SO.2D 470 (2000)

The Chancery Court of DeSoto County [Mississippi] found that a construction lien filed pursuant to Miss. Code Ann. § 85-7-131 by Richard Worton d/b/a Worton Asphalt & Paving, the appellee, was enforceable against Robert M. Bailey, the appellant and true owner of the subject property, having determined that there was sufficient evidence to establish that the general contractor, Ray and Associates, was an implied agent acting within the "apparent authority" granted by Bailey, in contracting with Worton. Having found no error, we affirm the judgment of the lower court.

FACTS

Robert M. Bailey, the appellant, and his partner were the developers of the College Hills Subdivision in Olive Branch where Worton Asphalt & Paving had installed a driveway on a lot the title of which is in the name of the appellant, Bailey. Bailey, in his effort to develop the area in the back portion of the subdivision where the subject lot is located, made an agreement with Billy and Sandra Ray d/b/a Ray & Associates, as builders and realtors, granting permission to them to build a house on the lot. The Rays were free to build the house as they wished, subject to the architectural approval consistent with the covenants of the subdivision. Ray was to secure a purchaser for the house and would pay Bailey for the lot when the house sold.

Bailey testified that he signed a note from the Bank of Tunica and loaned Ray the money on the lot for the house. Ray began construction and advertised the house for sale. The ad represented Ray & Associates as the sellers and real estate agents. The Rays later entered into a contract for the construction and sale of the house with Joe and Wendy Hill. Ms. Hill testified that she did not know at that time that Bailey was the owner of the lot. The contract with the Hills provided that the Hills would provide the labor for a portion of the construction of the house. Construction proceeded; however, the Rays developed financial problems and did not pay Worton Asphalt & Paving for the paving of the driveway of the house.

Ms. Hill testified that the asphalt work for the driveway was ordered by the Rays. Hill stated that she was present when Worton Asphalt arrived at the lot to pave the driveway. However, Worton Asphalt was prepared to leave the construction site without performing the work since neither of the Rays was present to sign the contract for $2,900. Hill managed to contact Sandra Ray by phone while Worton Asphalt was still at the site, and Ray authorized Worton to do the work. Billy Ray arrived at the site of the construction shortly thereafter, and the driveway was then paved. Bailey was not aware that the drive had been paved until several days later when he was driving through the subdivision. He stated that he was no more involved in the construction or progress of this house than he was with any other house in the subdivision, and his involvement was limited to getting paid for the lot when the house was sold.

Worton himself did not testify but his foreman, Mr. Collins, did. No testimony was offered regarding Bailey, and there was nothing to indicate that Worton relied on the Rays as agents of Bailey or had any knowledge that they were agents of Bailey. Hill was unequivocal in her testimony that Bailey was not involved with the negotiation and execution of the Hill contract with the Rays for the purchase of the house and that she did not even know of Bailey at the time that the contract for the house was signed. Bailey stated in his testimony that he met Ms. Hill for the first time when she stopped him in the road one day as he was driving through the subdivision. Hill knew who Bailey was because Sandra Ray made frequent references to him and had spoken with him on her speaker phone from her office in Hill's presence. Hill also testified that Ray periodically notified Bailey of the progress of the construction of the house. At the time that Hill stopped Bailey as he was driving, she expressed her problems to him regarding the Rays and told Bailey that she was prepared to hire an attorney. As a result of this conversation, Bailey said that he called Sandra Ray and asked her to get in touch with the Hills to work out their problem. Bailey also testified that he did not tell hill that he was the actual owner of the lot at that time because he did not realize that he was. He indicated that in the past such agreements for construction had been prompted by a conveyance of the lot thorough a second mortgage. He testified that the house was Sandra's and that he "had even forgotten about the title being in my name until they brought it up."

Worton Asphalt & Paving filed a construction lien pursuant to Miss. Code Ann. § 85-7-131 (1972) for $2,900 for the driveway and sought enforcement against Bailey. As to the claim of lien, Miss. Code Ann. § 85-7-131 (1972) reads as follows: "The lien declared in Section 85-7-131 shall exist only in favor of the person employed, or with whom the contract is made to perform such labor or furnish such materials or render such architectural service, and his assigns, and when the contract or employment is made by the owner, or by his agent, representative, guardian or tenant authorized, either expressly or impliedly, by the owner."

The Chancery Court of DeSoto County, having determined that there was sufficient evidence to establish an implied agency relationship between the general contractor with whom the appellee contracted and Bailey, found the lien to be enforceable against Bailey. Bailey appeals, claiming that the Rays' agreement with Worton does not bind him.

ISSUES

* * * * *

Looking at the facts in a light most favorable to the decision of the court below, it is not unreasonable to conclude that Worton relied on Ray and no one else because of her apparent authority. So far as third persons are concerned, the apparent powers of an agent are his real powers. 2 C.J.S. Agency §§ 95, 96. The power of an agent to bind his principal is not limited to the authority actually conferred upon the agent, but the principal is bound if the conduct of the principal is such that persons of reasonable prudence, ordinarily familiar with business practices, dealing with the agent might rightfully believe the agent to have the power he assumes to have. The agent's authority as to those with whom he deals is what it reasonably appears to be. McPherson v. McLendon, 221 So.2d 75, 78 (Miss.1969); Steen v. Andrews, 223 Miss. 694, 697, 78 So.2d 881, 883 (1955). Where the relationship of principal and agent exists, if the principal places his agent in a position where he appears, with reasonable certainty, to be acting for the principal, and his acts are within the apparent scope of his authority, such acts bind the principal. On principles of estoppel, a principal, having clothed an agent with semblance of authority, will not be permitted, after others have been led to act in reliance on appearances thus produce, to deny, to the prejudice of such others, what he has theretofore tacitly affirmed as to the agent's powers. General Contract Corp. v. Leggett, 224 Miss. 262, 269, 79 So.2d 843, 844 (1955). Where an agent, with the knowledge and consent of his principal, holds himself out as having certain powers and transacts business with a third person, the principal is estopped from denying the authority of the agent. Germania Life Ins. Co. v. Bouldin, 100 Miss. 660, 678, 56 So. 609, 613 (1911).

CONCLUSION

It is our opinion that the evidence was sufficient to show that the Rays were implied agents of Bailey vested with the apparent authority to bind Bailey on the construction lien filed by Worton Asphalt & Paving pursuant to Miss. Code Ann. § 85-7-131 (1972). Under Mississippi agency law, a principal is bound by the actions of its agent within the scope of that agent's real or apparent authority. Andrew Jackson Life Ins. Co. v. Williams, 566 So.2d 117, 1180 (Miss.1990); Ford v. Lamar Life Ins. Co., 513 So.2d 880, 888 (Miss.1987). "If an agent acted within his apparent authority, the issue of actual authority need not be reached." Andrew Jackson, 566 So.2d at 1180. Finding no error, we affirm the judgment of the chancellor.

AGENCY BY RATIFICATION

If an individual misrepresents himself as an agent and the principal accepts these unauthorized acts, the principal is said to ratify the agency relationship. The ratification is tantamount to the principal authorizing the agent's acts on the principal's behalf.

In order for ratification to occur the principal must have complete knowledge of the agent's action and at the time the agent's unauthorized acts occur, the third party must know of the existence of the principal.

DUTIES OF A PRINCIPAL TO AN AGENT

As a result of extensive case law on the subject, a generally accepted rule has evolved stating that a principal owes four duties to an agent. They are the duty to compensate the agent, a duty to reimburse and indemnify the agent, a duty to cooperate with the agent, and a duty to provide and maintain a safe work environment for the agent.

DUTIES OF AN AGENT TO A PRINCIPAL

On the other side of the coin are duties that the agent owes to the principal. An agent owes the principal a duty of loyalty, a duty of obedience, a duty of an accounting, and a duty of performance.

Carl Shen v. Leo A. Daly Company
222 F.3D 472 (2000)

Carl Shen is a former employee of Leo A. Daly Company's (Daly) Republic of China (Taiwan) office. Daly refused to pay taxes assessed by the Taiwanese government. As a result, Taiwan restricted Shen's travel, forbidding him from leaving the country. Shen then sued Daly on multiple theories of liability for damages and injunctive relief. Shen prevailed in part in the district court. Both he and Daly appeal the judgment. We affirm in part and reverse in part.

I. BACKGROUND

Shen is a United States citizen who retains dual Taiwanese citizenship. In 1989, Shen moved to Taiwan to become managing director of Daly's operation there.

To conduct business in Taiwan, Daly was required to designate a "responsible person," or legal representative in the country, and Shen was so designated. In November 1992, Daly decided to withdraw from Taiwan because of business setbacks. As a result, Shen was terminated but chose to remain in Taiwan. Daly, however, failed to remove Shen as its responsible person.

In December 1993, Shen received a notice from the Taiwan Tax Authority that it wanted to audit Daly's 1992 Taiwan tax returns. Shen, in turn, notified Daly's accounting firm in Taiwan and informed them he was concerned he could be held responsible for any deficiency because his "chop," the Taiwanese equivalent of a signature, was affixed to the returns. Daly responded that it was "inconceivable" any tax could be owed because Daly had suffered large losses in Taiwan. In January 1994, Shen asked Daly to indemnify him should the Taiwan Tax Authority impose the tax liability on him directly.

Following this request and until mid-October 1995, Shen, through a series of letters to Daly personnel and to Mr. Leo A. Daly III himself, implored Daly to resolve the tax dispute and remove him as the responsible person. In May 1994, the Taiwan Tax Authority assessed a tax liability of approximately $80,000 against Daly for 1991 and 1992. Daly did not appeal the assessment, and it became final in June 1995. In October 1995, the Taiwan Ministry of Finance and the Bureau of Entry and Exit informed Shen he was forbidden from leaving the country until resolution of the Daly tax issue. Daly's attempt to extricate Shen through diplomatic channels failed. Shen then brought suit for a declaratory judgment in Taiwan to remove himself as Daly's responsible person. Although the court recognized Shen was no longer an employee of Daly, it denied relief because Daly had not replaced him as the responsible person. The Ministry of Finance also denied an appeal by Shen.

In 1997, Shen sued Daly in the United States District Court for the District of Nebraska. He requested a preliminary injunction to force Daly to pay the taxes. The district court entered such an injunction on December 31, 1997. We assume Daly then paid the taxes because Taiwan lifted the travel restriction. The district court held a bench trial in February 1999, on the issue of a permanent injunction and damages. The district court found a violation of the implied covenant of good faith and fair dealing and granted a permanent injunction. Shen was also awarded attorney's fees and $4,760 in damages on his contractual claims. Shen, however, did not prevail on his claims for false imprisonment or intentional infliction of emotional distress. Both sides now appeal and we affirm in part and reverse in part.

II. DISCUSSION

This suit was brought under the court's diversity jurisdiction and therefore Nebraska law controls on all the issues presented in this appeal.

* * * * *

B. Injunctive Relief

* * * * *

The district court held that Daly breached the implied covenant of good faith and fair dealing based on the agency relationship between Daly and Shen. We agree. Under Nebraska law, whether a person is an agent is a question of fact. See McCurry v. School Dist. Of Valley, 242 Neb. 504, 496 N.W.2d 433, 439 (1993). The existence of an agency relationship does not depend on the terminology the parties use to characterize their relationship, but depends on the facts underlying the relationship. See Franksen v. Crossroads Joint Venture, 245 Neb. 863, 515 N.W.2d 794, 801 (1994); McCurry, 496 N.W.2d at 439. An agency relationship can be implied from words, conduct or circumstances that evidence an intent to create on. See McCurry, 496 N.W.2d at 439. For example, under agency principles, an agent can be given apparent or ostensible authority to act if the "alleged principal affirmatively, intentionally, or by lack of ordinary care causes third persons to act upon the apparent authority." See Franksen, 515 N.W.2d at 801. That is what happened in this case.

After Daly terminated Shen in December 1992, Daly did not remove Shen as its responsible person. When Shen entreated Daly to remove him as its responsible person in January 1994, Daly still did not act. In June 1994, Daly tried to have one of the employees of its accounting firm in Taiwan replace Shen and informed Shen that the employee had become Daly's new responsible person. The employee, however decided not to take the appointment, and Daly failed to inform Shen of this fact for seven months. By the time Shen learned there was no replacement for him, the threat of a travel restriction was looming, and Daly was unable to find anyone willing to take the appointment. The result of Daly's initial inaction and subsequent inability to replace Shen as a responsible person was that Shen remained Daly's agent regarding actions taken by Taiwan. Therefore, we find no error in the district court's factual finding of an agency relationship.

A principal and an agent are in a fiduciary relationship. See Andrews v. Schram, 252 Neb. 298, 562 N.W.2d 50, 54 (1997). Because of the fiduciary relationship, the principal owes the agent a duty of good faith and fair dealing in the incidents of their relationship. See Lawrence Warehouse Co. v Twohig, 224 F.2d 493, 497 (8th Cir.1995). Moreover, " '[c]orrelative with the duties of the agent to serve loyally and obediently are the principal's duties of compensation, indemnity, and protection.' " See Western Smelting & Ref. Co. v. First Nat'l Bank of Omaha, 150 Neb. 477, 35 N.W.2d 116, 121 (1948) (quoting Restatement of Agency Intro. Note, vol. 2, p. 999). Daly breached its duty as a fiduciary in the following ways: (1) Daly did not pay the tax when it was assessed; (2) it chose not to appeal the assessment through proper channels; and (3) Daly did not find a replacement for Shen as responsible person.

We recognize Daly believes the taxes were unfairly assessed and amount to little more than extortion. However, its dispute with Taiwan over the " 'principle of the thing' took place over the body of its innocent former employee and agent" and, thus, the district court did not abuse its discretion in granting the injunction based on Daly's breach of fiduciary duty. Shen v. Leo A. Daly Co., No 8:97CV441, Slip Op. at 14 (D.Neb. May 28, 1999).

* * * * *

III. CONCLUSION

Accordingly, we affirm the judgment of the district court with respect to injunctive relief and damages....

PRINCIPAL AND AGENT—LIABILITY TO THIRD PARTIES

Principals will usually be held liable for the acts of their agents if the actions are within the scope of the agents' employment. As such, principals will be legally responsible when agents contract with third parties, commit torts within the scope of the agency relationship, and commit crimes when acting on behalf of the principals.

LIABILITY FOR CONTRACTS

A major purpose of the agency relationship is to provide principals with the means to expand their business dealings. An agent is authorized to contact third parties, enter into contracts on behalf of the principal with third parties, and figuratively put the principal in several places at once. Further, ideally a good agent will be familiar with the ways of conducting business in a specific location, may have contacts in that location who are unknown or unfamiliar to the principal, and possess numerous other advantages not within the principal's scope.

This leads to liability issues where a principal is disclosed, partially disclosed or undisclosed. A disclosed principal is one whose identity a third party knows at the time she enters into an agreement; i.e., the third party knows the agent with whom she is dealing is acting on behalf of a known principal.

A partially disclosed principal is an individual whose identity is unknown to the third party at the time an agreement is reached; however, she does know the agent is representing some principal.

In either situation the principal is liable for acts committed by the agent within the scope of the agency relationship as the agent has actual authority.

If a third party does not know the principal and is unaware that an agency relationship exists, the agent (not the principal) may be liable to the third party if the principal fails to comply with his contractual obligations.

TORT LIABILITY

The doctrine of *Respondeat Superior* holds that a principal may be liable for the intentional and negligent torts of an agent when the tortuous behavior is committed within the scope of the agent's employment. Unauthorized acts committed outside the scope of employment are the legal responsibility of the agent.

Therefore, the crux of the issue to be determined by the courts is whether an agent was performing within or outside the bounds of his employment. The courts ask two questions: 1) Was the agent acting in the interest of the principal? and 2) Was the agent authorized to be in the place in which he was located when the tort occurred?

EXAMPLE:

Joe, a car mechanic for ABC Transmission, owned by Mr. Carr, goes to Jim's house on orders from Mr. Carr to pick up Jim's car and return it to the shop. On the way back to the shop, Joe stops at a bar, has two drinks and then hits another car parked legally in the bar's parking lot. Jim sues ABC Transmission and Joe. In this very simple example the court must decide if the company (the principal), Joe (the agent) or both parties are liable, jointly and severally. Actual cases are usually not so clear-cut.

CRIMINAL LIABILITY

Usually principals are not liable for the criminal conduct, e.g., murder, robbery, bribery, etc. of agents. It is too difficult to prove intent on the part of a principal, a requirement necessary to prove guilt for such crimes. Still, two exceptions exist: If a principal participates directly in an agent's crime, and if a principal has reason to know his agents or employees are violating a law.

TERMINATION OF AN AGENCY RELATIONSHIP

The agency relationship may end in two ways, by agreement or by operation of law.

TERMINATION BY AGREEMENT

Either a principal or an agent may terminate the agency relationship. When the relationship is terminated, the principal should provide actual notice to all third parties who dealt with the agent that the termination has occurred. Constructive notice may be provided to everyone else by ads in publications located where the agency relationship operated.

TERMINATION BY LAW

In this instance notification to third parties is not required. Five ways in which an agency relationship terminates by operation of law include: death of either the principal or agent, even if unknown by the survivor; insanity of either party; bankruptcy of the principal; impossibility of performance of the agency relationship, such as through a change in the law or the loss or destruction of the subject matter of the relationship; and the outbreak of war, especially if the countries of each party are at war.

CHAPTER QUESTIONS

1. How is an agency relationship formed?

2. Explain the legal principle of agency by estoppel.

3. What are the duties of a principal to an agent? An agent to a principal?

4. When might an agent be liable to a third party?

5. What is the difference between a disclosed and undisclosed principal?

6. Describe how an agency relationship may terminate or be terminated.

CHAPTER SEVENTEEN:
SOLE PROPRIETORSHIPS

The simplest form of business organization and operation is a sole proprietorship. This is the oldest means by which a business is created in the United States. As its name implies, individuals who wish to establish a business by themselves use this form. The person who runs the business is called a sole proprietor. He or she has complete managerial authority. The sole proprietorship is merely an extension of its owner. No one else owns any part of the business. However, the owner may employ as many individuals as are needed to run the business. Businesses that commonly utilize this form of organization are retail establishments, service businesses, and those businesses involved in agriculture. Many sole proprietorships are owned by a husband and/or wife. A sole proprietorship accounts for business income and expenses on federal schedule C. In addition, the sole proprietor is required to file schedule SE (self-employment tax) if the proprietorship makes a profit. In most states, a husband and wife may operate a sole proprietorship together.

FORMATION

A sole proprietorship is not a separate business entity, but rather, it is an extension of its owner. There are no complicated rules that must be followed in order to establish a sole proprietorship. Few legal requirements exist to establish them and minimal government rules have been enacted to regulate them. However, in most states if an individual is "doing business" in a name other than his own (called a trade name), he or she must file a disclosure form with the proper state authority to identify that party as the owner of the business. So, for example, if a creditor sues Ed's Auto Body Shop, owned by Edward Barnes, the creditor addresses the complaint to "Edward Barnes, doing business as Ed's Auto Body Shop." Further, certain types of businesses and businesses hiring employees must obtain special licenses or follow other legal requirements. For example, a delicatessen must obtain a special operating license and adhere to strict health code laws. If a sole proprietorship employs others, the Internal Revenue Service will have to issue an employer identification number [EIN] in order to have income and social security taxes withheld from the employees' wages. The owner will also have to follow state laws regarding workers' compensation insurance and unemployment insurance. These general requirements are not specific to sole proprietorships alone; they apply to other business entities as well.

TERMINATION

A proprietorship will be terminated when the proprietor closes the business or upon the death, insanity, or bankruptcy of the proprietor.

ADVANTAGES

The creation of a sole proprietorship is a simple and inexpensive process. A sole proprietor does not have to pay any fees for organizing his or her business as a sole proprietorship. The owner (proprietor) makes all the decisions and retains all profits accruing to the business. The net earnings are taxable as personal income and not subject to the corporate income tax. The business of a sole proprietor may be freely sold to another individual. However, because a sole proprietorship is merely an extension of the individual owner, a legal distinction exists because the sole proprietorship cannot be transferred from one person to another. The buyer must create his or her own form of business to conduct the business transferred.

DISADVANTAGES

A sole proprietorship is not a separate legal entity. It cannot sue or be sued in its own name. As such, the primary detriment of a sole proprietorship is the liability assumed by the owner. Liability is complete and unlimited. The proprietor is personally liable for all of the obligations and debts of the business. If the assets of the business are not sufficient to pay the claims of creditors, creditors may seek payment directly from the owner's personal assets. Therefore, the sole proprietor risks insolvency and may be exposed to personal bankruptcy. On the other hand, the proprietor must sue those who have caused damage to the proprietorship in his or her own name.

The sole proprietor who hires employees may be responsible for the torts of employees committed in the course of their employment. The proprietor is also liable for contracts entered into by an employee who has the authority to do so. The rules of agency apply in these situations. The theory under which the proprietor may be held liable for the wrongs of an employee is called *respondeat superior.* The act complained of must be "within the scope of employment." A proprietor may claim that the act should not be imputed to him or her because the employee is an independent contractor. An independent contractor controls his or her own "methods and means" of work and does not work under the control of the proprietor. The employer may also claim that the employee was, in effect, pursuing his or her own business or personal interests, under the "independent frolic" doctrine. Even if a court agrees that the employee was an independent contractor, the proprietor may still be held liable under a theory of "negligent selection" or because the duty was "non-delegable."

CHAPTER QUESTIONS

1. What is the purpose of a sole proprietorship?

2. Explain some advantages/disadvantages of this form of business entity.

3. Explain the concept of "*respondeat superior.*"

4. What is an independent contractor?

5. Is the proprietorship an entity for legal purposes?

CHAPTER EIGHTEEN:
PARTNERSHIPS

The Uniform Partnership Act (UPA) defines a partnership as "the association of two or more persons to carry on as co-owners of a business for profit." Essentially, a partnership requires that individuals pool capital resources or professional talents to obtain a profit. For this purpose, a "person" may include a corporation, a partnership, and other associations that are "artificial" persons, as well as natural persons. Some form of the UPA has been adopted by forty-nine states. Law, architectural, engineering, and accounting firms, as well as medical associations may operate as partnerships; however, a trend is emerging for such businesses to incorporate. Retail and service businesses may use the partnership form, as well as many individuals who intend to hold and manage real property together. When discussing partnerships we must differentiate between two distinct forms of this type of business organization, the general partnership and the limited partnership.

ATTRIBUTES OF A PARTNERSHIP

The UPA defines a partnership as an "association." Implicit in this concept is the voluntary nature of this business form. Therefore, a partnership is created by consent of the parties and is usually formed by executing a contract. For some purposes, the partnership is treated as a distinct entity, for others, the partners are treated as a group of individuals. In the former case, a partnership may buy, sell, and own property in the partnership's name and the partnership will file a federal income tax return for informational purposes in its own name to account for the income generated. At common law, a suit could never be brought by or against a partnership in its own name; each partner had to sue or be sued. However, while this principle is still generally true, many states now provide that a partnership can be treated as an entity for purposes of suing others or for being sued. State law must be consulted on this important matter.

The partnership as a separate entity does not pay income taxes. Instead, the income or losses incurred by it are "passed through" the partnership to the partners. Each partner is responsible for paying his or her portion of the taxes due on the profits received or may take deductions on his or her portion of losses incurred. A partnership dissolves on the death, retirement, or withdrawal of a partner. However, the more recently authored Revised Uniform Partnership Act (RUPA) adopted by eighteen states as of 1998, provides that a partnership does not automatically dissolve if a partner leaves the business; specifies fiduciary duties of the partners; and establishes a formula by which partnership interests may be valued in a buyout. The RUPA also establishes broader protective measures for limited liability partners. (See below, Dissolution and Termination of the Partnership)

A basic element of the partnership form requires partners to carry on as co-owners. This is demonstrated by sharing profits, joint ownership of property, making contributions of capital to the business, and joint participation in management decision-making. Finally, the UPA requires that the business be formed for profit. Therefore, businesses formed for religious, charitable, or fraternal purposes may not be a partnership.

FORMATION OF A PARTNERSHIP

A partnership may be formed by the voluntary actions of the parties or by implication through their ongoing conduct. The establishment of a partnership by voluntary means is usually most desirable because the rights and liabilities of each partner are best protected.

If, at the outset of a partnership, there is no written partnership agreement, partners split their capital contributions and divide the duties each will perform. Without a written agreement, the UPA controls. Therefore, without a partnership agreement, if the partnership consists of two partners and one does 70% of the work and the other only does 30%, each partner will receive 50% of the profits according to the UPA, no matter what the two partners intended.

In order to avoid this and numerous other problems—management responsibilities, profit distribution, borrowing authority, and so on—an agreement should be drawn up specifying each partner's rights, obligations and responsibilities. This agreement, called Articles of Partnership, fixes the expectations of the individuals.

With respect to the RUPA, this act is composed of rules that will apply to a partnership unless the partnership agreement states a requirement contrary to that stated in the Act.

Specific issues to consider in the formation of the partnership agreement run from the basic to the more complex: the name and address of the partnership, its purpose, the amount and type of investment each partner will contribute, managerial and voting power, dispute resolution, partner insurance (key man insurance), bookkeeping methods, banking responsibilities, borrowing rights, and employee issues.

A partnership can also be created involuntarily, i.e., when no express agreement exists and the parties do not call themselves partners. This is called a partnership by estoppel. In certain situations, a court may infer that a partnership exists despite the fact that the persons involved deny it. The courts will look beyond the form to the substance of the activities in making a determination. Section 16 of the UPA addresses this issue as follows:

> "When a person by words spoken or written or by conduct, represents himself, or consents to another representing him to anyone as a partner in an existing partnership or with one or more persons not actual partners, he is liable to any party to whom such representation has been made."

Section 7 of the UPA also deals with this circumstance from the aspect of profit sharing. The fact that two or more parties share the profits of a business gives rise to the rebuttable presumption that a partnership exists. This presumption may be overcome by evidence that the receipt of profits was for the purpose of repaying debts, paying wages or rent, paying a widow or personal representative of an estate, or paying for business goodwill and not as the result of any partnership relationship.

Also, if a partnership is created for a fixed term (two years, for example), and the partnership continues beyond the term without any express agreement, the UPA declares that the rights and duties of the partners remain the same as before the expiration of the term.

RELATIONSHIP OF THE PARTNERS

The UPA states that each partner must have a fiduciary relationship to the partnership. Usually each partner has one vote with respect to the management of a general partnership. Decisions are commonly made by a majority vote. Major decisions, such as whether to dissolve a partnership, merge with another business, or change the form of organization may require a unanimous vote.

The following rights and duties of partners should be addressed in a partnership agreement:

1. The right to be repaid the partner's contribution and to share equally in the partnership profits after partnership debts are paid;

2. The duty to contribute toward partnership losses (capital or other), generally according to the partner's share in the profits;

3. The right to be indemnified respecting personal liabilities reasonably incurred by a partner in the ordinary and proper conduct or preservation of the partnership business or property;

4. The right to be repaid, with interest, any payment or advance beyond the amount of capital contribution;

5. The right to manage the partnership along with the other partners;

6. The duty to keep partnership books and the right to inspect and copy such books;

7. The duty to render information to copartners regarding all things affecting the partnership;

8. A fiduciary duty to co-partners, much the same as that owed by an agent to a principal; and

9. The right to a formal accounting of partnership affairs if a partner is wrongfully excluded from the partnership business or possession of its property by the copartners; or if the right to an accounting is provided in the partnership agreement; or any other circumstances rendering an accounting just and reasonable.

PARTNERSHIP PROPERTY

Every partner has a right to possess partnership property in furtherance of the partnership business. Each partner also has an equal right to the use or possession of the property to advance the partnership business. Therefore, each partner's right in partnership property is not divisible; each has a full right in the whole.

Capital contributions are the initial funds invested by the partners and comprise the partnership property. Additional property acquired is partnership property. The intent of the parties determines whether an item is owned by a partner personally or by the partnership. The UPA explains that "[u]nless the contrary intention appears, property acquired with partnership funds is partnership property."

PARTNER INTERESTS

Partner interests in the partnership must be differentiated from partnership property. The partner's interest is a personal property interest that is owned by the partner. It may be sold or pledged as collateral to a creditor. Personal creditors may attach a partner's interest to collect debts.

The transfer of a partner's interest effects the partnership in several ways. Such a transfer does not cause the transferee to become a new partner in the business because all existing partners must agree to the addition of a new partner. Also, the transfer does not exempt the transferring partner from personal liability. Nor will a transfer of an interest eliminate individual liability to the partnership's existing creditors.

The partnership agreement may state limitations and restrictions on transfers of property. The partnership may have a right of first refusal if one partner wishes to transfer his or her interest in the business.

PROFIT SHARING

Unless otherwise expressed in the partnership agreement, partners share profits and losses equally. This may be modified by agreement of the partners. Partners may share profits in proportion to the individual capital contributions made to the partnership. The same may be applied to the losses incurred, if any; losses are normally distributed in the same proportion as are profits but the partnership agreement will control in this situation.

Normally, partners do not receive a "salary" unless the partnership agreement specifies to the contrary. This holds even if one partner performs most or even all of the work in running the business. A partner who is responsible for winding up (ending) the partnership is entitled to reasonable compensation performing these services. In terms of liability, partners are jointly and severally liable for partnership debt.

GENERAL PARTNERSHIP

This business organization provides that all profits and liabilities be divided among the partners. Therefore, all partnership profits are taxed at the personal income level of each partner and all partnership losses are deductible in similar fashion. Income is treated as ordinary income. Lost suits against the partnership are paid for out of the partners' personal resources.

LaSalle Partners v. United States
48 FED.CL. 797 (2001)

This case arises over a contract entered into in 1997 between the United States General Services Administration ("GSA"), LaSalle Partners ("LaSalle"), and, subject to dispute, Moore & Associates, Inc. ("Moore"). The contract was for the purpose of providing asset management and development services to the government in connection with a plan to convert the former Naval Surface Warfare Center in White Oak, Maryland into a campus for the Food and Drug Administration ("FDA"). Under the terms of the contract, a "public-private partnership" was formed to perform the work in two phases. Phase I called for creation of a business plan and negotiation of a proposed development agreement. Phase II provided the government with

an option to proceed with the development using the business plan. In the end, GSA and FDA did not go forward using the business plan that was produced by LaSalle and Moore in Phase I of the contract. Instead, the government proceeded with the development on its own, without the assistance of a private "partner." As a result, LaSalle and Moore claim that the government proceeded with the development on its own, without the assistance of a private "partner." As a result, LaSalle and Moore claim that the government breached their contract in numerous ways. In their seven-count complaint, LaSalle and Moore seek damages of $61 million.

This action comes before the court on the government's motion for dismissal of plaintiff Moore and for partial summary judgment. The government seeks to dismiss Moore on the grounds that Moore was LaSalle's subcontractor and was never in privity with the government. The government also moves for partial summary judgment on plaintiffs' claims for breach and damages arising from the government's decision not to use plaintiffs' services for the development of the White Oak site. The government contends that because it did not exercise its development option under Phase II of the contract, it never agreed to have plaintiffs develop the site and thus the government is not liable for lost development fees and profits associated with Phase II of the contract. For the same reason, the government argues that it is not liable for development-related damages arising from abrogation of the alleged "private-public partnership" with plaintiffs.

For the reasons that follow, the court GRANTS the government's motion to dismiss plaintiff Moore and for partial summary judgment.

FACTS

A. Background

1. The solicitation

The following facts are undisputed unless otherwise noted. On May 14, 1997, GSA released the final solicitation seeking private offerors to create a plan for the development of a consolidated headquarters for FDA upon the former site of the Naval Surface Warfare Center in White Oak, Maryland. The publication of the final solicitation followed the release of a draft request for proposals and a draft solicitation. In addition, a pre-proposal conference was held on April 3, 1997. The final solicitation, "A Public-Private Partnership Opportunity," described the plan envisioned by GSA for the White Oak site: a developer would be chosen to provide development, management and other services for the new FDA headquarters. Because conventional federal funding was not available at the time, GSA planned to "explore with the developer all opportunities and approaches with respect to financing for some or all of the project costs."

The solicitation identified a two-step process for the development of the White Oak site. As set forth in the Scope of Work, the awardee was to formulate a "business plan for the project." The solicitation provided that "the business plan (and all other written products) are works made for hire and are the property of the government." After approval of the business plan, the Scope of Work provided for a "project Implementation Option." The Scope of Work went on to state: "The government, at its sole discretion, may exercise the option to proceed with the project in accordance with the business plan....If the government exercises the option, the developer, working with the government will implement the business plan and will provide all support necessary [for the project]."

The solicitation summarized the acquisition process as follows:

> ...f. The developer will prepare draft portions of the business plan for review during the period of due diligence....
>
> g. The government will have the option to negotiate with the developer a development agreement for the purpose of implementing the business plan....
>
> h. If the government so elects, the developer will proceed with implementation of the strategy contained in the business plan.
>
> i. The selected developer, with full participation by the government, will conduct a competitive process for selection of...contractors....
>
> j. The government intends that its relationship with the developer will be one of mutual cooperation

and benefit; a relationship sometimes now commonly referred to as a "public-private partnership." Under the terms of the solicitation, the government agreed to pay the developer "a firm fixed price of $200,000 upon the completion of the business plan to the reasonable satisfaction of the Contracting Officer." With respect to implementation of the project, the solicitation provided that, "any fee for the project implementation phase will be negotiated between the government and the developer." In the Price Proposal section, the solicitation next provided that any proposal should include a discussion of "fee expectations." Under this section of the solicitation, the government provided:

The developer should discuss its fee expectations for the option phase (i.e. proceeding with the project (at the government's option) in accordance with the business plan)....Fee negotiations will take place during the preparation of the business plan. They should be concluded after approval of the business plan in connection with negotiation of a development agreement. Should the Government and the developer fail to negotiate a fee or development agreement, the Government at its option may direct that the developer cease all work on the project and may negotiate with other developers for preparation and/or implementation of the business plan.

Finally, the section of the solicitation titled "Option to Extend the Term of the Contract" provided:

The Government shall have the unilateral option of extending the term of this contract beyond the Base Contract for completion of the Option for a period of approximately sixteen (16) years. The same terms and conditions contained in this contract shall apply to the option, if exercised. The Option shall be exercised upon written notification (mailed or otherwise furnished) to the Contractor within four (4) years from the date of Notice to Proceed for the Base Contract....

The exercise of options is a Government prerogative, not a contractual right on the part of the Contractor. If the Government exercises the option(s) within the prescribed time frames, the Contractor shall be bound to perform the services for the option period(s) or be subject to the default provisions of the contract.

* * * * *

2. The offer and award

On June 16, 1997, LaSalle submitted an offer for the contract. LaSalle included a signed SF-33, its technical proposal, and one attachment: a copy of a June 13, 1997 letter from Herman Bulls of LaSalle to Moore memorializing the parties' response to the solicitation. The SF-33 identified only "Herman A. Bulls, Principal, LaSalle Partners" as the offeror. The technical proposal, however, stated that, "LaSalle Partners Limited and Moore & Associates, Inc. ("the Offeror") are pleased to present this proposal for partnership," and there are references throughout the proposal to both LaSalle and Moore. In particular, the proposal stated that, "LaSalle Partners will work with Moore7 Associates, in servicing GSA/FDA. Resources will be drawn from the Project Team's wide range of specialties to deliver the services required by the contract." The technical proposal also directed the government to refer to the June 13, 1997 letter, which it called a "Partnering Agreement" between LaSalle and Moore. That letter provided as follows:

LaSalle...& Moore...have agreed to submit a joint response to the Solicitation on the following terms and conditions... Each party shall bear all costs, risks and liabilities incurred by such party arising out of its obligations and performance under this agreement. LaSalle shall be the lead firm for production and submission of the response and shall be responsible for integrating the information provided by Moore. Moore shall submit all relevant information required by LaSalle for submission of the response and shall actively participate and review the response prior to its submission to GSA. In the event that the submission by LaSalle and Moore is accepted, the parties shall enter into an agreement to jointly provide the services to GSA, including the business plan required by the Solicitation....For purposes of submission of the response, Herman E. Bulls on behalf of LaSalle and Lloyd W. Moore on behalf of Moore shall be the parties' primary points of contact.

The letter is signed by the principals of each company, Mr. Bulls and Mr. Moore. The letter was not notarized nor did it carry a corporate seal from either party.

After the best and final offer signed by LaSalle was submitted on July 21, 1997, the contract was awarded to LaSalle on July 30, 1997. The contract provided for the development of a business pan, for which the SF-33 specified a fixed price of $200,000. In the letter sent to LaSalle transmitting the award, GSA's contracting officer Elizabeth Vitale wrote:

I am pleased to inform you that your offer…has been accepted as follows:

Initial Planning Phase:	$200,000
Project Implementation Option:	To be negotiated during
	Initial Planning Phase

A signed copy of Contract GS1P97MMC0020 is enclosed. Notice is hereby given to proceed with the Initial Planning Phase of the contract.

It is undisputed that after the contract was awarded, the government consistently recognized the participation of both LaSalle and Moore in the business plan development work. GSA's press release announced the "selection of LaSalle Partners Limited of Chicago, Illinois, and Moore & Associates, Inc., of Silver Spring, Maryland, to prepare a development plan for the former Naval Surface Warfare Center (NSWC) at White Oak, Maryland." An in an article co-written by Jag Bhargava, the GSA contracting officer's representative, and Nelson Alcalde, the source selection official, the authors stated that GSA had selected "the joint venture of LaSalle Partners and Moore & Associates as the government's development partner or the former Naval Surface Warfare Center at White Oak."

3. The business plan

Work commenced on the business plan on August 4, 1997, and until sometime in 1998, both LaSalle and Moore collaborated with the government to produce the business plan contemplated by the solicitation for the development of the White Oak project. It is undisputed that the government dealt with both LaSalle and Moore on a consistent basis in meetings and written communications, and recognized that both parties were playing a role in the contract work.

According to plaintiffs, LaSalle and Moore met with government representatives in December 1997 to begin negotiations on a development agreement as required by the contract; the parties agree that they never reached agreement on this development deal. Plaintiffs contend that starting in March 1998 the government began a pattern of conduct aimed at undermining the approach to development contemplated in the solicitation and in LaSalle and Moore's proposed business plan. Specifically, plaintiffs charge that because the government concluded late in the process that plaintiffs' initially-proposed business plan was inconsistent with certain Office of Management and Budget ("OMB") requirements knows as "scoring rules," the government abandoned its relationship with plaintiffs and thereby breached its contract with plaintiffs.

Eventually, at a meeting held on January 28, 1999, GSA notified LaSalle and Moore that it did not intend to use the business plan LaSalle and Moore submitted and that it intended to develop the project on its own. The contract relationship between LaSalle and Moore and the government therefore came to an end.

* * * * *

DISCUSSION

B. Moore Is Not in Privity with the Government and Thus Does Not Have Standing

The government argues that Moore does not have standing to maintain this action because Moore was never in privity with the government. The government contends that in such circumstances, Moore's claims must be dismissed.

1. There was no joint venture between LaSalle and Moore

LaSalle and Moore argue that they formed a joint venture as offerors for the White Oak project contract and that Moore has standing as a joint venturer. If Moore is a joint venturer, it would have standing as a member of the joint venture. See Ward-Schmid Co., Inc. v. United States, 18 Cl.Ct. 572, 575 (1989). However, if Moore was simply LaSalle's subcontractor, it would not have standing See Severin v. United States, 99 Ct.Cl. 435, 443, 1943 WL 4198 (1943).

Joint ventures are recognized legal entities for contracting with the government under the Federal Acquisition Regulations ("F.A.R."). The F.A.R. identifies two types of team arrangements: joint ventures and prime contractor-subcontractor relationships. Section 9.601 of the F.A.R. provides this definition:

"Contractor team arrangement" means an arrangement in which—Two or more companies form a partnership or joint venture to act as a potential prime contractor; or

A potential prime contractor agrees with one or more other companies to have them act as its subcontractors under a specified Government contract or acquisition program.

And Section 9.603 of the F.A.R. provides:

The Government will recognize the integrity and validity of contractor team arrangements; provided, the arrangements are identified and company relationships are fully disclosed in an offer....

In the instant case, even though plaintiffs assert that they formed a joint venture to perform this contract, they have not produced any evidence to support the existence of such a joint venture. First, plaintiffs concede they did not form a separate business entity for the joint venture. Second, plaintiffs concede they did not adhere to the terms of the solicitation for joint venturers. Under the solicitation, GSA expressly required the following information from joint venture teams:

A joint venture (team arrangements) shall meet the following requirements: All offers submitted by joint ventures must include a copy of the executed joint venture agreement.

All parties to the joint venture must sign the proposed contract documents prior to award (the requirement to sign the proposal notwithstanding). In the case of corporations that are venture entities, the corporation secretary must certify that the corporation is authorized to participate in the joint venture, by so certifying in the joint venture agreement and by submitting a separate certification to the Government prior to contract award. The joint venture must also provide a certificate which identifies a single point of contact, i.e., a principal representative (by name) of the joint venture for purposes of resolution of contractual matters and payment issues.

Plaintiffs acknowledge that they did not submit the necessary corporate certification from Moore's secretary, and they also acknowledge that Moore did not sign the contract. They nonetheless argue that the government "understood" that LaSalle and Moore had become joint venturers and that it would be contracting with both parties.

In support of their contention that LaSalle and Moore formed a joint venture, plaintiffs rely on a June 13, 1997 letter from Herman Bulls of LaSalle to Moore which was submitted to the government with the solicitation. The letter includes the following statements: "LaSalle Partners Limited…and Moore & Associates, Inc.…have agreed to submit a joint response to the Solicitation on the following terms and conditions"; "LaSalle shall be the lead firm for production and submission of the response and shall be responsible for integrating the information provided by Moore."; and "In the event the submission by LaSalle and Moore is accepted, the parties shall enter into an agreement to jointly provide the services to the GSA, including the business plan required by the Solicitation."

The court concludes that this letter is not by its terms "an executed joint venture agreement" as required by the solicitation, and does not prove the existence of a joint venture. At best, the letter expresses the plaintiffs' intention to form a joint venture in the future, upon the award of the contract.

* * * * *

D. There Was No Partnership Agreement Between LaSalle and the Government That Guaranteed LaSalle the Right to Be the White Oak Project Developer

LaSalle also supports its claim for lost development fees and profits on the theory that in forming a "public-private partnership" with the government, LaSalle was guaranteed the right to develop the White Oak site regardless of whether LaSalle's business plan for the development was adopted. LaSalle alleges that the government breached its partnership obligations when it decided to proceed without LaSalle using only government funds.

LaSalle asserts that the words of the contract itself constitute an express partnership agreement. LaSalle states correctly that a "public-private partnership" was formed between LaSalle and the government. However, LaSalle's contention that a "public-private partnership" is the legal equivalent of a commercial "partnership" is not supported. LaSalle contends that the nature of its relationship with the government is spelled out in the Government Accounting Office ("GAO") publication titled, "Public-Private Partnerships: Terms Related to Building and Facility Partnerships." LaSalle claims that this pamphlet defines "public-private partnerships" as synonymous with commercial partnerships. The term "partnership" appears in the glossary of the GAO pamphlet accompanied by the following definition: "A partnership is a legal relationship existing between two entities contractually associated as joint principles in a business." LaSalle argues that the inclusion of this definition in the GAO publication is conclusive proof that the government sees "public-private partnerships" as legally-binding relationships.

The government acknowledges that the GAO pamphlet includes a definition of general commercial partnerships, but asserts that the pamphlet by its terms does not suggest that a "partnership" was created here. The court agrees. Besides defining commercial partnerships, the GAO pamphlet also includes a separate definition for the term "public-private partnership," and the definition for a "public-private partnership" is quite different from that of a general commercial partnership:

Under a public-private partnership, sometime referred to as a public-private venture, a contractual arrangement is formed between public- and private-section partners. These arrangements typically involve a government agency contracting with a private partner to renovate, construct, operate, maintain, and/or manage a facility or system, in whole or in part, that provides a public service.

Under these arrangements, the agency may retain ownership of the public facility or system, but the private party generally invests its own capital to design and develop the properties. Typically, each partner shares in income resulting from the partnership. Such a venture, although a contractual arrangement, differs from typical service contracting in t that the private-sector partner usually makes a substantial cash, at-risk, equity investment in the project, and the public sector gains access to new revenue or service delivery capacity without having to pay the private-sector partner.

Public-Private Partnerships: Terms Related to Building and Facility Partnerships, GAO/GDD-99-71, April 1999.

Thus, a "public-private partnership" is quite different form a commercial partnership. A legally-binding commercial partnership is defined as "an association of two or more persons to carry on as co-owners [of] a business for profit." Revised Uniform Partnership Act (1994) (U.L.A.) § 101. "[T]he attribute of co-ownership distinguishes a partnership from a mere agency relationship." Id. § 202 (in Comment). "A partnership is established through the voluntary agreement of the parties." In re Ashline, 37 B.R. 136 140 (Bankr.N.D.N.Y.1984). See also 59A AM. JUR.2d Partnership § 148 (1987 & Supp.2000). The essential characteristics which generally are used to support the conclusion that a partnership exists are: 1) the intentions of the parties; 2) co-ownership of the business property; and 3) sharing of the profits and generally the losses as well; and 4) evidence that each alleged partner participated in the management of the business or had some right to control the function or conduct of the business. Coca-Cola Bottling Co. of Elizabethtown, Inc. v. Coca-Cola Co., 696 F.Supp. 57, 74 D.Del.1988) ("The necessary indicia of a legal partnership...include one party having a voice in the management of the other's manner of conducting business, sharing of risks, and joint control or ownership of assets."); H.C. Nelson v. Seaboard Surety Co., 269 F.2d 882, 887 (8th Cir.1959)(holding that whether a partnership exists depends on whether parties exhibited an objective intent to satisfy the requirements of partnership. See generally 59 AM. JUR. § § 148–175.

Tested against these general commercial partnership standards, there can be no doubt that the agreement between LaSalle and the government never rose to the level of a legally-binding commercial partnership in which each side owes a fiduciary responsibility to the other. See id. § 421. The contract awarded to LaSalle, by its terms, did not contain any of the defining aspects required to create a commercial partnership. The contract did not make LaSalle a co-owner of the White Oak site or any other government assets, nor did the contract provide for any sharing of profits or losses. Indeed, the fee for preparing a satisfactory business plan was fixed at $200,000, and the contract plainly identified the work as "work for hire" and "property of the government."

Further, plaintiffs were not given any control over the project.

* * * * *

CONCLUSION

For all the reasons discussed above, plaintiffs have failed to demonstrate plaintiff Moore's standing or raise any material facts which would preclude summary judgment for the government. Accordingly, the government's motion to dismiss Moore for lack of standing and for partial summary judgment is GRANTED. In granting this motion, the court has determined that plaintiffs' claims for $59 million in lost development fees and profits fail as a matter of law....

DISSOLUTION AND TERMINATION OF THE PARTNERSHIP

Partnerships do not exist perpetually as corporations may. A partnership can terminate when one or more partners withdraw from the partnership, it merges with another partnership, the partnership agreement expires, or the partnership becomes bankrupt.

The process of terminating a partnership is called dissolution and winding up. Dissolution prevents the commencement of new business and winding up ends all old matters, pays outstanding debts, distributes any profits and assets that remain. One must differentiate between a dissolution and termination of a partnership. These terms are not interchangeable. Under the UPA, dissolution occurs when one partner ceases to be associated with carrying on the business. Therefore, if a partner dies, retires, or otherwise leaves, a partnership is dissolved, but is not necessarily terminated. The structure of the partnership changes, but this may or may not affect the business itself. The partnership may reorganize and continue without the exiting partner. Remember, however, that the Revised Uniform Partnership Act (RUPA), provides that a partnership does not automatically dissolve if a partner leaves the business.

Alternatively, dissolution of the partnership may lead to its termination. This means that the business stops; the assets are liquidated and distributed among the creditors; and the remaining amounts, if any, are distributed to partners to reimburse capital contributions and distribute any remaining profits. There are three general types of dissolution.

DISSOLUTION BY JUDICIAL DECREE

If members of the partnership are no longer able to work together they may petition a court for dissolution in the interest of preserving their investment and the property of the partnership.

DISSOLUTION BY AGREEMENT

The partnership agreement may include a limitation on the duration of the partnership. At the end of the time limit, the partnership is dissolved. Without such a limitation, or if no partnership agreement exists, the partners can unanimously consent to dissolve the partnership. In international business, parties frequently enter into relationships, termed "joint ventures," which are organized for a set time period and for a limited, specified purpose. At the end of that period or at the attainment of the purpose for which the joint venture was formed the joint venture may be terminated.

DISSOLUTION BY OPERATION OF LAW

Certain events may evolve that cause dissolution. The death of one partner automatically dissolves the partnership, but the partnership itself may survive. The partnership buys out the deceased partner's interest, which is paid to the estate of the deceased partner. Bankruptcy of the partnership or of an individual partner will also dissolve the partnership. State law should be consulted concerning these issues. "Buy-sell" agreements are often concerned with dissolution of the partnership.

LIMITED PARTNERSHIPS

The law governing limited partnerships is contained in the Revised Uniform Limited Partnership Act (RULPA), adopted by almost every state. Limited partnerships evolve when partners in a general partnership accept investments from another or others, called limited partner(s). A limited partnership must have a least one general partner and one limited partner. Also, the word "limited" must be spelled out or abbreviated in the partnership's name. The general partner(s) manages the partnership and assumes responsibility for the debts of the partnership. The limited partner(s) contributes cash or other property and owns an interest in the business, but does not participate in its management. Limited partners do no incur unlimited liability in the partnership: they are not personally liable for the debts of the partnership beyond the amount invested. This protection may be forfeited if a limited partner engages in the "management and control" of the business, that is, involves itself in the "day to day" operation of the partnership. The fact that limited partners avoid personal liability for the debts of the business provides the main advantage of a limited partnership over that of a partnership.

With the exception of the way limited partners are treated under the law and the need for legal adherence to state law in the formation of limited partnerships, general and limited partnerships function in the same way. The Revised Uniform Limited Partnership Act (RULPA) has been adopted by forty-eight states and is the primary law applicable to this business form. Limited partnerships are discussed further in Chapter Twenty.

CHAPTER QUESTIONS

1. Describe the ways in which a partnership may be created.

2. What impact does the transfer of a partner's interest have on the partnership?

3. Explain how a partnership may be dissolved.

4. Differentiate between a general partnership and a limited partnership.

5. Explain the taxation of a partnership.

Chapter Nineteen:
Corporations

A corporation is the creation of statutory law. It is an artificial person and operates as an entity separate from the person or persons who own it. It is created under state law and issues shares of ownership called stock to investors who are the owners of the corporation. However, some public corporations can be created under special provisions of federal law. The individual state corporate laws are not uniform. A codification of modern corporate law exists—the Model Business Corporation Act (MBCA) and the Revised Model Business Corporation Act (RMBCA)—neither of which has been adopted in its entirety by any state.

The corporation is the most important type of business organization in the United States. It has existed in its current form for over 100 years. The U.S. has more businesses organized in the corporate form than in any other.

Characteristics

A corporation has several advantages which may be found in its important characteristics.

A corporation has unlimited duration or perpetual succession. A corporation may continue as an entity "forever" or for a specific period of time, no matter how often ownership of its stock changes, free transferability of interest, limited liability, continuity, and centralized management. In the eyes of the law it is considered a person and can hold title to property.

Corporate Name

A corporation's name identifies it. The RMBCA requires that the corporate name contains the word "corporation," "company," "incorporated," "limited," or an abbreviation of one of these terms. The name cannot be the same as that of another corporation, nor can it be so similar to another's name so as to deceive the public. Each state keeps a registry of available corporate names. The corporation may sue or be sued in the corporate name, and is taxed as a separate entity—all activities attributable to natural persons.

Because a corporation is recognized under state and federal law as a person, it can take advantage of many of the same rights and privileges that U.S. citizens enjoy. The Bill of Rights guarantees certain protections to persons as citizens and a corporation is included within its meaning for purposes of equal protection under the Fourteenth Amendment. A corporation has access to the courts and it is entitled to due process before being denied life, liberty, or property. A corporation is also protected from unreasonable search, seizure, and double jeopardy.

The First Amendment likewise applies to a corporation. A corporation is entitled to freedom of speech. However, the Fifth Amendment protection against self-incrimination does not apply to a corporation; it applies to the corporation's individual officers and employees. The privileges and immunities clause of the U.S. Constitution (requiring each state to treat citizens of other states equally with respect to access to courts, travel rights, etc.) does not apply to a corporation (or an unincorporated association).

One difficulty existing with respect to the corporate form has to do with criminal acts committed by a corporation. Obviously, a corporation cannot be imprisoned, even though it is a "person." Instead, most courts usually fine a corporation that has violated a criminal statute. In recent years, criminal conduct that is attributable to a corporation's officers or agents may subject those individuals to possible imprisonment. Violation of the Foreign Corrupt Practices Act, for example, may subject an individual to criminal liability.

TYPES OF CORPORATIONS

Corporations may be categorized in terms of their relationship to the public, the nature of their activities, and the source of their authority. A corporation may be broadly described as public or private. More specifically, corporations may be characterized as closely held, publicly held, Subchapter S, limited liability, professional, or multinational.

CLOSELY HELD CORPORATIONS

In this form, variously called a closed corporation or family or privately held corporation, the shares of the corporation are held by one or a few shareholders. In many cases, the shareholders are members of a single family who retain complete control of all corporate-related matters. The stock issued by a closely held corporation is not publicly traded, that is, it is not bought and sold on any national stock exchange, the New York Stock Exchange or Chicago Board of Trade, for example.

PUBLICLY HELD CORPORATIONS

Conversely, this corporate form's stock is traded on one or more U.S. stock exchanges. The operation of a publicly held corporation is vastly different from that of a closely held corporation; the former is subject to national securities laws, the Securities Exchange Commission and laws of the state in which it is incorporated, does business, and has its headquarters.

Although shareholders own a publicly held corporation, control lies with the corporation's officers and managers. Of all the forms of business discussed, the corporation has the largest effect on the public at large. One reason is sheer wealth—corporations possess more money and have more assets than other entities and their regulation makes the greatest impact on society.

MULTINATIONAL CORPORATIONS

Also called transnational corporations, this type of publicly held corporation is globally preeminent. This type of publicly held corporation produces, exports, imports, and distributes its product and resource necessary to manufacture its product, worldwide. Its stock may be traded on one or more foreign stock exchanges and its officers and directors may be citizens of several nations. Their existence may have a far larger impact on society than publicly held corporations that "reside" in one country only.

SUBCHAPTER S CORPORATIONS

This form of business is referred to by the subchapter of the Internal Revenue Code, which governs its establishment. Shareholders of a close corporation who meet the requirements of the IRC may elect S status. A Subchapter S corporation is a combination of the corporate and partnership entities. It operates as a corporation, but it is taxed like a partnership. This allows shareholders to be treated as partners for tax purposes, while retaining the benefit of limited liability provided by the corporate form. An S corporation currently may not have more than 75 shareholders. All shareholders must be U.S. citizens or permanent residents of the United States. The corporation may only issue one class of stock. Not all domestic general business corporations are eligible for Subchapter S status.

PROFESSIONAL CORPORATIONS

This form of corporate entity is usually formed by doctors, accountants, lawyers, and other professionals. Benefits include tax advantages for deductions such as health benefits and pension plans. However, individuals who incorporate professionally are not protected against liability for negligent performance of their professional acts.

CLASSIFICATIONS OF CORPORATIONS

PUBLIC, PRIVATE, AND QUASI-PUBLIC CORPORATIONS

A public corporation is one established for governmental purposes and for the administration of public affairs. A city is a public or municipal corporation, acting under authority granted to it by the state. A private corporation on the other hand, is organized for charitable and benevolent purposes or for purposes of finance, industry, and commerce. It is owned by private individuals rather than by the government. A quasi-public corporation, also called a public service corporation or public utility, is a private corporation furnishing services upon which the public is especially dependent, such as water, natural gas, or electricity.

Public authorities are created by the government as a service provider. The government can render services directly or through a separate corporation or authority. The Port Authority of New York and New Jersey and the Tennessee Valley Authority are examples of public authorities. Municipal parking authorities and low-cost public housing projects may operate as public authorities.

Special Service Corporations are created to perform a particular service—transportation, savings and loan operations, insurance, banking and similar specialized purposes—and are subject to separate codes or statutes with respect to organization. Federal and state laws and administrative agencies regulate the particularities of the way in which these businesses are conducted.

PROFESSIONAL CORPORATIONS

This type of corporation is organized to conduct professional services, such as a law firm, or a medical association.

NONPROFIT CORPORATIONS

These corporations are organized for charitable (eleemosynary), scientific, cultural, educational or benevolent purposes. They are usually private and may be used in conjunction with an ordinary corporation to facilitate making contracts with the government. Examples include hospitals, nursing homes, universities, sports associations, and fraternal organizations. Many of these nonprofit corporations receive tax-deductible donations from third parties. Many are tax-exempt under state law.

Corporations are considered Domestic, Foreign or Alien depending upon where the corporation was incorporated and where it is doing business. A corporation is domestic with respect to the state under whose laws it is incorporated and foreign in all other states. A foreign corporation cannot automatically do business in another state. It must obtain a certificate of authority in the states in which it plans to operate. An alien corporation is one that is incorporated in a foreign country.

FORMATION

As was previously stated, a corporation must normally be formed in compliance with state laws. Every corporation is created under the law of one state or another. All fifty states have enacted their own laws to govern incorporation as has the District of Columbia, Guam and Puerto Rico. These statutes specify what must be included in the articles of incorporation: identifying the corporation's name, registered address and resident agent, its general purpose, the class or classes of stock to be issued, the stocks face values, and the names and addresses of the incorporators of the business. Together with any required fees, this information is sent to and filed with the secretary of state of the incorporating state. The secretary issues a certificate of incorporation (also called a charter or articles of incorporation) upon satisfaction of all requirements.

One way in which corporations are formed is through the use of promoters to create the corporation and subscribers who invest in the proposed corporation. The promoters (incorporators) take care of the plans for financing a corporation and create the corporate charter. Promoters also sell stock subscriptions and obtain loans, materials, and supplies needed to start the corporation. At this point, they are personally liable for the contracts executed because the corporation has not yet been "born." Once the corporation is formed, it may adopt the promoters' actions and agree to indemnify them for any such actions previously undertaken.

Once the state receives the filing and issues a charter or certificate of incorporation, the corporation calls its first board meeting. The board of directors is elected, stock certificates are issued, and a set of bylaws to govern the operation of the corporation is adopted. The board of directors convenes at the second meeting to elect officers and address those issues necessary to begin business.

Up to this time, Delaware is the major state of registration of corporations. The Supreme Court of Delaware is the most influential of all the courts of this country with respect to the governance of corporations. About one-half of the nation's 500 largest corporations are incorporated in Delaware, as are one-third of the corporations listed on the New York Stock Exchange. Incorporation fees and corporate taxes are comparatively low and the corporation laws are favorable, allowing corporations to operate with minimal state interference. Delaware also maintains a separate Chancery Court that, over time, has developed a staff of judges who have accumulated specialized knowledge in the laws of corporations and who are attuned to their special needs and problems. Almost any conceivable issue involving corporate law has been presented in the Chancery Court. Therefore, corporate directors and managers and their attorneys can rely on the decisional law in planning corporate changes and legal strategies. This is especially true in cases involving corporate takeovers.

IMPROPER FORMATION

Once the formation procedures are complete a *de jure* corporation results. Neither the state nor any party may question its existence. However, sometimes the incorporators, in making a good faith effort to comply with the states incorporation laws, fail. The court will then find that a *de facto* corporation exists, i.e., although there has not been total compliance, the entity created is treated as a corporation for legal and other purposes.

The *de facto* corporation must act as a corporation in order to exist. In this situation, only the state may challenge its existence. Shareholders in the *de facto* corporation maintain limited liability, to the extent of their capital contribution.

Sometimes an entity substantially deviates from the prescribed statutory procedure. In this case the entity is neither a *de jure* nor a *de facto* corporation. Numerous states require the business to file its articles of incorporation before a corporation emerges. The court may still treat the business that has not filed its articles as a corporation by estoppel. A business that acts like a corporation, follows the tax laws applicable to corporations and issues stock as a corporation is not permitted to deny the existence of the corporate form for purposes of avoiding payment of dividends of its stock.

PIERCING THE CORPORATE VEIL

There are instances in which individuals will attempt to create a corporation for illegal purposes or to hide the assets of stockholders, thereby shielding them from personal liability. The business acts like a corporation, but exists in name only. Such an entity is considered the alter ego of the shareholders. In such cases, the "corporation" usually does not hold shareholder meetings, board of director meetings, does not keep minutes of meetings, nor maintain financial books for the "corporation." The sham operation attempts to protect the assets of the individuals from creditors. If a creditor sues the "corporation," the court is able to pierce the corporate veil and hold the shareholders personally liable for the "corporation's" debts. A similar result would obtain where the shareholders commingle corporation and business assets or where corporate assets are used to pay the personal, private debt of a shareholder. The corporate form may also be pierced if the corporation fails to file required forms, informational documents, or fails to pay taxes as required. These actions are termed as a violation of the "corporate formalities" doctrine.

FINANCING THE CORPORATION

In order to operate and expand its market present, a corporation will endeavor to obtain debt and equity. Loans of the corporation are debts and the sale of interests in the corporation, i.e., ownership, is equity.

Debt is made up of three general types of instruments: notes (short-term loans, bonds), long-term loans (secured by a lien or mortgage on corporate assets) and debentures (unsecured long-term loans). Generally, the corporation must make interest payments periodically on the loans. The interest paid on debt securities is tax deductible to the corporation. However, dividend payments to the owners of equity interests in the corporation are not tax deductible. This makes debt financing an especially appealing means for a corporation to obtain financing. Risks are present as well. If a corporation is financed too heavily with debt, the IRS may consider it too thinly capitalized and loans made by shareholder will be characterized as capital contributions.

Equity is raised by corporations through the sale of shares of stock. Stock represents an ownership interest in a corporation. Shareholders, the corporation's owners, possess rights to control the business by voting, receive income through the distribution of dividends, and, if and when a corporation dissolves, share in its net assets. All of this is proportionate to the number of shares of stock in a corporation that each person owns.

A corporation must authorize the number of shares of stock in its articles of incorporation. However, not all shares must be issued or sold. The Revised Model Business Corporations Act (RMBCA) requires that articles of incorporation authorize one or more classes of stock entitling owners to unlimited voting rights and one or more classes of stock entitling owners to share the net assets of the corporation upon its dissolution. One class of stock may contain both of these provisions.

CLASSES OF STOCK

Common Stock generally gives owners the right to vote, receive income through dividend distribution and receive net assets upon the sale of stock. No preferential benefits attach to ownership so shareholders of common stock bear the greater risk of financial downturns.

Preferred stock contains some form of dividend payment or asset distribution rights not given to shares of common stock. For example, preferred stock shareholders may receive dividends before common stock shareholders at a specific rate of return expressed in the articles of incorporation. A cumulative preferred stockholder will not lose the right to receive dividends in a year when holders of other classes of stock in a corporation do not receive any dividends at all. However, they do not receive the actual dividend in that year, it is postponed (accumulated) to a year in which dividends are distributed. Additionally, they receive all past and current dividends due before holders of common stock receive any dividends.

Participating preferred stock is where owners receive dividends first and at a rate higher than the common stock shareholders do. Any remaining income is shared by both types of shareholders based on the number of shares owned.

If there is liquidation preferred stock, shares may be sold at par (face) value or a previously specified amount first. Then common stock may be sold based on the assets remaining in the corporation. This stock type may carry participation rights, also.

Convertible stock may be exchanged for common stock at an established price ratio.

Preferred stock is limited in its voting rights and a corporation usually has the right to redeem or exchange it for a previously established amount of money.

The irrelevance of these classification may increase as more states adopt the RMBCA. The act states that the articles of incorporation of a company must express the classes of stock and number of shares in each class, but does not refer to specific classes of stock as common or preferred. Thus, if only one class of stock is created in the articles of incorporation, under the RMBCA, the stock carries with it voting rights and participation rights in corporate assets. If more than one class of stock is created, the board of directors of the corporation must authorize or designate the distinguishing elements of each class.

Such powers given to a board of directors is considerable and provides broad flexibility in building the capital structure of the corporation. Shareholders however, do not benefit because it dilutes their interest in the corporation. Presently, these board powers are contrary to business trends and securities regulation.

Stock warrants—A corporation may issue the right to purchase a specific number of shares of stock at a specific price for a specific period of time. Stock warrants certify this right and may be traded as the stock is itself. If an employee receives such rights as compensation it is called a stock option. The employee may not trade these rights, however.

HOW A CORPORATION OPERATES

Management of a corporation is in the hands of shareholders, the board of directors, and corporate officers and managers. To what extent each group has superior power over the other varies within each corporation.

SHAREHOLDERS

Shareholders own the corporation, yet they have no direct control over it as one would expect owners to possess. They have no agency relationship with a corporation. All shareholders may do is exercise their right to vote for individuals: the winners of such vote becoming members of the board of directors. Shareholders' meetings are usually held annually at a time expressed in the corporate bylaws. The board of directors may call special shareholders' meetings.

Shareholders do not have to go to shareholders' meetings in order to cast their votes. They may delegate their power to vote through a proxy, a written authorization to cast votes. The SEC established proxy rules, which provide for the use of a ballot form to solicit proxies. The form must state that the shareholder's wishes will be carried out with respect to his voting instructions. Alternatively, a shareholder may give the proxy committee the power to vote his shares as they see fit. The proxy committee sends each shareholder a list of candidates and short biographies of each person up for election. They also send a statement of resolutions upon which shareholders vote.

Because most shareholders do not attend meetings, their power ostensibly rests with the corporation's management. An individual shareholder of a large corporation could not hope to have a director of his choosing placed on a ballot and actually win election. The management team actually selects those individuals it wants on the board. The shareholders provide either tacit approval by voting for them or not. As the proxy committee has access to corporate funds and a shareholder may only resort to personal funds, it is not hard to see who holds the true power in electing a board of directors.

THE BOARD OF DIRECTORS

Most boards of publicly held corporations do not actually manage a corporation in the true sense of the word. They are more likely to act as overseers and set a corporation's policy. It is in this role that the board authorizes dividend payment, alters a corporations' capital structure, selects and removes corporate officers and executive personnel, decides on the amount of compensation payable to executives, approves of executives' pension plans, and changes a corporation's bylaws. Often, however, the board simply approves of the plans the corporation's officers and management team want to effectuate. So, like shareholders to some extent, the board really does not assume the power it may theoretically seem to possess.

THE OFFICERS AND MANAGEMENT TEAM OF A CORPORATION

The power to control a corporation usually lies here. These individuals act on behalf of the corporation as its agents and are directly responsible for the day-to-day business operations. Usually, a corporation must have a president, vice-president and treasurer, but the RMBCA does not express this requirement.

Corporations, especially very large ones, tend to operate on a more impersonal level than smaller entities such as partnerships. However, the law requires that corporate management incur certain responsibilities. Officers and directors of the corporation are fiduciaries: they have a legally enforceable fiduciary obligation to shareholders. The RMBCA states these duties expressly. Managers must exercise the obligations in good faith, with the care an ordinarily prudent person in a like position would exercise under similar circumstances; and in a manner he reasonably believes to be in the best interests of the corporation. See Section 8.30 and 8.42 of the RMBCA.

Under the corporate opportunity doctrine a corporate officer or director may breach her fiduciary duty if she takes advantage of an opportunity that should belong to the corporation.

In Re Cumberland Farms, Inc., Debtor,
Demetrios B. Haseotes v. Cumberland Farms, Inc.
284 F.3D 216 (2002)

In 1992, Cumberland Farms, Inc. ("Cumberland"), a close corporation owned by the six siblings of the Haseotes family, filed a petition for reorganization under Chapter 11 of the Bankruptcy Act. Demetrios B. Haseotes—one of Cumberland's directors and the appellant here—filed claims against the corporation for roughly $3 million of pre-petition indebtedness owed on certain promissory notes. In response, Cumberland asserted a set-off claim of approximately $5.75 million, arguing that Haseotes breached his duty of loyalty when he caused his wholly-owned company to pay down a debt owed to him, while ignoring a much larger dept owed to Cumberland. The bankruptcy court agreed, and disallowed Haseotes's claims against Cumberland. On appeal, the district court affirmed. Haseotes then appealed to this court. We affirm.

* * * * *

III.

As a member of Cumberland's board of directors, Haseotes owed the corporation a fiduciary duty of loyalty and fair dealing. As the bankruptcy court observed, the principles governing a director's duty of loyalty are "broad and pervasive." In re Cumberland Farms, 249 B.R. 341, 350 (Bankr.D.Mass.2000). Corporate directors must "act with absolute fidelity to the corporation] and must place their duties to the corporation above every other financial or business obligation." Demoulas v. Demoulas Super Markets, Inc., 424 Mass. 501, 677 N.E.2d 159, 179–80 (Mass.1997).

The fiduciary duty is "especially exacting where the corporation is closely held." Cooke v. Lynn Sand & Stone Co., 37 Mass.App.Ct. 490, 640 N.E.2d 786, 791 (Mass.App.Ct. 1994) (citing Donahue v. Rodd Electrotype Co., 367 Mass. 578, 328 N.E.2d 505 (Mass.1975)). In a close corporation like Cumberland, "the relationship among the stockholders must be one of trust, confidence and absolute loyalty if the enterprise is to succeed....All participants rely on the fidelity and abilities of those stockholders who hold office. Disloyalty and self-seeking conduct on the part of any stockholder will engender bickering, corporate stalemates, and perhaps, efforts to achieve dissolution." Donahue, 328 N.E.2d at 512.

In an attempt to give substance to the general duty of loyalty, courts have recognized several more specific obligations. We focus here on a particular variant known as the corporate opportunity doctrine, which prohibits a director "from taking, for personal benefit, an opportunity or advantage that belongs to the corporation." Demoulas, 677 N.E.2d at 180.

The corporate opportunity doctrine is best understood as a "rule of disclosure." Martin v. Kagan (In re Tufts Elecs., Inc.), 746 F.2d 915, 917 (1st Cir.1984). When a corporate director learns of an opportunity that could benefit the corporation, she must inform the disinterested shareholders of all the material details of the opportunity so that they may decide whether the corporation can and should take advantage of it. Demoulas, 677 N.E.2d at 180. ("To satisfy the principle of fairness to the corporation and to meet his duty of loyalty, the fiduciary must fully disclose to the corporation, all material facts concerning the opportunity.") It is inherently unfair for the director to deny the corporation that choice and instead take the opportunity for herself. Thus, Massachusetts courts hold that "[t]he nondisclosure of a corporate opportunity is, in itself, unfair to a corporation and a breach of fiduciary duty." Id. at 183.

Accordingly, it makes no difference whether, as Haseotes insists, his decision to cause Cumberland Crude Processing, Inc. ("CCP") to repay the shipping operation before Cumberland was "a business judgment that seemed fair at the time." Haseotes argues at length that the $5.75 million at issue was best spent paying down the loan from the shipping operation. He maintains that "the bulk of the funds" was simply funneled through the shipping operation to Chemical Bank, to repay the $50 million loan that he had personally guaranteed. A default on the Chemical Bank loan, Haseotes insists, would have had catastrophic results for the whole enterprise. Be that as it may, the decision as to how to use that money was not his to make if the availability of the $5.75 million was an "opportunity" that rightfully belonged to Cumberland. We must determine, therefore, whether the availability of money in CCP constituted an "opportunity" within the meaning of the corporate opportunity doctrine.

A. Existence of a Corporate Opportunity

Normally, a corporate opportunity is thought of as a business or investment opportunity within the sphere of, or somehow related to, the corporation's own activities. See Durfee v. Durfee Canning, Inc., 323 Mass. 187, 80 N.E.2d 522, 528 (Mass.1948). So, for example, if one of Cumberland's directors learned of a gas station for sale in the New England area, she would be obligated to disclose that fact to Cumberland before purchasing the station for herself.

Although the facts here diverge somewhat from the prototypical corporate opportunity case, we agree with the Bankruptcy court that the disputed repayments fall well within the contours of the doctrine. In Demoulas, the Supreme Judicial Court of Massachusetts ("SJC") noted that recent formulations of the corporate opportunity doctrine have "given a...broad definition to the scope of potential corporate interests, and have focused on the responsibility of the fiduciary to present these possibilities to the corporation for its consideration." 677 N.E.2d at 180 (citing Victor Brudney & Robert Charles Clark, A New Look at Corporate Opportunities, 94 Harv. L.Rev. 997, 1032 n.108 (1981)) (stating that the definition of "corporate opportunity" should leave little room for the director to appropriate any opportunity conceivably advantageous to the corporation, without its consent)). The court explained that, "[I]n selecting a test for determining which ventures rightfully belong to a corporation, and are subject to the corporate opportunity doctrine, the corporation deserves broad protection....[T]he focus is on the paramount obligations of the fiduciary." Id.

Here, any funds that became available in CCP provided an opportunity to pay down CCP's $50 million debt to Cumberland. That opportunity was more than "conceivably advantageous" to Cumberland; it was desperately needed. Moreover, there is no question that the money was within Cumberland's sphere of interests—not only was it owed to Cumberland under the promissory note, but the subordination agreement explicitly required Haseotes to apply any available money toward Cumberland's loan before paying down CCP's debt to himself or other family member. Yet, instead of attempting to repay Cumberland's loan, Haseotes had CCP pay more that $5 million on the loan from his own shipping operation, which in turn was financed by the loan from Chemical Bank. In so doing, Haseotes took for himself an opportunity that properly belonged to Cumberland, in violation of his duty of loyalty.

Haseotes contends that Cumberland would have chosen (as he did) to use the money to repay Chemical Bank or other creditor of the refinery, in order to preserve the chance of selling the refinery. That argument amounts to little more than a claim that Cumberland would not have been able to take advantage of the corporate opportunity, making disclosure an empty gesture. However, the Masssachusetts courts consistently have held that "the existence of any impediment [to the corporation making use of the opportunity] does not excuse the failure of a fiduciary to present the opportunity to the board and to disclose all material details before pursuing it himself." Demoulas, 677 N.E.2d at 183; accord Durfee, 80 N.E.2d at 530. ("[T]he argument that a fiduciary is not subject to the general rule [regarding corporate opportunities] where the corporation itself is unable to take advantage of [the opportunity] is not persuasive.") To the contrary, the duty of loyalty requires that "opportunities must be presented to the corporation without regard to possible impediments, and material facts must be fully disclosed, so that the corporation may consider whether and how to address these obstacles." Demoulas, 677 N.E.2d at 181.

Nor does the fact that Haseotes may not have profited personally from the disputed repayments alter our analysis. The key point is that he "placed himself in a position in which…his own pecuniary interests could have prevented him from acting in [Cumberland's] best interest." Geller v. Allied-Lyons PLC, 42 Mass.App.Ct. 120, 674 N.E.2d 1334, 1337 (Mass.App.Ct.1997). In such circumstances, Haseotes was obligated to seek approval from Cumberland's board before acting. The requirement of disclosure "takes from the fiduciary the power to decide whether the opportunity or self-dealing transaction is in the corporation's interest and removes the temptation posed by a 'conflict between self-interest and integrity.' " Demoulas, 677 N.E.2d at 181 (quoting Durfee, 80 N.E.2ds at 528).

B. Disclosure

We turn, then, to the question whether Haseotes disclosed the opportunity to Cumberland. As a matter of law, any disclosure must be "full." Dynan v. Fritz, 400 Mass. 230, 508 N.E.2d 1371, 1378 (Mass.1987) ("[G]ood faith requires full and honest disclosure of all relevant circumstances to permit a disinterested decision maker to exercise its informed judgment.") A director plainly violates his duty of loyalty if his disclosure of the corporate opportunity is "misleading, inaccurate, and materially incomplete." Demoulas, 677 N.E.2d at 185. Similarly, "sotto voce indications do not fulfill a fiduciary's duty of full disclosure." Geller, 674 N.E.2d at 1338 (citing cases); see also id. at 1339 & n. 9 (rejecting inference that disinterested director's lack of response to alleged disclosure constituted acquiescence).

Haseotes does not attempt to show that he made the kind of full and explicit disclosure required by Massachusetts law. Instead, he argues that disclosure was unnecessary because the other members of Cumberland's board know that money was available in CCP, and that Haseotes was using it to repay the loan from his shipping operation. It is not clear whether such an argument is a viable defense to liability under the corporate opportunity doctrine. As noted above, Massachusetts courts hold that the failure to disclose a corporate opportunity is, in and of itself, a breach of the duty of loyalty. Demoulas, 677 N.E.2d at 183. We need not resolve that question here, however, because the bankruptcy court found that Cumberland's directors were not aware of the opportunity for repayment. We reverse the bankruptcy court's findings of fact only if, on the entire evidence, we are " 'left with the definite and firm conviction that a mistake has been committed.' " In re GSF Corp., 938 F.2d 1467, 1474 (1st Cir.1991) (quoting Anderson v. City of Bessemer City, 470 U.S. 564, 573 (1985) (describing standard for clear error)). We find no such clear error here. Based on the evidence presented at trial, the bankruptcy court determined that Bentas and the other members of Cumberland's board were not aware of the 1992 and 1993 payments from CCP to Haseotes and the shipping operation. Moreover, the court concluded that Haseotes knew that such payments would be viewed with disapproval by Cumberland's other directors. Not only did they violate the 1988 subordination agreement, but memos from Bentas to Haseotes—first in 1990, and again in 1992—made clear that she opposed any payments from CCP to the shipping operation or Haseotes's other enterprises.

Not surprisingly, Haseotes takes a different view of the facts. To support his claim that Bentas and the other members of Cumberland's board of directors must have known of the payments from CCP to the shipping operation, Haseotes points to testimony by Donna Walsh, Cumberland's assistant treasurer, that she sent quarterly reports to Bentas listing the balances of various shareholder accounts. One of the columns on those reports was devoted to CCP's debt to Haseotes. By comparing the balance on that account from one report to the next, Bentas could have discovered that Haseotes was causing CCP to pay down its debt to him.

However, Walsh testified that the quarterly reports were not always issued promptly. In particular, it appears that the reports for September and December, 1992, were not issued until July, 1993. Moreover, Bentas herself testified that she did not compare the quarterly reports, and was not aware of the payments from CCP to the shipping operations at the time they were made. Arthur Koumantzelis, Cumberland's chief financial officer during the relevant period and another recipient of the quarterly reports, also denied any knowledge of the challenged payments. The bankruptcy court did not commit clear error in crediting that testimony, and in concluding that Cumberland's directors were not aware of the payments made by CCP in 1992 and 1993.

Haseotes also argues that Cumberland's directors should have known that money was available in CCP and that Haseotes was using it to repay the loan from the shipping operation. Emphasizing that the quarterly reports were available for scrutiny, and that he never attempted to hide his actions, he "implies that Cumberland was negligent in not acquiring all the information pertaining to [the repayments]." In re Cumberland Farms, 249 B.R. at 354.

That argument turns the duty of disclosure on its head. "While it is true that officers and directors have a duty of reasonable supervision, this duty is for the benefit of the corporation, not the wrongdoer." Puritan Med. Ctr. v. Cashman, 413 Mass. 167, 596 N.E.2d 1004, 1008 (Mass.1992). Thus, it is not enough that, through their own investigations, the members of Cumberland's board might have learned—or at least suspected—that money was available in CCP.

The mere existence of a suspicion that there has been a breach of trust is not sufficient to constitute a confirmation. For a cestui que trust to "ratify" or confirm a breach of trust, he must be apprised of all the material facts and as well of their legal effect. No half-hearted disclosure or partial discovery is sufficient in either respect. The trustee's duty of disclosure is not discharged by leaving the cestui to draw doubtful inferences, conclusions and suspicions. Durfee, 80 N.E.2d at 531.

In sum, we conclude that the bankruptcy court did not err in finding that Haseotes breached his duty of loyalty to Cumberland when, without informing Cumberland's board of directors that money had become available in CCP, he caused CCP to apply the money toward it debt to Haseotes's shipping operation, rather than its larger debt to Cumberland. The judgment of the district court is affirmed. So ordered.

If a corporation wants to take advantage of an opportunity, but for the lack of financial wherewithal cannot, directors and officers must try to secure the needed funds, short of putting up their own, in order to secure the opportunity. Where personal advantage is taken of an opportunity and a corporation was obviously unable to utilize the opportunity for lack of finances, the courts are divided as to whether the officer or director has breached a fiduciary obligation.

Conflicts of interest also present numerous issues over which litigation results. The conflict arises when an officer, director or corporation in which an officer or director holds an interest, becomes involved in a transaction with the corporation. Under the RMBCA, a transaction in which a conflict of interest exists will not be voided under three basic circumstances: 1) If the material facts of the transaction and those of the director's or officer's interest were disclosed or otherwise known to the board or one of its committees and it authorized or otherwise approved the transaction; 2) If the material facts of the transaction and the director's or officer's interest were known to the shareholders entitled to vote and they approved the transaction; or 3) If the transaction was fair to the corporation. This last method is very broad and may be problematic.

Business Judgment Rule

Officer, directors, and stockholders are obligated to control, manage, and invest the corporation's assets for its benefit and owe both the stockholders and the corporation a duty to act honestly and with due diligence. These are legal duties. The duty of honesty explicitly forbids individuals acting as fiduciaries from personally profiting at the corporation's expense. As agents of the corporation, they must maintain loyalty to it; they are forbidden from subsuming its interest to their own. Due diligence means that fiduciaries must exercise reasonable care in managing the corporation's affairs. They may be held personally liable for acting negligently in running the corporation and making irrational or careless decisions on its behalf. In performing their responsibilities to the corporation with reasonable care, a director will be protected by the business judgment rule.

Officers and directors are legally obligated to perform their duties as they would reasonably believe to be in the corporation's best interests. They will not be held liable for making an honest mistake. If a director or officer makes a business decision in good faith and without consideration of personal gain, courts will refrain from questioning the virtue of the decision.

Guidance is also provided in the RMBCA. A director is entitled to rely on reports and other information obtained from officers or employees of the corporation whom the director reasonably believes are reliable and competent. A director also may rely on the advice of legal advisors or accountants on matters within their respective scopes of expertise; or a committee of directors (but not a committee upon which the director serves) if the director reasonably believes the committee deserves his confidence.

William Brehm, et al, v. Michael D. Eisner, et al and the Walt Disney Company 746 A.2d 244 (2000)

In this appeal from the Court of Chancery, we agree with the holding of the Court of Chancery that the stockholder derivative Complaint was subject to dismissal for failure to set forth particularized facts creating a reasonable doubt that the director defendants were disinterested and independent or that their conduct was protected by the business judgment rule. Our affirmance, however, is in part based on a somewhat different analysis than that of the Court below or the parties. Accordingly, in the interests of justice, we reverse only to the extent of providing that one aspect of the dismissal shall be without prejudice, and we remand to the Court of Chancery to provide plaintiffs a reasonable opportunity to file a further amended complaint consistent with this opinion.

The Claims before us are that: (a) the board of directors of The Walt Disney Company ("Disney") as it was constituted in 1995 (the "Old Board") breached its fiduciary duty in approving an extravagant and wasteful Employment Agreement of Michael S. Ovitz as president of Disney; (b) the Disney board of directors as it was constituted in 1996 (the "New Board") breached its fiduciary duty in agreeing to a "non-fault" termination of the Ovitz Employment Agreement, a decision that was extravagant and wasteful; and (c) the directors were not disinterested and independent.

* * * * *

Facts

This statement of facts is taken from the Complaint. We have attempted to summarize here the essence of Plaintiffs' factual allegations on the key issues before us, disregarding the many conclusions that are not supported by factual allegations.

A. The 1995 Ovitz Employment Agreement

By an agreement dated October 1, 1995, Disney hired Ovitz as its president. He was a long-time friend of Disney Chairman and CEO Michael Eisner. At the time, Ovitz was an important talent broker in Hollywood. Although he lacked experience managing a diversified public company, other companies with entertainment operations had been interested in hiring him for high-level executive positions. The Employment Agreement was unilaterally negotiated by Eisner and approved by the Old Board. Their judgment was that Ovitz was a valuable person to hire as president of Disney, and they agreed ultimately with Eisner's recommendation in awarding him an extraordinarily lucrative contract.

Ovitz' Employment Agreement had an initial term of five years and required that Ovitz "devote his full time and best efforts exclusively to the Company," with exceptions for volunteer work, service on the board of another company, and managing his passive investments. In return, Disney agreed to give Ovitz a base salary of $1 million per year, a discretionary bonus, and two sets of stock options (the "A" options and the "B" options) that collectively would enable Ovitz to purchase 5 million shares of Disney common stock.

The "A" options were scheduled to vest in three annual increments of 1 million shares each, beginning on September 30, 1998 (i.e., at the end of the third full year of employment) and continuing for the following two years (through September 2000). The agreement specifically provided that the "A" options would vest immediately if Disney granted Ovitz a non-fault termination of the Employment Agreement. The "B" options, consisting of 2 million shares, differed in two important respects. Although scheduled to vest annually starting in September 2001 (i.e., the year after the last "A" option would vest), the "B" options were conditioned on Ovitz and Disney first having agreed to extend his employment beyond the five-year term of the Employment Agreement. Furthermore, Ovitz would forfeit the right to qualify for the "B" options if his initial employment term of five years ended prematurely for any reason, even if from a non-fault termination.

The employment Agreement provided for three ways by which Ovitz' employment might end. He might serve his five years and Disney might decide against offering him a new contract. If so, Disney would owe Ovitz a $10 million termination payment. Before the end of the initial term, Disney could terminate Ovitz for "good cause" only if Ovitz committed gross negligence or malfeasance, or if Ovitz resigned voluntarily. Disney would owe Ovitz no additional compensation if it terminated him for "good cause." Termination without cause (non-fault termination) would entitle Ovitz to the present value of his remaining salary payments through September 30, 2000, a $10 million severance payment, an additional $7.5 million for each fiscal year remaining under the agreement, and the immediate vesting of the first 3 million stock options (the "A" options).

Plaintiffs allege that the Old Board knew that Disney needed a strong second-in-command. Disney had recently made several acquisitions, and questions lingered about Eisner's health due to major heart surgery. The Complaint further alleges that "Eisner had demonstrated little or no capacity to work with important or well-known subordinate executives who wanted to position themselves to succeed him," citing the departures of Disney executives Jeffrey Katzenberg, Richard Frank, and Stephen Bollenbach as examples. Thus, the Board knew that, to increase the chance for long-term success, it had to take extra care in reviewing a decision to hire Disney's new president.

But Eisner's decision that Disney should hire Ovitz as its president was not entirely well-received. When Eisner told three member of the Old Board in mid-August 1995 that he had decided to hire Ovitz, all three "denounced the decision." Although not entirely clear from the Complaint, the vote of the Old Board approving the Ovitz Employment Agreement two months later appears to have been unanimous. . . .

The Complaint then alleges that the Old Board failed properly to inform itself about the total costs and incentives of the Ovitz Employment Agreement, especially the severance package. This is the key allegation related to this issue on appeal. Specifically, plaintiffs allege that the Board failed to realize that the contract gave Ovitz an incentive to find a way to exit the Company via a non-fault termination as soon as possible because doing so would permit him to earn more than he could by fulfilling his contract. * * * * * As has been conceded by Graef Crystal, the executive compensation consultant who advised the Old Board with respect to the Ovitz Employment Agreement, the Old Board never considered the costs that would be incurred by Disney in the event Ovitz was terminated from the Company for a reason other than cause prior to the natural expiration of the Ovitz Employment Agreement.

Although repeated in various forms in the Complaint, these quoted admissions by Crystal constitute the extent of the factual support for the allegation that the Old Board failed properly to consider the severance elements of the agreement. This Court, however, must juxtapose these allegations with the legal presumption that the Old Board's conduct was a proper exercise of business judgment. That presumption includes the statutory protection for a board that relies in good faith on an expert advising the Board. We must decide whether plaintiffs' factual allegations, if proven, would rebut that presumption.

* * * * *

On December 11, 1996, Eisner and Ovitz agreed to arrange for Ovitz to leave Disney on the non-fault basis provided for in the 1995 employment Agreement. Eisner then "caused" the New Board "to rubber-stamp his decision (by 'mutual consent')." This decision was implemented by a December 27, 1996 letter to Ovitz from defendant Sanford M. Litvack, an officer and director Disney.

* * * * *

The Complaint charges the New Board with waste, computing the value of the severance package agreed to by the Board at over $140 million, consisting of cash payment of about $39 million and the value of the immediately vesting "A" options of over $101 million. The Complaint quotes Crystal, the Old Board's expert, as saying in January 1997 that Ovitz' severance package was a "shocking amount of severance." * * * * *

Analytical Framework for the Informational Component of Directorial Decision Making

Plaintiffs claim that the Court of Chancery erred when it concluded that a board of directors in "not required to be informed of every fact, but rather is required to be reasonably informed." Applying that conclusion, the Court of Chancery held that the Complaint did not create a reasonable doubt that the Old Board had satisfied the requisite informational component when it approved the Ovitz contract in 1995. In effect, Plaintiffs argue that being "reasonably informed" is too lax a standard to satisfy Delaware's legal test for the informational component of board decisions. They contend that the Disney directors on the Old Board did not avail themselves of all material information reasonably available in approving Ovitz' 1995 contract, and thereby violated their fiduciary duty of care.

The "reasonably informed" language used by the Court of Chancery here may have been a short-hand attempt to paraphrase the Delaware jurisprudence that, in making business decisions, directors must consider all material information reasonably available, and that the directors' process is actionable only if grossly negligent. The question is whether the trial court's formulation is consistent with our objective test of reasonableness, the test of materiality and concepts of gross negligence. We agree with the Court of Chancery that the standard for judging the informational component of the directors' decision making does not mean that the Board must be informed of every fact. The Board is responsible for considering only material facts that are reasonably available, not those that are immaterial or out of the Board's reasonable reach.

* * * * *

Plaintiffs' Contention that the Old Board Violated the Process Duty of Care in Approving the Ovitz Employment Agreement

Certainly in this case the economic exposure of the corporation to the payout scenarios of the Ovitz contract was material, particularly given its large size, for purposes of the directors' decision-making process. And those dollar exposure numbers were reasonably available because the logical inference from plaintiffs' allegations is that Crystal or the New Board could have calculated the numbers. Thus, the objective tests of reasonable availability and materiality were satisfied by this Complaint. But that is not the end of the inquiry for liability purposes.

The Court of Chancery interpreted the Complaint to allege that only Crystal—and not the Board itself—failed to bring to bear all the necessary information because he (Crystal) did not quantify for the Board the maximum payout to Ovitz under the non-fault termination scenario.

Alternatively, the Court of Chancery reasoned that even if the Old Board failed to make the calculation, that fact does not raise a reasonable doubt of due care because Crystal did not consider it critical to ascertain the potential costs of Ovitz' severance package. The Court's language is as follows: With regard to the alleged breach of the duty of care, Plaintiffs claim that the directors were not properly informed before they adopted the Employment Agreement because they did not know the value of the compensation package offered to Ovitz. To that end, Plaintiffs offer several statements made by Graef Crystal, the financial expert who advised the Board on the Employment Agreement, including his admission that "[n]obody quantified the total cost of the severance package and I wish we had."

The fact that Crystal did not quantify the potential severance benefits to Ovitz for terminating early without cause (under the terms of the Employment Agreement) does not create a reasonable inference that the Board failed to consider the potential cost to Disney in the event that they decided to terminate Ovitz without cause. But, even if the Board did fail to calculate the potential cost to Disney, I nevertheless think that this allegation fails to create a reasonable doubt that the former Board exercised due care. Disney's expert did not consider an inquiry into the potential cost of Ovitz' severance benefits to be critical or relevant to the Board's consideration of the Employment Agreement. Merely because Crystal now regrets not having calculated the package is not reason enough to overturn the judgment of the Board then. It is the essence of the business judgment rule that a court will not apply 20/20 hindsight to second guess a board's decision, except "in rare cases [where] a transaction may be so egregious on its face that the board approval cannot meet the test of business judgment." Because the Board's reliance on Crystal and his decision not to fully calculate the amount of severance lack "egregiousness," this is not that rare case. I think it a correct statement of law that the duty of care is still fulfilled even if a Board does not know the exact amount of a severance payout but nonetheless is fully informed about the manner in which such a payout would be calculated. A board is not required to be informed of every fact, but rather is required to be reasonably informed. Here the Plaintiffs have failed to plead facts giving rise to a reasonable doubt that the Board, as a matter of law, was reasonably informed on this issue.

* * * * *

Although the Court of Chancery did not expressly predicate its decision on 8 Del.C. Section 141(e), Crystal is presumed to be an expert on whom the board was entitled to rely in good faith under Section 141(e) in order to be "fully protected." Plaintiffs must rebut the presumption that the directors properly exercised their business judgment, including their good faith reliance on Crystal's expertise. What Crystal now believes in hindsight that he and the Board should have done in 1995 does not provide that rebuttal.

* * * * *

As for the plaintiffs' contention that the directors failed to exercise "substantive due care," we should note that such a concept is foreign to the business judgment rule. Courts do not measure, weigh or quantify directors' judgments. We do not even decide if they are reasonable in this context. Due care in the decision making context is process due care only. Irrationality is the outer limit of the business judgment rule. Irrationality may be the functional equivalent of the waste test or it may tend to show that the decision is not made in good faith, which is a key ingredient of the business judgment rule. [FN66] The business judgment rule has been well formulated by Aronson and other cases. See, e.g., Aronson v. Lewis, Del.Supr., 473 A.2d 805, 812 (1984) ("it is a presumption that in making a business decision the directors...acted on an informed basis, in good faith and in the honest belief that the action taken was in the best interests of the corporation."). Thus, directors' decisions will be respected by courts unless the directors are interested or lack independence relative to the decision, do not act in good faith, act in a manner that cannot be attributed to a rational business purpose or reach their decision by a grossly negligent process that includes the failure to consider all material facts reasonably available.

* * * * *

We agree with the conclusion of the Court of Chancery: The Board made a business decision to grant Ovitz a Non-Fault Termination. Plaintiffs may disagree with the Board's judgment as to how this matter should have been handled. But where, as here, there is no reasonable doubt as to the disinterest of or absence of fraud by the Board, mere disagreement cannot serve as grounds for imposing liability based on alleged breaches of fiduciary duty and waste. There is no allegation that the Board did not consider the pertinent issues surrounding Ovitz' termination. Plaintiffs' sole argument appears to be that they do not agree with the course of action taken by the Board regarding Ovitz' separation from Disney. This will not suffice to create a reasonable doubt that the Board's decision to grant Ovitz a Non-Fault Termination was the product of an exercise of business judgment. * * * * *

CORPORATE LIABILITY

Because a corporation is a distinct legal entity, it can execute its own contracts. Those individuals working for the corporation—agents, officers, directors, managers, and shareholders—are not personally liable for the corporation's contracts. However, if any of these persons personally guaranteed performance of a corporation's contract, he or she is held liable if the corporation fails to perform. Frequently, officers or stockholders in small corporations having limited capital resources must make personal guarantees on the corporation's contracts. If this occurs, the individual is personally liable for the contract so guaranteed, but not for any other corporate debts. Naturally, an agent acting without the required authorization may be held liable to third parties damaged by the unauthorized acts of the agent.

Torts committed against a third party by a corporate agent or employee will result in personal liability by the tortfeasor (the technical name for the person who committed the tort) to the third party for any damages suffered. If a tort is committed within the scope of an agent's or employee's duties, the corporation is liable for those tort damages. Usually, a court will award punitive damages only if an intentional tort is committed by or approved by an employee at the management level. Others within the corporate structure—shareholders, directors, managers, officers, agents, employees—are not personally liable for a tort they did not commit or approve. The actual tortfeasor and the corporation itself are liable.

The obligations of majority shareholders to minority shareholders are more difficult to define. Some courts hold that the majority has a fiduciary duty to the minority, but this duty is not absolute. Obviously, all stockholders have the right to vote their shares in their own best interest and as they see fit. If the result is disadvantageous to the minority, not much can be done, nor should it. This is the premise of majority rule in a corporation.

Nevertheless, some limitations do apply. Where the majority's decision results in an abuse of the minority shareholders or deprives them of a previously agreed upon benefit, a court may intervene. This typically occurs in small, closely-held corporations where an individual shareholder may sue the corporation because of a disagreement with an action taken by the majority under certain circumstances. This suit is termed as a derivative suit.

POWERS OF CORPORATIONS

The following are corporate powers.

CORPORATE SEAL

A corporation may have its own distinctive seal. Its use is not required unless it is mandated by statute or unless a natural person is required to use it in transacting corporate business. The use of the seal authenticates the power of the officer to conduct business on behalf of the corporation.

BYLAWS

The rules and regulations enacted by a corporation to govern its business and its shareholders, directors, and officers are called bylaws. They are usually adopted by stockholders, but in some states they may be adopted by the directors. The state of incorporation is not required to approve bylaws or an amendment made to the corporate charter. They are generally private matters for the corporation.

Corporate bylaws are subordinate to the laws of the state of incorporation, the statute under which the corporation is formed, and the charter of the corporation. A bylaw that conflicts with one of these superior controls or that is intrinsically unreasonable is invalid. Valid bylaws are binding on all stockholders, but not on third parties unless they have notice or knowledge of them.

STOCK

A corporation may issue certificates of stock representing a fractional interest in the ownership of the property possessed by the corporation. Shareholders do not own or hold an interest in any specific property of the corporation. The corporation owns all of its property.

REPURCHASING STOCK

A corporation may purchase its own stock if it is solvent at the time of purchase and it does not impair capital assets. This type of stock is then typically called treasury stock. Such shares can be sold by the corporation at any price. They can be sold at less than par value, unlike original shares, which cannot. (The RMBCA has eliminated the concept of par value and the technical differences between original shares and treasury shares that are written into conventional statutes.) Treasury stock has the character of outstanding stock. However, it cannot be voted and dividends cannot be paid.

EXECUTION OF CONTRACTS

A corporation may execute contracts in its own name.

BORROWING MONEY

A corporation has the implied power to borrow money for authorized business purposes. A corporation may issue bonds as a means for borrowing money.

EXECUTION OF COMMERCIAL PAPER

Corporations are empowered to issue or indorse commercial paper and to accept drafts.

PROPERTY

In order to carry out its express powers, property owned by the corporation may be acquired, leased, assigned for the benefit of creditors, or even sold. A number of states require that a solvent corporation may not transfer all of its property without obtaining the consent of all or a substantial its property as security or collateral for those debts. Franchises of public service companies, such as a public transportation system or public utility company, cannot mortgage or pledge their property.

DOING BUSINESS IN A FOREIGN STATE

A corporation has the express authority to engage in business in other states. It must adhere to the laws of the foreign state in which it does business.

PARTICIPATION IN OTHER BUSINESSES

A corporation, like a natural person, may participate in joint ventures and partnerships (as a general partner or in a limited partnership). The RMBCA permits a corporation to be "a promoter, partner, member, associate, or manager of any partnership, joint venture, trust, or other entity."

EMPLOYEE BENEFITS

The RMBCA grants a corporation the power "to pay pensions and establish pension plans, pension trusts, profit-sharing plans, share bonus plans, share option plans, and benefit or incentive plans for any or all of its current or former directors, officers, employees, and agents."

CHARITABLE CONTRIBUTIONS

The RMBCA authorizes a corporation "to make donations for the public welfare or for charitable, scientific, or educational purposes." No limit is placed on the amount that may be donated; however, some states through tax provisions may limit the amount that can be donated for charitable purposes. Corporations are generally prohibited from making political contribution to individual candidate for public office, but not to political action committees (PACs).

ULTRA VIRES ACTS

A corporation acting in excess of or beyond the scope of the powers granted by its charter and the statute under which it was organized, is said to be acting *ultra vires,* literally, beyond its powers. This is comparable to an agent acting beyond the scope of authority given by his or her principal. Such conduct also is inappropriate for stockholders and creditors of the corporation.

A corporation becomes a recognized entity upon the filing of its articles of incorporation with the Secretary of State as long as these articles conform to the state statute governing incorporation. Generally, the statute declares that every corporation formed under the state's law will have certain powers unless the articles of incorporation expressly exclude some of the listed powers. The statute then lists every possible power necessary to run a business. Some states make a blanket grant of all powers that a natural person running the business would possess. As a result, the modern corporation has such a broad range of powers that it is almost impossible to find an action this is *ultra vires,* unless specifically excluded.

Nonprofit corporations are more restricted as to the range of powers granted to them. Certain actions not authorized by the charters of nonprofit corporations may be determined to be *ultra vires.*

Usually, *ultra vires* cannot be raised to attack the validity of any act, contract, or transfer of property unless such act, contract, or transfer of property is extreme. For example, if a garbage removal corporation suddenly began a movie production company, it could be determined that the act was *ultra vires.* Other states still recognize the rule that an *ultra vires* contract has no effect because it was not authorized and, as such went beyond the power of the corporation.

If an *ultra vires* contract is completely performed, most states will not allow either party to claim the act was *ultra vires* in an attempt to rescind the contract. However, if neither party to the *ultra vires* contract has performed, the courts will not enforce the contract or hold either party liable for its breach.

Every state permits shareholders to obtain an injunction or to file a derivative suit to stop a corporation's board of directors or other persons involved from entering into an *ultra vires* transaction. A corporation, or a shareholder acting on its behalf, may sue those individuals who made or approved the contract in order to recover damages for the loss incurred by the corporation resulting from the *ultra vires* contract. Finally, a state attorney general may bring an action to revoke a corporation's charter if it repeatedly acts *ultra vires.*

DISSOLUTION

Theoretically, a corporation can function in perpetuity. It will expire under certain circumstances that can be either voluntary or involuntary. Voluntary dissolution occurs when the corporation files a certificate of dissolution with the Secretary of State. The board of directors and shareholders usually must approve the dissolution. This form of dissolution may occur when a company ceases to make a profit or if it is attempting to fend off a hostile takeover.

Involuntary dissolution results from an administrative or judicial procedure; usually when a corporation fails to comply with administrative requirements, such as paying taxes, maintaining a statutory agent, or failing to file required forms. A shareholder also may sue to dissolve a corporation based on gross mismanagement or unfair treatment of the stockholders.

Once the corporation is dissolved, the board of directors or a court-appointed trustee must wind up its affairs, including liquidating all corporate assets and distributing the proceeds. The proceeds are distributed to creditors first and then to shareholders. In certain cases, debts to shareholders may be subordinated to the debts of other creditors. In other cases, the debt to a shareholder who has acted improperly may be converted to shareholder equity.

Students will learn much more about the nature and function of corporations in their classes in accounting, corporate finance, and individual and entity taxation.

CHAPTER QUESTIONS

1. Why is the corporate form the most popular means for conducting business?

2. What constitutional benefits are conferred on corporations?

3. How is a corporation formed?

4. What is meant by "piercing the corporate veil"?

5. When may a director of a corporation be held personally liable for wrongful act committed against a third party in the name of the corporation?

6. Mark Stone signed articles of incorporation for the Lume-A-Star Corporation. The articles did not fully conform to the state's laws of incorporation, and, therefore, the Secretary of State did not issue a certificate of incorporation. The Acme Earth-Moving Company leased equipment to Lume-A-Star that refused to pay for it. May Acme sue Lume-A-Star for nonpayment of the rented equipment? Why or why not? May ACME sue Mark?

7. What obligations do officers and directors of a corporation owe to the corporation and its shareholders?

8. What is meant by acting *ultra vires*?

9. When may an involuntary dissolution of a corporation occur?

10. What is the difference between a *de jure* and *de facto* corporation?

11. What is the business judgment rule?

12. What is the stakeholder theory?

CHAPTER TWENTY:
LIMITED LIABILITY CORPORATIONS AND
LIMITED PARTNERSHIPS

The two most common forms of business organization selected by two or more persons entering into business together are the partnership and the corporation. As explained in previous chapters, each form has distinct advantages and disadvantages. For partnerships, the advantage is that partnership income is taxed only once (all income is "passed through" the partnership entity to the partners themselves, who are taxed only as individuals); the disadvantage is the personal liability of the partners. For corporations, the advantage is the limited liability of shareholders; the disadvantage is the double taxation of corporate income. For many entrepreneurs and investors, the ideal business form would combine the tax advantages of the partnership form of business with the limited liability of the corporate enterprise.

A relatively new form of business organization called the limited liability company (LLC) is a hybrid form that meets these needs by offering the limited liability of the corporation and the tax advantages of a partnership. Increasingly, LLCs are becoming an organizational form of choice among businesspersons—a trend encouraged by state statutes permitting their use.

In this chapter, we begin by examining the LLC. We then look at a similar type of entity that is also relatively new—the limited liability partnership (LLP). The chapter concludes with a discussion of the limited partnership, a special type of traditional partnership in which some of the partners have limited liability, and the limited liability limited partnership (LLLP). Note that although some scholars have proposed that states enact statutes allowing for limited liability sole proprietorships, to date, no state has done so.

LIMITED LIABILITY COMPANIES

Limited liability companies are governed by state LLC statutes. These laws vary, of course, from state to state. In an attempt to create more uniformity among the states in this respect, in 1995 the National Conference of Commissioners on Uniform State Laws issued the Uniform Limited Liability Company Act (ULLCA). To date, less than one-fourth of the states have adopted the ULLCA, and thus the law governing LLCs remains far from uniform. Some provisions are common to most state statutes however, and we base our discussion of LLCs in this section on these common elements.

EVOLUTION OF THE LLC

In 1977, Wyoming became the first state to pass legislation authorizing the creation of an LLC. Although LLCs emerged in the United States only in 1977, they have been in existence for over a century in other areas, including several European and South American nations. Part of the impetus behind creating LLCs in this country is that foreign investors are allowed to become LLC members.

Generally, the LLC offers U.S. firms and potential investors from other countries flexibility and opportunities greater than those available through partnerships or corporations.

In the United States, after Wyoming's adoption of an LLC statute, it still was not known how the Internal Revenue Service (IRS) would treat the LLC for tax purposes. In 1988, however, the IRS ruled that Wyoming LLCs would be taxed as partnerships instead of corporations, providing that certain requirements were met. Prior to this ruling, only one other state—Florida, in 1982—had authorized LLCs. The 1988 ruling encouraged other states to enact LLC statutes and, in less than a decade, all states had done so.

IRS rules that went into effect on January 1, 1997, encouraged even more widespread use of LLCs in the business world. These rules provide that any unincorporated business will automatically be taxed as a partnership unless it indicates otherwise on the tax form. The exceptions involve publicly traded companies, companies formed under a state incorporation statute, and certain foreign-owned companies. If a business chooses to be taxed as a corporation, it can indicate this choice by checking a box on the IRS form.

THE NATURE OF THE LLC

LLCs share many characteristics with corporations. Like corporations, LLCs are creatures of the state. In other words, they must be formed and operated in compliance with state law. Also like corporations, LLCs are legal entities apart from their owners, who are called members. As a legal person, the LLC can sue or be sued, enter into contracts, and hold title to property [ULLCA 201]. The terminology used to describe LLCs formed in other states or nations is also similar to the terminology used in corporate law. For example, an LLC formed in one state but doing business in another state is referred to in the second state as a foreign LLC.

Like shareholders in a corporation, members of an LLC enjoy limited liability [ULLCA 303]. Members of an LLC can also bring derivative actions on behalf of the LLC [ULLCA 101]. As with the corporate shareholder's derivative suit, any damages recovered go to the LLC, not to the members personally. Recall from Chapter Nineteen that courts, on occasion, will disregard the corporate entity ("pierce the corporate veil") and hold a shareholder personally liable for corporate obligations.

At issue in the following case was whether this same principle should be extended to an LLC. Could the managing member of an LLC be held personally liable for property damage caused by the LLC?

Kaycee Land and Livestock v. Flahive.
2002 WY. 73, 46 P.3D 323 (2002)

Background and Facts

Roger Flahive is the managing member of Flahive Oil & Gas LLC. To exercise mineral rights beneath certain real property, Flahive Oil & Gas entered into a contract with Kaycee Land and Livestock in Johnson County, Wyoming, allowing Flahive Oil & Gas to use the surface of Kaycee's land. Later, alleging environmental contamination to its property, Kaycee filed a suit in a Wyoming state court against Flahive and his LLC. On discovering that Flahive Oil & Gas had no assets as of the time of the suit, Kaycee asked the court to disregard the LLC entity and hold Flahive personally liable for the contamination. Before issuing a judgment in the case,

the court submitted this question to the Wyoming Supreme Court: "[I]s a claim to pierce the Limited Liability entity veil or disregard the Limited Liability Company entity in the same manner as a court would pierce a corporate veil or disregard a corporate shield, an available remedy" against an LLC? Unlike some states' statutes, Wyoming's LLC provisions do not address this issue.

KITE, Justice.

* * * * *

DECISION AND REMEDY

Every state that has enacted LLC piercing legislation has chosen to follow corporate law standards and not develop a separate LLC standard. Statutes [that] create corporations and LLCs have the same basic purpose—to limit the liability of individual investors with a corresponding benefit to economic development. Statutes created the legal fiction of the corporation being a completely separate entity which could act independently from individual persons. If the corporation were created and operated in conformance with the statutory requirements, the law would treat it as a separate entity and shelter the individual shareholders from any liability caused by corporate action, thereby encouraging investment. However, courts throughout the country have consistently recognized certain unjust circumstances can arise if immunity from liability shelters those who have failed to operate a corporation as a separate entity. Consequently, when corporations fail to follow the statutorily mandated formalities, co-mingle funds, or ignore the restrictions in their articles of incorporation regarding separate treatment of corporate property, the courts deem it appropriate to disregard the separate identity and do not permit shareholders to be sheltered from liability to third parties for damages caused by the corporations' acts.

We can discern no reason, in either law or policy, to treat LLCs differently than we treat corporations. If the members and officers of an LLC fail to treat it as a separate entity as contemplated by statute, they should not enjoy immunity from individual liability for the LLC's acts that cause damage to third parties.

* * * * *

Certainly, the various factors which would justify piercing an LLC veil would not be identical to the corporate situation for the obvious reason that many of the organizational formalities applicable to corporations do not apply to LLCs. The LLC's operation is intended to be much more flexible than a corporation's. Factors relevant to determining when to pierce the corporate veil have developed over time in a multitude of cases. It would be inadvisable in this case * * * * * to attempt to articulate all the possible factors to be applied to LLCs in Wyoming in the future. For guidance, we direct attention to commentators who have opined on the appropriate factors to be applied in the LLC context.

The Wyoming Supreme Court held that the LLC entity could be disregarded. The court concluded that there was no reason to treat an LLC differently than a corporation when considering whether to disregard the legal entity and hold its members personally liable. The court remanded the case for a determination as to whether piercing the veil was appropriate in the circumstances.

Suppose that Flahive had scrupulously followed all statutorily mandated formalities, had not commingled personal and LLC funds, and had always treated LLC property as separate and distinct from his personal property. Would the decision in this case likely have been different?

LLC FORMATION

To form an LLC, articles of organization must be filed with a central state agency—usually the secretary of state's office. Typically, the articles are required to include such information as the name of the business, its principal address, the name and address of a registered agent, the names of the owners, and information on how the LLC will be managed. The business's name must include the words Limited Liability Company or the initials LLC. In addition to filing the articles of organization, a few states require that a notice of the intention to form an LLC be published in a local newspaper.

About one-fourth of the states specifically require LLCs to have at least two owners, or members. The rest of the states usually permit one-member LLCs, although some LLC statutes are silent on this issue.

JURISDICTIONAL REQUIREMENTS

One of the significant differences between LLCs and corporations has to do with federal jurisdictional requirements. The federal jurisdiction statute provides that a corporation is deemed to be a citizen of the state where it is incorporated and maintains its principal place of business. The statute does not mention the state citizenship of partnerships, LLCs, and other unincorporated associations, but the courts have tended to regard these entities as citizens of every state in which their members are citizens.

The state citizenship of LLCs may come into play when a party sues an LLC based on diversity of citizenship. Remember that in some circumstances, such as when parties to a lawsuit are from different states, a federal court can exercise diversity jurisdiction in cases in which the amount in controversy exceeds $75,000. Total diversity of citizenship must exist, however. For example, a citizen of New York will not be able to bring a suit in federal court—on the basis of diversity jurisdiction—against multiple defendants if one of the defendants is also a citizen of New York.

ADVANTAGES AND DISADVANTAGES OF THE LLC

Although the LLC offers many advantages to businesspersons, it also has some disadvantages. We look now at some of the advantages and disadvantages of the LLC.

Advantages of the LLC

A key advantage of the LLC is that the liability of members is limited to the amount of their investments. Another advantage is the flexibility that the LLC offers in regard to business operations and management—as will be discussed shortly.

Yet another advantage is that an LLC with two or more members can choose to be taxed either as a partnership or as a corporation. An LLC that wants to distribute profits to the members may prefer to be taxed as a partnership to avoid the "double taxation" characteristic of the corporate entity. Remember that a corporation as an entity pays income taxes on its profits, and the shareholders pay personal income taxes on profits distributed as dividends. Unless an LLC indicates that it wishes to be taxed as a corporation, it is automatically taxed as a partnership by the IRS. This means that the LLC as an entity pays no taxes; rather, as in a partnership, profits are "passed through" the LLC to the members who then personally pay taxes on the profits. If LLC members want to reinvest profits in the business, however, rather than distribute the profits to members, they may prefer to be taxed as a corporation if corporate income tax rates are lower than personal tax rates. Part of the attractiveness of the LLC is this flexibility with respect to taxation.

For federal income tax purposes, one-member LLCs are automatically taxed as sole proprietorships unless they indicate that they wish to be taxed as corporations. With respect to state taxes, most states follow the IRS rules.

Disadvantages of the LLC

The disadvantages of the LLC are relatively few. Although initially there was uncertainty over how LLCs would be taxed, that disadvantage no longer exists. One remaining disadvantage is that state LLC statutes are not yet uniform. Until all of the states have adopted the ULLCA, an LLC in one state will have to check the rules in the other states in which the firm does business to ensure that it retains its limited liability. Generally, though, most—if not all—states apply to a foreign LLC (an LLC formed in another state) the law of the state where the LLC was formed.

Still another disadvantage is the lack of case law dealing with LLCs. How the courts interpret statutes provides important guidelines for businesses. Given the relative newness of the LLC as a business form in the United States, there is not, as yet, a substantial body of case law to provide this kind of guidance.

THE LLC OPERATING AGREEMENT

In an LCC, the members themselves can decide how to operate the various aspects of the business by forming an operating agreement [ULLCA 103(a)]. Operating agreements typically contain provisions relating to management, how profits will be divided, the transfer of membership interests, whether the LLC will be dissolved on the death or departure of a member, and other important issues.

An operating agreement need not be in writing and indeed need not even be formed for an LLC to exist. Generally, though, LLC members should protect their interests by forming a written operating agreement. As with any business arrangement, disputes may arise over any number of issues. If there is no agreement covering the topic under dispute, such as how profits will be divided, the state LLC statute will govern the outcome. For example, most LLC statutes provide that if the members have not specified how profits will be divided, they will be divided equally among the members.

Generally, when an issue is not covered by an operating agreement or by an LLC statute, the principles of partnership law are applied. At issue in the following case was whether partnership law should apply to a dispute between LLC members as to how business receipts were to be divided on the firm's dissolution.

Hurwitz v. Padden
581 N.W. 2D 359 (1998)

Background and Facts

Thomas Hurwitz and Michael Padden formed a two-person law firm as a partnership without a written agreement. They shared all proceeds on a fifty-fifty basis and reported all income as partnership income. Less than eighteen months later, Hurwitz filed articles of organization with the state of Minnesota to establish the firm as an LLC. More than three years later, Padden told Hurwitz that he wanted to dissolve their professional relationship. They resolved all business issues between them, except for a division of fees from several of the firm's cases. Hurwitz filed a suit in a Minnesota state court against Padden, seeking, among other things, a distribution of the fees on a fifty-fifty basis. The court applied the principles of partnership law, ruled that the fees should be divided equally, and entered a judgment in favor of Hurwitz for $101,750. Padden appealed, arguing in part that these principles of partnership law should not apply to an LLC.

SHORT, Judge.

* * * * *

* * * * * [T]he Minnesota Limited Liability Company Act specifically incorporates the definition and use of the term "dissolution" from the Uniform Partnership Act [UPA]. Under both statutes, the entity is not terminated upon dissolution, but continues until all business issues are resolved. Thus, the UPA provides guidance when examining the end stages of either entity's life. * * * * *

It is undisputed: (1) the firm had no written or oral agreement regarding the division of * * * * * fees upon dissolution; (2) the firm existed for approximately five-and-a-half years before Padden requested dissolution; (3) a little over five months elapsed between the date of dissolution and the date the parties [filed a suit] to settle the firm's remaining issues; (4) the firm's [disputed] fee cases were acquired before the firm's dissolution; (5) prior to its dissolution, the firm divided fees equally between the parties; and (6) at the time the parties filed suit, the firm was in a winding-up phase. Under these circumstances, partnership principles * * * * * govern the division of fees obtained from pre-dissolution * * * * * files. Thus, the * * * * * fees obtained from pre-dissolution case files must be divided equally between the parties, which is consistent with the pre-dissolution method of allocation.

The state intermediate appellate court affirmed the decision of the lower court. The appellate court concluded that the disputed fees should be divided equally, as all fees had been divided before the dissolution.

LLC MANAGEMENT

Basically, the members have two options for managing an LLC. The members may decide in their operating agreement to be either a "member-managed" LLC or a "manager-managed" LLC. Most LLC statutes and the ULLCA provide that unless the articles of organization specify otherwise, an LLC is assumed to be member managed [ULLCA 203(a)(6)].

Participation in Management

In a member-managed LLC, all of the members participate in management, and decisions are made by majority vote [ULLCA 404(a)]. In a manager-managed LLC, the members designate a group of persons to manage the firm. The management group may consist of only members, both members and nonmembers, or only nonmembers. Managers in a manager-managed LLC owe fiduciary duties to the LLC and its members, including the duty of loyalty and the duty of care [ULLCA 409(a), 409(h)], just as corporate directors and officers owe fiduciary duties to the corporation and its shareholders.

Operating Procedures

The members of an LLC can include provisions governing decision-making procedures in their operating agreement. For example, the agreement can include procedures for choosing or removing managers. Although most LLC statutes are silent on this issue, the ULLCA provides that members may choose and remove managers by majority vote [ULLCA 404(b)(3)].

The members are also free to include in the agreement provisions designating when and for what purposes formal members' meetings will be held. In contrast to state laws governing corporations, most state LLC statutes have no provisions regarding members' meetings.

Members may also specify in their agreement how voting rights will be apportioned. If they do not, LLC statutes in most states provide that voting rights are apportioned according to each member's capital contributions. Some states provide that, in the absence of an agreement to the contrary, each member has one vote.

LIMITED LIABILITY PARTNERSHIPS

The limited liability partnership (LLP) is similar to the LLC. The difference between an LLP and an LLC is that the LLP is designed more for professionals who normally do business as partners in a partnership. The major advantage of the LLP is that it allows a partnership to continue as a pass-through entity for tax purposes but limits the personal liability of the partners.

The first state to enact an LLP statute was Texas, in 1991. Other states quickly followed suit, and by 1997, virtually all of the states had enacted LLP statutes. Like LLCs, LLPs must be formed and operated in compliance with state statutes. The appropriate form must be filed with a central state agency, usually the secretary of state's office, and the business's name must include either the words "Limited Liability Partnership" or the initials "LLP."

In most states, it is relatively easy to convert a traditional partnership into an LLP because the firm's basic organizational structure remains the same. Additionally, all of the statutory and common law rules governing partnerships still apply (apart from those modified by the LLP statute). Normally, LLP statutes are simply amendments to a state's already existing partnership law.

The LLP form is especially attractive for two categories of businesses: professional services and family businesses. Professional service firms include law firms and accounting firms. Family limited liability partnerships are basically business organizations in which all of the partners are related.

LIABILITY IN AN LLP

Many professionals, such as attorneys and accountants, work together using the business form of the partnership. Remember that a major disadvantage of the partnership is the unlimited personal liability of its owner-partners. Partners are also subject to joint and several (individual) liability for partnership obligations. For example, suppose that a group of lawyers is operating as a partnership. A client sues one of the attorneys for malpractice and wins a large judgment, and the firm's malpractice insurance is insufficient to cover the obligation. When the attorney's personal assets are exhausted, the personal assets of the other, innocent partners can be used to satisfy the judgment.

The LLP allows professionals to avoid personal liability for the malpractice of other partners. Although LLP statutes vary from state to state, generally each state statute limits the liability of partners in some way. For example, Delaware law protects each innocent partner from the "debts and obligations of the partnership arising from negligence, wrongful acts, or misconduct." In North Carolina, Texas, and Washington, D.C., the statutes protect innocent partners from obligations arising from "errors, omissions, negligence, incompetence, or malfeasance." Although the language of these statutes may seem to apply specifically to attorneys, virtually any group of professionals can use the LLP.

Questions remain, however, regarding the exact limits of this exemption from liability. One question concerns limits on liability outside the state in which the LLP was formed. Another question is whether liability should be imposed to some extent on a negligent partner's supervising partner.

Liability outside the State of Formation

Because state LLP statutes are not uniform, a question arises when an LLP formed in one state does business in another state. If the LLP statutes in the two states provide different liability protection, which law applies? Most states apply the law of the state in which the LLP was formed, even when the firm does business in another state. Some states, though, do not expressly recognize foreign LLPs (that is, LLPs formed in another state), and others do not require foreign LLPs to register before doing business. Although there have been no cases to date in these states, disputes will likely arise over which law to apply.

Supervising Partner's Liability

A partner who commits a wrongful act, such as negligence, is liable for the results of the act. Also liable is the partner who supervises the party who commits a wrongful act. This principle generally applies to all types of partners and partnerships, including LLPs.

When the partners are members of an LLP and more than one member is negligent, how should liability be shared? Is each partner jointly and severally liable for the entire result, as a general partner would be in most states? Some states provide for proportionate liability—that is, for separate determinations of the negligence of the partners.

For example, suppose that accountants Don and Jane are partners in an LLP, with Don supervising Jane. Jane negligently fails to file tax returns for their client, Centaur Tools. Centaur files a suit against Don and Jane. In a state that does not allow for proportionate liability, Don can be held liable for the entire loss. Under a proportionate liability statute, Don will be liable for no more than his portion of the responsibility for the missed tax deadline. (Even if Jane settles the case quickly, Don will still be liable for his portion.)

FAMILY LIMITED LIABILITY PARTNERSHIPS

A family limited liability partnership (FLLP) is a limited liability partnership in which the majority of the partners are persons related to each other, essentially as spouses, parents, grandparents, siblings, cousins, nephews, or nieces. A person acting in a fiduciary capacity for persons so related can also be a partner. All of the partners must be natural persons or persons acting in a fiduciary capacity for the benefit of natural persons.

Probably the most significant use of the FLLP form of business organization is in agriculture. Family-owned farms sometimes find this form to their benefit. The FLLP offers the same advantages as other LLPs and provides some additional advantages, such as, in Iowa, an exemption from real estate transfer taxes when partnership real estate is transferred among partners.

LIMITED PARTNERSHIPS

To this point, we have been discussing relatively new forms of limited liability business organizations. We now look at a far older business organizational form that limits the liability of some of its owners—the limited partnership. Limited partnerships originated in medieval Europe and have been existence in the United States since the early 1800s. In many ways, limited partnerships are like general partnerships, but they also differ from general partnerships in several ways. Because of this, they are sometimes referred to as special partnerships.

A limited partnership consists of at least one general partner and one or more limited partners. A general partner assumes management responsibility for the partnership and so has full responsibility for the partnership and for all debts of the partnership. A limited partner contributes cash or other property and owns an interest in the firm but does not undertake any management duties and is not personally liable for partnership debts beyond the amount of her or his investment. A limited partner can forfeit limited liability by taking part in the management of the business. A comparison of the basic characteristics of general partnerships and limited partnerships appears in Exhibit 20-1.

Until 1976, the law governing limited partnerships in all states except Louisiana was the Uniform Limited Partnership Act (ULPA). Since 1976, most states and the District of Columbia have adopted the revised version of the ULPA, known as the Revised Uniform Limited Partnership Act (RULPA). Because the RULPA is the dominant law governing limited partnerships in the United States, we will refer to the RULPA in the following discussion.

FORMATION OF A LIMITED PARTNERSHIP

Compared with the informal, private, and voluntary agreement that usually suffices for a general partnership, the formation of a limited partnership is a public and formal proceeding that must follow statutory requirements. A limited partnership must have at least one general partner and one limited partner, as mentioned previously. Additionally, the partners must sign a certificate of limited partnership, which requires information similar to that found in a corporate charter. The certificate must be filed with the designated state official—under the RULPA, the secretary of state. The certificate is usually open to public inspection.

RIGHTS AND LIABILITIES OF PARTNERS

General partners, unlike limited partners, are personally liable to the partnership's creditors; thus, at least one general partner is necessary in a limited partnership so that someone has personal liability. This policy can be circumvented in states that allow a corporation to be the general partner in a partnership. Because the corporation has limited liability by virtue of corporate laws, if a corporation is the general partner, no one in the limited partnership has personal liability.

Rights of Limited Partners

Subject to the limitations that will be discussed shortly, limited partners have essentially the same rights as general partners, including the right of access to partnership books and the right to other information regarding partnership business. On dissolution of the partnership, limited partners are entitled to a return of their contributions in accordance with the partnership certificate [RULPA 201(a)(10)]. They can also assign their interests subject to the certificate [RULPA 702, 704].

The RULPA provides that a limited partner has the right to sue an outside party on behalf of the firm if the general partners with authority to do so have refused to file suit [RULPA 1001]. In addition, investor protection legislation, such as securities laws, may give some protection to limited partners.

Liabilities of Limited Partners

In contrast to the personal liability of general partners, the liability of a limited partner is limited to the capital that she or he contributes or agrees to contribute to the partnership [RULPA 502].

Exhibit 20-1:　A Comparison of General Partnerships and Limited Partnerships

Characteristic	General Partnership (UPA)	Limited Partnership (RULPA)
Creation	By agreement of two or more persons to carry on a business as co-owners for profit.	By agreement of two or more persons to carry on a business as co-owners for profit. Must include one or more general partners and one or more limited partners. Filing of a certificate with the Secretary of State is required.
Sharing of Profits and Losses	By agreement; or, in the absence of agreement, profits are shared equally by the partners, and losses are shared in the same ratio as profits.	Profits are shared as required in the certificate agreement, and losses are shared likewise, up to the amount of the limited partners' capital contributions. In the absence of a provision in the certificate agreement, profits and losses are shared on the basis of percentages of capital contributions.
Liability	Unlimited personal liability of all partners.	Unlimited personal liability of all general partners; limited partners liable only to the extent of their capital contributions.
Capital Contribution	No minimum or mandatory amount; set by agreement.	Set by agreement.
Management	By agreement, or in the absence of agreement, all partners have an equal voice.	General partners by agreement, or else each has an equal voice. Limited partners have no voice or else are subject to liability as general partners (but only if a third party has reason to believe that the limited partner is a general partner). A limited partner may act as an agent or employee of the partnership and vote on amending the certificate or on the sale or dissolution of the partnership.
Duration	By agreement, or can be dissolved by action of the partners (withdrawal), operation of law (death or bankruptcy), or court decree.	By agreement in certificate or by withdrawal, death, or mental incompetence of a general partner in absence of the right of the other general partners to continue the partnership. Death of a limited partner, unless he or she is the only remaining limited partner, does not terminate the partnership.
Distribution of Assets on Liquidation—Order of Priorities	1. Outside creditors. 2. Partner creditors. 3. Partners, according to capital contributions. 4. Partners, according to profits.	1. Outside creditors and partner creditors. 2. Partners and former partners entitled to distributions before withdrawal under the agreement or the RULPA. 3. Partners, according to capital contributions. 4. Partners, according to profits.

A limited partnership is formed by good faith compliance with the requirements for signing and filing the certificate, even if it is incomplete or defective. When a limited partner discovers a defect in the formation of the limited partnership, she or he can avoid future liability by causing an appropriate amendment or certificate to be filed or by renouncing an interest in the profits of the partnership [RULPA 304]. If the limited partner takes neither of these actions on discovery of the defect, however, the partner can be held personally liable by the firm's creditors. Liability for false statements in a partnership certificate runs in favor of persons relying on the false statements and against partners who know of the falsity but still sign the certificate [RULPA 207].

Limited Partners and Management

Limited partners enjoy limited liability so long as they do not participate in management [RULPA 303]. A limited partner who participates in management will be just as liable as a general partner to any creditor who transacts business with the limited partnership and believes, based on the limited partner's conduct, that the limited partner is a general partner [RULPA 303]. How much actual review and advisement a limited partner can engage in before being exposed to liability is an unsettled question. A limited partner who knowingly permits his or her name to be used in the name of the limited partnership is liable to creditors who extend credit to the limited partnership without knowledge that the limited partner is not a general partner [RULPA 102, 303(d)].

Although limited partners cannot participate in management, this does not mean that the general partners are totally free of restrictions in running the business. The general partners in a limited partnership have fiduciary obligations to the partnership and to the limited partners, as the following case illustrates.

BT-I v. Equitable Life Assurance Society of the United States
75 CAL.APP.4th 1406, 76 CAL.APP.4th 684E, 89 CAL.RPTR.2D 811 (1999)

Background and Facts

BT-I, a general partnership, entered into a general partnership with Equitable Life Assurance Society of the United States to develop and operate an office building and retail complex in California. Banque Paribas lent the firm $62.5 million for the project. Six years later, BT-I and Equitable dissolved their general partnership and entered into a limited partnership, with Equitable as general partner and BT-I as limited partner. Equitable was given title to the retail complex and the sole right to manage the partnership. Paragraph 5.1(c) of the limited partnership agreement gave Equitable broad powers, "provided, however, * * * * * that in no event shall the General Partner be required to take any action * * * * * to prevent Banque Paribas or any other lender from exercising any remedies in connection with any loan made to the Partnership." Later, when Banque Paribas solicited bids to "sell" its loan, Equitable (in its capacity as a corporate entity) bought it for $38.5 million. On the due date, Equitable demanded full payment from the partnership, but none was made. A month later, Equitable offered to sell the loan to the partnership, but the offer was not accepted. Equitable scheduled a foreclosure sale. Three days before the sale, BT-I offered $ 39 million for the project, but Equitable turned it down. At the sale, Equitable bought the partnership's office building. BT-I filed a suit in a California state court against Equitable, alleging in part breach of fiduciary duty. Equitable argued that the partnership agreement allowed it to buy the loans and foreclose the same as any other lender. The court entered a judgment in Equitable's favor.

BT-I appealed to a state intermediate appellate court.

BEDSWORTH, J. [Judge]

* * * * *

In general, under the California Revised Limited Partnership Act, partners may determine by agreement many aspects of their relationship. But there are limitations. A general partner of a limited partnership is subject to the same restrictions, and has the same liabilities to the partnership and other partners, as in a general partnership. * * * * *

* * * * *

We do not believe the partnership agreement can be read as permitting Equitable to purchase the loans for its own account and foreclose. Certainly, it does not expressly allow such conduct. Even if the language were broad enough to justify such an interpretation, we hold a partnership agreement cannot relieve a general partner of its fiduciary duties to a limited partner and the partnership where the purchase and foreclosure of partnership debt is involved.

Paragraph 5.1(c) provides Equitable did not have to contribute any more money to the partnership or otherwise take any action to prevent foreclosure by any lender. Fairly read, this absolves Equitable of the duty to act affirmatively to bail out the partnership from the consequences of default. But Equitable's conduct in buying and foreclosing the loans went far beyond whatever safe harbor might be found in the partnership agreement. It is one thing simply to do nothing and suffer the consequences equally with all other partners. It is another to step out of the role of partner and into that of an aggressive (and apparently greedy) lender in the marketplace. * * * * * Equitable was BT-I's partner, not its lender, and it lost sight of this most basic distinction in its haste to pounce upon the loan.

Nor can we agree with Equitable that the Revised Uniform Limited Partnership Act * * * * * [justifies] what it did. It is true the act permits the parties to vary its effect * * * * *. But the fact that the act allows the parties to structure many aspects of their relationship is not a license to freely engage in self-dealing—it remains our responsibility to delimit the outer boundaries of permissible conduct by a fiduciary. In view of the rule against waiving fundamental fiduciary duties, we cannot stretch these general provisions to include giving Equitable a free hand to act for its own self-interest. Equitable was still a fiduciary, and its conduct must be measured by fiduciary standards.

The state intermediate appellate court reversed the judgment of the lower court. A general partner in a limited partnership has the same fiduciary obligation as a general partner in a general partnership, and this duty cannot be contracted away.

DISSOLUTION OF THE LIMITED PARTNERSHIP

A limited partnership is dissolved in much the same way as an ordinary partnership. The retirement, death, or mental incompetence of a general partner can dissolve the partnership, but not if the business can be continued by one or more of the other general partners in accordance with their certificate of limited partnership or by the consent of all of the members [RULPA 801]. The death or assignment of interest of a limited partner does not dissolve the limited partnership [RULPA 702, 704, 705]. A limited partnership can be dissolved by court decree [RULPA 802].

Bankruptcy or the withdrawal of a general partner dissolves a limited partnership. Bankruptcy of a limited partner, however, does not dissolve the partnership unless it causes the bankruptcy of the limited partnership. The retirement of a general partner causes a dissolution unless the members consent to a continuation by the remaining general partners or unless this contingency is provided for in the certificate.

On dissolution, creditors' rights, including those of partners who are creditors, take first priority. Then partners and former partners receive unpaid distributions of partnership assets and, except as otherwise agreed, amounts representing returns on their contributions and amounts proportionate to their shares of the distributions [RULPA 804].

LIMITED LIABILITY LIMITED PARTNERSHIPS

A limited liability limited partnership (LLLP) is a type of limited partnership. An LLLP differs from a limited partnership in that the liability of a general partner in an LLLP is the same as the liability of a limited partner. That is, the liability of all partners in an LLLP is limited to the amount of their investments in the firm.

A few states provide expressly for LLLPs. In states that do not provide for LLLPs but do allow for limited partnerships and limited liability partnerships, a limited partnership should probably still be able to register with the state as an LLLP.

MAJOR BUSINESS FORMS COMPARED

When deciding which form of business organization would be most appropriate, businesspersons normally take several factors into consideration. As mentioned earlier, these factors include ease of creation, the liability of the owners, tax considerations, and the need for capital. Each major form of business organization offers distinct advantages and disadvantages with respect to these and other factors.

For example, the sole proprietorship has the advantage of being easily and inexpensively established, but the owner faces personal liability for business obligations as well as restrictions on obtaining capital for additional financing. The partnership is relatively easy to establish and provides a way for the business to obtain capital (from partners' contributions). It enjoys tax benefits as well. The partnership also has a major disadvantage: the personal liability of the partners. One of the advantages of the corporate form is that capital for expansion can be obtained by the issuance of shares of stock. Another advantage is the limited liability of the shareholder-owners. The limited liability company and the limited liability partnership increasingly are becoming forms of choice because of the many advantages they offer with respect to both the liability of the owners and taxation. Refer to Exhibit 20-2, following, for major forms of business compared.

EXHIBIT 20-2: MAJOR FORMS OF BUSINESS COMPARED

Characteristic	Sole Proprietorship	Partnership	Corporation
Method of Creation	Created at will by owner.	Created by agreement of the parties.	Charter issued by state—created by statutory authorization.
Legal Position	Not a separate entity; owner if the business.	Not a separate legal entity in many states.	Always a legal entity separate and distinct from its owners—a legal fiction for the purposes of owning property and being a party to litigation.
Liability	Unlimited liability	Unlimited liability.	Limited liability of shareholders—shareholders are not liable for the debts of the corporation.
Duration	Determined by owner; automatically dissolved on owner's death.	Terminated by agreement of the partners, by the death of one or more of the partners, by withdrawal of a partner, by bankruptcy, and so on.	Can have perpetual existence.
Transferability of Interest	Interest can be transferred, but individual's proprietorship then ends.	Although partnership interest can be assigned, assignee does not have full rights of a partner.	Shares of stock can be transferred.
Management	Completely at owner's discretion.	Each general partner has a direct and equal voice in management unless expressly agreed otherwise in the partnership agreement.	Shareholders elect directors, who set policy and appoint officers.
Taxation	Owner pays personal taxes on business income.	Each partner pays pro rata share of income taxes on net profits, whether or not they are distributed.	Double taxation—corporation pays income tax on net profits, with no deduction for dividends, and shareholders pay income tax on disbursed dividends they receive.
Organizational Fees, Annual License Fees, and Annual Reports	None.	None.	All required.
Transaction of Business in other states	Generally, no limitation.	Generally no limitation. (A few states have enacted statues requiring that foreign partnerships qualify to do business there.)	Normally must qualify to do business and obtain certificate of authority.

EXHIBIT 20-2: MAJOR FORMS OF BUSINESS COMPARED (CONTINUED)

Characteristic	Limited Partnership	Limited Liability Company	Limited Liability Partnership
Method of Creation	Created by agreement to carry on a business for profit. At least one party must be a general partner and the other(s) limited partner(s). Certificate of limited partnership is filed. Charter must be issued by the state.	Created by an agreement of the owner-members of the company. Articles of organization are filed. Charter must be issued by the state.	Created by an agreement of the partners. Certificate of a limited liability partnership is filed. Charter must be issued by state.
Legal Position	Treated as a legal entity.	Treated as a legal entity.	Generally, treated same as a general partnership.
Liability	Unlimited liability of all general partners; limited partners are liable only to the extent of capital contributions.	Member-owners' liability is limited to the amount of capital contributions or investments.	Varies from state to state but usually limits liability of a partner for certain acts committed by other partners.
Duration	By agreement in certificate, or by termination of the last general partner (withdrawal, death, and so on) or last limited partner.	Unless a single-member LLC, can have perpetual existence (same as corporation).	Terminated by agreement of partners, by death or withdrawal of a partner, or by law (such as bankruptcy).
Transferability of Interest	Interest can be assigned (same as general partnership), but if assignee becomes a member with consent of other partners, certificate must be amended.	Member interests are freely transferable.	Interest can be assigned same as in a general partnership.
Management	General partners have equal voice or by agreement. Limited partners may not retain limited liability if they actively participate in management.	Member-owners can fully participate in management, or member-owners can select managers to manage the firm on behalf of the members.	Same as a general partnership.
Taxation	Generally taxed as a partnership.	LLC is not taxed, and members are taxed personally on profits	Same as a general partnership.
Organizational Fees, Annual License Fees, and Annual Reports	Organizational fee required; usually not others.	Organizational fee required; others vary with states.	Organizational fee required (such as a set amount per partner); usually not others.
Transaction of Business in other states	Generally, no limitation.	Generally, no limitation but may vary depending on state.	Generally, no limitation, but state laws vary as to formation and limitation of liability.

Unit IV
Appendices

Appendix A:
Constitution of the United States

We the People of the United States, in Order to form a more perfect Union, establish Justice, insure domestic Tranquility, provide for the common defense, promote the general Welfare, and secure the Blessings of Liberty to ourselves and our Posterity, do ordain and establish this Constitution for the United States of America.

Article I
Section 1
All legislative Powers herein granted shall be vested in a Congress of the United States, which shall consist of a Senate and House of Representatives.

Section 2
The House of Representatives shall be composed of Members chosen every second Year by the People of the several States, and the Electors in each State shall have the Qualifications requisite for Electors of the most numerous Branch of the State Legislature.

No Person shall be a Representative who shall not have attained to the Age of twenty five Years, and been seven Years a Citizen of the United States, and who shall not, when elected, be an Inhabitant of that State in which he shall be chosen.

Representatives and direct Taxes shall be apportioned among the several States which may be included within this Union, according to their respective Numbers, which shall be determined by adding to the whole Number of free Persons, including those bound to Service for a Term of Years, and excluding Indians not taxed, three fifths of all other Persons. The actual Enumeration shall be made within three Years after the first Meeting of the Congress of the United States, and within every subsequent Term of ten Years, in such Manner as they shall by Law direct. The number of Representatives shall not exceed one for every thirty Thousand, but each State shall have at Least one Representative; and until such enumeration shall be made, the State of New Hampshire shall be entitled to chuse three, Massachusetts eight, Rhode Island and Providence Plantations one, Connecticut five, New-York six, New Jersey four, Pennsylvania eight, Delaware one, Maryland six, Virginia ten, North Carolina five, South Carolina five, and Georgia three.

When vacancies happen in the Representation from any State, the Executive Authority thereof shall issue Writs of Election to fill such vacancies.

The House of Representatives shall chuse their Speaker and other Officers; and shall have the sole Power of Impeachment.

SECTION 3

The Senate of the United States shall be composed of two Senators from each State, chosen by the Legislature thereof, for six Years; and each Senator shall have one Vote.

Immediately after they shall be assembled in Consequence of the first Election, they shall be divided as equally as may be into three Classes. The Seats of the Senators of the first Class shall be vacated at the Expiration of the second Year, of the second Class at the Expiration of the fourth Year, and of the third Class at the Expiration of the sixth Year, so that one third may be chosen every second Year; and if Vacancies happen by Resignation or otherwise, during the Recess of the Legislature of any State, the Executive thereof may make temporary Appointments until the next Meeting of the Legislature, which shall then fill such Vacancies.

No Person shall be a Senator who shall not have attained to the Age of thirty Years, and been nine Years a Citizen of the United States, and who shall not, when elected, be an Inhabitant of that State for which he shall be chosen.

The Vice President of the United States shall be President of the Senate, but shall have no Vote, unless they be equally divided.

The Senate shall chuse their other Officers, and also a President pro tempore, in the Absence of the Vice President, or when he shall exercise the Office of President of the United States.

The Senate shall have the sole power to try all Impeachments. When sitting for that Purpose, they shall be an Oath or Affirmation. When the President of the United States is tried, the Chief Justice shall preside: And no Person shall be convicted without the Concurrence of two thirds of the Members present.

Judgment in Cases of Impeachment shall not extend further than to removal from Office, and disqualification to hold and enjoy any Office of honor, Trust or Profit under the United States: but the Party convicted shall nevertheless be liable and subject to Indictment, Trial, Judgment and Punishment, according to Law.

SECTION 4

The Times, Places and Manner of holding Elections for Senators and Representatives, shall be prescribed in each State by the Legislature thereof: but the Congress may at any time by Law make or alter such Regulations, except as to the Places of chusing Senators.

The Congress shall assemble at least once in every Year, and such Meeting shall be on the first Monday in December, unless they shall by Law appoint a different Day.

SECTION 5

Each House shall be the Judge of the Elections, Returns and Qualifications of its own Members, and a Majority of each shall constitute a Quorum to do Business; but a smaller Number may adjourn from day to day, and may be authorized to compel the Attendance of absent Members, in such Manner, and under such Penalties as each House may provide.

Each House may determine the Rules of its Proceedings, punish its Members for disorderly Behaviour, and, with the Concurrence of two thirds, expel a Member.

Each House shall keep a Journal of its Proceedings, and from time to time publish the same, excepting such Parts as may in their Judgment require Secrecy; and the Yeas and Nays of the Members of either House on any question shall, at the Desire of one fifth of those Present, be entered on the Journal.

Neither House, during the Session of Congress, shall, without the Consent of the other, adjourn for more than three days, nor to any other Place than that in which the two Houses shall be sitting.

SECTION 6

The Senators and Representatives shall receive a Compensation for their Services, to be ascertained by Law, and paid out of the Treasury of the United States. They shall in all Cases, except Treason, Felony and Breach of the Peace, be privileged from Arrest and Breach of the Peace, be privileged from Arrest during their Attendance at the Session of their respective Houses, and in going to and returning from the same; and for any Speech or Debate in either House, they shall not be questioned in any other Place.

No Senator or Representative shall, during the Time for which he was elected, be appointed to any civil Office under the Authority of the United States, which shall have been created, or the Emoluments whereof shall have been encreased during such time; and no Person holding any Office under the United States, shall be a Member of either House during his Continuance in Office.

SECTION 7

All Bills for raising Revenue shall originate in the House of Representatives; but the Senate may propose or concur with Amendments as on other Bills.

Every Bill which shall have passed the House of Representatives and the Senate, shall, before it become a Law, be presented to the President of the United States; If he approve he shall sign it, but if not he shall return it, with his Objections to that House in which it shall have originated, who shall enter the Objections at large on their Journal, and proceed to reconsider it. If after such Reconsideration two thirds of that House shall agree to pass the Bill, it shall be sent, together with the Objections, to the other House, by which it shall likewise be reconsidered, and if approved by two thirds of that House, it shall become a Law. But in all such Cases the Votes of both Houses shall be determined by Yeas and Nays, and the Names of the Persons voting for and against the Bill shall be entered on the Journal of each House respectively. If any Bill shall not be returned by the President within ten Days (Sundays excepted) after it shall have been presented to him, the Same shall be a Law, in like Manner as if he had signed it, unless the Congress by their Adjournment prevent its Return, in which Case it shall not be a Law.

Every Order, Resolution, or Vote to which the Concurrence of the Senate and House of Representatives may be necessary (except on a question of Adjournment) shall be presented to the President of the United States; and before the Same shall take Effect, shall be approved by him, or being disapproved by him, shall be repassed by two thirds of the Senate and House of Representatives, according to the Rules and Limitations prescribed in the Case of a Bill.

SECTION 8

The Congress shall have Power to lay and collect Taxes, Duties, Imposts and Excises, to pay the Debts and provide for the common Defense and general Welfare of the United States; but all Duties, Imposts and Excises shall be uniform throughout the United States;

To borrow Money on the credit of the United States;

To regulate Commerce with foreign Nations, and among the several States, and with the Indian Tribes;

To establish an uniform Rule of Naturalization, and uniform Laws on the subject of Bankruptcies throughout the United States;

To coin Money, regulate the Value thereof, and of foreign Coin, and fix the Standard of Weights and Measures;

To provide for the Punishment of counterfeiting the Securities and current Coin of the United States;

To establish Post Offices and post Roads;

To promote the Progress of Science and useful Arts, by securing for limited Times to Authors and Inventors the exclusive Right to their respective Writings and Discoveries;

To constitute Tribunals inferior to the supreme Court;

To define and punish Piracies and Felonies committed on the high Seas, and Offenses against the Law of Nations;

To declare War, grant Letters of Marque and Reprisal, and make Rules concerning Captures on Land and Water;

To raise and support Armies, but no Appropriation of Money to that Use shall be for a longer Term than two Years;

To provide and maintain a Navy;

To make Rules for the Government and Regulation of the land and naval Forces;

To provide for calling forth the Militia to execute the Laws of the Union, suppress Insurrections and repel Invasions;

To provide for organizing, arming, and disciplining, the Militia, and for governing such Part of them as may be employed in the Service of the United States, reserving to the States respectively, the Appointment of the Officers, and the Authority of training the Militia according to the discipline described by Congress;

To exercise exclusive Legislation in all Cases whatsoever, over such District (not exceeding ten Miles square) as may, by Cession of particular States, and the Acceptance of Congress, become the Seat of the Government of the United States, and to exercise like Authority over all Places purchased by the Consent of the Legislature of the State in which the Same shall be, for the Erection of Forts, Magazines, Arsenals, dock-Yards, and other needful Buildings;—And

To make all Laws which shall be necessary and proper for carrying into Execution the foregoing Powers, and all other Powers vested by this Constitution in the Government of the United States, or in any Department or Officer thereof.

SECTION 9

The Migration or Importation of such Persons as any of the States now existing shall think proper to admit, shall not be prohibited by the Congress prior to the Year one thousand eight hundred and eight, but a Tax of Duty may be imposed on such Importation, not exceeding ten dollars for each Person.

The Privilege of the Writ of Habeas Corpus shall not be suspended, unless when in Cases of Rebellion or Invasion the public Safety may require it.

No Bill of Attainder or ex post facto Law shall be passed.

No Capitation, or other direct, Tax shall be laid, unless in

Proportion to the Census or Enumeration herein before directed to be taken.

No Tax or Duty shall be laid on Articles exported from any State.

No Preference shall be given by any Regulation of Commerce or Revenue to the Ports of one State over those of another; nor shall Vessels bound to, or from, one State, be obliged to enter, clear, or pay Duties in another.

No Money shall be drawn from the Treasury, but in Consequence of Appropriations made by Laws; and a regular Statement and Account of the Receipts and Expenditures of all public Money shall be published from time to time.

No Title of Nobility shall be granted by the United States: And no Person holding any Office of Profit or Trust under them, shall, without the Consent of the Congress, accept of any present, Emolument, Office, or Title, of any kind whatever, from any King, Prince, or foreign State.

SECTION 10
No State shall enter into any Treaty, Alliance, or Confederation; grant Letters of Marque and Reprisal; coin Money; emit Bills of Credit; make any Thing but gold and silver Coin a Tender in Payment of Debts; pass any Bill of Attainder, ex post facto Law, or Law impairing the Obligation of Contracts, or grant any Title of Nobility.

No State shall, without the Consent of the Congress, lay any Imposts or Duties on Imports or Exports, except what may be absolutely necessary for executing its inspection Laws: and the net Produce of all Duties and Imposts, laid by any State on Imports or Exports, shall be for the Use of the Treasury of the United States; and all such Laws shall be subject to the Revision and Controul of the Congress.

No State shall, without the Consent of Congress, lay any Duty of Tonnage, keep Troops, or Ships of War in time of Peace, enter into any Agreement or Compact with another State, or with a foreign Power, or engage in War, unless actually invaded, or in such imminent Danger as will not admit of delay.

ARTICLE II
SECTION 1
The executive Power shall be vested in a President of the United States of America. He shall hold his Office during the Term of four Years, and, together with the Vice President, chosen for the same Term, be elected, as follows:

Each State shall appoint, in such Manner as the Legislature thereof may direct, a Number of Electors, equal to the whole Number of Senators and Representatives to which the State may be entitled in the Congress: but no Senator or Representative, or Person holding an Office of Trust or Profit under the United States, shall be appointed an Elector.

The Electors shall meet in their respective States, and vote by Ballot for two Persons, of whom one at least shall not be an Inhabitant of the same State with themselves. And they shall make a list of all the Persons voted for, and of the Number of Votes for each; which List they shall sign and certify, and transmit sealed to the Seat of the Government of the United States, directed to the President of the Senate. The President of the Senate shall, in the presence of the Senate and House of Representatives, open all the Certificates, and the Votes shall be counted. The Person having the greatest Number of Votes shall be the President, if such Number be a Majority of the whole Number of Electors appointed; and if there be more than one who have such Majority, and have an equal Number of Votes, then the House of Representatives shall immediately chuse by Ballot one of them for President; and if no Person have a Majority, then from the five highest on the List the said House shall in like Manner chuse the President. But in chusing the President, the Votes shall be taken by States, the Representation from each State having one Vote; A quorum for this Purpose shall consist of a Member or Members from two thirds of the States, and a Majority of all the States shall be necessary to a Choice. In every Case, after the Choice of the President, the Person having the Greatest Number of Votes of the Electors shall be the Vice President. But if there should remain two or more who have equal Votes, the Senate shall chuse from them by Ballot the Vice President.

The Congress may determine the Time of Chusing the Electors, and the Day on which they shall give their Votes; which Day shall be the same throughout the United States.

No Person except a natural born Citizen, or a Citizen of the United States, at the time of the Adoption of this Constitution, shall be eligible to the Office of President; neither shall any Person be eligible to that Office who shall not have attained to the Age of thirty five Years, and been fourteen Years a Resident within the United States.

In Case of the Removal of the President from Office, or of his Death, Resignation, or Inability to discharge the Powers and Duties of the said Office, the Same shall devolve on the Vice President, and the Congress may by Law provide for the Case of Removal, Death, Resignation or Inability, both of the President and Vice President, declaring what Officer shall then act as President, and such Officer shall act accordingly, until the Disability be removed, or a President shall be elected.

The President shall, at stated Times, receive for his Services, a Compensation, which shall neither be encreased nor diminished during the Period for which he shall have been elected, and he shall not receive within that Period any other Emolument from the United States, or any of them.

Before he enter on the Execution of his Office, he shall take the following Oath or Affirmation:—"I do solemnly swear (or affirm) that I will faithfully execute the Office of President of the United States, and will to the best of my Ability, preserve, protect and defend the Constitution of the United States."

Section 2

The President shall be Commander in Chief of the Army and Navy of the United States, and of the Militia of the several States, when called into the actual Service of the United States; he may require the Opinion, in writing, of the principal Officer in each of the executive Departments, upon any Subject relating to the Duties of their respective Offices, and he shall have Power to grant Reprieves and Pardons for Offences against the United States, except in Cases of Impeachment.

He shall have Power, by and with the Advice and Consent of the Senate, to make Treaties, providing two thirds of the Senators present concur; and he shall nominate, and by and with the Advice and Consent of the Senate, shall appoint Ambassadors, other public Ministers and Consuls, Judges of the supreme Court, and all other Officers of the United States, whose Appointments are not herein otherwise provided for, and which shall be established by Law: but the Congress may by Law vest the Appointment of such inferior Officers, as they think proper, in the President alone, in the Courts of Law, or in the Heads of Departments.

The President shall have Power to fill up all Vacancies that may happen during the Recess of the Senate, by granting Commissions which shall expire at the End of their next Session.

SECTION 3

He shall from time to time give to the Congress Information of the State of the Union, and recommend to their Consideration such Measures as he shall judge necessary and expedient; he may, on extraordinary Occasions, convene both Houses, or either of them, and in Case of Disagreement between them, with Respect to the Time of Adjournment, he may adjourn them to such Time as he shall think proper, he shall receive Ambassadors and other public Ministers; he shall take Care that the Laws be faithfully executed, and shall Commission all the Offices of the United States.

SECTION 4

The President, Vice President and all civil Officers of the United States, shall be removed from Office on Impeachment for, and Conviction of, Treason, Bribery, or other Crimes and Misdemeanors.

ARTICLE III

SECTION 1

The judicial Power of the United States, shall be vested in one supreme Court, and in such inferior Courts as the Congress may from time to time ordain and establish. The Judges, both of the supreme and inferior Courts, shall hold their Offices during good Behaviour, and shall, at Times, receive for their Services, a Compensation, which shall not be diminished during their Continuance in Office.

SECTION 2

The judicial Power shall extend to all Cases, in Law and Equity, arising under this Constitution, the Laws of the United States, and Treaties made, or which shall be made, under their Authority;—to all Cases affecting Ambassadors, other public Ministers and Consuls;—to all Cases of admiralty and maritime Jurisdiction;—to Controversies to which the United States shall be a Party;—to controversies between two or more States;—between a State and Citizens of another State;—between Citizens of different States;—between Citizens of the same State claiming Lands under Grants of different States; and between a State, or the Citizens thereof, and foreign States, Citizens or Subjects.

In all Cases affecting Ambassadors, other public Ministers and Consuls, and those in which a State shall be Party, the supreme Court shall have original Jurisdiction. In all the other Cases before mentioned, the supreme Court shall have appellate Jurisdiction, both as to Law and Fact, with such Exceptions, and under such Regulations as the Congress shall make.

The Trial of all Crimes, except in Cases of Impeachment, shall be by Jury; and such Trial shall be held in the State where the said Crimes shall have been committed; but when not committed within any State, the Trial shall be at such Place or Places as the Congress may by Law have directed.

SECTION 3

Treason against the United States, shall consist only in levying War against them, or in adhering to their Enemies, giving them Aid and Comfort. No Person shall be convicted of Treason unless on the Testimony of two Witnesses to the same overt Act, or on Confession in open Court.

The Congress shall have Power to declare the Punishment of Treason, but no Attainder of Treason shall work Corruption of Blood, or Forfeiture except during the Life of the Person attainted.

ARTICLE IV
SECTION 1

Full Faith and Credit shall be given in each State to the public Acts, Records, and judicial Proceedings of every other State. And the Congress may by general Laws prescribe the Manner in which such Arts, Records and Proceedings shall be proved, and the Effect thereof.

SECTION 2

The Citizens of each State shall be entitled to all Privileges and Immunities of Citizens in the several States.

A Person charged in any State with Treason, Felony, or other Crime, who shall flee from Justice, and be found in another State, shall on Demand of the executive Authority of the State from which he fled, be delivered up, to be removed to the State having Jurisdiction of the Crime.

No Person held to Service or Labour in one State, under the Laws thereof, escaping into another, shall, in Consequence of any Law or Regulation therein, be discharged from such Service or Labour, but shall be delivered up on Claim of the Party to whom such Service or Labour may be due.

SECTION 3

New States may be admitted by the Congress into this Union; but no new State shall be formed or erected within the Jurisdiction of any other State; nor any State be formed by the Junction of two or more States, or Parts of States, without the Consent of the Legislatures of the States concerned as well as the Congress.

The Congress shall have Power to dispose of and make all needful Rules and Regulations respecting the Territory or other Property belonging to the United States; and nothing in this Constitution shall be so construed as to Prejudice any Claims of the United States, or of any particular State.

SECTION 4

The United States shall guarantee to every State in this Union a Republican Form of Government, and shall protect each of them against Invasion; and on Application of the Legislature, or of the Executive (when the Legislature cannot be convened) against domestic Violence.

ARTICLE V

The Congress, whenever two thirds of both Houses shall deem it necessary, shall propose Amendments to this Constitution, or, on the Application of the Legislatures of two thirds of the several States, shall call a Convention for proposing Amendments, which, in either Case, shall be valid to all Intents and Purposes, as Part of this Constitution, when ratified by the Legislatures of three fourths of the several States, or by Conventions in three fourths thereof, as the one or the other Mode of Ratification may be proposed by the Congress; Provided that no Amendment which may be made prior to the Year One thousand eight hundred and eight shall in any Manner affect the first and fourth Clauses in the Ninth Section of the first Article; and that no State, without its Consent, shall be deprived of its equal Suffrage in the Senate.

ARTICLE VI

All Debts contracted and Engagements entered into, before the Adoption of this Constitution, shall be as valid against the United States under this Constitution, as under the Confederation.

This Constitution, and the Laws of the United States which shall be made in Pursuance thereof; and all Treaties made, or which shall be made, under the Authority of the United States, shall be the supreme Law of the Land; and the Judges in every State shall be bound thereby, any Thing in the Constitution or Laws of any State to the Contrary notwithstanding.

The Senators and Representatives before mentioned, and the Members of the several State Legislatures, and all executive and judicial Officers, both of the United States and of the Several States, shall be bound by Oath or Affirmation, to support this Constitution; but no religious Test shall ever be required as a Qualification to any Office or public Trust under the United States.

ARTICLE VII

The Ratification of the Conventions of nine States, shall be sufficient for the Establishment of this Constitution between the States so ratifying the Same.

AMENDMENT I [1791]

Congress shall make no law respecting an establishment of religion, or prohibiting the free exercise thereof; or abridging the freedom of speech, or the press; or the right of the people peaceably to assemble, and to petition the Government for a redress of grievances.

AMENDMENT II [1791]

A well regulated Militia, being necessary to the security for a free State, the right of the people to keep and bear Arms, shall not be infringed.

AMENDMENT III [1791]

No Soldier shall, in time of peace be quartered in any house, without the consent of the Owner, nor in time of war, but in a manner to be prescribed by law.

AMENDMENT IV [1791]

The right of the people to be secure in their persons, houses, papers, and effects, against unreasonable searches and seizures, shall not be violated, and no Warrants shall issue, but upon probable cause, supported by Oath or Affirmation, and particularly describing the place to be searched, and the persons or things to be seized.

AMENDMENT V [1791]

No person shall be held to answer for a capital, or otherwise infamous crime, unless on a presentment or indictment of a Grand Jury, except in cases arising in the land or naval forces, or in the Militia, when in actual service in time of War or public danger; nor shall any person be subject for the same offense to be twice put in jeopardy of life or limb; nor shall be compelled in any criminal case to be a witness against himself, nor be deprived of life, liberty, or property, without due process of law; nor shall private property be taken for public use, without just compensation.

AMENDMENT VI [1791]

In all criminal prosecutions, the accused shall enjoy the right to a speedy and public trial, by an impartial jury of the State and district wherein the crime shall have been committed, which district shall have been previously ascertained by law, and to be informed of the nature and cause of the accusation; to be confronted with the Witnesses against him; to have compulsory process for obtaining witnesses in his favor, and to have the Assistance of counsel for his defense.

AMENDMENT VII [1791]

In suits at common law, where the value in controversy shall exceed twenty dollars, the right of trial by jury shall be preserved, and no fact tried by a jury, shall be otherwise re-examined in any Court of the United States, than according to the rules of the common law.

AMENDMENT VIII [1791]

Excessive bail shall not be required, no excessive fines imposed, nor cruel and unusual punishments inflicted.

AMENDMENT IX [1791]

The enumeration in the Constitution, of certain rights, shall not be construed to deny or disparage others retained by the people.

AMENDMENT X [1791]

The powers not delegated to the United States by the Constitution, nor prohibited by it to the States, are reserved to the States respectively, or to the people.

AMENDMENT XI [1798]

The judicial power of the United States shall not be construed to extend to any suit in law or equity, commenced or prosecuted against one of the United States by Citizens of another State, or by Citizens or Subjects of any Foreign State.

AMENDMENT XII [1804]

The Electors shall meet in their respective states and vote by ballot for President and Vice-President, one of whom, at least, shall not be an inhabitant of the same state with themselves; they shall name in their ballots the person voted for as President, and in distinct ballots the person voted for as Vice-President, and they shall make distinct lists of all persons voted for as President, and of all persons voted for as Vice-President, and of the number of votes for each, which lists they shall sign and certify, and transmit sealed to the seat of the government of the United States, directed to the President of the Senate;—The President of the Senate shall, in the presence of the Senate and House of Representatives, open all the certificates and the votes shall then be counted;—The person having the greatest number of votes for President, shall be the President, if such a number be a majority of the whole number of Electors appointed; and if no person have such majority, then from the persons having the highest numbers not exceeding three on the list of those voted for as President, the House of Representatives shall choose immediately, by ballot, the President. But in choosing the President, the votes shall be taken by states, the representation from each state having one vote; a quorum for this purpose shall consist of a member or members from two-thirds of the states, and a majority of all the states shall be necessary to a choice. And if the House of Representatives shall not choose a President whenever the right of choice shall devolve upon them, before the fourth day of March next following, then the Vice-President shall act as President, as in the case of the death or other constitutional disability of the President. The person having the greatest number of votes as Vice-President, shall be the Vice-president, if such number be a majority of the whole number of Electors appointed, and if no person have a majority, then from the two highest numbers on the list, the Senate shall choose the Vice-President; a quorum for the purpose shall consist of two-thirds of the whole number of Senators, and a majority of the whole number shall be necessary to a choice. But no person constitutionally ineligible to the office of President shall be eligible to that of the Vice-President of the United States.

AMENDMENT XIII [1865]

SECTION 1

Neither slavery nor involuntary servitude, except as a punishment for crime whereof the party shall have been duly convicted, shall exist within the United States, or any place subject to their jurisdiction.

SECTION 2

Congress shall have power to enforce this article by appropriate legislation.

AMENDMENT XIV [1868]

SECTION 1

All persons born or naturalized in the United States, and subject to the jurisdiction thereof, are citizens of the United States and of the State wherein they reside. No State shall make or enforce any law which shall abridge the privileges or immunities of citizens of the United States; nor shall any State deprive any person of life, liberty, or property, without due process of law; nor deny to any person within its jurisdiction the equal protection of the laws.

SECTION 2

Representatives shall be appointed among the several States according to their respective numbers, counting the whole number of persons in each State, excluding Indians not taxed. But when the right to vote at any election for the choice of electors for President and Vice President of the United States, Representatives in Congress, the Executive and Judicial officers of a State, or the members of the Legislature thereof, is denied to any of the male inhabitants of such State, being twenty-one years of age, and citizens of the United States, or in any way abridged, except for participation in rebellion, or other crime, the basis of representation therein shall be reduced in the proportion which the number of such male citizens shall bear the whole number of male citizens twenty-one years of age in such State.

SECTION 3

No person shall be a Senator or Representative in Congress, or elector of President and Vice President, or hold any office, civil or military, under the United States, or under any State, who, having previously taken an oath, as a member of Congress, or as an officer of the United States, or as a member of any State legislature, or as an executive or judicial officer of any State, to support the Constitution of the United States, shall have engaged in insurrection or rebellion against the same, or given aid or comfort to the enemies thereof. But Congress may by a vote of two-thirds of each House, remove such disability.

SECTION 4

The validity of the public debt of the United States, authorized by law, including debts incurred for payment of pensions and bounties for services in suppressing insurrection or rebellion, shall not be questioned. But neither the United States nor any State shall assume or pay any debt or obligation incurred in aid of insurrection of rebellion against the United States, or any claim for the loss or emancipation of any slave; but all such debts, obligations and claims shall be held illegal and void.

SECTION 5

The Congress shall have power to enforce, by appropriate legislation, the provisions of this article.

AMENDMENT XV [1870]

SECTION 1

The right of citizens of the United States to vote shall not be denied or abridged by the United States or by any State on account of race, color, or previous condition of servitude.

SECTION 2

The Congress shall have power to enforce this article by appropriate legislation.

AMENDMENT XVI [1913]

The Congress shall have power to lay and collect taxes on incomes, from whatever source derived, without apportionment among the several States, and without regard to any census or enumeration.

AMENDMENT XVII [1913]

The Senate of the United States shall be composed of two Senators from each State, elected by the people thereof, for six years; and each Senator shall have one vote. The electors in each State shall have the qualifications requisite for electors of the most numerous branch of the State legislatures.

When vacancies happen in the representation of any State in the Senate, the executive authority of each State shall issue writs of election to fill such vacancies; Provided, That the legislature of any State may empower the executive thereof to make temporary appointments until the people fill the vacancies by election as the legislature may direct.

This amendment shall not be construed as to affect the election or term of any Senator chosen before it becomes valid as part of the Constitution.

AMENDMENT XVIII [1919]

SECTION 1

After one year from the ratification of this article the manufacture, sale, or transportation of intoxicating liquors within, the importation thereof into, or the exportation thereof from the United States and all territory subject to the jurisdiction thereof for beverage purposes is hereby prohibited.

SECTION 2

The Congress and the several States shall have concurrent power to enforce this article by appropriate legislation.

SECTION 3

This article shall be inoperative unless it shall have been ratified as an amendment to the Constitution by the legislatures of the several States, as provided in the Constitution, within seven years from the date of the submission hereof to the States by the Congress.

AMENDMENT XIX [1920]

The right of citizens of the United States to vote shall not be denied or abridged by the United States or by any State on account of sex.

Congress shall have power to enforce this article by appropriate legislation.

AMENDMENT XX [1933]

SECTION 1

The terms of the President and Vice President shall end at noon on the 20th day of January, and the terms of Senators and Representatives at noon on the 3d day of January, of the years in which such terms would have ended if this article had not been ratified; and the terms of their successors shall then begin.

SECTION 2

The Congress shall assemble at least once in every year, and such meeting shall begin at noon on the 3d day of January, unless they shall by law appoint a different day.

SECTION 3

If, at the time fixed for the beginning of the term of the President, the President elect shall have died, the Vice President elect shall become President. If a President shall not have been chosen before the time fixed for the beginning of his term, or if the President elect shall have failed to qualify, then the Vice President elect shall act as President until a President shall have qualified; and the Congress may by law provide for the case wherein neither a President elect nor a Vice President elect shall have qualified, declaring who shall then act as President, or the manner in which one who is to act shall be selected, and such person shall act accordingly until a President or Vice President shall have qualified.

SECTION 4

The Congress may by law provide for the case of the death of any of the persons from whom the House of Representatives may choose a President whenever the right of choice shall have devolved upon them, and for the case of the death of any of the persons from whom the Senate may choose a Vice President whenever the right of choice shall have devolved upon them.

Section 5

Sections 1 and 2 shall take effect on the 15th day of October following the ratification of this article.

Section 6

This article shall be inoperative unless it shall have been ratified as an amendment to the Constitution by the legislatures of three-fourths of the several States within seven years from the date of its submission.

Amendment XXI [1933]

Section 1

The eighteenth article of amendment to the Constitution of the United States is hereby repealed.

Section 2

The transportation or importation into any State, Territory, or possession of the United States for delivery or use therein of intoxicating liquors, in violation of the laws thereof, is hereby prohibited.

Section 3

This article shall be inoperative unless it shall have been ratified as an amendment to the Constitution by conventions in the several States, as provided in the Constitution, within seven years from the date of the submission hereof to the States by the Congress.

Amendment XXII [1951]

Section 1

No person shall be elected to the office of the President more than twice, and no person who has held the office of President, or acted as President, for more than two years of a term to which some other person was elected President shall be elected to the office of the President more than once. But this Article shall not apply to any person holding the office of President when this Article was proposed by the Congress, and shall not prevent any person who may be holding the office of President, or acting as President, during the term within which this Article becomes operative from holding the office of President, or acting as President during the remainder of such term.

Section 2

This article shall be inoperative unless it shall have been ratified as an amendment to the Constitution by the legislatures of three-fourths of the several States within seven years from the date of its submission to the States by the Congress.

Amendment XXIII [1961]

Section 1

The District constituting the seat of Government of the United States shall appoint in such manner as the Congress may direct:

A number of electors of President and Vice President equal to the whole number of Senators and Representatives in Congress to which the District would be entitled if it were a State, but in no event more than the least populous State; they shall be in addition to those appointed by the States, but they shall be considered, for the purposes of the election of President and Vice President, to be electors appointed by a State; and they shall meet in the District and perform such duties as provided by the twelfth article of amendment.

SECTION 2

The Congress shall have power to enforce this article by appropriate legislation.

AMENDMENT XXIV [1964]

SECTION 1

The right of citizens of the United States to vote in any primary or other election for President or Vice President, for electors for President or Vice President or for Senator or Representative in Congress, shall not be denied or abridged by the United States or any State by reason of failure to pay any poll tax or other tax.

SECTION 2

The Congress shall have power to enforce this article by appropriate legislation.

AMENDMENT XXV [1967]

SECTION 1

In case of the removal of the President from office or of his death or resignation, the Vice President shall become President.

SECTION 2

Whenever there is a vacancy in the office of the Vice President, the President shall nominate a Vice President who shall take office upon confirmation by a majority vote of both Houses of Congress.

SECTION 3

Whenever the President transmits to the President pro tempore of the Senate and the Speaker of the House of Representatives his written declaration that he is unable to discharge the powers and duties of his office, and until he transmits to them a written declaration to the contrary, such powers and duties shall be discharged by the Vice President as Acting President.

SECTION 4

Whenever the Vice President and a majority of either the principal officers of the executive departments or of such other body as Congress may by law provide, transmit to the President pro tempore of the Senate and the Speaker of the House of Representatives their written declaration that the President is unable to discharge the powers and duties of his office, the Vice President shall immediately assume the powers and duties of the office as Acting President.

Thereafter, when the President transmits to the President pro tempore of the Senate and the Speaker of the House of Representatives his written declaration that no inability exists, he shall resume the powers and duties of his office unless the Vice President and a majority of either the principal officers of the executive department or of such other body as Congress may by law provide, transmit within four days to the President pro tempore of the Senate and the Speaker of the House of Representatives their written declaration that the President is unable to discharge the powers and duties of his office. Thereupon Congress shall decide the issue, assembling within forty-eight hours for that purpose if not in session. If the Congress, within twenty-one days after receipt of the latter written declaration, or, if Congress is not in session, within twenty-one days after Congress is required to assemble, determines by two-thirds vote of both Houses that the President is unable to discharge the powers and duties of his office, the Vice President shall continue to discharge the same as Acting President; otherwise, the President shall resume the powers and duties of his office.

AMENDMENT XXVI [1971]

SECTION 1
The right of citizens of the United States, who are eighteen years of age or older, to vote shall not be denied or abridged by the United States or by any State on account of age.

SECTION 2
The Congress shall have power to enforce this article by appropriate legislation.

AMENDMENT XXVII [1992]
No law, varying the compensation for the services of the Senators and Representatives, shall take effect, until an election of Representatives shall have intervened.

APPENDIX B:
FUNDAMENTALS OF LEGAL RESEARCH

ABBREVIATIONS:

F. Supp.   **The Federal Supplement.** Contains cases decided by the United States District Courts.

F. 2d   **The Federal Reporter, Second Series.** Contains cases decided by the United States Courts of Appeals.

DECISIONS OF THE UNITED STATES SUPREME COURT ARE REPORTED IN THE FOLLOWING THREE PUBLICATIONS:

U.S.   **United States Reports**

S. C.   **Supreme Court Reporter**

L. Ed. 2d   **Lawyers Edition, Second Series**

OTHER FEDERAL REPORTERS

L.W.   **United States Law Week.** From time to time a Supreme Court decision will be reported in Law Week before it is published in the other reporters. This citation is sometimes used in order to publish the brief of the decision as soon as possible.

F.R.D.   **Federal Rules Decisions.** Reports decisions of the United States District Courts not reported in the Federal Supplement.

Westlaw   Database that includes decisions of the US Supreme court, Federal courts, state courts, legal periodicals, etc.

Lexis-Nexis   Database that includes decisions of the US Supreme Court, Federal courts, state courts, legal periodicals, etc.

Findlaw   General legal source finder

DECISIONS OF STATE COURTS ARE REPORTED IN REGIONAL REPORTERS AS LISTED BELOW:

N.E. 2d   **Northeastern Reporter, Second Series.** Cases decided in the state courts of Massachusetts, Rhode Island, New York, Ohio, Indiana and Illinois.

A. 2d   **Atlantic Reporter, Second Series.** Cases decided in the state courts of Maine, New Hampshire, Vermont, Connecticut, New Jersey, Pennsylvania, Delaware and Maryland.

So. 2d	**Southern Reporter, Second Series.** Cases decided in the state courts of Florida, Alabama, Mississippi and Louisiana.
S.E. 2d	**Southeastern Reporter, Second Series.** Cases decided in the state courts of Virginia, West Virginia, North Carolina, South Carolina and Georgia.
S.W. 2d	**Southwestern Reporter, Second Series.** Cases decided in the state courts of Kentucky, Tennessee, Missouri, Arkansas and Texas.
P. 2d	**Pacific Reporter, Second Series.** Cases decided in the state courts of Montana, Wyoming, Idaho, Kansas, Colorado, Oklahoma, New Mexico, Utah, Arizona, Nevada, Washington, Oregon and California.
N.W. 2d	**Northwestern Reporter, Second Series.** Cases decided in the state courts of Michigan, Wisconsin, Iowa, Minnesota, North Dakota, South Dakota and Nebraska.

OTHER PUBLICATIONS

N.Y.S. 2d	**New York Supplement, Second Series.** Cases decided in certain New York state courts. Some of these cases may also be reported in N.E. 2d.
Cal. Rptr.	**California Reporter.** Cases decided in the state courts of California. Some of these cases will also appear in P.2d. The Cal. Reporter was started in 1960 and California cases decided prior to 1960 can be found in P.2d.
U.S.C.	**United States Code.** This contains a codification of the laws passed by Congress.
U.S.C.A.	**United States Code Annotated.** This contains the annotations to the United States Code and, therefore includes cases that have been decided which interpret sections of the Code.
P.E.R.B.	**Public Employment Relations Board.**
P.E.R.C.	**Public Employees Relations Commission.** Various states have established such boards or commissions to conduct proceedings relating to collective bargaining by public employees in the state.
N.L.R.B.	**National Labor Relations Board.** The NLRB has jurisdiction over private employers covered by the National Labor Relations Act.
L.R.R.M.	**Labor Relations Reporting Manual.**
C.F.R.	**Code of Federal Regulations.** Federal Regulations are promulgated by federal agencies given the power by statute to adopt rules and regulations to carry out the purpose of the statute which that particular agency administers. Regulations have the force of law.
A.L.R. 3d	**American Law Reports, Third Series.** This reporter is annotated and contains discussion and other citations to similar cases after the reported case.

Appendix C:
Elements of the Brief

Name of Case: Plaintiff (Abbreviated) v. Defendant (Abbreviated)

You must be very careful that you read the facts of the case attentively to differentiate between the plaintiff and the defendant and the appellant and the appellee. Sometimes in the case name as it appears in a text, the names of the parties have been reversed if the plaintiff was successful at the trial level and the defendant has now filed an appeal. In the appellate case, the defendant's name may be listed first because he or she has now become the appellant, the party bringing the appeal. Thus, a case originally brought under the name of *Smith v. Jones* may now be cited as *Jones v. Smith* because Jones, the original defendant and party who lost at the trial level, is now the appellant. As such, Jones's name will be listed first. Since most of the cases you will read will be appellate cases, you must be especially mindful of this point.

Facts

A very brief, short-hand statement of why the parties are in court must be made. The facts should at a minimum include the key elements of the dispute, the theory of the plaintiff's case, and the defense raised by the defendant, if any. At the conclusion of the facts, always state who was the prevailing or winning party at the trial level and which party filed the appeal.

Issue or Question

This is the key to the case! What is the very specific issue or question the court was called upon to decide? Formulating the issue is a very important task and it takes practice to state the issue precisely and not in too general terms. Sometimes the court may help you by using the words "issue" or "question." Sometimes the task is much more difficult. Remember, just as in *Jeopardy*, the issue or question should always be stated in the form of a question!

Decision

The decision, of course, will state the party who won the case and the party for whom the judgment was rendered. Was the decision of the trial court upheld, reversed, modified, etc? What was the final ruling of the court? Be sure you are careful in stating the decision of the court. State precisely what remedy the court ordered, what the court decided, or what it ordered the parties to do. Sometimes a court will use the word "holding" to state its decision.

Reason or Rule

This is perhaps the most important part of a case. It is the statement of the legal principle or rule which not only helped to decide this case, but which will be helpful in deciding all future cases which involve similar facts. In many cases, this may be considered the precedent or rule of the case. Note that if the case cites or refers to other cases, a Restatement of one of the various areas of the law (contracts, torts, agency, etc.), a special text (Wigmore, Corbin, Williston, etc.), or statute, you should cite these under an "authority for the rule." Finally, if a rule has several elements, you should state these elements clearly and distinctly.

REACTION

A personal comment might be in order for some cases. Do you agree that the case was decided in a proper way? Did the "right person" win? Is the decision legally correct? Is the decision "ethically" correct? This is generally not a required part of the brief, but it is, of course, an important part of the process of legal reasoning, of "thinking like a lawyer." In some cases, however, you will be required to write a brief, one paragraph reaction to the result reached in the case. These "reaction paragraphs" (usually dealing with an issue involving ethics) will be specially noted in the course outline and will answer some specific questions raised in the cases.

Once you have "briefed" a case, the important part of the case—what you will need to remember and recall—will generally be the legal rule or precedent established in the case. It might be well to keep a special portion of your notebook reserved for restating these important legal rules. These precedents or legal rules will help you in deciding future cases, solving problems, etc., since, as you are aware, law is deductive in nature; that is, we use general rules to solve important problems and to resolve specific questions. In some cases, a rule becomes so identified with a particular case that you will remember the rule as the "Rule of X Case", or the "X Principle" or the "Rule of *X v. Y.*" An example might be the Rule of *Lucy v. Zehmer*, concerning the objective test used to determine if an offer has been made.

All of this will become second nature to you by the time you complete your first course in law at Seton Hall University. Briefing a case is an important tool in helping to "think like a lawyer."

APPENDIX D:
CONTRACT PROBLEMS

PROBLEM SET 1

1. X and Y entered into an express oral contract for the purchase of a certain amount of wood saws. X delivered the saws to Y and Y refuses to pay for them, stating that there was no agreement as to price. Is there an obligation to pay? Why? What price?

2. Carol read an ad in the local newspaper offering a baby grand piano for sale for $350.00. Carol visited the home of the offeror and gave the seller a check for $350.00, promising to return in the afternoon to pick up the piano. The seller then went off to church and after Mass, she stopped off at her good friend's home where the general opinion of several of her friends was that the piano was worth much more than $350.00. The seller had the piano appraised and found that it was indeed worth around $2,000.00. The seller then called Carol and said that "I've changed my mind and I'm not going to sell." The seller mails the check back to Carol. Is there a contract? Can Carol get the piano? Why? Might the seller claim unconscionability?

3. Tom is a local franchisee of the Popeye's Chicken Corp. A provision in the franchise agreement calls for the payment of $2,000 if the franchisee "fails to perform any of the terms or conditions of the contract." Tom runs into some economic difficulties and misses a one month payment of the franchise fee and the franchiser now seeks to enforce the $2,000 clause. Is such a clause enforceable? What standard?

4. X agreed to supply Y with all of his requirements of ice for his fishing boat fleet if Y would agree to purchase all his ice and other ice products from X. Is this contract enforceable?

5. X and Y were involved in an automobile accident on South Orange Avenue right near Center Street. Y claimed that X was responsible for the accident and X agreed to pay all of Y's expenses and doctor bills rather than risk a potential lawsuit where X might lose his license. About a month later, X receives a letter from a Mr. Simeri (who lives on the intersection) in which Mr. Simeri says that he saw the entire accident clearly and Y definitely went through the red traffic light. X now refuses to honor his promise and Y sues for breach of contract. Who will win? Why? What test will the court apply?

6. Fred paid Johnny $1.00 for an option to purchase a piece of real estate worth approximately $1,000,000. When Johnny later receives an offer for $1,500,000 for the property, he attempts to back out of the earlier option claiming that "$1 just isn't enough to bind me for a million dollar deal; be serious." Who is right? What rule?

7. Liam bought a 1998 automobile for the purchase price of $800.00. At the time of the purchase, Liam was 16 years old. At a party the evening of the purchase, Liam had a bit too much to drink and started to drive home, whereupon he had an auto accident. The next morning, Liam calls the car dealer and tells him that he is "going to cancel the contract." May he do so? Majority rule? New York rule? Third rule? Suppose that Liam had lied about his age at the time of the purchase. Would that change the result?

8. Rick Veldman signs up for Karate lessons and agrees to a 36 lesson package at $25.00 each. After taking the lessons, Rick attempts to get his money back, claiming that he was a minor when the contract was entered into. Does Rick have a legitimate argument? Suppose that Rick had waited until 8 months after reaching his age of majority? What rule do courts apply to service contracts?

9. X, an 18 year old boy, agrees to pay back $1,000 to a local bank, in return for a loan to help pay for his college education. Later, X receives a gift from his grandfather and attempts to cancel his contract with the bank. X not only wants to return the $1,000, but also wants to avoid paying the reasonable interest charges, claiming that he was a minor when he entered into the contract. Is X correct? What rule?

10. X, a salesman for a natural gas company, falsely assured Y, a buyer of residential natural gas for home building purposes, that a certain minimum pressure would be all that would be needed to insure adequate home heating pressure. X knew that the specifications he had given out were false. However, Y was very knowledgeable in the area of natural gas and knew that X's assurances were "probably unrealistic or false," but Y went through with the deal because the "price was right." Later, when the gas was shown to have improper pressure, Y sues X for fraud. What result? Reasons?

11. X, an infant, signed an agreement with a baby-sitting contracting firm, whereby X would receive 8 jobs per month in return for paying 15% back to the babysitting company. After X worked for the company for 3 months, she received a bill for $37.50, the share she had promised to pay. X now refuses to pay the bill claiming that she is a minor. Is she correct? What rule should the court apply?

12. Fred bought a stereo system from Radio Shack at a cost of $150.00. Fred reached his 18th birthday (the age of majority) and made a payment on account. Then Fred tried to rescind the contract using age as a defense. Can he now do so?

13. X and Y were both minors and entered into a contract for the purchase and sale of a motor bike. X later tries to rescind the sale. Is a minor's contract with another minor voidable?

14. John owed $25,000 to his neighbor Jim. When Jim requested payment, John admitted that he was unable to do so. Jim then told John that if he did not make an immediate payment, he would be forced to sue John or possibly put a lien on John's house. John thereupon agreed to re-finance the amount of the loan at a higher interest rate. Later, when Jim tried to enforce the new agreement, John defended on grounds that he entered into this agreement under "duress." Who is right? Why?

15. Fran agreed to purchase certain items on credit from the XYZ Corporation. The agreement called for the payment of substantial late fees and other charges and also called for a total repossession of all items if any individual payments were missed, Fran is a recent immigrant from Haiti who has great difficulty reading and writing English. In fact, Fran signed the contract using only a simple "X" When the XYZ Corporation sought to enforce the contract after Fran defaulted, what defense might be available to Fran? Discuss.

16. X sold Y a TV repair business. The contract contained a clause which prohibited X from opening up a similar business in a 10 mile radius for a period of 5 years. Is such a clause enforceable? Why or why not? What rule?

17. X went to work as president of a hat factory. X learned that the factory was having some difficulty in making its payroll, so X assured the workers (8) that if the factory was unable to meet the monthly payments to its workers, X would do so. Later, X had a disagreement with his Board of Directors and quit his job. When the factory was unable to meet its payroll, the workers contacted X, reminding him of his earlier promise. Can X be compelled to honor his promise if his promise was made orally? What defense might be available? Any exception?

18. X orally sold a piece of real estate to Y. Y moved on to the premises and put in an "in-ground" swimming pool, and made other improvements to the property. Later X tried to deny that a contract for sale had been entered into and claimed the Statute of Frauds as an absolute defense. Who is right? Why?

19. Elvis Presley agreed orally to hire a booking agent to represent him for a three-year period or "until such time as you secure for me 12 major contract bookings." Later, Elvis fires the agent and the agent sues for breach of contract. Elvis's lawyer asserts the Statute of Frauds as a defense. Who is right? Discuss. Suppose the contract was for an 18-month period?

20. Andrew entered into an oral contract for the purchase of $2750 worth of sporting goods and other athletic supplies. Later, Andrew refused to accept the goods and was sued for breach of contract. What defense might be available to Andrew? Suppose the goods had been specially manufactured for use by Andrew. Might that change the result? What is a specially manufactured good?

21. X set his son up in a printing business. When his son began to experience some financial setbacks, X called various suppliers and orally promised:

    A.   I'll stand behind any losses my son incurs; or

    B.   If my son can't pay, just send me the bills and I'll make good on them.

    Later, the business experiences real difficulty and various creditors contact X and seek payment. What defense might be available to X? How would you counter this argument? Discuss.

22. Sears sold a TV set to Homer. When Homer got the TV set home, he found out that it had a non-functioning tube and it didn't work correctly. Meanwhile, however, Sears had assigned the right to collect payment to the Sears Credit Corporation. Sears Credit maintains that they only are there "to enforce payment" and "we are not concerned about any problems with the TV." Will Seats Credit Corp. be able to enforce payment without admitting responsibility for the defective product? What rule?

23. John Grill purchases an insurance policy on his life, naming "my grandchildren" as beneficiaries. After John's death, Junior Grill becomes concerned about the great delay that has taken place in settling his grandfather's estate. After a further delay of 5 months, Junior seeks to file suit to compel payment to himself and his other cousins. Does Junior have standing to sue?

24. Fred was promised S600 a month in expense money for so long as he remained "in good standing at the University of Wisconsin Medical School." The money had been put up by a local medical foundation which raises funds through private contributions. Later, Fred is flunked out of school because it is learned that he was involved in a major cheating scandal. Townspeople, who live in the same town where the funds have been raised, learn about the scandal and seek to have Fred repay all monies paid to him for the two-year period during which he received funds. Will the townspeople have standing to sue?

25. Peter Grace promises the Trustees of the local University that he will be giving the University a $7 million dollar gift for the construction of a modern residence dormitory. Invited to the campus, Mr. Grace comes under attack by various student radicals for alleged involvement in covert CIA activities. Incensed, Grace cancels his pledge to the University. However, in the meantime, the University had expended considerable sums to hire an architect, draw up plans and break ground for the new structure, all costing around $2 million dollars. Is Mr. Grace's promise to the University enforceable? On what showing? Discuss.

26. X contracted to purchase 100,000 bushels of apples from a certain fruit farmer in Spokane, Washington. Just prior to the delivery date, a major volcano erupts and the entire crop is destroyed. Might the farmer be compelled to complete delivery of the contracted for apples? Explain. What defense might be available?

Problem Set 2

1. XYZ Corporation sent a letter to Harry Hotdog, in which it offered Harry employment as a managerial trainee at an annual salary of $15,000. Harry wrote back, stating: "I will accept, but would you consider raising the salary to $16,000? I don't feel that I can work for any less than $16,000 per year." Can XYZ Corporation now offer the job to someone else?

2. Fly-By-Night Construction Company agreed to construct a one car garage for Innocent, who agreed to pay $1,500. Before the garage was built, Innocent promised to pay Fly-By-Night an additional $1,700 if it would build a two car garage instead of a one car garage. After Fly-By-Night had completed the two car garage, Innocent paid $1,500, but refused to pay any more. Fly-By-Night sues Innocent for the additional $1,700.

Can Fly-By-Night collect? Is there a "consideration problem" here?

3. For fifteen years, Jim has mowed John's lawn on Friday afternoons during the months of April through October, and John has paid Jim ten dollars for each mowing. One Friday, Jim brings his mower to John's house, says hello to John, and mows John's lawn. During this time, John watches Jim but says nothing. Later, John refuses to pay, alleging that he and Jim had not entered into an express agreement for mowing the lawn. Can Jim collect? Upon what theory?

4. Southampton Gallery advertised its annual Spring art auction as an auction "without reserve." Nuvo Reesh submitted the highest bid for an original Schmutz lithograph, but the auctioneer refused to sell it, stating that the highest bid was still not high enough. Must the Gallery turn over the painting?

5. Sonny borrowed $3,000 at no interest from his father. The loan was to be repaid January 1, 2001. On that date, Sonny called his father and said that he only had $2,000. He asked if his father would accept the $2,000 as full satisfaction of the debt. The father agreed. After having received the $2,000, the father asked for an additional $1,000. Sonny refused to pay it, and the father sued. Who will win, and why?

6. Uncle promised 16-year old Nephew a gold watch if Nephew would refrain from smoking until his 21st birthday. Nephew did refrain from smoking until age 21, but when he tried to collect the watch, Uncle refused. Can the Uncle be compelled to pay?

7. Craig wanted to stage a production of the well-known play, "Kick Your Dog Down a Dusty Road." He wrote Natalie, a famous actress, offering her the lead in the play at $10,000 per week for six weeks. His letter also stated "Offer ends in one week." Natalie received the letter the next day and immediately mailed an acceptance. Natalie's letter was temporarily lost in the mail and did not arrive until five days after she had dispatched it. Craig, not hearing from Natalie, decided to abandon the project. If Natalie sues Craig, what will be the result?

8. Jack offered to sell a prime piece of real estate to I.O.U., a private university. I.O.U. paid Jack $500 to keep his offer open for 6 months, from September 1 to March 1. In October, Jack wants to sell the property to a third party, Industrialist. May Jack do so?

9. In January, Two & Two (an accounting firm of national reputation based in New York) procured lists of all senior accounting students in the nation who ranked in the top 10 percent of their graduating classes. Two & Two sent out form letters on firm stationary which congratulated each recipient on his or her fine academic record. The letter also stated, in pertinent part:

> "We are proud of the fact that our salary and benefit schedule for the first year associates is slightly higher than the average among firms of our stature. A typical Two & Two associate becomes a partner within eight years, and Two & Two has a policy of a mandatory four week vacation during the first year. We hope that you will consider a position with Two & Two upon graduation. We would be pleased to call anyone with your credentials our associate."
>
> Best of Luck
> Leonard Lifo

for Two & Two,
a Professional Corporation

Should this letter be characterized as an offer? Why or why not?

10. Thrifty promised to donate $500 to his favorite charity, the Irwin Home for Impoverished Lawyers. In reliance on Thrifty's pledge, the Home immediately ordered some badly needed three-piece suits for some of its inmates. Thrifty later changed his mind and refused to make the donation. Can Thrifty be compelled to make the donation? What showing?

11. On June 1, 1998 the Management Group, Inc. offered Hilary a position as house counsel, to begin September 1, 1998. Hilary did not communicate with the Management Group until October 1, 1998, when she showed up at its offices and announced that she wanted the job. The Management Group had already hired someone else. Is Hilary entitled to the job?

12. While Hank Homeowner is away on vacation, workmen from the Cosine, Construction Company erroneously re-surface Hank's dilapidated driveway, mistaking Hank's house for the house on which they were supposed to be working. Cosmo later bills Hank, and Hank refuses to pay. Cosmo then sues Hank, arguing that Hank received a benefit, and thus should be required to pay. Discuss Cosino's chances of success under both contractual and quasi-contractual theories.

13. Farthing published an advertisement in the newspaper offering a reward of $500 for the return of her cat. After several weeks, she changed her mind, and posted several signs around town that stated that her offer was withdrawn. Goodguy saw the newspaper ad but did not see the signs. He returned the cat and claimed the reward. Must Farthing pay him?

14. Black wrote to Berin: "I have decided to sell my farm, Blackacre. I would want around $65,000 for it. Let's have lunch next week and discuss it." Has Black made an offer? Why or why not?

15. Widow offered a reward of $50,000 for the apprehension of the person who had killed her husband. Sheriff Goodguy saw the reward offer. In the course of his duties, he apprehended the killer. Several days later, he claimed the reward, but the widow refused to pay. Should the Sheriff collect?

16. The Klotts signed an agreement to purchase a house owned by the Stewarts. The day after the Klotts moved into the house they became aware of a malfunctioning water well in need of major repairs. During the negotiations for the sale of the house, no mention was ever made about the water supply. The Klotts did not ask for any information; they had assumed the water came from the city well. Nor did the Stewarts volunteer any information. The Klotts sue the Stewarts for damages, claiming that there was a fraudulent nondisclosure and concealment of the faulty well. Assuming the Stewarts were aware of the faulty condition of the well at the time of the sale, are they liable for damages for not disclosing this information?

17. Wilson had been working for the telephone company when Hayes and the Winslow Construction Co. promised her a job as a flag girl on a construction job. Wilson was

told to quit her present job, which she did. Hayes and the Winslow Construction Co. did not fulfill their promise to employ Wilson, and she sues to recover lost wages during her period of unemployment. Are Hayes and Winslow Construction Co. liable on their promise? What theory?

18. Rose, a minor under the age of 21, purchased an automobile from a Buick dealer. Seven months later, Rose declared the contract invalid since, as a minor, she wasn't permitted by law to make a contract for the purchase of an automobile. Rose demanded: (1) that the contract be declared invalid and (2) that the entire purchase price of the automobile be refunded to her. Will her demands be honored?

19. Tovar, a Kansas physician, sought employment in an Illinois hospital as a resident physician. Terms of employment were agreed upon and Tovar signed a contract. After two weeks of employment with the Illinois hospital, Tovar was summarily dismissed on the grounds that he did not have a valid Illinois medical license. Tovar sues the hospital for wrongful termination of his employment contract, despite acknowledging that he did not have an Illinois license. Tovar claims that the license is not necessary to the fulfillment of the terms of the contract. Is the hospital liable on the contract?

20. On October 20, 1973, Uscian and Blacconeri entered into a written contract for the sale of a certain parcel of land owned by Uscian. The contract was expressly contingent upon Uscian obtaining approval from the city to subdivide the property. Uscian's application for subdivision was denied by the city. Thereafter, in December of 1973, the parties orally agreed to sell the property without first obtaining a subdivision. Later Uscian backed out of the deal. Blacconeri now sues for specific performance of the written contract. Uscian sets up the Statute of Frauds as his defense. Is this a good defense? Explain.

PROBLEM SET 3
SHORT ANSWERS

1. Torbert accepted Jordan's proposal that they go to the Fall Cotillion together. In return for Jordan's willingness to purchase tickets and pay all expenses, Torbert set aside the time and restricted herself from doing anything else on the evening of the dance. Jordan cancels the date at the last minute. Any possible basis of recovery? How much? (What is the measure of the damages?)

2. Faulkner, nineteen years old, realized that his contracts were not enforceable because of his age. He bought an expensive television set, for which he agreed to pay $47.50 per month for twelve months, The seller did not know that Faulkner was a minor. After using the set for two months, Faulkner refused to make additional payments and demanded return of all monies paid. General Rule? Exceptions? State law exceptions?

3. Reynolds, a minor, purchased a winter coat at a reasonable price. After wearing the coat for more than three months, she returned it to the store and demanded her money back, Will she recover? Why or why not?

4. Colby was unconscious as a result of a hit-and-run accident. He was taken to the hospital, where he underwent emergency treatment and surgery. After regaining consciousness, Colby denied any responsibility for the hospital charges, stating that he had

5. Engineering Research, Ltd., hired Jacobs to work on a research project that would require at least three years to complete. The offer of salary and employment were oral and Jacobs accepted it. Is the agreement enforceable?

6. Zabinsky, an artist, was commissioned to do a portrait of Governor Simms. When he was called to Europe to do portraits of several members of a wealthy family, he assigned the duty to a famous artist who had taught him in graduate school. Is such an assignment possible? Why or why not? What showing?

7. Stabler contracted with EHS for installation of an electric heating system in her residence. The contractor assured Stabler that she would be delighted with the work and "If it is not satisfactory, you won't have to pay us a cent..." Stabler claimed dissatisfaction and refused to pay. What rule? What standard?

8. Wendel, an Olympic Skater, turned professional skater and signed an agreement with Ice Shows. After four weeks of practice, Wendel suffered a broken ankle. Any further obligations required of either party?

9. Stolts agreed to buy an 18th century chest from Empire Antiques for $4700. When Stolts went to pick up the chest, Empire refused delivery, stating that the chest was going to be given to a museum. Can Stolts get the chest?

10. Goldstein found a watch with no identification so he could not locate the owner. An advertisement in the paper on Tuesday identified the watch and offered a $25 reward. Goldstein responded to the ad and returned the watch. The owner refused to pay the reward stating that the ad was "merely an invitation to trade" and not a firm offer. May Goldstein recover the $25 reward?

11. While intoxicated, Russ bought a fur jacket from Sam paying her with a check for $1300. Several hours later, remembering what he had done, he stopped payment on the check. Sam sued Russ for the $1300 and refused to accept the return of the cost. Will the suit succeed? Why or why not?

12. In a state where gambling is illegal, Hopkins agreed to act as a bookie. Hopkins's boss refused to pay him for work done in the bookie establishment. Hopkins sues. Will he collect?

13. Raphael owns and operates a Nursing Home. He recently purchased this business from its former owners, Lullaby House. Along with the various service contracts inherited by Raphael is one for furnishing laundry. After using the laundry service for six months, Raphael receives a bill for laundry and cleaning. He refuses to pay asserting that he never had made a contract with the laundry. Is he right? Evaluate.

14. Mrs. Williams uses various items from a local retail store totaling almost $1800. She signs a printed form which provided for installment payments and forfeiture of all items purchased if one of the installments was not paid on time. Mrs. Williams sues to set the contract aside. What basis? Discuss.

15. Freddy sends Larry an offer to purchase gasoline. Larry receives the offer on August 12 and immediately wires Freddy that he is not interested in the deal. Prior to the receipt of this wire, Larry calls Freddy and says that he accepts. Is there a contract? Why?

16. Under what circumstances might a newspaper ad be considered as an offer?

17. Gerry bids on a construction job as a subcontractor. The contractor receives his bid but prior to the awarding of the contract, Gerry notices that he has made a clerical error and attempts to notify the contractor of this fact. Are there any circumstances where a revocation at this point might be possible?

18. Freddy calls his friend Joe on the phone and states: "Remember those three pieces of land in Arkansas you were interested in buying? I'll make them available to you for three weeks." Three days later, however, Freddy sent Joe a letter and says: "Lots sold. Sorry." Joe contends that he had a firm option for three weeks. Is he correct?

19. How would the Common law have treated the following difference in an offer and an acceptance: OFFER: Three lathes (wood); packed in styrofoam; seller to pay shipping cost; green cabinets; ACCEPTANCE: Accept offer but only desire two lathes.

20. How does the U.C.C. define goods? merchant? unconscionability?

21. OFFER: Will sell between 6 and 7 thousand tons of potatoes: ACCEPTANCE: Will purchase 6,550 tons of potatoes. Is there a contract?

GLOSSARY

A

Abandoned property

Property with which the owner has voluntarily parted, with no intention of recovering it.

Abandonment

In landlord-tenant law, a tenant's departure from leased premises completely, with no intention of returning before the end of the lease term.

Abatement

A process by which legatees receive reduced benefits if the assets of an estate are insufficient to pay in full all general bequests provided for in the will.

Abus de droit

A doctrine developed in the French courts. The doctrine modified employment at will and protected workers exercising their rights from wrongful discharge and other employer abuses.

Acceleration clause

A clause in an installment contract that provides for all future payments to become due immediately on the failure to tender timely payments or on the occurrence of a specified event.

Acceptance

(1) In contract law, the offeree's notification to the offeror that the offeree agrees to be bound by the terms of the offeror's proposal. Although historically the terms of acceptance had to be the mirror image of the terms of the offer, the Uniform Commercial Code provides that even modified terms of the offer in a definite expression of acceptance constitute a contract. (2) In negotiable instruments law, the drawee's signed agreement to pay a draft when presented.

Acceptor

The person (the drawee) who accepts a draft and who agrees to be primarily responsible for its payment.

Access contract

A contract formed for the purpose of obtaining, by electronic means, access to another's database or information processing system.

Accession

Occurs when an individual adds value to personal property by either labor or materials. In some situations, a person may acquire ownership rights in another's property through accession.

Accommodation party

A person who signs an instrument for the purpose of lending his or her name as credit to another party on the instrument.

Accord and satisfaction

An agreement for payment (or other performance) between two parties, one of whom has a right of action against the other. After the payment has been accepted or other performance has been made, the "accord and satisfaction" is complete and the obligation is discharged.

Accredited investors

In the context of securities offerings, "sophisticated" investors, such as banks, insurance companies, investment companies, the issuer's executive officers and directors, and persons whose income or net worth exceeds certain limits.

Acquittal

A certification or declaration following a trial that the individual accused of a crime is innocent, or free from guilt, and is thus absolved of the charges.

Act of state doctrine

A doctrine that provides that the judicial branch of one country will not examine the validity of public acts committed by a recognized foreign government within its own territory.

Actionable

Capable of serving as the basis of a lawsuit.

Actual authority

Authority of an agent that is express or implied.

Actual malice

Real and demonstrable evil intent. In a defamation suit, a statement made about a public figure normally must be made with actual malice (with either knowledge of its falsity or a reckless disregard of the truth) for liability to be incurred.

Actus reus (pronounced ak-tus ray-uhs)

A guilty (prohibited) act. The commission of a prohibited act is one of the two essential elements required for criminal liability, the other element being the intent to commit a crime.

Adequate protection doctrine

In bankruptcy law, a doctrine that protects secured creditors from losing their security as a result of an automatic stay on legal proceedings by creditors against the debtor once the debtor petitions for bankruptcy relief. In certain circumstances, the bankruptcy court may provide adequate protection by requiring the debtor or trustee to pay the creditor or provide additional guaranties to protect the creditor against the losses suffered by the creditor as a result of the stay.

Adhesion contract

A "standard-form" contract, such as that between a large retailer and a consumer, in which the stronger party dictates the terms.

Adjudicate

To render a judicial decision. In the administrative process, the proceeding in which an administrative law judge hears and decides on issues that arise when an administrative agency charges a person or a firm with violating a law or regulation enforced by the agency.

Adjudication

The process of adjudicating. *See Adjudicate*

Administrative agency

A federal, state, or local government agency established to perform a specific function. Administrative agencies are authorized by legislative acts to make and enforce rules to administer and enforce the acts.

Administrative law

The body of law created by administrative agencies (in the form of rules, regulations, orders, and decisions) in order to carry out their duties and responsibilities.

Administrative law judge (ALJ)

One who presides over an administrative agency hearing and who has the power to administer oaths, take testimony, rule on questions of evidence, and make determinations of fact.

Administrative process

The procedure used by administrative agencies in the administration of law.

Administrator

One who is appointed by a court to handle the probate (disposition) of a person's estate if that person dies intestate (without a valid will) or if the executor named in the will cannot serve.

Adverse possession

The acquisition of title to real property by occupying it openly, without the consent of the owner, for a period of time specified by a state statute. The occupation must be actual, open, notorious, exclusive, and in opposition to all others, including the owner.

Affidavit

A written or printed voluntary statement of facts, confirmed by the oath or affirmation of the party making it and made before a person having the authority to administer the oath or affirmation.

Affirm

To validate; to give legal force to. *See also Ratification*

Affirmative action

Job-hiring policies that give special consideration to members of protected classes in an effort to overcome present effects of past discrimination.

Affirmative defense

A response to a plaintiff's claim that does not deny the plaintiff's facts but attacks the plaintiff's legal right to bring an action. An example is the running of the statute of limitations.

After-acquired evidence

A type of evidence submitted in support of an affirmative defense in employment discrimination cases. Evidence that, prior to the employer's discriminatory act, the employee engaged in misconduct sufficient to warrant dismissal had the employer known of it earlier.

After-acquired property

Property of the debtor that is acquired after the execution of a security agreement.

Age of majority

The age at which an individual is considered legally capable of conducting himself or herself responsibly. A person of this age is entitled to the full rights of citizenship, including the right to vote in elections. In contract law, one who is no longer an infant and can no longer disaffirm a contract.

Agency

A relationship between two parties in which one party (the agent) agrees to represent or act for the other (the principal).

Agency by estoppel

Arises when a principal negligently allows an agent to exercise powers not granted to the agent, thus justifying others in believing that the agent possesses the requisite agency authority. *See also Promissory estoppel*

Agent

A person who agrees to represent or act for another, called the principal.

Aggressor

The acquiring corporation in a takeover attempt.

Agreement

A meeting of two or more minds in regard to the terms of a contract; usually broken down into two events—an offer by one party to form a contract, and an acceptance of the offer by the person to whom the offer is made.

Alien corporation

A designation in the United States for a corporation formed in another country but doing business in the United States.

Alienation

In real property law, the voluntary transfer of property from one person to another (as opposed to a transfer by operation of law).

Allegation

A statement, claim, or assertion.

Allege

To state, recite, assert, or charge.

Allonge *(pronounced uh-lohnj)*

A piece of paper firmly attached to a negotiable instrument, on which transferees can make indorsements if there is no room left on the instrument itself.

Alteration

In the context of leaseholds, an improvement or change made that materially affects the condition of the property. Thus, for example, erecting an additional structure probably would (and painting interior walls would not) be considered making an alteration.

Alternative dispute resolution (ADR)

The resolution of disputes in ways other than those involved in the traditional judicial process. Negotiation, mediation, and arbitration are forms of ADR.

Amend

To change and improve through a formal procedure.

American Arbitration Association (AAA)

The major organization offering arbitration services in the United States.

Analogy

In logical reasoning, an assumption that if two things are similar in some respects, they will be similar in other respects also. Often used in legal reasoning to infer the appropriate application of legal principles in a case being decided by referring to previous cases involving different facts but considered to come within the policy underlying the rule.

Annuity

An insurance policy that pays the insured fixed, periodic payments for life or for a term of years, as stipulated in the policy, after the insured reaches a specified age.

Annul

To cancel; to make void.

Answer procedurally

A defendant's response to the plaintiff's complaint.

Antecedent claim

A preexisting claim. In negotiable instruments law, taking an instrument in satisfaction of an antecedent claim is taking the instrument for value—that is, for valid consideration.

Anticipatory repudiation

An assertion or action by a party indicating that he or she will not perform an obligation that the party is contractually obligated to perform at a future time.

Antitrust law

The body of federal and state laws and statutes protecting trade and commerce from unlawful restraints, price discrimination, price fixing, and monopolies. The principal federal antitrust statues are the Sherman Act of 1890, the Clayton Act of 1914, and the Federal Trade Commission Act of 1914.

Apparent authority

Authority that is only apparent, not real. In agency law, a person may be deemed to have had the power to act as an agent for another party if the other party's manifestations to a third party led the third party to believe that an agency existed when, in fact, it did not.

Appeal

Resort to a superior court, such as an appellate court, to review the decision of an inferior court, such as a trial court or an administrative agency.

Appellant

The party who takes an appeal from one court to another.

Appellate court

A court having appellate jurisdiction. Each state court system has at least one level of appellate courts. In the federal court system, the appellate courts are the circuit courts of appeals (intermediate appellate courts) and the United States Supreme Court (the highest appellate court in the federal system).

Appellate jurisdiction

Courts having appellate jurisdiction act as reviewing courts, or appellate courts. Generally, cases can be brought before appellate courts only on appeal from an order or a judgment of a trial court or other lower court.

Appellee

The party against whom an appeal is taken—that is, the party who opposes setting aside or reversing the judgment.

Appraisal right

The right of a dissenting shareholder, if he or she objects to an extraordinary transaction of the corporation (such as a merger or consolidation), to have his or her shares appraised and to be paid the fair value of his or her shares by the corporation.

Appropriation

In tort law, the use by one person of another person's name, likeness, or other identifying characteristic without permission and for the benefit of the user.

Arbitrary and capricious test

The court reviewing an informal administrative agency action applies this test to determine whether or not that action was in clear error. The court gives wide discretion to the expertise of the agency and decides if the agency had sufficient factual information on which to base its action. If no clear error was made, then the agency's action stands.

Arbitration

The settling of a dispute by submitting it to a disinterested third party (other than a court), who renders a decision. The decision may or may not be legally binding.

Arbitration clause

A clause in a contract that provides that, in the event of a dispute, the parties will submit the dispute to arbitration rather than litigate the dispute in court.

Arraignment

A procedure in which an accused person is brought before the court to plead to the criminal charge in the indictment or information. The charge is read to the person, and he or she is asked to enter a plea—such as "guilty" or "not guilty."

Arson

The malicious burning of another's dwelling. Some statutes have expanded this to include any real property regardless of ownership and the destruction of property by other means—for example, by explosion.

Articles of incorporation

The document filed with the appropriate governmental agency, usually the secretary of state, when a business is incorporated; state statutes usually prescribe what kind of information must be contained in the articles of incorporation.

Articles of organization

The document filed with a designated state official by which a limited liability company is formed.

Articles of partnership

A written agreement that sets forth each partner's rights and obligations with respect to the partnership.

Artisan's lien

A possessory lien given to a person who has made improvements and added value to another person's personal property as security for payment for services performed.

Assault

Any word or action intended to make another person fearful of immediate physical harm; a reasonably believable threat.

Assignee

The person to whom contract rights are assigned.

Assignment

The act of transferring to another all or part of one's rights arising under a contract.

Assignor

The person who assigns contract rights.

Assumption of risk

A defense against negligence that can be used when the plaintiff is aware of a danger and voluntarily assumes the risk of injury from that danger.

Attachment

(1) In the context of secured transactions, the process by which a security interest in the property of another becomes enforceable. (2) In the context of judicial liens, a court-ordered seizure and taking into custody of property prior to the securing of a judgment for a past-due debt.

Attempted monopolization

Any actions by a firm to eliminate competition and gain monopoly power.

Attractive nuisance doctrine

A common law doctrine under which a landowner or landlord may be held liable for injuries incurred by children who are lured onto the property by something dangerous and enticing thereon.

Authenticate

To sign a record, or with the intent to sign a record, to execute or to adopt an electronic sound, symbol, or the like to link with the record. A record is retrievable information inscribed on a tangible medium or stored in an electronic or other medium.

Authority

In agency law, the agent's permission to act on behalf of the principal. An agent's authority may be actual (express or implied) or apparent. *See also Actual authority; Apparent authority*

Authorized means

In contract law, the means of acceptance authorized by the offeror.

Automatic stay

In bankruptcy proceedings, the suspension of virtually all litigation and other action by creditors against the debtor or the debtor's property; the stay is effective the moment the debtor files a petition in bankruptcy.

Award

In the context of litigation, the amount of money awarded to a plaintiff in a civil lawsuit as damages. In the context of arbitration, the arbitrator's decision.

B

Bail

An amount of money set by the court that must be paid by a criminal defendant to the court before the defendant will be released from custody. Bail is set to assure that an individual accused of a crime will appear for further criminal proceedings. If the accused provides bail, whether in cash or in a surety bond, then he or she is released from jail.

Bailee

One to whom goods are entrusted by a bailor. Under the Uniform Commercial Code, a party who, by a bill of lading, warehouse receipt, or other document of title, acknowledges possession of goods and contracts.

Bailee's lien

A possessory lien, or claim, that a bailee entitled to compensation can place on the bailed property to ensure that he or she will be paid for the services provided. The lien is effective as long as the bailee retains possession of the bailed goods and has not agreed to extend credit to the bailor. Sometimes referred to as an artisan's lien.

Bailment

A situation in which the personal property of one person (a bailor) is entrusted to another (a bailee), who is obligated to return the bailed property to the bailor or dispose of it as directed.

Bailor

One who entrusts goods to a bailee.

Bait-and-switch advertising

Advertising a product at a very attractive price (the "bait") and then informing the consumer, once he or she is in the store, that the advertised product is either not available or is of poor quality; the customer is then urged to purchase ("switched" to) a more expensive item.

Banker's acceptance

A negotiable instrument that is commonly used in international trade. A banker's acceptance is drawn by a creditor against the debtor, who pays the draft at maturity. The drawer creates a draft without designating a payee. The draft can pass through many parties' hands before a bank (drawee) accepts it, transforming the draft into a banker's acceptance. Acceptances can be purchased and sold in a way similar to securities.

Bankruptcy court

A federal court of limited jurisdiction that handles only bankruptcy proceedings. Bankruptcy proceedings are governed by federal bankruptcy law.

Bargain

A mutual undertaking, contract, or agreement between two parties; to negotiate over the terms of a purchase or contract.

Basis of the bargain

In contract law, the affirmation of fact or promise on which the sale of goods is predicated, creating an express warranty.

Battery

The unprivileged, intentional touching of another.

Beachhead acquistion

The gradual accumulation of a bloc of a target corporation's shares by an aggressor during an attempt to obtain control of the corporation.

Bearer

A person in the possession of an instrument payable to bearer or indorsed in blank.

Bearer instrument

Any instrument that is not payable to a specific person, including instruments payable to the bearer or to "cash."

Beneficiary

One to whom life insurance proceeds are payable or for whose benefit a trust has been established or property under a will has been transferred.

Bequest

A gift by will of personal property (from the verb—to bequeath).

Beyond a reasonable doubt

The standard used to determine the guilt or innocence of a person criminally charged. To be guilty of a crime, one must be proved guilty "beyond and to the exclusion of every reasonable doubt." A reasonable doubt is one that would cause a prudent person to hesitate before acting in matters important to him or her.

Bilateral contract

A type of contract that arises when a promise is given in exchange for a return promise.

Bill of lading

A document that serves both as evidence of the receipt of goods for shipment and as documentary evidence of title to the goods.

Bill of Rights

The first ten amendments to the U.S. Constitution.

Binder

A written, temporary insurance policy.

Binding authority

Any source of law that a court must follow when deciding a case. Binding authorities include constitutions, statutes, and regulations that govern the issue being decided, as well as court decisions that are controlling precedents within the jurisdiction.

Blank indorsement

An indorsement that specifies no particular indorsee and can consist of a mere signature. An order instrument that is indorsed in blank becomes a bearer instrument.

Blue laws

State or local laws that prohibit the performance of certain types of commercial activities on Sunday.

Blue sky laws

State laws that regulate the offer and sale of securities.

Bona fide

Good faith. A bona fide obligation is one made in good faith—that is, sincerely and honestly.

Bona fide occupational qualification (BFOQ)

Identifiable characteristics reasonably necessary to the normal operation of a particular business. These characteristics can include gender, national origin, and religion, but not race.

Bond

A certificate that evidences a corporate (or government) debt. It is a security that involves no ownership interest in the issuing entity.

Bond indenture

A contract between the issuer of a bond and the bondholder.

Bounty payment

A reward (payment) given to a person or persons who perform a certain service—such as informing legal authorities of illegal actions.

Boycott

A concerted refusal to do business with a particular person or entity in order to obtain concessions or to express displeasure with certain acts or practices of that person or business. *See also Secondary boycott*

Breach

To violate a law, by an act or an omission, or to break a legal obligation that one owes to another person or to society.

Breach of contract

The failure, without legal excuse, of a promisor to perform the obligations of a contract.

Bribery

The offering, giving, receiving, or soliciting of anything of value with the aim of influencing an official action or an official's discharge of a legal or public duty or (with respect to commercial bribery) a business decision.

Brief

A formal legal document submitted by the attorney for the appellant—or the appellee (in answer to the appellant's brief)—to an appellate court when a case is appealed. The appellant's brief outlines the facts and issues of the case, the judge's rulings or jury's findings that should be reversed or modified, the applicable law, and the arguments on the client's behalf.

Browse-wrap terms

Terms and conditions of use that are presented to an Internet user at the time certain products, such as software, are being downloaded but that need not be agreed to (by clicking "I agree," for example) before being able to install or use the product.

Bulk transfer

A bulk sale or transfer, not made in the ordinary course of business, of a major part of the materials, supplies, merchandise, or other inventory of an enterprise.

Bureaucracy

A large organization that is structured hierarchically to carry out specific functions.

Burglary

The unlawful entry into a building with the intent to commit a felony. (Some state statutes expand this to include the intent to commit any crime.)

Business ethics

Ethics in a business context; a consensus of what constitutes right or wrong behavior in the world of business and the application of moral principles to situations that arise in a business setting.

Business invitees

Those people, such as customers or clients, who are invited onto business premises by the owner of those premises for business purposes.

Business judgment rule

A rule that immunizes corporate management from liability for actions that result in corporate losses or damages if the actions are undertaken in good faith and are within both the power of the corporation and the authority of management to make.

Business necessity

A defense to allegations of employment discrimination in which the employer demonstrates that an employment practice that discriminates against members of a protected class is related to job performance.

Business plan

A document describing a company, its products, and its anticipated future performance. Creating a business plan is normally the first step in obtaining loans or venture-capital funds for a new business enterprise.

Business tort

The wrongful interference with the business rights of another.

Business trust

A voluntary form of business organization in which investors (trust beneficiaries) transfer cash or property to trustees in exchange for trust certificates that represent their investment shares. Management of the business and trust property is handled by the trustees for the use and benefit of the investors. The certificate holders have limited liability (are not responsible for the debts and obligations incurred by the trust) and share in the trust's profits.

Buyer in the ordinary course of business

A buyer who, in good faith and without knowledge that the sale to him or her is in violation of the ownership rights or security interest of a third party in the goods, purchases goods in the ordinary course of business from a person in the business of selling goods of that kind.

Buy-sell agreement

In the context of partnerships, an express agreement made at the time of partnership formation for one or more of the partners to buy out the other or others should the situation warrant—and thus provide for the smooth dissolution of the partnership.

Bylaws

A set of governing rules adopted by a corporation or other association.

Bystander

A spectator, witness, or person standing nearby when an event occurred and who did not engage in the business or act leading to the event.

C

C.I.F. or C.&F.

Cost, insurance, and freight—or just cost and freight. A pricing term in a contract for the sale of goods requiring, among other things, that the seller place the goods in the possession of a carrier before risk passes to the buyer.

C.O.D.

Cash on delivery. In sales transactions, a term meaning that the buyer will pay for the goods on delivery and before inspecting the goods.

Callable bond

A bond that may be called in and the principal repaid at specified times or under conditions specified in the bond when it is issued.

Cancellation

The act of nullifying, or making void. *See also Rescission*

Capital

Accumulated goods, possessions, and assets used for the production of profits and wealth; the equity of owners in a business.

Carrier

An individual or organization engaged in transporting passengers or goods for hire. *See also Common carrier*

Case law

The rules of law announced in court decisions. Case law includes the aggregate of reported cases that interpret judicial precedents, statutes, regulations, and constitutional provisions.

Case on point

A previous case involving factual circumstances and issues that are similar to the case before the court.

Cash surrender value

The amount that the insurer has agreed to pay to the insured if a life insurance policy is canceled before the insured's death.

Cashier's check

A check drawn by a bank on itself.

Categorical imperative

A concept developed by the philosopher Immanuel Kant as an ethical guideline for behavior. In deciding whether an action is right or wrong, or desirable or undesirable, a person should evaluate the action in terms of what would happen if everybody else in the same situation, or category, acted the same way.

Causation in fact

An act or omission without ("but for") which an event would not have occurred.

Cause of action

A situation or state of facts that would entitle a party to sustain a legal action and give the party a right to seek a judicial remedy.

Cease-and-desist order

An administrative or judicial order prohibiting a person or business firm from conducting activities that an agency or court has deemed illegal.

Certificate of deposit (CD)

A note of a bank in which a bank acknowledges a receipt of money from a party and promises to repay the money, with interest, to the party on a certain date.

Certificate of incorporation

The primary document that evidences corporate existence (referred to as articles of incorporation in some states).

Certificate of limited partnership

The basic document filed with a designated state official by which a limited partnership is formed.

Certification

In negotiable instruments law, the act of certifying a check. *See Certified check*

Certification mark

A mark used by one or more persons, other than the owner, to certify the region, materials, mode of manufacture, quality, or accuracy of the owner's goods or services. When used by members of a cooperative, association, or other organization, such a mark is referred to as a collective mark. Examples of certification marks include the "Good Housekeeping Seal of Approval" and "UL Tested."

Certified check

A check that has been accepted by the bank on which it is drawn. Essentially, the bank, by certifying (accepting) the check, promises to pay the check at the time the check is presented.

Certiorari

See Writ of certiorari

Chain-style business franchise

A franchise that operates under a franchisor's trade name and that is identified as a member of a select group of dealers that engage in the franchisor's business. The franchisee is generally required to follow standardized or prescribed methods of operation. Examples of this type of franchise are McDonald's and most other fast-food chains.

Chancellor

An adviser to the king at the time of the early king's courts of England. Individuals petitioned the king for relief when they could not obtain an adequate remedy in a court of law, and these petitions were decided by the chancellor.

Charging order

In partnership law, an order granted by a court to a judgment creditor that entitles the creditor to attach profits or assets of a partner on dissolution of the partnership.

Charitable trust

A trust in which the property held by a trustee must be used for a charitable purpose, such as the advancement of health, education, or religion.

Charter

See Corporate charter

Chattel

All forms of personal property.

Chattel paper

Any writing or writings that show both a debt and the fact that the debt is secured by personal property. In many instances, chattel paper consists of a negotiable instrument coupled with a security agreement.

Check

A draft drawn by a drawer ordering the drawee bank or financial institution to pay a certain amount of money to the holder on demand.

Checks and balances

The national government is composed of three separate branches: the executive, the legislative, and the judicial branches. Each branch of the government exercises a check on the actions of the others.

Choice-of-language clause

A clause in a contract designating the official language by which the contract will be interpreted in the event of a future disagreement over the contract's terms.

Choice-of-law clause

A clause in a contract designating the law (such as the law of a particular state or nation) that will govern the contract.

Citation

A reference to a publication in which a legal authority—such as a statute or a court decision—or other source can be found.

Civil law

The branch of law dealing with the definition and enforcement of all private or public rights, as opposed to criminal matters.

Civil law system

A system of law derived from that of the Roman Empire and based on a code rather than case law; the predominant system of law in the nations of continental Europe and the nations that were once their colonies. In the United States, Louisiana is the only state that has a civil law system.

Claim

As a verb, to assert or demand. As a noun, a right to payment.

Clearinghouse

A system or place where banks exchange checks and drafts drawn on each other and settle daily balances.

Click-on agreement

An agreement that arises when a buyer, engaging in a transaction on a computer, indicates his or her assent to be bound by the terms of an offer by clicking on a button that says, for example, "I agree"; sometimes referred to as a click-on license or a click-wrap agreement.

Close corporation

A corporation whose shareholders are limited to a small group of persons, often including only family members. The rights of shareholders of a close corporation usually are restricted regarding the transfer of shares to others.

Closed shop

A firm that requires union membership by its workers as a condition of employment. The closed shop was made illegal by the Labor-Management Relations Act of 1947.

Closing

The final step in the sale of real estate—also called settlement or closing escrow. The escrow agent coordinates the closing with the recording of deeds, the obtaining of title insurance, and other concurrent closing activities. A number of costs must be paid, in cash, at the time of closing, and they can range from several hundred to several thousand dollars, depending on the amount of the mortgage loan and other conditions of the sale.

Closing argument

An argument made after the plaintiff Closing arguments are made prior to the jury charges.

Codicil

A written supplement or modification to a will. A codicil must be executed with the same formalities as a will.

Collateral

Under Article 9 of the Uniform Commercial Code, the property subject to a security interest, including accounts and chattel paper that have been sold.

Collateral promise

A secondary promise that is ancillary (subsidiary) to a principal transaction or primary contractual relationship, such as a promise made by one person to pay the debts of another if the latter fails to perform. A collateral promise normally must be in writing to be enforceable.

Collecting bank

Any bank handling an item for collection, except the payor bank.

Collective bargaining

The process by which labor and management negotiate the terms and conditions of employment, including working hours and workplace conditions.

Collective mark

A mark used by members of a cooperative, association, or other organization to certify the region, materials, mode of manufacture, quality, or accuracy of the specific goods or services. Examples of collective marks include the labor union marks found on tags of certain products and the credits of movies, which indicate the various associations and organizations that participated in the making of the movies.

Comity

A deference by which one nation gives effect to the laws and judicial decrees of another nation. This recognition is based primarily on respect.

Comment period

A period of time following an administrative agency's publication or a notice of a proposed rule during which private parties may comment in writing on the agency proposal in an effort to influence agency policy. The agency takes any comments received into consideration when drafting the final version of the regulation.

Commerce clause

The provision in Article I, Section 8, of the U.S. Constitution that gives Congress the power to regulate interstate commerce.

Commercial impracticability

A doctrine under which a seller may be excused from performing a contract when (1) a contingency occurs, (2) the contingency's occurrence makes performance impracticable, and (3) the nonoccurrence of the contingency was a basic assumption on which the contract was made. Despite the fact that UCC 2-615 expressly frees only sellers under this doctrine, courts have not distinguished between buyers and sellers in applying it.

Commercial paper

See Negotiable instrument

Commingle

To mix together. To put funds or goods together into one mass so that the funds or goods are so mixed that they no longer have separate identities. In corporate law, if personal and corporate interests are commingled to the extent that the corporation has no separate identity, a court may "pierce the corporate veil" and expose the shareholders to personal liability.

Common area

In landlord-tenant law, a portion of the premises over which the landlord retains control and maintenance responsibilities. Common areas may include stairs, lobbies, garages, hallways, and other areas in common use.

Common carrier

A carrier that holds itself out or undertakes to carry persons or goods of all persons indifferently, or of all who choose to employ it.

Common law

That body of law developed from custom or judicial decisions in English and U.S. courts, not attributable to a legislature.

Common stock

Shares of ownership in a corporation that give the owner of the stock a proportionate interest in the corporation with regard to control, earnings, and net assets; shares of common stock are lowest in priority with respect to payment of dividends and distribution of the corporation's assets on dissolution.

Community property

A form of concurrent ownership of property in which each spouse technically owns an undivided one-half interest in property acquired during the marriage. This form of joint ownership occurs in only nine states and Puerto Rico.

Comparative law

The study and comparison of legal systems and laws across nations.

Comparative negligence

A theory in tort law under which the liability for injuries resulting from negligent acts is shared by all parties who were negligent (including the injured party), on the basis of each person's proportionate negligence.

Compensatory damages

A money award equivalent to the actual value of injuries or damages sustained by the aggrieved party.

Complaint

The pleading made by a plaintiff alleging wrongdoing on the part of the defendant; the document that, when filed with a court, initiates a lawsuit.

Complete performance

Performance of a contract strictly in accordance with the contract's terms.

Composition agreement

See Creditors' composition agreement

Computer crime

Any wrongful act that is directed against computers and computer parties, or wrongful use or abuse of computers or software.

Computer information

As defined by the Uniform Computer Information Transactions Act, "information in an electronic form obtained from or through use of a computer, or that is in digital or an equivalent form capable of being processed by a computer."

Concentrated industry

An industry in which a large percentage of market sales is controlled by either a single firm or a small number of firms.

Conciliation

A form of alternative dispute resolution in which the parties reach an agreement themselves with the help of a neutral third party, called a conciliator, who facilitates the negotiations.

Concurrent conditions

Conditions in a contract that must occur or be performed at the same time; they are mutually dependent. No obligations arise until these conditions are simultaneously performed.

Concurrent jurisdiction

Jurisdiction that exists when two different courts have the power to hear a case. For example, some cases can be heard in either a federal or a state court.

Concurrent ownership

Joint ownership.

Concurring opinion

A written opinion outlining the views of a judge or justice to make or emphasize a point that was not made or emphasized in the majority opinion.

Condemnation

The process of taking private property for public use through the government's power of eminent domain.

Condition

A possible future event, the occurrence or nonoccurrence of which will trigger the performance of a legal obligation or terminate an existing obligation under a contract.

Condition precedent

A condition in a contract that must be met before a party's promise becomes absolute.

Condition subsequent

A condition in a contract that operates to terminate a party's absolute promise to perform.

Conditional contract

A contract subject to a condition that must be met for the contract to be enforceable. *See Condition precedent*

Confession of judgment

The act of a debtor in permitting a judgment to be entered against him or her by a creditor, for an agreed sum, without the institution of legal proceedings.

Confiscation

A government's taking of privately owned business or personal property without a proper public purpose or an award of just compensation.

Conforming goods

Goods that conform to contract specifications.

Confusion

The mixing together of goods belonging to two or more owners so that the separately owned goods cannot be identified.

Conglomerate merger

A merger between firms that do not compete with each other because they are in different markets (as opposed to horizontal and vertical mergers).

Consent

Voluntary agreement to a proposition or an act of another. A concurrence of wills.

Consequential damages

Special damages that compensate for a loss that is not direct or immediate (for example, lost profits). The special damages must have been reasonably foreseeable at the time the breach or injury occurred in order for the plaintiff to collect them.

Consideration

Generally, the value given in return for a promise or a performance. The consideration, which must be present to make the contract legally binding, must be something of legally sufficient value and bargained for.

Consignee

One to whom goods are delivered on consignment. *See also Consignment*

Consignment

A transaction in which an owner of goods (the consignor) delivers the goods to another (the consignee) for the consignee to sell. The consignee pays the consignor for the goods when they are sold by the consignee.

Consignor

One who consigns goods to another. *See also Consignment*

Consolidation

A contractual and statutory process in which two or more corporations join to become a completely new corporation. The original corporations cease to exist, and the new corporation acquires all their assets and liabilities.

Constitutional law

Law that is based on the U.S. Constitution and the constitutions of the various states.

Constructive condition

A condition in a contract that is neither expressed nor implied by the contract but rather is imposed by law for reasons of justice.

Constructive delivery

An act equivalent to the actual, physical delivery of property that cannot be physically delivered because of difficulty or impossibility; for example, the transfer of a key to a safe constructively delivers the contents of the safe.

Constructive eviction

A form of eviction that occurs when a landlord fails to perform adequately any of the undertakings (such as providing heat in the winter) required by the lease, thereby making the tenant's further use and enjoyment of the property exceedingly difficult or impossible.

Constructive trust

An equitable trust that is imposed in the interests of fairness and justice when someone wrongfully holds legal title to property. A court may require the owner to hold the property in trust for the person or persons who rightfully should own the property.

Consumer credit

Credit extended primarily for personal or household use.

Consumer-debtor

An individual whose debts are primarily consumer debts (debts for purchases made primarily for personal or household use).

Consumer goods

Goods that are primarily for personal or household use.

Consumer law

The body of statutes, agency rules, and judicial decisions protecting consumers of goods and services from dangerous manufacturing techniques, mislabeling, unfair credit practices, deceptive advertising, and so on. Consumer laws provide remedies and protections that are not ordinarily available to merchants or to businesses.

Contingency fee

An attorney's fee that is based on a percentage of the final award received by his or her client as a result of litigation.

Continuation statement

A statement that, if filed within six months prior to the expiration date of the original financing statement, continues the perfection of the original security interest for another five years. The perfection of a security interest can be continued in the same manner indefinitely.

Contract

An agreement that can be enforced in court; formed by two or more parties, each of whom agrees to perform or to refrain from performing some act now or in the future.

Contract implied in law

See Quasi contract

Contract under seal

A formal agreement in which the seal is a substitute for consideration. A court will not invalidate a contract under seal for lack of consideration.

Contractual agreement

See Contract

Contractual capacity

The threshold mental capacity required by the law for a party who enters into a contract to be bound by that contract.

Contribution

See Right of contribution

Contributory negligence

A theory in tort law under which a complaining party's own negligence contributed to or caused his or her injuries. Contributory negligence is an absolute bar to recovery in a minority of jurisdictions.

Conversion

The wrongful taking, using, or retaining possession of personal property that belongs to another.

Convertible bond

A bond that can be exchanged for a specified number of shares of common stock under certain conditions.

Conveyance

The transfer of a title to land from one person to another by deed; a document (such as a deed) by which an interest in land is transferred from one person to another.

Conviction

The outcome of a criminal trial in which the defendant has been found guilty of the crime with which he or she was charged and on which sentencing, or punishment, is based.

Cooperative

An association that is organized to provide an economic service to its members (or shareholders). An incorporated cooperative is a nonprofit corporation. It will make distributions of dividends, or profits, to its owners on the basis of their transactions with the cooperative rather than on the basis of the amount of capital they contributed. Examples of cooperatives are consumer purchasing cooperatives, credit cooperatives, and farmers' cooperatives.

Co-ownership

Joint ownership.

Copyright

The exclusive right of authors to publish, print, or sell an intellectual production for a statutory period of time. A copyright has the same monopolistic nature as a patent or trademark, but it differs in that it applies exclusively to works of art, literature, and other works of authorship, including computer programs.

Corporate charter

The document issued by astate agency or authority (usually the secretary of state) that grants a corporation legal existence and the right to function.

Corporate social responsibility

The concept that corporations can and should act ethically and be accountable to society for their actions.

Corporation

A legal entity formed in compliance with statutory requirements. The entity is distinct from its shareholders-owners.

Cosign

The act of signing a document (such as a note promising to pay another in return for a loan or other benefit) jointly with another person and thereby assuming liability for performing what was promised in the document.

Cost-benefit analysis

A decision-making technique that involves weighing the costs of a given action against the benefits of the action.

Co-surety

A joint surety. One who assumes liability jointly with another surety for the payment of an obligation.

Counteradvertising

New advertising that is undertaken pursuant to a Federal Trade Commission order for the purpose of correcting earlier false claims that were made about a product.

Counterclaim

A claim made by a defendant in a civil lawsuit that in effect sues the plaintiff.

Counteroffer

An offeree's response to an offer in which the offeree rejects the original offer and at the same time makes a new offer.

Course of dealing

Prior conduct between parties to a contract that establishes a common basis for their understanding.

Course of performance

The conduct that occurs under the terms of a particular agreement; such conduct indicates what the parties to an agreement intended it to mean.

Court of equity

A court that decides controversies and administers justice according to the rules, principles, and precedents of equity.

Court of law

A court in which the only remedies that could be granted were things of value, such as money damages. In the early English king's courts, courts of law were distinct from courts of equity.

Covenant against encumbrances

A grantor's assurance that on land conveyed there are no encumbrances—that is, that no third parties have rights to or interests in the land that would diminish its value to the grantee.

Covenant not to compete

A contractual promise to refrain from competing with another party for a certain period of time (not excessive in duration) and within a reasonable geographic area. Although covenants not to compete restrain trade, they are commonly found in partnership agreements, business sale agreements, and employment contracts. If they are ancillary to such agreements, covenants not to compete will normally be enforced by the courts unless the time period or geographic area is deemed unreasonable.

Covenant not to sue

An agreement to substitute a contractual obligation for some other type of legal action based on a valid claim.

Covenant of quiet enjoyment

A promise by a grantor (or landlord) that the grantee (or tenant) will not be evicted or disturbed by the grantor or a person having a lien or superior title.

Covenant of the right to convey

A grantor's assurance that he or she has sufficient capacity and title to convey the estate that he or she undertakes to convey by deed.

Covenant running with the land

An executory promise made between a grantor and a grantee to which they and subsequent owners of the land are bound.

Cover

A buyer or lessee's purchase on the open market of goods to substitute for those promised but never delivered by the seller. Under the Uniform Commercial Code, if the cost of cover exceeds the cost of the contract goods, the buyer or lessee can recover the difference, plus incidental and consequential damages.

Cram-down provision

A provision of the Bankruptcy Code that allows a court to confirm a debtor's Chapter 11 reorganization plan even though only one class of creditors has accepted it. To exercise the court's right under this provision, the court must demonstrate that the plan does not discriminate unfairly against any creditors and is fair and equitable.

Crashworthiness doctrine

A doctrine that imposes liability for defects in the design or construction of motor vehicles that increase the extent of injuries to passengers if an accident occurs. The doctrine holds even when the defects do not actually cause the accident.

Creditor

A person to whom a debt is owed by another person (the debtor).

Creditor beneficiary

A third party beneficiary who has rights in a contract made by the debtor and a third person. The terms of the contract obligate the third person to pay the debt owed to the creditor. The creditor beneficiary can enforce the debt against either party.

Creditors' composition agreement

An agreement formed between a debtor and his or her creditors in which the creditors agree to accept a lesser sum than that owed by the debtor in full satisfaction of the debt.

Crime

A wrong against society proclaimed in a statute and, if committed, punishable by society through fines and/or imprisonment—and, in some cases, death.

Criminal act

See Actus reus

Criminal intent

See Mens rea

Criminal law

Law that defines and governs actions that constitute crimes. Generally, criminal law has to do with wrongful actions committed against society for which society demands redress.

Cross-border pollution

Pollution across national boundaries; air and water degradation in one nation resulting from pollution-causing activities in a neighboring country.

Cross-collateralization

The use of an asset that is not the subject of a loan to collateralize that loan.

Cross-examination

The questioning of an opposing witness during the trial.

Cumulative voting

A method of shareholder voting designed to allow minority shareholders to be represented on the board of directors. With cumulative voting, the number of members of the board to be elected is multiplied by the total number of voting shares held. The result equals the number of votes a shareholder has, and this total can be cast for one or more nominees for director.

Cure

Under the Uniform Commercial Code, the right of a party who tenders nonconforming performance to correct his or her performance within the contract period.

Cyber crime

A crime that occurs online, in the virtual community of the Internet, as opposed to the physical world.

Cyber hate speech

Extreme hate speech on the Internet. Racist materials and Holocaust denials disseminated on the Web are examples.

Cyber mark

A trademark in cyberspace.

Cyber stalker

A person who commits the crime of stalking in cyberspace. Generally, stalking consists of harassing a person and putting that person in reasonable fear for his or her safety or the safety of the person's immediate family.

Cyber terrorist

A hacker whose purpose is to exploit a target computer for a serious impact, such as the corruption of a program to sabotage a business.

Cyber tort

A tort committed via the Internet.

Cybernotary

A legally recognized authority that can certify the validity of digital signatures.

D

Damages

Money sought as a remedy for a breach of contract or for a tortious act.

Debenture bond

A bond for which no specific assets of the corporation are pledged as backing; rather, the bond is backed by the general credit rating of the corporation, plus any assets that can be seized if the corporation allows the debentures to go into default.

Debtor

Under Article 9 of the Uniform Commercial Code, a debtor is any party who owes payment or performance of a secured obligation, whether or not the party actually owns or has rights in the collateral.

Debtor in possession (DIP)

In Chapter 11 bankruptcy proceedings, a debtor who is allowed to continue in possession of the estate in property (the business) and to continue business operations.

Declaratory judgment

A court's judgment on a justiciable controversy when the plaintiff is in doubt as to his or her legal rights; a binding adjudication of the rights and status of litigants even though no consequential relief is awarded.

Decree

The judgment of a court of equity.

Deed

A document by which title to property (usually real property) is passed.

Defalcation

The misuse of funds.

Defamation

Any published or publicly spoken false statement that causes injury to another's good name, reputation, or character.

Default

The failure to observe a promise or discharge an obligation. The term is commonly used to mean the failure to pay a debt when it is due.

Default judgment

A judgment entered by a court against a defendant who has failed to appear in court to answer or defend against the plaintiff's claim.

Defendant

One against whom a lawsuit is brought; the accused person in a criminal proceeding.

Defense

Reasons that a defendant offers in an action or suit as to why the plaintiff should not obtain what he or she is seeking.

Deficiency judgment

A judgment against a debtor for the amount of a debt remaining unpaid after collateral has been repossessed and sold.

Delegatee

One to whom contract duties are delegated by another, called the delegator.

Delegation

The transfer of a contractual duty to a third party. The party delegating the duty (the delegator) to the third party (the delegatee) is still obliged to perform on the contract should the delegatee fail to perform.

Delegation doctrine

A doctrine based on Article I, Section 8, of the U.S. Constitution, which has been construed to allow Congress to delegate some of its power to make and implement laws to administrative agencies. The delegation is considered to be proper as long as Congress sets standards outlining the scope of the agency's authority.

Delegator

One who delegates his or her duties under a contract to another, called the delegatee.

Delivery

In contract law, the one party's act of placing the subject matter of the contract within the other party's possession or control.

Delivery ex ship

Delivery from the carrying ship. A contract term indicating that risk of loss will not pass to the buyer until the goods leave the ship or are otherwise properly unloaded.

Delivery order

A written order to deliver goods directed to a warehouser, carrier, or other person who, in the ordinary course of business, issues warehouse receipts or bills of lading [UCC 7-102(1)(d)].

Demand deposit

Funds (accepted by a bank) subject to immediate withdrawal, in contrast to a time deposit, which requires that a depositor wait a specific time before withdrawing or pay a penalty for early withdrawal.

Demurrer

See Motion to dismiss

De novo

Anew; afresh; a second time. In a hearing de novo, an appellate court hears the case as a court of original jurisidction—that is, as if the case had not previously been tried and a decision rendered.

Depositary bank

The first bank to receive a check for payment.

Deposition

The testimony of a party to a lawsuit or a witness taken under oath before a trial.

Destination contract

A contract in which the seller is required to ship the goods by carrier and deliver them at a particular destination. The seller assumes liability for any losses or damage to the goods until they are tendered at the destination specified in the contract.

Devise

To make a gift of real property by will.

Dilution

With respect to trademarks, a doctrine under which distinctive or famous trademarks are protected from certain unauthorized uses of the marks regardless of a showing of competition or a likelihood of confusion. Congress created a federal cause of action for dilution in 1995 with the passage of the Federal Trademark Dilution Act.

Direct examination

The examination of a witness by the attorney who calls the witness to the stand to testify on behalf of the attorney's client.

Directed verdict

See Motion for a directed verdict

Disaffirmance

The legal avoidance, or setting aside, of a contractual obligation.

Discharge

The termination of an obligation. (1) In contract law, discharge occurs when the parties have fully performed their contractual obligations or when events, conduct of the parties, or operation of the law releases the parties from performance. (2) In bankruptcy proceedings, the extinction of the debtor's dischargeable debts.

Discharge in bankruptcy

The release of a debtor from all debts that are provable, except those specifically excepted from discharge by statute.

Disclosed principal

A principal whose identity is known to a third party at the time the agent makes a contract with the third party.

Discovery

A phase in the litigation process during which the opposing parties may obtain information from each other and from third parties prior to trial.

Dishonor

To refuse to accept or pay a draft or a promissory note when it is properly presented. An instrument is dishonored when presentment is properly made and acceptance or payment is refused or cannot be obtained within the prescribed time.

Disparagement of property

An economically injurious false statement made about another's product or property. A general term for torts that are more specifically referred to as slander of quality or slander of title.

Disparate-impact discrimination

A form of employment discrimination that results from certain employer practices or procedures that, although not discriminatory on their face, have a discriminatory effect.

Disparate-treatment discrimination

A form of employment discrimination that results when an employer intentionally discriminates against employees who are members of protected classes.

Dissenting opinion

A written opinion by a judge or justice who disagrees with the majority opinion.

Dissolution

The formal disbanding of a partnership or a corporation. It can take place by (1) acts of the partners or, in a corporation, of the shareholders and board of directors; (2) the death of a partner; (3) the expiration of a time period stated in a partnership agreement or a certificate of incorporation; or (4) judicial decree.

Distribution agreement

A contract between a seller and a distributor of the seller's products setting out the terms and conditions of the distributorship.

Distributorship

A business arrangement that is established when a manufacturer licenses a dealer to sell its product. An example of a distributorship is an automobile dealership.

Diversity of citizenship

Under Article III, Section 2, of the Constitution, a basis for federal court jurisdiction over a lawsuit between (1) citizens of different states, (2) a foreign country and citizens of a state or of different states, or (3) citizens of a state and citizens or subjects of a foreign country. The amount in controversy must be more than $75,000 before a federal court can take jurisdiction in such cases.

Divestiture

The act of selling one or more of a company's parts, such as a subsidiary or plant; often mandated by the courts in merger or monopolization cases.

Dividend

A distribution to corporate shareholders of corporate profits or income, disbursed in proportion to the number of shares held.

Docket

The list of cases entered on a court's calendar and thus scheduled to be heard by the court.

Document of title

Paper exchanged in the regular course of business that evidences the right to possession of goods (for example, a bill of lading or a warehouse receipt).

Domain name

The series of letters and symbols used to identify site operators on the Internet; Internet "addresses."

Domestic corporation

In a given state, a corporation that does business in, and is organized under the laws of, that state.

Domestic relations court

A court that deals with domestic (household) relationships, such as adoption, divorce, support payments, child custody, and the like.

Donee beneficiary

A third party beneficiary who has rights under a contract as a direct result of the intention of the contract parties to make a gift to the third party.

Double jeopardy

A situation occurring when a person is tried twice for the same criminal offense; prohibited by the Fifth Amendment to the Constitution.

Double taxation

A feature (and disadvantage) of the corporate form of business. Because a corporation is a separate legal entity, corporate profits are taxed by state and federal governments. Dividends are again taxable as ordinary income to the shareholders receiving them.

Draft

Any instrument (such as a check) drawn on a drawee (such as a bank) that orders the drawee to pay a certain sum of money, usually to a third party (the payee), on demand or at a definite future time.

Dram shop act

A state statute that imposes liability on the owners of bars and taverns, as well as those who serve alcoholic drinks to the public, for injuries resulting from accidents caused by intoxicated persons when the sellers or servers of alcoholic drinks contributed to the intoxication.

Drawee

The party that is ordered to pay a draft or check. With a check, a financial institution is always the drawee.

Drawer

The party that initiates a draft (writes a check, for example), thereby ordering the drawee to pay.

Due diligence

A required standard of care that certain professionals, such as accountants, must meet to avoid liability for securities violations. Under securities law, an accountant will be deemed to have exercised due diligence if he or she followed generally accepted accounting principles and generally accepted auditing standards and had, "after reasonable investigation, reasonable grounds to believe and did believe, at the time such part of the registration statement became effective, that the statements therein were true and that there was no omission of a material fact required to be stated therein or necessary to make the statements therein not misleading."

Due negotiation

The transfer of a document of title in such form that the transferee becomes a holder [UCC 7-501].

Due process clause

The provisions of the Fifth and Fourteenth Amendments to the Constitution that guarantee that no person shall be deprived of life, liberty, or property without due process of law. Similar clauses are found in most state constitutions.

Dumping

The selling of goods in a foreign country at a price below the price charged for the same goods in the domestic market.

Durable power of attorney

A document that authorizes a person to act on behalf of an incompetent person—write checks, collect insurance proceeds, and otherwise manage the disabled person's affairs, including health care—when he or she becomes incapacitated. Spouses often give each other durable power of attorney and, if they are advanced in age, may give a second such power of attorney to an older child.

Duress

Unlawful pressure brought to bear on a person, causing the person to perform an act that he or she would not otherwise perform.

Duty of care

The duty of all persons, as established by tort law, to exercise a reasonable amount of care in their dealings with others. Failure to exercise due care, which is normally determined by the "reasonable person standard," constitutes the tort of negligence.

E

E-agent

A computer program, electronic, or other automated means used to perform specific tasks without review by an individual.

E-commerce

Business transacted in cyberspace.

E-contract

A contract that is entered into in cyberspace and is evidenced only by electronic impulses (such as those that make up a computer's memory), rather than, for example, a typewritten form.

E-money

Prepaid funds recorded on a computer or a card (such as a smart card).

E-signature

As defined by the Uniform Electronic Transactions Act, "an electronic sound, symbol, or process attached to or logically associated with a record and executed or adopted by a person with the intent to sign the record."

Early neutral case evaluation

A form of alternative dispute resolution in which a neutral third party evaluates the strengths and weakness of the disputing parties' positions; the evaluator's opinion forms the basis for negotiating a settlement.

Easement

A nonpossessory right to use another's property in a manner established by either express or implied agreement.

Ejectment

The eviction of a tenant from leased premises. A remedy at common law to which the landlord can resort when a tenant fails to pay rent for leased premises. To obtain possession of the premises, the landlord must appear in court and show that the defaulting tenant is in wrongful possession.

Elder law

A relatively new area of legal practice in which attorneys assist older persons in dealing with such problems as disability, long-term health care, age discrimination, grandparents' visitation rights, and other problems relating to age.

Electronic fund transfer (EFT)

A transfer of funds with the use of an electronic terminal, a telephone, a computer, or magnetic tape.

Emancipation

In regard to minors, the act of being freed from parental control; occurs when a child's parent or legal guardian relinquishes the legal right to exercise control over the child. Normally, a minor who leaves home to support himself or herself is considered emancipated.

Embezzlement

The fraudulent appropriation of money or other property by a person to whom the money or property has been entrusted.

Eminent domain

The power of a government to take land for public use from private citizens for just compensation.

Employee

A person who works for an employer for a salary or for wages.

Employer

An individual or business entity that hires employees, pays them salaries or wages, and exercises control over their work.

Employment at will

A common law doctrine under which either party may terminate an employment relationship at any time for any reason, unless a contract specifies otherwise.

Employment discrimination

Treating employees or job applicants unequally on the basis of race, color, national origin, religion, gender, age, or disability; prohibited by federal statutes.

Enabling legislation

A statute enacted by Congress that authorizes the creation of an administrative agency and specifies the name, composition, purpose, and powers of the agency being created.

Encryption

The process by which a message (plaintext) is transformed into something (ciphertext) that the sender and receiver intend third parties not to understand.

Endowment insurance

A type of insurance that combines life insurance with an investment so that if the insured outlives the policy, the face value is paid to him or her; if the insured does not outlive the policy, the face value is paid to his or her beneficiary.

Entrapment

In criminal law, a defense in which the defendant claims that he or she was induced by a public official—usually an undercover agent or police officer—to commit a crime that he or she would otherwise not have committed.

Entrepreneur

One who initiates and assumes the financial risks of a new enterprise and who undertakes to provide or control its management.

Entrustment

The transfer of goods to a merchant who deals in goods of that kind and who may transfer those goods and all rights to them to a buyer in the ordinary course of business [UCC 2-403(2)].

Environmental impact statement (EIS)

A statement required by the National Environmental Policy Act for any major federal action that will significantly affect the quality of the environment. The statement must analyze the action's impact on the environment and explore alternative actions that might be taken.

Environmental law

The body of statutory, regulatory, and common law relating to the protection of the environment.

Equal dignity rule

In most states, a rule stating that express authority given to an agent must be in writing if the contract to be made on behalf of the principal is required to be in writing.

Equal protection clause

The provision in the Fourteenth Amendment to the Constitution that guarantees that no state will "deny to any person within its jurisdiction the equal protection of the laws." This clause mandates that state governments treat similarly situated individuals in a similar manner.

Equitable maxims

General propositions or principles of law that have to do with fairness (equity).

Equity of redemption

The right of a mortgagor who has breached the mortgage agreement to redeem or purchase the property prior to foreclosure proceedings.

Escheat

The transfer of property to the state when the owner of the property dies without heirs.

Escrow account

An account that is generally held in the name of the depositor and escrow agent; the funds in the account are paid to a third person only on fulfillment of the escrow condition.

Establishment clause

The provision in the First Amendment to the U.S. Constitution that prohibits Congress from creating any law "respecting an establishment of religion."

Estate

The interest that a person has in real and personal property.

Estate planning

Planning in advance how one's property and obligations should be transferred on one's death. Wills and trusts are two basic devices used in the process of estate planning.

Estop

To bar, impede, or preclude.

Estoppel

The principle that a party's own acts prevent him or her from claiming a right to the detriment of another who was entitled to and did rely on those acts. *See also Agency by estoppel; Promissory estoppel*

Estray statute

A statute defining finders' rights in property when the true owners are unknown.

Ethical reasoning

A reasoning process in which an individual links his or her moral convictions or ethical standards to the particular situation at hand.

Ethics

Moral principles and values applied to social behavior.

Evidence

Proof offered at trial—in the form of testimony, documents, records, exhibits, objects, and so on—for the purpose of convincing the court or jury of the truth of a contention.

Eviction

A landlord's act of depriving a tenant of possession of the leased premises.

Ex parte contact

Communications with an administrative agency that are not placed in the record.

Ex ship

See Delivery ex ship

Exclusionary rule

In criminal procedure, a rule under which any evidence that is obtained in violation of the accused's constitutional rights guaranteed by the Fourth, Fifth, and Sixth Amendments, as well as any evidence derived from illegally obtained evidence, will not be admissible in court.

Exclusive distributorship

A distributorship in which the seller and the distributor of the seller's products agree that the distributor has the exclusive right to distribute the seller's products in a certain geographic area.

Exclusive jurisdiction

Jurisdiction that exists when a case can be heard only in a particular court or type of court, such as a federal court or a state court.

Exclusive-dealing contract

An agreement under which a seller forbids a buyer to purchase products from the seller's competitors.

Exculpatory clause

A clause that releases a contractual party from liability in the event of monetary or physical injury, no matter who is at fault.

Executed contract

A contract that has been completely performed by both parties.

Execution

An action to carry into effect the directions in a court decree or judgment.

Executive agency

An administrative agency within the executive branch of government. At the federal level, executive agencies are those within the cabinet departments.

Executor

A person appointed by a testator to see that his or her will is administered appropriately.

Executory contract

A contract that has not as yet been fully performed.

Export

To sell products to buyers located in other countries.

Express authority

Authority expressly given by one party to another. In agency law, an agent has express authority to act for a principal if both parties agree, orally or in writing, that an agency relationship exists in which the agent had the power (authority) to act in the place of, and on behalf of, the principal.

Express contract

A contract in which the terms of the agreement are fully and explicitly stated in words, oral or written.

Express warranty

A seller's or lessor's oral or written promise, ancillary to an underlying sales or lease agreement, as to the quality, description, or performance of the goods being sold or leased.

Expropriation

The seizure by a government of privately owned business or personal property for a proper public purpose and with just compensation.

Extension clause

A clause in a time instrument that allows the instrument's date of maturity to be extended into the future.

F

F.A.S.

Free alongside. A contract term that requires the seller, at his or her own expense and risk, to deliver the goods alongside the ship before risk passes to the buyer.

F.O.B.

Free on board. A contract term that indicates that the selling price of the goods includes transportation costs (and that the seller carries the risk of loss) to the specific F.O.B. place named in the contract. The place can be either the place of initial shipment (for example, the seller's city or place of business) or the place of destination (for example, the buyer's city or place of business).

Family limited liability partnership (FLLP)

A limited liability partnership (LLP) in which the majority of the partners are persons related to each other, essentially as spouses, parents, grandparents, siblings, cousins, nephews, or nieces. A person acting in a fiduciary capacity for persons so related could also be a partner. All of the partners must be natural persons or persons acting in a fiduciary capacity for the benefit of natural persons.

Federal form of government

A system of government in which the states form a union and the sovereign power is divided between a central government and the member states.

Federal question

A question that pertains to the U.S. Constitution, acts of Congress, or treaties. A federal question provides a basis for federal jurisdiction.

Federal Reserve System

A network of twelve central banks, located around the country and headed by the Federal Reserve Board of Governors. Most banks in the United States have Federal Reserve accounts.

Federal Rules of Civil Procedure (FRCP)

The rules controlling procedural matters in civil trials brought before the federal district courts.

Federal system

A system of government in which power is divided by a written constitution between a central government and regional, or subdivisional, governments. Each level must have some domain in which its policies are dominant and some genuine political or constitutional guarantee of its authority.

Fee simple

An absolute form of property ownership entitling the property owner to use, possess, or dispose of the property as he or she chooses during his or her lifetime. On death, the interest in the property passes to the owner's heirs; a fee simple absolute.

Fee simple absolute

An ownership interest in land in which the owner has the greatest possible aggregation of rights, privileges, and power. Ownership in fee simple absolute is limited absolutely to a person and his or her heirs.

Fellow-servant doctrine

A doctrine that bars an employee from suing his or her employer for injuries caused by a fellow employee.

Felony

A crime—such as arson, murder, rape, or robbery—that carries the most severe sanctions, usually ranging from one year in a state or federal prison to the forfeiture of one's life.

Fictitious payee

A payee on a negotiable instrument whom the maker or drawer does not intend to have an interest in the instrument. Indorsements by fictitious payees are not treated as unauthorized under Article 3 of the Uniform Commercial Code.

Fiduciary

As a noun, a person having a duty created by his or her undertaking to act primarily for another's benefit in matters connected with the undertaking. As an adjective, a relationship founded on trust and confidence.

Fiduciary duty

The duty, imposed on a fiduciary by virtue of his or her position, to act primarily for another's benefit.

Filtering software

A computer program that includes a pattern through which data are passed. When designed to block access to certain Web sites, the pattern blocks the retrieval of a site whose URL or key words are on a list within the program.

Final order

The final decision of an administrative agency on an issue. If no appeal is taken, or if the case is not reviewed or considered anew by the agency commission, the administrative law judge's initial order becomes the final order of the agency.

Financial institution

An organization authorized to do business under state or federal laws relating to financial institutions. For example, under the Electronic Fund Transfer Act, financial institutions include banks, savings and loan associations, credit unions, and other business entities that directly or indirectly hold accounts belonging to consumers.

Financing statement

A document prepared by a secured creditor and filed with the appropriate government official to give notice to the public that the creditor claims an interest in collateral belonging to the debtor named in the statement. The financing statement must contain the names and addresses of both the debtor and the creditor, and describe the collateral by type or item.

Firm offer

An offer (by a merchant) that is irrevocable without consideration for a period of time (not longer than three months). A firm offer by a merchant must be in writing and must be signed by the offeror.

Fitness for a particular purpose

See *Implied warranty of fitness for a particular purpose*

Fixture

A thing that was once personal property but that has become attached to real property in such a way that it takes on the characteristics of real property and becomes part of that real property.

Flame

An online message in which one party attacks another in harsh, often personal, terms.

Floating lien

A security interest in proceeds, after-acquired property, or property purchased under a line of credit (or all three); a security interest in collateral that is retained even when the collateral changes in character, classification, or location.

Force majeure (*pronounced mah-zhure*) clause

A provision in a contract stipulating that certain unforeseen events—such as war, political upheavals, acts of God, or other events—will excuse a party from liability for nonperformance of contractual obligations.

Foreclosure

A proceeding in which a mortgagee either takes title to or forces the sale of the mortgagor's property in satisfaction of a debt.

Foreign corporation

In a given state, a corporation that does business in the state without being incorporated therein.

Foreseeable risk

In negligence law, the risk of harm or injury to another that a person of ordinary intelligence and prudence should have reasonably anticipated or foreseen when undertaking an action or refraining from undertaking an action.

Forfeiture

The termination of a lease, according to its terms or the terms of a statute, when one of the parties fails to fulfill a condition under the lease and thereby breaches it.

Forgery

The fraudulent making or altering of any writing in a way that changes the legal rights and liabilities of another.

Formal contract

A contract that by law requires for its validity a specific form, such as executed under seal.

Forum

A jurisdiction, court, or place in which disputes are litigated and legal remedies are sought.

Forum-selection clause

A provision in a contract designating the court, jurisdiction, or tribunal that will decide any disputes arising under the contract.

Franchise

Any arrangement in which the owner of a trademark, trade name, or copyright licenses another to use that trademark, trade name, or copyright, under specified conditions or limitations, in the selling of goods and services.

Franchise tax

A state or local government tax on the right and privilege of carrying on a business in the form of a corporation.

Franchisee

One receiving a license to use another's (the franchisor's) trademark, trade name, or copyright in the sale of goods and services.

Franchisor

One licensing another (the franchisee) to use his or her trademark, trade name, or copyright in the sale of goods or services.

Fraud

Any misrepresentation, either by misstatement or omission of a material fact, knowingly made with the intention of deceiving another and on which a reasonable person would and does rely to his or her detriment.

Fraud in the execution

In the law of negotiable instruments, a type of fraud that occurs when a person is deceived into signing a negotiable instrument, believing that he or she is signing something else (such as a receipt); also called fraud in the inception. Fraud in the execution is a universal defense to payment on a negotiable instrument.

Fraud in the inducement

Ordinary fraud. In the law of negotiable instruments, fraud in the inducement occurs when a person issues a negotiable instrument based on false statements by the other party. The issuing party will be able to avoid payment on that instrument unless the holder is a holder in due course; in other words, fraud in the inducement is a personal defense to payment on a negotiable instrument.

Fraudulent misrepresentation (fraud)

Any misrepresentation, either by misstatement or omission of a material fact, knowingly made with the intention of deceiving another and on which a reasonable person would and does rely to his or her detriment.

Free exercise clause

The provision in the First Amendment to the U.S. Constitution that prohibits Congress from making any law "prohibiting the free exercise" of religion.

Frustration of purpose

A court-created doctrine under which a party to a contract will be relieved of his or her duty to perform when the objective purpose for performance no longer exists (due to reasons beyond that party's control).

Full faith and credit clause

A clause in Article IV, Section 1, of the Constitution that provides that "Full Faith and Credit shall be given in each State to the public Acts, Records, and Judicial Proceedings of every other State." The clause ensures that rights established under deeds, wills, contracts, and the like in one state will be honored by the other states and that any judicial decision with respect to such property rights will be honored and enforced in all states.

Full warranty

A warranty as to full performance covering generally both labor and materials.

Fungible goods

Goods that are alike by physical nature, by agreement, or by trade usage. Examples of fungible goods are wheat, oil, and wine that are identical in type and quality.

G

Garnishment

A legal process used by a creditor to collect a debt by seizing property of the debtor (such as wages) that is being held by a third party (such as the debtor's employer).

General jurisdiction

Exists when a court's subject-matter jurisdiction is not restricted. A court of general jurisdiction normally can hear any type of case.

General partner

In a limited partnership, a partner who assumes responsibility for the management of the partnership and liability for all partnership debts.

General partnership

See Partnership

Generally accepted accounting principles (GAAP)

The conventions, rules, and procedures necessary to define accepted accounting practices at a particular time. The source of the principles is the Federal Accounting Standards Board.

Generally accepted auditing standards (GAAS)

Standards concerning an auditor's professional qualities and the judgment exercised by him or her in the performance of an examination and report. The source of the standards is the American Institute of Certified Public Accountants.

Genuineness of assent

Knowing and voluntary assent to the terms of a contract. If a contract is formed as a result of a mistake, misrepresentation, undue influence, or duress, genuineness of assent is lacking, and the contract will be voidable.

Gift

Any voluntary transfer of property made without consideration, past or present.

Gift *causa mortis*

A gift made in contemplation of death. If the donor does not die of that ailment, the gift is revoked.

Gift *inter vivos*

A gift made during one's lifetime and not in contemplation of imminent death, in contrast to a gift causa mortis.

Good faith

Under the Uniform Commercial Code good faith means honesty in fact; with regard to merchants, good faith means honesty in fact and the observance of reasonable commercial standards of fair dealing in the trade.

Good faith purchaser

A purchaser who buys without notice of any circumstance that would put a person of ordinary prudence on inquiry as to whether the seller has valid title to the goods being sold.

Good Samaritan statute

A state statute that provides that persons who rescue or provide emergency services to others in peril—unless they do so recklessly, thus causing further harm—cannot be sued for negligence.

Grand jury

A group of citizens called to decide, after hearing the state's evidence, whether a reasonable basis (probable cause) exists for believing that a crime has been committed and whether a trial ought to be held.

Grant deed

A deed that simply recites words of consideration and conveyance. Under statute, a grant deed may impliedly warrant that at least the grantor has not conveyed the property's title to someone else.

Grantee

One to whom a grant (of land or property, for example) is made.

Grantor

A person who makes a grant, such as a transferor of property or the creator of a trust.

Group boycott

The refusal to deal with a particular person or firm by a group of competitors; prohibitedby the Sherman Act.

Guarantor

A person who agrees to satisfy the debt of another (the debtor) only after the principal debtor defaults; a guarantor's liability is thus secondary.

H

Habitability

See Implied warranty of habitability

Hacker

A person who uses one computer to break into another. Professional computer programmers refer to such persons as "crackers."

Health-care power of attorney

A document that designates a person who will have the power to choose what type of and how much medical treatment a person who is unable to make such a choice will receive.

Hearsay

An oral or written statement made out of court that is later offered in court by a witness (not the person who made the statement) to prove the truth of the matter asserted in the statement. Hearsay is generally inadmissible as evidence.

Hirfindahl-Hirschman Index (HHI)

An index of market power used to calculate whether a merger of two businesses will result in sufficient monopoly power to violate antitrust laws.

Historical school

A school of legal thought that emphasizes the evolutionary process of law and that looks to the past to discover what the principles of contemporary law should be.

Holder

Any person in the possession of an instrument drawn, issued, or indorsed to him or her, to his or her order, to bearer, or in blank.

Holder in due course (HDC)

A holder who acquires a negotiable instrument for value; in good faith; and without notice that the instrument is overdue, that it has been dishonored, that any person has a defense against it or a claim to it, or that the instrument contains unauthorized signatures, alterations, or is so irregular or incomplete as to call into question its authenticity.

Holographic will

A will written entirely in the signer's handwriting and usually not witnessed.

Homestead exemption

A law permitting a debtor to retain the family home, either in its entirety or up to a specified dollar amount, free from the claims of unsecured creditors or trustees in bankruptcy.

Horizontal merger

A merger between two firms that are competing in the same market.

Horizontal restraint

Any agreement that in some way restrains competition between rival firms competing in the same market.

Hot-cargo agreement

An agreement in which employers voluntarily agree with unions not to handle, use, or deal in nonunion-produced goods of other employers; a type of secondary boycott explicitly prohibited by the Labor-Management Reporting and Disclosure Act of 1959.

Hung jury

A jury whose members are so irreconcilably divided in their opinions that they cannot come to a verdict by the requisite number of jurors. The judge in this situation may order a new trial.

I

Identification

In a sale of goods, the express designation of the specific goods provided for in the contract.

Illusory promise

A promise made without consideration, which renders the promise unenforceable.

Immunity

A status of being exempt, or free, from certain duties or requirements. In criminal law, the state may grant an accused person immunity from prosecution—or agree to prosecute for a lesser offense—if the accused person agrees to give the state information that would assist the state in prosecuting other individuals for crimes. In tort law, freedom from liability for defamatory speech. *See also Privilege*

Implied authority

Authority that is created not by an explicit oral or written agreement but by implication. In agency law, implied authority (of the agent) can be conferred by custom, inferred from the position the agent occupies, or implied by virtue of being reasonably necessary to carry out express authority.

Implied warranty

A warranty that the law derives by implication or inference from the nature of the transaction or the relative situation or circumstances of the parties.

Implied warranty of fitness for a particular purpose

A warranty that goods sold or leased are fit for a particular purpose. The warranty arises when any seller or lessor knows the particular purpose for which a buyer or lessee will use the goods and knows that the buyer or lessee is relying on the skill and judgment of the seller or lessor to select suitable goods.

Implied warranty of habitability

An implied promise by a landlord that rented residential premises are fit for human habitation—that is, in a condition that is safe and suitable for people to live in.

Implied warranty of merchantability

A warranty that goods being sold or leased are reasonably fit for the ordinary purpose for which they are sold or leased, are properly packaged and labeled, and are of fair quality. The warranty automatically arises in every sale or lease of goods made by a merchant who deals in goods of the kind sold or leased.

Implied-in-fact contract

A contract formed in whole or in part from the conduct of the parties (as opposed to an express contract).

Impossibility of performance

A doctrine under which a party to a contract is relieved of his or her duty to perform when performance becomes impossible or totally impracticable (through no fault of either party).

Imposter

One who, by use of the mail, telephone, or personal appearance, induces a maker or drawer to issue an instrument in the name of an impersonated payee. Indorsements by imposters are not treated as unauthorized under Article 3 of the Uniform Commercial Code.

In pari delicto

At equal fault.

***In personam* jurisdiction**

Court jurisdiction over the "person" involved in a legal action; personal jurisdiction.

***In rem* jurisdiction**

Court jurisdiction over a defendant's property.

Incidental beneficiary

A third party who incidentally benefits from a contract but whose benefit was not the reason the contract was formed; an incidental beneficiary has no rights in a contract and cannot sue to have the contract enforced.

Incidental damages

Losses reasonably associated with, or related to, actual damages resulting from a breach of contract.

Indemnify

To compensate or reimburse another for losses or expenses incurred.

Independent contractor

One who works for, and receives payment from, an employer but whose working conditions and methods are not controlled by the employer. An independent contractor is not an employee but may be an agent.

Independent regulatory agency

An administrative agency that is not considered part of the government's executive branch and is not subject to the authority of the president. Independent agency officials cannot be removed without cause.

Indictment *(pronounced in-dyte-ment)*

A charge by a grand jury that a reasonable basis (probable cause) exists for believing that a crime has been committed and that a trial should be held.

Indorsee

The person to whom a negotiable instrument is transferred by indorsement.

Indorsement

A signature placed on an instrument for the purpose of transferring one's ownership rights in the instrument.

Indorser

A person who transfers an instrument by signing (indorsing) it and delivering it to another person.

Industry-wide liability

Product liability that is imposed on an entire industry when it is unclear which of several sellers within the industry manufactured a particular product. *See also Market-share liability*

Informal contract

A contract that does not require a specified form or formality in order to be valid.

Information

A formal accusation or complaint (without an indictment) issued in certain types of actions (usually criminal actions involving lesser crimes) by a law officer, such as a magistrate.

Information return

A tax return submitted by a partnership that only reports the income earned by the business. The partnership as an entity does not pay taxes on the income received by the partnership. A partner's profit from the partnership (whether distributed or not) is taxed as individual income to the individual partner.

Infringement

A violation of another's legally recognized right. The term is commonly used with reference to the invasion by one party of another party's rights in a patent, trademark, or copyright.

Initial order

In the context of administrative law, an agency's disposition in a matter other than a rulemaking. An administrative law judge's initial order becomes final unless it is appealed.

Injunction

A court decree ordering a person to do or refrain from doing a certain act or activity.

Innkeeper

An owner of an inn, hotel, motel, or other lodgings.

Innkeeper's lien

A possessory or statutory lien allowing the innkeeper to take the personal property of a guest, brought into the hotel, as security for nonpayment of the guest's bill (debt).

Innocent misrepresentation

A false statement of fact or an act made in good faith that deceives and causes harm or injury to another.

Insider

A corporate director or officer, or other employee or agent, with access to confidential information and a duty not to disclose that information in violation of insider-trading laws.

Insider trading

The purchase or sale of securities on the basis of "inside information" (information that has not been made available to the public) in violation of a duty owed to the company whose stock is being traded.

Insolvent

Under the Uniform Commercial Code, a term describing a person who ceases to pay "his debts in the ordinary course of business or cannot pay his debts as they become due or is insolvent within the meaning of federal bankruptcy law" [UCC 1-201(23)].

Installment contract

Under the Uniform Commercial Code, a contract that requires or authorizes delivery in two or more separate lots to be accepted and paid for separately.

Instrument

See Negotiable instrument

Insurable interest

An interest either in a person's life or well-being or in property that is sufficiently substantial that insuring against injury to (or the death of) the person or against damage to the property does not amount to a mere wagering (betting) contract.

Insurance

A contract in which, for a stipulated consideration, one party agrees to compensate the other for loss on a specific subject by a specified peril.

Intangible property

Property that is incapable of being apprehended by the senses (such as by sight or touch); intellectual property is an example of intangible property.

Integrated contract

A written contract that constitutes the final expression of the parties' agreement. If a contract is integrated, evidence extraneous to the contract that contradicts or alters the meaning of the contract in any way is inadmissible.

Intellectual property

Property resulting from intellectual, creative processes. Patents, trademarks, and copyrights are examples of intellectual property.

Intended beneficiary

A third party for whose benefit a contract is formed; an intended beneficiary can sue the promisor if such a contract is breached.

Intentional tort

A wrongful act knowingly committed.

***Inter vivos* gift**

See *Gift inter vivos*

***Inter vivos* trust**

A trust created by the grantor (settlor) and effective during the grantor's lifetime (that is, a trust not established by a will).

Intermediary bank

Any bank to which an item is transferred in the course of collection, except the depositary or payor bank.

International law

The law that governs relations among nations. International customs and treaties are generally considered to be two of the most important sources of international law.

International organization

In international law, a term that generally refers to an organization composed mainly of nations and usually established by treaty. The United States is a member of more than one hundred multilateral and bilateral organizations, including at least twenty through the United Nations.

Interpretive rule

An administrative agency rule that is simply a statement or opinion issued by the agency explaining how it interprets and intends to apply the statutes it enforces. Such rules are not automatically binding on private individuals or organizations.

Interrogatories

A series of written questions for which written answers are prepared and then signed under oath by a party to a lawsuit, usually with the assistance of the party's attorney.

Intestacy laws

State statutes that specify how property will be distributed when a person dies intestate (without a valid will); statutes of descent and distribution.

Intestate

As a noun, one who has died without having created a valid will; as an adjective, the state of having died without a will.

Investment company

A company that acts on behalf of many smaller shareholder-owners by buying a large portfolio of securities and professionally managing that portfolio.

Invitee

A person who, either expressly or impliedly, is privileged to enter onto another's land. The inviter owes the invitee (for example, a customer in a store) the duty to exercise reasonable care to protect the invitee from harm.

Irrevocable offer

An offer that cannot be revoked or recalled by the offeror without liability. A merchant's firm offer is an example of an irrevocable offer.

Issue

The first transfer, or delivery, of an instrument to a holder.

J

Joint and several liability

In partnership law, a doctrine under which a plaintiff may sue, and collect a judgment from, one or more of the partners separately (severally, or individually) or all of the partners together (jointly). This is true even if one of the partners sued did not participate in, ratify, or know about whatever it was that gave rise to the cause of action.

Joint liability

Shared liability. In partnership law, partners incur joint liability for partnership obligations and debts. For example, if a third party sues a partner on a partnership debt, the partner has the right to insist that the other partners be sued with him or her.

Joint stock company

A hybrid form of business organization that combines characteristics of a corporation (shareholder-owners, management by directors and officers of the company, and perpetual existence) and a partnership (it is formed by agreement, not statute; property is usually held in the names of the members; and the shareholders have personal liability for business debts). Usually, the joint stock company is regarded as a partnership for tax and other legally related purposes.

Joint tenancy

The joint ownership of property by two or more co-owners in which each co-owner owns an undivided portion of the property. On the death of one of the joint tenants, his or her interest automatically passes to the surviving joint tenants.

Joint venture

A joint undertaking of a specific commercial enterprise by an association of persons. A joint venture is normally not a legal entity and is treated like a partnership for federal income tax purposes.

Judgment

The final order or decision resulting from a legal action.

Judgment n.o.v.

See Motion for judgment n.o.v.

Judgment rate of interest

A rate of interest fixed by statute that is applied to a monetary judgment from the moment the judgment is awarded by a court until the judgment is paid or terminated.

Judicial lien

A lien on property created by a court order.

Judicial process

The procedures relating to, or connected with, the administration of justice through the judicial system.

Judicial review

The process by which courts decide on the constitutionality of legislative enactments and actions of the executive branch.

Jurisdiction

The authority of a court to hear and decide a specific action.

Jurisprudence

The science or philosophy of law.

Justiciable *(pronounced jus-tish-a-bul)* **controversy**

A controversy that is not hypothetical or academic but real and substantial; a requirement that must be satisfied before a court will hear a case.

K

King's court

A medieval English court. The king's courts, or curiae regis, were established by the Norman conquerors of England. The body of law that developed in these courts was common to the entire English realm and thus became known as the common law.

L

Laches

The equitable doctrine that bars a party's right to legal action if the party has neglected for an unreasonable length of time to act on his or her rights.

Landlord

An owner of land or rental property who leases it to another person, called the tenant.

Landlord's lien

A landlord's remedy for a tenant's failure to pay rent. When permitted under a statute or the lease agreement, the landlord may take and keep or sell whatever of the defaulting tenant's property is on the leased premises.

Larceny

The wrongful taking and carrying away of another person's personal property with the intent to permanently deprive the owner of the property. Some states classify larceny as either grand or petit, depending on the property's value.

Last clear chance

A doctrine under which a plaintiff may recover from a defendant for injuries or damages suffered, notwithstanding the plaintiff's own negligence, when the defendant had the opportunity—a last clear chance—to avoid harming the plaintiff through the exercise of reasonable care but failed to do so.

Law

A body of enforceable rules governing relationships among individuals and between individuals and their society.

Lawsuit

The litigation process. *See Litigation*

Lease

In real property law, a contract by which the owner of real property (the landlord, or lessor) grants to a person (the tenant, or lessee) an exclusive right to use and possess the property, usually for a specified period of time, in return for rent or some other form of payment.

Lease agreement

In regard to the lease of goods, an agreement in which one person (the lessor) agrees to transfer the right to the possession and use of property to another person (the lessee) in exchange for rental payments.

Leasehold estate

An estate in realty held by a tenant under a lease. In every leasehold estate, the tenant has a qualified right to possess and/or use the land.

Legacy

A gift of personal property under a will.

Legal *positivists*

Adherents to the positivist school of legal thought. This school holds that there can be no higher law than a nation's positive law—law created by a particular society at a particular point in time. In contrast to the natural law school, the positivist school maintains that there are no "natural" rights; rights come into existence only when there is a sovereign power (government) to confer and enforce those rights.

Legal rate of interest

A rate of interest fixed by statute as either the maximum rate of interest allowed by law or a rate of interest applied when the parties to a contract intend, but do not fix, an interest rate in the contract. In the latter case, the rate is frequently the same as the statutory maximum rate permitted.

Legal realism

A school of legal thought that was popular in the 1920s and 1930s and that challenged many existing jurisprudential assumptions, particularly the assumption that subjective elements play no part in judicial reasoning. Legal realists generally advocated a less abstract and more pragmatic approach to the law, an approach that would take into account customary practices and the circumstances in which transactions take place. The school left a lasting imprint on American jurisprudence.

Legal reasoning

The process of reasoning by which a judge harmonizes his or her decision with the judicial decisions of previous cases.

Legatee

One designated in a will to receive a gift of personal property.

Legislative rule

An administrative agency rule that carries the same weight as a congressionally enacted statute.

Lessee

A person who acquires the right to the possession and use of another's property in exchange for rental payments.

Lessor

A person who sells the right to the possession and use of property to another in exchange for rental payments.

Letter of credit

A written instrument, usually issued by a bank on behalf of a customer or other person, in which the issuer promises to honor drafts or other demands for payment by third persons in accordance with the terms of the instrument.

Leveraged buyout (LBO)

A corporate takeover financed by loans secured by the acquired corporation's assets or by the issuance of corporate bonds, resulting in a high debt load for the corporation.

Levy

The obtaining of money by legal process through the seizure and sale of property, usually done after a writ of execution has been issued.

Liability

Any actual or potential legal obligation, duty, debt, or responsibility.

Libel

Defamation in writing or other form (such as in a videotape) having the quality of permanence.

License

A revocable right or privilege of a person to come on another person's land.

Licensee

One who receives a license to use, or enter onto, another's property.

Lien *(pronounced leen)*

A claim against specific property to satisfy a debt.

Lien creditor

One whose claim is secured by a lien on particular property, as distinguished from a general creditor, who has no such security.

Life estate

An interest in land that exists only for the duration of the life of some person, usually the holder of the estate.

Limited jurisdiction

Exists when a court's subject-matter jurisdiction is limited. Bankruptcy courts and probate courts are examples of courts with limited jurisdiction.

Limited liability

Exists when the liability of the owners of a business is limited to the amount of their investments in the firm.

Limited liability company (LLC)

A hybrid form of business enterprise that offers the limited liability of the corporation but the tax advantages of a partnership.

Limited liability limited partnership (LLLP)

A type of limited partnership. The difference between a limited partnership and an LLLP is that the liability of the general partner in an LLLP is the same as the liability of the limited partner. That is, the liability of all partners is limited to the amount of their investments in the firm.

Limited liability partnership (LLP)

A form of partnership that allows professionals to enjoy the tax benefits of a partnership while limiting their personal liability for the malpractice of other partners.

Limited partner

In a limited partnership, a partner who contributes capital to the partnership but has no right to participate in the management and operation of the business. The limited partner assumes no liability for partnership debts beyond the capital contributed.

Limited partnership

A partnership consisting of one or more general partners (who manage the business and are liable to the full extent of their personal assets for debts of the partnership) and one or more limited partners (who contribute only assets and are liable only to the extent of their contributions).

Limited-payment life

A type of life insurance for which premiums are payable for a definite period, after which the policy is fully paid.

Limited warranty

A written warranty that fails to meet one or more of the minimum standards for a full warranty.

Liquidated damages

An amount, stipulated in the contract, that the parties to a contract believe to be a reasonable estimation of the damages that will occur in the event of a breach.

Liquidated debt

A debt that is due and certain in amount.

Liquidation

(1) In regard to bankruptcy, the sale of all of the nonexempt assets of a debtor and the distribution of the proceeds to the debtor's creditors. Chapter 7 of the Bankruptcy Code provides for liquidation bankruptcy proceedings. (2) In regard to corporations, the process by which corporate assets are converted into cash and distributed among creditors and shareholders according to specific rules of preference.

Litigant

A party to a lawsuit.

Litigation

The process of resolving a dispute through the court system.

Living will

A document that allows a person to control the methods of medical treatment that may be used after a serious accident or illness.

Loan workout

See Workout

Long arm statute

A state statute that permits a state to obtain personal jurisdiction over nonresident defendants. A defendant must have "minimum contacts" with that state for the statute to apply.

Lost property

Property with which the owner has involuntarily parted and then cannot find or recover.

M

Magistrate's court

A court of limited jurisdiction that is presided over by a public official (magistrate) with certain judicial authority, such as the power to set bail.

Mailbox rule

A rule providing that an acceptance of an offer becomes effective on dispatch (on being placed in a mailbox), if mail is, expressly or impliedly, an authorized means of communication of acceptance to the offeror.

Main purpose rule

A rule of contract law under which an exception to the Statute of Frauds is made if the main purpose in accepting secondary liability under a contract is to secure a personal benefit. If this situation exists, the contract need not be in writing to be enforceable.

Majority

See Age of majority

Majority opinion

A court's written opinion, outlining the views of the majority of the judges or justices deciding the case.

Maker

One who promises to pay a certain sum to the holder of a promissory note or certificate of deposit (CD).

Malpractice

Professional misconduct or the failure to exercise the requisite degree of skill as a professional. Negligence—the failure to exercise due care—on the part of a professional, such as a physician or an attorney, is commonly referred to as malpractice.

Manufacturing or processing-plant franchise

A franchise that is created when the franchisor transmits to the franchisee the essential ingredients or formula to make a particular product. The franchisee then markets the product either at wholesale or at retail in accordance with the franchisor's standards. Examples of this type of franchise are Coca-Cola and other soft-drink bottling companies.

Marine insurance

Insurance protecting shippers and vessel owners from losses or damages sustained by a vessel or its cargo during the transport of goods or materials by water.

Mark

See Trademark

Market concentration

A situation that exists when a small number of firms share the market for a particular good or service. For example, if the four largest grocery stores in Chicago accounted for 80 percent of all retail food sales, the market clearly would be concentrated in those four firms.

Market power

The power of a firm to control the market price of its product. A monopoly has the greatest degree of market power.

Marketable title

Title to real estate that is reasonably free from encumbrances, defects in the chain of title, and other events that affect title, such as adverse possession.

Market-share liability

A method of sharing liability among several firms that manufactured or marketed a particular product that may have caused a plaintiff's injury. This form of liability sharing is used when the true source of the product is unidentifiable. Each firm's liability is proportionate to its respective share of the relevant market for the product. Market-share liability applies only if the injuring product is fungible, the true manufacturer is unidentifiable, and the unknown character of the manufacturer is not the plaintiff's fault.

Market-share test

The primary measure of monopoly power. A firm's market share is the percentage of a market that the firm controls.

Marshalling assets

The arrangement or ranking of assets in a certain order toward the payment of debts. In equity, when two creditors have recourse to the same property of the debtor, but one has recourse to other property of the debtor, that creditor must resort first to those assets of the debtor that are not available to the other creditor.

Mass-market license

An e-contract that is presented with a package of computer information in the form of a click-on license or a shrink-wrap license.

Material alteration

See Alteration

Material fact

A fact to which a reasonable person would attach importance in determining his or her course of action. In regard to tender offers, for example, a fact is material if there is a substantial likelihood that a reasonable shareholder would consider it important in deciding how to vote.

Mechanic's lien

A statutory lien on the real property of another, created to ensure payment for work performed and materials furnished in the repair or improvement of real property, such as a building.

Mediation

A method of settling disputes outside of court by using the services of a neutral third party, called a mediator. The mediator acts as a communicating agent between the parties and suggests ways in which the parties can resolve their dispute.

Member

The term used to designate a person who has an ownership interest in a limited liability company.

Mens rea (pronounced mehns ray-uh)

Mental state, or intent. A wrongful mental state is as necessary as a wrongful act to establish criminal liability. What constitutes a mental state varies according to the wrongful action. Thus, for murder, the mens rea is the intent to take a life; for theft, the mens rea must involve both the knowledge that the property belongs to another and the intent to deprive the owner of it.

Merchant

A person who is engaged in the purchase and sale of goods. Under the Uniform Commercial Code, a person who deals in goods of the kind involved in the sales contract; for further definitions, see UCC 2-104.

Merger

A contractual and statutory process in which one corporation (the surviving corporation) acquires all of the assets and liabilities of another corporation (the merged corporation). The shareholders of the merged corporation receive either payment for their shares or shares in the surviving corporation.

Meta tags

Words inserted into a Web site's key words field to increase the site's appearance in search engine results.

Minimum-contacts requirement

The requirement that before a state court can exercise jurisdiction over a foreign corporation, the foreign corporation must have sufficient contacts with the state. A foreign corporation that has its home office in the state or that has manufacturing plants in the state meets this requirement.

Minimum wage

The lowest wage, either by government regulation or union contract, that an employer may pay an hourly worker.

Mini-trial

A private proceeding in which each party to a dispute argues its position before the other side and vice versa. A neutral third party may be present and act as an adviser if the parties fail to reach an agreement.

Mirror image rule

A common law rule that requires, for a valid contractual agreement, that the terms of the offeree's acceptance adhere exactly to the terms of the offeror's offer.

Misdemeanor

A lesser crime than a felony, punishable by a fine or imprisonment for up to one year in other than a state or federal penitentiary.

Mislaid property

Property with which the owner has voluntarily parted and then cannot find or recover.

Misrepresentation

A false statement of fact or an action that deceives and causes harm or injury to another. *See also Fraudulent misrepresentation (fraud); Innocent misrepresentation*

Mitigation of damages

A rule requiring a plaintiff to have done whatever was reasonable to minimize the damages caused by the defendant.

Money laundering

Falsely reporting income that has been obtained through criminal activity as income obtained through a legitimate business enterprise—in effect, "laundering" the "dirty money."

Monopolization

The possession of monopoly power in the relevant market and the willful acquisition or maintenance of that power, as distinguished from growth or development as a consequence of a superior product, business acumen, or historic accident.

Monopoly

A term generally used to describe a market in which there is a single seller or a limited number of sellers.

Monopoly power

The ability of a monopoly to dictate what takes place in a given market.

Moral minimum

The minimum degree of ethical behavior expected of a business firm, which is usually defined as compliance with the law.

Mortgage

A written instrument giving a creditor (the mortgagee) an interest in (a lien on) the debtor's (mortgagor's) property as security for a debt.

Mortgage bond

A bond that pledges specific property. If the corporation defaults on the bond, the bondholder can take the property.

Mortgagee

Under a mortgage agreement, the creditor who takes a security interest in the debtor's property.

Mortgagor

Under a mortgage agreement, the debtor who gives the creditor a security interest in the debtor's property in return for a mortgage loan.

Most-favored-nation status

A status granted in an international treaty by a provision stating that the citizens of the contracting nations may enjoy the privileges accorded by either party to citizens of the most favored nations. Generally, most-favored-nation clauses are designed to establish equality of international treatment.

Motion

A procedural request or application presented by an attorney to the court on behalf of a client.

Motion for a directed verdict

In a jury trial, a motion for the judge to take the decision out of the hands of the jury and direct a verdict for the moving party on the ground that the other party has not produced sufficient evidence to support his or her claim; referred to as a motion for judgment as a matter of law in the federal courts.

Motion for a new trial

A motion asserting that the trial was so fundamentally flawed (because of error, newly discovered evidence, prejudice, or other reason) that a new trial is necessary to prevent a miscarriage of justice.

Motion for judgment n.o.v.

A motion requesting the court to grant judgment in favor of the party making the motion on the ground that the jury verdict against him or her was unreasonable and erroneous.

Motion for judgment on the pleadings

A motion by either party to a lawsuit at the close of the pleadings requesting the court to decide the issue solely on the pleadings without proceeding to trial. The motion will be granted only if no facts are in dispute.

Motion for summary judgment

A motion requesting the court to enter a judgment without proceeding to trial. The motion can be based on evidence outside the pleadings and will be granted only if no facts are in dispute.

Motion to dismiss

A pleading in which a defendant asserts that the plaintiff's claim fails to state a cause of action (that is, has no basis in law) or that there are other grounds on which a suit should be dismissed.

Multiple product order

An order issued by the Federal Trade Commission to a firm that has engaged in deceptive advertising by which the firm is required to cease and desist from false advertising not only in regard to the product that was the subject of the action but also in regard to all the firm's other products.

Municipal court

A city or community court with criminal jurisdiction over traffic violations and, less frequently, with civil jurisdiction over other minor matters.

Mutual assent

The element of agreement in the formation of a contract. The manifestation of contract parties' mutual assent to the same bargain is required to establish a contract.

Mutual fund

A specific type of investment company that continually buys or sells to investors shares of ownership in a portfolio.

Mutual rescission

An agreement between the parties to cancel their contract, releasing the parties from further obligations under the contract. The object of the agreement is to restore the parties to the positions they would have occupied had no contract ever been formed. *See also Rescission*

N

National law

Law that pertains to a particular nation (as opposed to international law).

Natural law

The belief that government and the legal system should reflect universal moral and ethical principles that are inherent in human nature. The natural law school is the oldest and one of the most significant schools of legal thought.

Necessaries

Necessities required for life, such as food, shelter, clothing, and medical attention; may include whatever is believed to be necessary to maintain a person's standard of living or financial and social status.

Necessity

In criminal law, a defense against liability; under Section 3.02 of the Model Penal Code, this defense is justifiable if "the harm or evil sought to be avoided" by a given action "is greater than that sought to be prevented by the law defining the offense charged."

Negligence

The failure to exercise the standard of care that a reasonable person would exercise in similar circumstances.

Negligence per se

An act (or failure to act) in violation of a statutory requirement.

Negligent misrepresentation

Any manifestation through words or conduct that amounts to an untrue statement of fact made in circumstances in which a reasonable and prudent person would not have done (or failed to do) that which led to the misrepresentation. A representation made with an honest belief in its truth may still be negligent due to (1) a lack of reasonable care in ascertaining the facts, (2) the manner of expression, or (3) the absence of the skill or competence required by a particular business or profession.

Negotiable instrument

A signed writing that contains an unconditional promise or order to pay an exact sum of money, on demand or at an exact future time, to a specific person or order, or to bearer.

Negotiation

(1) In regard to dispute settlement, a process in which parties attempt to settle their dispute without going to court, with or without attorneys to represent them. (2) In regard to instruments, the transfer of an instrument in such a way that the transferee (the person to whom the instrument is transferred) becomes a holder.

Nominal damages

A small monetary award (often one dollar) granted to a plaintiff when no actual damage was suffered or when the plaintiff is unable to show such loss with sufficient certainty.

Nonconforming goods

Goods that do not conform to contract specifications.

No-par shares

Corporate shares that have no face value—that is, no specific dollar amount is printed on their face.

Notary public

A public official authorized to attest to the authenticity of signatures.

Note

A written instrument signed by a maker unconditionally promising to pay a fixed amount of money to a payee or a holder on demand or on a specific date.

Notice-and-comment rulemaking

An administrative rulemaking procedure that involves the publication of a notice of a proposed rulemaking in the Federal Register, a comment period for interested parties to express their views on the proposed rule, and the publication of the agency's final rule in the Federal Register.

Notice of Proposed Rulemaking

A notice published (in the Federal Register) by an administrative agency describing a proposed rule. The notice must give the time and place for which agency proceedings on the proposed rule will be held, a description of the nature of the proceedings, the legal authority for the proceedings (which is usually the agency's enabling legislation), and the terms of the proposed rule or the subject matter of the proposed rule.

Novation

The substitution, by agreement, of a new contract for an old one, with the rights under the old one being terminated. Typically, there is a substitution of a new person who is responsible for the contract and the removal of an original party's rights and duties under the contract.

Nuisance

A common law doctrine under which persons may be held liable for using their property in a manner that unreasonably interferes with others' rights to use or enjoy their own property.

Nuncupative will

An oral will (often called a deathbed will) made before witnesses; usually limited to transfers of personal property.

O

Objective theory of contracts

A theory under which the intent to form a contract will be judged by outward, objective facts (what the party said when entering into the contract, how the party acted or appeared, and the circumstances surrounding the transaction) as interpreted by a reasonable person, rather than by the party's own secret, subjective intentions.

Obligee

One to whom an obligation is owed.

Obligor

One that owes an obligation to another.

Offer

A promise or commitment to perform or refrain from performing some specified act in the future.

Offeree

A person to whom an offer is made.

Offeror

A person who makes an offer.

Omnibus clause

A provision in an automobile insurance policy that protects the vehicle owner who has taken out the insurance policy and anyone who drives the vehicle with the owner's permission.

Online Dispute Resolution (ODR)

The resolution of disputes with the assistance of organizations that offer dispute-resolution services via the Internet.

Opening statement

A statement made to the jury at the beginning of a trial by a party's attorney, prior to the presentation of evidence. The attorney briefly outlines the evidence that will be offered and the legal theory that will be pursued.

Operating agreement

In a limited liability company, an agreement in which the members set forth the details of how the business will be managed and operated.

Operation of law

A term expressing the manner in which certain rights or liabilities may be imposed on a person by the application of established rules of law to the particular transaction, without regard to the actions or cooperation of the party himself or herself.

Opinion

A statement by the court expressing the reasons for its decision in a case.

Optimum profits

The amount of profits that a business can make and still act ethically, as opposed to maximum profits, defined as the amount of profits a firm can make if it is willing to disregard ethical concerns.

Option contract

A contract under which the offeror cannot revoke his or her offer for a stipulated time period, and the offeree can accept or reject the offer during this period without fear that the offer will be made to another person. The offeree must give consideration for the option (the irrevocable offer) to be enforceable.

Order for relief

A court's grant of assistance to a complainant. In bankruptcy proceedings, the order relieves the debtor of the immediate obligation to pay the debts listed in the bankruptcy petition.

Order instrument

A negotiable instrument that is payable "to the order of an identified person" or "to an identified person or order."

Ordinance

A law passed by a local governing unit, such as a municipality or a county.

Original jurisdiction

Courts having original jurisdiction are courts of the first instance, or trial courts—that is, courts in which lawsuits begin, trials take place, and evidence is presented.

Output contract

An agreement in which a seller agrees to sell and a buyer agrees to buy all or up to a stated amount of what the seller produces.

Overdraft

A check written on a checking account in which there are insufficient funds to cover the amount of the check.

P

Parent-subsidiary merger

A merger of companies in which one company (the parent corporation) owns most of the stock of the other (the subsidiary corporation). A parent-subsidiary merger (short-form merger) can use a simplified procedure when the parent corporation owns at least 90 percent of the outstanding shares of each class of stock of the subsidiary corporation.

Parol evidence

A term that originally meant "oral evidence," but which has come to refer to any negotiations or agreements made prior to a contract or any contemporaneous oral agreements made by the parties.

Parol evidence rule

A substantive rule of contracts under which a court will not receive into evidence the parties' prior negotiations, prior agreements, or contemporaneous oral agreements if that evidence contradicts or varies the terms of the parties' written contract.

Partially disclosed principal

A principal whose identity is unknown by a third person, but the third person knows that the agent is or may be acting for a principal at the time the agent and the third person form a contract.

Partner

A co-owner of a partnership.

Partnering agreement

An agreement between a seller and a buyer who frequently do business with each other on the terms and conditions that will apply to all subsequently formed electronic contracts.

Partnership

An agreement by two or more persons to carry on, as co-owners, a business for profit.

Partnership by estoppel

A judicially created partnership that may, at the court's discretion, be imposed for purposes of fairness. The court can prevent those who present themselves as partners (but who are not) from escaping liability if a third person relies on an alleged partnership in good faith and is harmed as a result.

Par-value shares

Corporate shares that have a specific face value, or formal cash-in value, written on them, such as one dollar.

Past consideration

An act done before the contract is made, which ordinarily, by itself, cannot be consideration for a later promise to pay for the act.

Patent

A government grant that gives an inventor the exclusive right or privilege to make, use, or sell his or her invention for a limited time period. The word patent usually refers to some invention and designates either the instrument by which patent rights are evidenced or the patent itself.

Payee

A person to whom an instrument is made payable.

Payor bank

The bank on which a check is drawn (the drawee bank).

Penalty

A sum inserted into a contract, not as a measure of compensation for its breach but rather as punishment for a default. The agreement as to the amount will not be enforced, and recovery will be limited to actual damages.

Per capita

A Latin term meaning "per person." In the law governing estate distribution, a method of distributing the property of an intestate's estate in which each heir in a certain class (such as grandchildren) receives an equal share.

Per curiam

By the whole court; a court opinion written by the court as a whole instead of being authored by a judge or justice.

Per se

A Latin term meaning "in itself" or "by itself."

***Per se* violation**

A type of anticompetitive agreement—such as a horizontal price-fixing agreement—that is considered to be so injurious to the public that there is no need to determine whether it actually injures market competition; rather, it is in itself (per se) a violation of the Sherman Act.

Per stirpes

A Latin term meaning "by the roots." In the law governing estate distribution, a method of distributing an intestate's estate in which each heir in a certain class (such as grandchildren) takes the share to which his or her deceased ancestor (such as a mother or father) would have been entitled.

Perfect tender rule

A common law rule under which a seller was required to deliver to the buyer goods that conformed perfectly to the requirements stipulated in the sales contract. A tender of nonconforming goods would automatically constitute a breach of contract. Under the Uniform Commercial Code, the rule has been greatly modified.

Perfection

The legal process by which secured parties protect themselves against the claims of third parties who may wish to have their debts satisfied out of the same collateral; usually accomplished by the filing of a financing statement with the appropriate government official.

Performance

In contract law, the fulfillment of one's duties arising under a contract with another; the normal way of discharging one's contractual obligations.

Periodic tenancy

A lease interest in land for an indefinite period involving payment of rent at fixed intervals, such as week to week, month to month, or year to year.

Personal defense

A defense that can be used to avoid payment to an ordinary holder of a negotiable instrument but not a holder in due course (HDC) or a holder with the rights of an HDC.

Personal identification number (PIN)

A number given to the holder of an access card (debit card, credit card, ATM card, or the like) that is used to conduct financial transactions electronically. Typically, the card will not provide access to a system without the number, which is meant to be kept secret to inhibit unauthorized use of the card.

Personal jurisdiction

See In personam jurisdiction

Personal property

Property that is movable; any property that is not real property.

Personalty

Personal property.

Petition in bankruptcy

The document that is filed with a bankruptcy court to initiate bankruptcy proceedings. The official forms required for a petition in bankruptcy must be completed accurately, sworn to under oath, and signed by the debtor.

Petitioner

In equity practice, a party that initiates a lawsuit.

Petty offense

In criminal law, the least serious kind of criminal offense, such as a traffic or building-code violation.

Pierce the corporate veil

To disregard the corporate entity, which limits the liability of shareholders, and hold the shareholders personally liable for a corporate obligation.

Plaintiff

One who initiates a lawsuit.

Plea

In criminal law, a defendant's allegation, in response to the charges brought against him or her, of guilt or innocence.

Plea bargaining

The process by which a criminal defendant and the prosecutor in a criminal case work out a mutually satisfactory disposition of the case, subject to court approval; usually involves the defendant's pleading guilty to a lesser offense in return for a lighter sentence.

Pleadings

Statements made by the plaintiff and the defendant in a lawsuit that detail the facts, charges, and defenses involved in the litigation; the complaint and answer are part of the pleadings.

Pledge

A common law security device (retained in Article 9 of the Uniform Commercial Code) in which personal property is turned over to the creditor as security for the payment of a debt and retained by the creditor until the debt is paid.

Police powers

Powers possessed by states as part of their inherent sovereignty. These powers may be exercised to protect or promote the public order, health, safety, morals, and general welfare.

Policy

In insurance law, a contract between the insurer and the insured in which, for a stipulated consideration, the insurer agrees to compensate the insured for loss on a specific subject by a specified peril.

Positive law

The body of conventional, or written, law of a particular society at a particular point in time.

Positivist school

A school of legal thought whose adherents believe that there can be no higher law than a nation's positive law—the body of conventional, or written, law of a particular society at a particular time.

Possessory lien

A lien that allows one person to retain possession of another's property as security for a debt or obligation owed by the owner of the property to the lienholder. An example of a possessory lien is an artisan's lien.

Potential competition doctrine

A doctrine under which a conglomerate merger may be prohibited by law because it would be injurious to potential competition.

Potentially responsible party (PRP)

A potentially liable party under the Comprehensive Environmental Response, Compensation and Liability Act (CERCLA). Any person who generated the hazardous waste, transported the hazardous waste, owned or operated a waste site at the time of disposal, or currently owns or operates a site may be responsible for some or all of the cleanup costs involved in removing the hazardous chemicals.

Power of attorney

A written document, which is usually notarized, authorizing another to act as one's agent; can be special (permitting the agent to do specified acts only) or general (permitting the agent to transact all business for the principal).

Preauthorized transfer

A transaction authorized in advance to recur at substantially regular intervals. The terms and procedures for preauthorized electronic fund transfers through certain financial institutions are subject to the Electronic Fund Transfer Act.

Precedent

A court decision that furnishes an example or authority for deciding subsequent cases involving identical or similar facts.

Predatory pricing

The pricing of a product below cost with the intent to drive competitors out of the market.

Preemption

A doctrine under which certain federal laws preempt, or take precedence over, conflicting state or local laws.

Preemptive rights

Rights held by shareholders that entitle them to purchase newly issued shares of a corporation's stock, equal in percentage to shares presently held, before the stock is offered to any outside buyers. Preemptive rights enable shareholders to maintain their proportionate ownership and voice in the corporation.

Preference

In bankruptcy proceedings, property transfers or payments made by the debtor that favor (give preference to) one creditor over others. The bankruptcy trustee is allowed to recover payments made both voluntarily and involuntarily to one creditor in preference over another.

Preferred stock

Classes of stock that have priority over common stock both as to payment of dividends and distribution of assets on the corporation's dissolution.

Prejudgment interest

Interest that accrues on the amount of a court judgment from the time of the filing of a lawsuit to the court's issuance of a judgment.

Preliminary hearing

An initial hearing used in many felony cases to establish whether or not it is proper to detain the defendant. A magistrate reviews the evidence and decides if there is probable cause to believe that the defendant committed the crime with which he or she has been charged.

Premium

In insurance law, the price paid by the insured for insurance protection for a specified period of time.

Prenuptial agreement

An agreement made before marriage that defines each partner's ownership rights in the other partner's property. Prenuptial agreements must be in writing to be enforceable.

Preponderance of the evidence

A standard in civil law cases under which the plaintiff must convince the court that, based on the evidence presented by both parties, it is more likely than not that the plaintiff's allegation is true.

Presentment

The act of presenting an instrument to the party liable on the instrument to collect payment; presentment also occurs when a person presents an instrument to a drawee for acceptance.

Presentment warranties

Any person who presents an instrument for payment or acceptance impliedly warrants that (1) he or she is entitled to enforce the instrument or authorized to obtain payment or acceptance on behalf of a person who is entitled, (2) the instrument has not been altered, and (3) he or she has no knowledge that the signature of the drawer is unauthorized.

Pretrial conference

A conference, scheduled before the trial begins, between the judge and the attorneys litigating the suit. The parties may settle the dispute, clarify the issues, schedule discovery, and so on during the conference.

Pretrial motion

A written or oral application to a court for a ruling or order, made before trial.

Price discrimination

Setting prices in such a way that two competing buyers pay two different prices for an identical product or service.

Price-fixing agreement

An agreement between competitors in which the competitors agree to fix the prices of products or services at a certain level; prohibited by the Sherman Act.

Prima facie case

A case in which the plaintiff has produced sufficient evidence of his or her conclusion that the case can go to a jury; a case in which the evidence compels the plaintiff's conclusion if the defendant produces no evidence to disprove it.

Primary liability

In negotiable instruments law, absolute responsibility for paying a negotiable instrument. Makers and acceptors are primarily liable.

Principal

In agency law, a person who agrees to have another, called the agent, act on his or her behalf.

Principle of rights

The principle that human beings have certain fundamental rights (to life, freedom, and the pursuit of happiness, for example). Those who adhere to this "rights theory" believe that a key factor in determining whether a business decision is ethical is how that decision affects the rights of others. These others include the firm's owners, its employees, the consumers of its products or services, its suppliers, the community in which it does business, and society as a whole.

Privatization

The replacement of government-provided products and services by private firms.

Privilege

In tort law, the ability to act contrary to another person's right without that person's having legal redress for such acts. Privilege may be raised as a defense to defamation.

Privileges and immunities clause

Special rights and exceptions provided by law. Article IV, Section 2, of the Constitution requires states not to discriminate against one another's citizens. A resident of one state cannot be treated as an alien when in another state; he or she may not be denied such privileges and immunities as legal protection, access to courts, travel rights, or property rights.

Privity of contract

The relationship that exists between the promisor and the promisee of a contract.

Pro rata

Proportionately; in proportion.

Probable cause

Reasonable grounds to believe the existence of facts warranting certain actions, such as the search or arrest of a person.

Probate

The process of proving and validating a will and the settling of all matters pertaining to administration, guardianship, and the like.

Probate court

A state court of limited jurisdiction that conducts proceedings relating to the settlement of a deceased person's estate.

Procedural due process

The requirement that any government decision to take life, liberty, or property must be made fairly. For example, fair procedures must be used in determining whether a person will be subjected to punishment or have some burden imposed on him or her.

Procedural law

Rules that define the manner in which the rights and duties of individuals may be enforced.

Procedural unconscionability

Occurs when, due to one contractual party's vastly superior bargaining power, the other party lacks a knowledge or understanding of the contract terms due to inconspicuous print or the lack of an opportunity to read the contract or to ask questions about its meaning. Procedural unconscionability often involves an adhesion contract, which is a contract drafted by the dominant party and then presented to the other—the adhering party—on a take-it-or-leave-it basis.

Proceeds

Under Article 9 of the Uniform Commercial Code, whatever is received when the collateral is sold or otherwise disposed of, such as by exchange.

Product liability

The legal liability of manufacturers, sellers, and lessors of goods to consumers, users, and bystanders for injuries or damages that are caused by the goods.

Product misuse

A defense against product liability that may be raised when the plaintiff used a product in a manner not intended by the manufacturer. If the misuse is reasonably foreseeable, the seller will not escape liability unless measures were taken to guard against the harm that could result from the misuse.

Professional corporation

A corporation formed by professional persons, such as physicians, lawyers, dentists, and accountants, to gain tax benefits. Subject to certain exceptions (when a court may treat a professional corporation as a partnership for liability purposes), the shareholders of a professional corporation have the limited liability characteristic of the corporate form of business.

Profit

In real property law, the right to enter onto and remove things from the property of another (for example, the right to enter onto a person's land and remove sand and gravel therefrom).

Promise

A person's assurance that he or she will or will not do something.

Promisee

A person to whom a promise is made.

Promisor

A person who makes a promise.

Promissory estoppel

A doctrine that applies when a promisor makes a clear and definite promise on which the promisee justifiably relies; such a promise is binding if justice will be better served by the enforcement of the promise. *See also Estoppel*

Promissory note

A written promise made by one person (the maker) to pay a fixed sum of money to another person (the payee or a subsequent holder) on demand or on a specified date.

Promoter

A person who takes the preliminary steps in organizing a corporation, including (usually) issuing a prospectus, procuring stock subscriptions, making contract purchases, securing a corporate charter, and the like.

Property

Legally protected rights and interests in anything with an ascertainable value that is subject to ownership.

Prospectus

A document required by federal or state securities laws that describes the financial operations of the corporation, thus allowing investors to make informed decisions.

Protected class

A class of persons with identifiable characteristics who historically have been victimized by discriminatory treatment for certain purposes. Depending on the context, these characteristics include age, color, gender, national origin, race, and religion.

Proximate cause

Legal cause; exists when the connection between an act and an injury is strong enough to justify imposing liability.

Proxy

In corporation law, a written agreement between a stockholder and another under which the stockholder authorizes the other to vote the stockholder's shares in a certain manner.

Proxy fight

A conflict between an individual, group, or firm attempting to take control of a corporation and the corporation's management for the votes of the shareholders.

Public figures

Individuals who are thrust into the public limelight. Public figures include government officials and politicians, movie stars, well-known businesspersons, and generally anybody who becomes known to the public because of his or her position or activities.

Public policy

A government policy based on widely held societal values and (usually) expressed or implied in laws or regulations.

Public prosecutor

An individual, acting as a trial lawyer, who initiates and conducts criminal cases in the government's name and on behalf of the people.

Puffery

A salesperson's exaggerated claims concerning the quality of property offered for sale. Such claims involve opinions rather than facts and are not considered to be legally binding promises or warranties.

Punitive damages

Money damages that may be awarded to a plaintiff to punish the defendant and deter future similar conduct.

Purchase-money security interest (PMSI)

A security interest that arises when a seller or lender extends credit for part or all of the purchase price of goods purchased by a buyer.

Q

Qualified indorsement

An indorsement on a negotiable instrument in which the indorser disclaims any contract liability on the instrument; the notation "without recourse" is commonly used to create a qualified indorsement.

Quantum meruit (pronounced kwahn-tuhm mehr-oo-wuht)

Literally, "as much as he deserves"—an expression describing the extent of liability on a contract implied in law (quasi contract). An equitable doctrine based on the concept that one who benefits from another's labor and materials should not be unjustly enriched thereby but should be required to pay a reasonable amount for the benefits received, even absent a contract.

Quasi contract

A fictional contract imposed on parties by a court in the interests of fairness and justice; usually, quasi contracts are imposed to avoid the unjust enrichment of one party at the expense of another.

Question of fact

In a lawsuit, an issue involving a factual dispute that can only be decided by a judge (or, in a jury trial, a jury).

Question of law

In a lawsuit, an issue involving the application or interpretation of a law; therefore, the judge, and not the jury, decides the issue.

Quiet enjoyment

See Covenant of quiet enjoyment

Quitclaim deed

A deed intended to pass any title, interest, or claim that the grantor may have in the property but not warranting that such title is valid. A quitclaim deed offers the least amount of protection against defects in the title.

Quorum

The number of members of a decision-making body that must be present before business may be transacted.

Quota

An assigned import limit on goods.

R

Ratification

The act of accepting and giving legal force to an obligation that previously was not enforceable.

Reaffirmation agreement

An agreement between a debtor and a creditor in which the debtor reaffirms, or promises to pay, a debt dischargeable in bankruptcy. To be enforceable, the agreement must be made prior to the discharge of the debt by the bankruptcy court.

Real defense

See Universal defense

Real property

Land and everything attached to it, such as foliage and buildings.

Reasonable care

The degree of care that a person of ordinary prudence would exercise in the same or similar circumstances.

Reasonable doubt

See Beyond a reasonable doubt

Reasonable person standard

The standard of behavior expected of a hypothetical "reasonable person." The standard against which negligence is measured and that must be observed to avoid liability for negligence.

Rebuttal

The refutation of evidence introduced by an adverse party's attorney.

Receiver

In a corporate dissolution, a court-appointed person who winds up corporate affairs and liquidates corporate assets.

Record

According to the Uniform Electronic Transactions Act, information that is either inscribed on a tangible medium or stored in an electronic or other medium and that is retrievable. The Uniform Computer Information Transactions Act uses the term record instead of writing.

Recording statutes

Statutes that allow deeds, mortgages, and other real property transactions to be recorded so as to provide notice to future purchasers or creditors of an existing claim on the property.

Red herring

A preliminary prospectus that can be distributed to potential investors after the registration statement (for a securities offering) has been filed with the Securities and Exchange Commission. The name derives from the red legend printed across the prospectus stating that the registration has been filed but has not become effective.

Redemption

A repurchase, or buying back. In secured transactions law, a debtor's repurchase of collateral securing a debt after a creditor has taken title to the collateral due to the debtor's default but before the secured party disposes of the collateral.

Reformation

A court-ordered correction of a written contract so that it reflects the true intentions of the parties.

Regulation E

A set of rules issued by the Federal Reserve System's board of governors under the authority of the Electronic Fund Transfer Act to protect users of electronic fund transfer systems.

Regulation Z

A set of rules promulgated by the Federal Reserve Board to implement the provisions of the Truth-in-Lending Act.

Reimbursement

See Right of reimbursement

Rejection

In contract law, an offeree's express or implied manifestation not to accept an offer. In the law governing contracts for the sale of goods, a buyer's manifest refusal to accept goods on the ground that they do not conform to contract specifications.

Rejoinder

The defendant's answer to the plaintiff's rebuttal.

Release

A contract in which one party forfeits the right to pursue a legal claim against the other party.

Relevant evidence

Evidence tending to make a fact at issue in the case more or less probable than it would be without the evidence. Only relevant evidence is admissible in court.

Remainder

A future interest in property held by a person other than the original owner.

Remanded

Sent back. If an appellate court disagrees with a lower court's judgment, the case may be remanded to the lower court for further proceedings in which the lower court's decision should be consistent with the appellate court's opinion on the matter.

Remedy

The relief given to an innocent party to enforce a right or compensate for the violation of a right.

Remedy at law

A remedy available in a court of law. Money damages are awarded as a remedy at law.

Remedy in equity

A remedy allowed by courts in situations where remedies at law are not appropriate. Remedies in equity are based on settled rules of fairness, justice, and honesty, and include injunction, specific performance, rescission and restitution, and reformation.

Remitter

A person who sends money, or remits payment.

Rent

The consideration paid for the use or enjoyment of another's property. In landlord-tenant relationships, the payment made by the tenant to the landlord for the right to possess the premises.

Rent escalation clause

A clause providing for an increase in rent during a lease term.

Repair-and-deduct statutes

Statutes providing that a tenant may pay for repairs and deduct the cost of the repairs from the rent, as a remedy for a landlord's failure to maintain leased premises.

Replevin *(pronounced ruh-pleh-vin)*

An action to recover specific goods in the hands of a party who is wrongfully withholding them from the other party.

Reply

Procedurally, a plaintiff's response to a defendant's answer.

Reporter

A publication in which court cases are published, or reported.

Repudiation

The renunciation of a right or duty; the act of a buyer or seller in rejecting a contract either partially or totally. *See also Anticipatory repudiation*

Requirements contract

An agreement in which a buyer agrees to purchase and the seller agrees to sell all or up to a stated amount of what the buyer needs or requires.

***Res ipsa loquitur** (pronounced rehs ehp-suh low-quuh-tuhr)*

A doctrine under which negligence may be inferred simply because an event occurred, if it is the type of event that would not occur in the absence of negligence. Literally, the term means "the facts speak for themselves."

Resale price maintenance agreement

An agreement between a manufacturer and a retailer in which the manufacturer specifies the minimum retail price of its products. Resale price maintenance agreements are illegal per se under the Sherman Act.

Rescind *(pronounced reh-sihnd)*

To cancel. *See also Rescission*

Rescission *(pronounced reh-sih-zhen)*

A remedy whereby a contract is canceled and the parties are returned to the positions they occupied before the contract was made; may be effected through the mutual consent of the parties, by their conduct, or by court decree.

Residuary

The surplus of a testator's estate remaining after all of the debts and particular legacies have been discharged.

***Respondeat superior** (pronounced ree-spahn-dee-uht soo-peer-ee-your)*

In Latin, "Let the master respond." A doctrine under which a principal or an employer is held liable for the wrongful acts committed by agents or employees while acting within the course and scope of their agency or employment.

Respondent

In equity practice, the party who answers a bill or other proceeding.

Restitution

An equitable remedy under which a person is restored to his or her original position prior to loss or injury, or placed in the position he or she would have been in had the breach not occurred.

Restraint on trade

Any contract or combination that tends to eliminate or reduce competition, effect a monopoly, artificially maintain prices, or otherwise hamper the course of trade and commerce as it would be carried on if left to the control of natural economic forces.

Restrictive covenant

A private restriction on the use of land that is binding on the party that purchases the property originally as well as on subsequent purchasers. If its benefit or obligation passes with the land's ownership, it is said to "run with the land."

Restrictive indorsement

Any indorsement on a negotiable instrument that requires the indorsee to comply with certain instructions regarding the funds involved. A restrictive indorsement does not prohibit the further negotiation of the instrument.

Resulting trust

An implied trust arising from the conduct of the parties. A trust in which a party holds the actual legal title to another's property but only for that person's benefit.

Retained earnings

The portion of a corporation's profits that has not been paid out as dividends to shareholders.

Retainer

An advance payment made by a client to a law firm to cover part of the legal fees and/or costs that will need to be incurred on that client's behalf.

Retaliatory eviction

The eviction of a tenant because of the tenant's complaints, participation in a tenant's union, or similar activity with which the landlord does not agree.

Reverse

To reject or overrule a court's judgment. An appellate court, for example, might reverse a lower court's judgment on an issue if it feels that the lower court committed an error during the trial or that the jury was improperly instructed.

Reverse discrimination

Discrimination against majority groups, such as white males, that results from affirmative action programs, in which preferences are given to minority members and women.

Reversible error

An error by a lower court that is sufficiently substantial to justify an appellate court's reversal of the lower court's decision.

Reversionary interest

A future interest in property retained by the original owner.

Revocation

In contract law, the withdrawal of an offer by an offeror. Unless an offer is irrevocable, it can be revoked at any time prior to acceptance without liability.

Right of contribution

The right of a co-surety who pays more than his or her proportionate share on a debtor's default to recover the excess paid from other co-sureties.

Right of entry

The right to peaceably take or resume possession of real property.

Right of first refusal

The right to purchase personal or real property—such as corporate shares or real estate—before the property is offered for sale to others.

Right of redemption

See Equity of redemption; Redemption

Right of reimbursement

The legal right of a person to be restored, repaid, or indemnified for costs, expenses, or losses incurred or expended on behalf of another.

Right of subrogation

The right of a person to stand in the place of (be substituted for) another, giving the substituted party the same legal rights that the original party had.

Right-to-work law

A state law providing that employees are not to be required to join a union as a condition of obtaining or retaining employment.

Risk

A prediction concerning potential loss based on known and unknown factors.

Risk management

Planning that is undertaken to protect one's interest should some event threaten to undermine its security. In the context of insurance, risk management involves transferring certain risks from the insured to the insurance company.

Robbery

The act of forcefully and unlawfully taking personal property of any value from another; force or intimidation is usually necessary for an act of theft to be considered a robbery.

Rule of four

A rule of the United States Supreme Court under which the Court will not issue a *writ of certiorari* unless at least four justices approve of the decision to issue the writ.

Rule of reason

A test by which a court balances the positive effects (such as economic efficiency) of an agreement against its potentially anticompetitive effects. In antitrust litigation, many practices are analyzed under the rule of reason.

Rule 10b-5

See SEC Rule 10b-5

Rulemaking

The process undertaken by an administrative agency when formally adopting a new regulation or amending an old one. Rulemaking involves notifying the public of a proposed rule or change and receiving and considering the public's comments.

Rules of evidence

Rules governing the admissibility of evidence in trial courts.

S

S corporation

A close business corporation that has met certain requirements as set out by the Internal Revenue Code and thus qualifies for special income tax treatment. Essentially, an S corporation is taxed the same as a partnership, but its owners enjoy the privilege of limited liability.

Sale

The passing of title (evidence of ownership rights) from the seller to the buyer for a price.

Sale on approval

A type of conditional sale in which the buyer may take the goods on a trial basis. The sale becomes absolute only when the buyer approves of (or is satisfied with) the goods being sold.

Sale or return

A type of conditional sale in which title and possession pass from the seller to the buyer; however, the buyer retains the option to return the goods during a specified period even though the goods conform to the contract.

Sales contract

A contract for the sale of goods under which the ownership of goods is transferred from a seller to a buyer for a price.

Satisfaction

See Accord and satisfaction

Scienter *(pronounced sy-en-ter)*

Knowledge by the misrepresenting party that material facts have been falsely represented or omitted with an intent to deceive.

Search warrant

An order granted by a public authority, such as a judge, that authorizes law enforcement personnel to search particular premises or property.

Seasonably

Within a specified time period, or, if no period is specified, within a reasonable time.

SEC Rule 10b-5

A rule of the Securities and Exchange Commission that makes it unlawful, in connection with the purchase or sale of any security, to make any untrue statement of a material fact or to omit a material fact if such omission causes the statement to be misleading.

Secondary boycott

A union's refusal to work for, purchase from, or handle the products of a secondary employer, with whom the union has no dispute, for the purpose of forcing that employer to stop doing business with the primary employer, with whom the union has a labor dispute.

Secondary liability

In negotiable instruments law, the contingent liability of drawers and indorsers. A secondarily liable party becomes liable on an instrument only if the party that is primarily liable on the instrument dishonors it or, in regard to drafts and checks, the drawee fails to pay or to accept the instrument, whichever is required.

Secured party

A lender, seller, or any other person in whose favor there is a security interest, including a person to whom accounts or chattel paper has been sold.

Secured transaction

Any transaction in which the payment of a debt is guaranteed, or secured, by personal property owned by the debtor or in which the debtor has a legal interest.

Securities

Generally, corporate stocks and bonds. A security may also be a note, debenture, stock warrant, or any document given as evidence of an ownership interest in a corporation or as a promise of repayment by a corporation.

Security agreement

An agreement that creates or provides for a security interest between the debtor and a secured party.

Security interest

Any interest "in personal property or fixtures which secures payment or performance of an obligation" [UCC 1-201(37)].

Self-defense

The legally recognized privilege to protect one's self or property against injury by another. The privilege of self-defense protects only acts that are reasonably necessary to protect one's self or property.

Seniority system

In regard to employment relationships, a system in which those who have worked longest for the company are first in line for promotions, salary increases, and other benefits; they are also the last to be laid off if the work force must be reduced.

Service mark

A mark used in the sale or the advertising of services, such as to distinguish the services of one person from the services of others. Titles, character names, and other distinctive features of radio and television programs may be registered as service marks.

Service of process

The delivery of the complaint and summons to a defendant.

Settlor

One creating a trust.

Severance pay

A payment by an employer to an employee that exceeds the employee's wages due on termination.

Sexual harassment

In the employment context, the granting of job promotions or other benefits in return for sexual favors or language or conduct that is so sexually offensive that it creates a hostile working environment.

Sham transaction

A false transaction without substance that is undertaken with the intent to defraud a creditor or the government. An example of a sham transaction is the sale of assets to a friend or relative for the purpose of concealing assets from creditors or a bankruptcy court.

Share

A unit of stock. *See also Stock*

Shareholder

One who purchases shares of a corporation's stock, thus acquiring an equity interest in the corporation.

Shareholder's derivative suit

A suit brought by a shareholder to enforce a corporate cause of action against a third person.

Shari'a

Civil law principles of some Middle Eastern countries that are based on the Islamic directives that follow the teachings of the prophet Mohammed.

Shelter principle

The principle that the holder of a negotiable instrument who cannot qualify as a holder in due course (HDC), but who derives his or her title through an HDC, acquires the rights of an HDC.

Sheriff's deed

The deed given to the purchaser of property at a sheriff's sale as part of the foreclosure process against the owner of the property.

Shipment contract

A contract in which the seller is required to ship the goods by carrier. The buyer assumes liability for any losses or damage to the goods after they are delivered to the carrier. Generally, all contracts are assumed to be shipment contracts if nothing to the contrary is stated in the contract.

Short-form merger

A merger between a subsidiary corporation and a parent corporation that owns at least 90 percent of the outstanding shares of each class of stock issued by the subsidiary corporation. Short-form mergers can be accomplished without the approval of the shareholders of either corporation.

Short-swing profits

Profits made by officers, directors, and certain large stockholders resulting from the use of nonpublic (inside) information about their companies; prohibited by Section 12 of the 1934 Securities Exchange Act.

Shrink-wrap agreement

An agreement whose terms are expressed in a document located inside a box in which goods (usually software) are packaged; sometimes called a shrink-wrap license.

Sight draft

In negotiable instruments law, a draft payable on sight—that is, when it is presented for payment.

Signature

Under the Uniform Commercial Code, "any symbol executed or adopted by a party with a present intention to authenticate a writing."

Slander

Defamation in oral form.

Slander of quality (trade libel)

The publication of false information about another's product, alleging that it is not what its seller claims.

Slander of title

The publication of a statement that denies or casts doubt on another's legal ownership of any property, causing financial loss to that property's owner.

Small claims courts

Special courts in which parties may litigate small claims (usually, claims involving $2,500 or less). Attorneys are not required in small claims courts, and in many states attorneys are not allowed to represent the parties.

Smart card

Prepaid funds recorded on a microprocessor chip embedded on a card. One type of e-money.

Sociological school

A school of legal thought that views the law as a tool for promoting justice in society.

Sole proprietorship

The simplest form of business, in which the owner is the business; the owner reports business income on his or her personal income tax return and is legally responsible for all debts and obligations incurred by the business.

Sovereign immunity

A doctrine that immunizes foreign nations from the jurisdiction of U.S. courts when certain conditions are satisfied.

Spam

Bulk, unsolicited ("junk") e-mail.

Special indorsement

An indorsement on an instrument that indicates the specific person to whom the indorser intends to make the instrument payable; that is, it names the indorsee.

Special warranty deed

A deed in which the grantor only covenants to warrant and defend the title against claims and demands of the grantor and all persons claiming by, through, and under the grantor.

Specific performance

An equitable remedy requiring the breaching party to perform as promised under the contract; usually granted only when money damages would be an inadequate remedy and the subject matter of the contract is unique (for example, real property).

Spendthrift trust

A trust created to prevent the beneficiary from spending all the money to which he or she is entitled. Only a certain portion of the total amount is given to the beneficiary at any one time, and most states prohibit creditors from attaching assets of the trust.

Spot zoning

Granting a zoning classification to a parcel of land that is different from the classification given to other land in the immediate area.

Stale check

A check, other than a certified check, that is presented for payment more than six months after its date.

Standing to sue

The requirement that an individual must have a sufficient stake in a controversy before he or she can bring a lawsuit. The plaintiff must demonstrate that he or she either has been injured or threatened with injury.

Stare decisis (pronounced ster-ay dih-si-ses)

A common law doctrine under which judges are obligated to follow the precedents established in prior decisions.

Statute of Frauds

A state statute under which certain types of contracts must be in writing to be enforceable.

Statute of limitations

A federal or state statute setting the maximum time period during which a certain action can be brought or certain rights enforced.

Statute of repose

Basically, a statute of limitations that is not dependent on the happening of a cause of action. Statutes of repose generally begin to run at an earlier date and run for a longer period of time than statutes of limitations.

Statutory law

The body of law enacted by legislative bodies (as opposed to constitutional law, administrative law, or case law).

Statutory lien

A lien created by statute.

Statutory period of redemption

A time period (usually set by state statute) during which the property subject to a defaulted mortgage, land contract, or other contract can be redeemed by the debtor after foreclosure or judicial sale.

Stock

An equity (ownership) interest in a corporation, measured in units of shares.

Stock certificate

A certificate issued by a corporation evidencing the ownership of a specified number of shares in the corporation.

Stock option

See Stock warrant

Stock warrant

A certificate that grants the owner the option to buy a given number of shares of stock, usually within a set time period.

Stockholder

See Shareholder

Stop-payment order

An order by a bank customer to his or her bank not to pay or certify a certain check.

Strict liability

Liability regardless of fault. In tort law, strict liability may be imposed on defendants in cases involving abnormally dangerous activities, dangerous animals, or defective products.

Strike

An extreme action undertaken by unionized workers when collective bargaining fails; the workers leave their jobs, refuse to work, and (typically) picket the employer's workplace.

Subject-matter jurisdiction

Jurisdiction over the subject matter of a lawsuit.

Sublease

A lease executed by the lessee of real estate to a third person, conveying the same interest that the lessee enjoys but for a shorter term than that held by the lessee.

Subpoena

A document commanding a person to appear at a certain time and place or give testimony concerning a certain matter.

Subrogation

See Right of subrogation

Subscriber

An investor who agrees, in a subscription agreement, to purchase capital stock in a corporation.

Substantial evidence test

The test applied by a court reviewing an administrative agency's informal action. The court determines whether the agency acted unreasonably and overturns the agency's findings only if unsupported by a substantial body of evidence.

Substantial performance

Performance that does not vary greatly from the performance promised in a contract; the performance must create substantially the same benefits as those promised in the contract.

Substantive due process

A requirement that focuses on the content, or substance, of legislation. If a law or other governmental action limits a fundamental right, such as the right to travel or to vote, it will be held to violate substantive due process unless it promotes a compelling or overriding state interest.

Substantive law

Law that defines the rights and duties of individuals with respect to each other, as opposed to procedural law, which defines the manner in which these rights and duties may be enforced.

Substantive unconscionability

Results from contracts, or portions of contracts, that are oppressive or overly harsh. Courts generally focus on provisions that deprive one party of the benefits of the agreement or leave that party without remedy for nonperformance by the other. An example of substantive unconscionability is the agreement by a welfare recipient with a fourth-grade education to purchase a refrigerator for $2,000 under an installment contract.

Suit

See Lawsuit; Litigation

Summary judgment

See Motion for summary judgment

Summary jury trial (SJT)

A method of settling disputes in which a trial is held, but the jury's verdict is not binding. The verdict acts only as a guide to both sides in reaching an agreement during the mandatory negotiations that immediately follow the summary jury trial.

Summons

A document informing a defendant that a legal action has been commenced against him or her and that the defendant must appear in court on a certain date to answer the plaintiff's complaint. The document is delivered by a sheriff or any other person so authorized.

Superseding cause

An intervening force or event that breaks the connection between a wrongful act and an injury to another; in negligence law, a defense to liability.

Supremacy clause

The provision in Article VI of the Constitution that provides that the Constitution, laws, and treaties of the United States are "the supreme Law of the Land." Under this clause, state and local laws that directly conflict with federal law will be rendered invalid.

Surety

A person, such as a cosigner on a note, who agrees to be primarily responsible for the debt of another.

Suretyship

An express contract in which a third party to a debtor-creditor relationship (the surety) promises to be primarily responsible for the debtor's obligation.

Surviving corporation

The remaining, or continuing, corporation following a merger. The surviving corporation is vested with the merged corporation's legal rights and obligations.

Syllogism

A form of deductive reasoning consisting of a major premise, a minor premise, and a conclusion.

Symbolic speech

Nonverbal conduct that expresses opinions or thoughts about a subject. Symbolic speech is protected under the First Amendment's guarantee of freedom of speech.

Syndicate

An investment group of persons or firms brought together for the purpose of financing a project that they would not or could not undertake independently.

T

Tag

A key word in a document that can serve as an index reference to the document. On the Web, search engines return results based, in part, on the tags in Web documents.

Takeover

The acquisition of control over a corporation through the purchase of a substantial number of the voting shares of the corporation.

Taking

The taking of private property by the government for public use. Under the Fifth Amendment to the Constitution, the government may not take private property for public use without "just compensation."

Tangible property

Property that has physical existence and can be distinguished by the senses of touch, sight, and so on. A car is tangible property; a patent right is intangible property.

Target corporation

The corporation to be acquired in a corporate takeover; a corporation to whose shareholders a tender offer is submitted.

Tariff

A tax on imported goods.

Technology licensing

Allowing another to use and terms are expressed in a document located inside a box in which goods (usually software) are packaged; sometimes called a shrink-wrap license.

Teller's check

A negotiable instrument drawn by a bank on another bank or drawn by a bank and payable at or payable through a bank.

Tenancy at sufferance

A type of tenancy under which one who, after rightfully being in possession of leased premises, continues (wrongfully) to occupy the property after the lease has been terminated. The tenant has no rights to possess the property and occupies it only because the person entitled to evict the tenant has not done so.

Tenancy at will

A type of tenancy under which either party can terminate the tenancy without notice; usually arises when a tenant who has been under a tenancy for years retains possession, with the landlord's consent, after the tenancy for years has terminated.

Tenancy by the entirety

The joint ownership of property by a husband and wife. Neither party can transfer his or her interest in the property without the consent of the other.

Tenancy for years

A type of tenancy under which property is leased for a specified period of time, such as a month, a year, or a period of years.

Tenancy in common

Co-ownership of property in which each party owns an undivided interest that passes to his or her heirs at death.

Tenancy in partnership

Co-ownership of partnership property.

Tenant

One who has the temporary use and occupation of real property owned by another person, called the landlord; the duration and terms of the tenancy are usually established by a lease.

Tender

An unconditional offer to perform an obligation by a person who is ready, willing, and able to do so.

Tender of delivery

Under the Uniform Commercial Code, a seller's or lessor's act of placing conforming goods at the disposal of the buyer or lessee and giving the buyer or lessee whatever notification is reasonably necessary to enable the buyer or lessee to take delivery.

Tender offer

An offer to purchase made by one company directly to the shareholders of another (target) company; often referred to as a "takeover bid."

Term insurance

A type of life insurance policy for which premiums are paid for a specified term. Payment on the policy is due only if death occurs within the term period. Premiums are less expensive than for whole life or limited-payment life, and there is usually no cash surrender value.

Testamentary trust

A trust that is created by will and therefore does not take effect until the death of the testator.

Testate

The condition of having died with a valid will.

Testator

One who makes and executes a will.

Third party beneficiary

One for whose benefit a promise is made in a contract but who is not a party to the contract.

Time draft

A draft that is payable at a definite future time.

Tippee

A person who receives inside information.

Title insurance

Insurance commonly purchased by a purchaser of real property to protect against loss in the event that the title to the property is not free from liens or superior ownership claims.

Tombstone ad

An advertisement, historically in a format resembling a tombstone, of a securities offering. The ad informs potential investors of where and how they may obtain a prospectus.

Tort

A civil wrong not arising from a breach of contract. A breach of a legal duty that proximately causes harm or injury to another.

Tortfeasor

One who commits a tort.

Totten trust

A trust created by the deposit of a person's own money in his or her own name as a trustee for another. It is a tentative trust, revocable at will until the depositor dies or completes the gift in his or her lifetime by some unequivocal act or declaration.

Toxic tort

Failure to use or to clean up properly toxic chemicals that cause harm to a person or society.

Trade acceptance

A draft that is drawn by a seller of goods ordering the buyer to pay a specified sum of money to the seller, usually at a stated time in the future. The buyer accepts the draft by signing the face of the draft, thus creating an enforceable obligation to pay the draft when it comes due. On a trade acceptance, the seller is both the drawer and the payee.

Trade dress

The image and overall appearance of a product—for example, the distinctive decor, menu, layout, and style of service of a particular restaurant. Basically, trade dress is subject to the same protection as trademarks.

Trade fixture

The personal property of a commercial tenant that has been installed or affixed to real property for a business purpose. When the lease ends, the tenant can remove the fixture but must repair any damage to the real property caused by the fixture's removal.

Trade libel

The publication of false information about another's product, alleging it is not what its seller claims; also referred to as slander of quality.

Trade name

A term that is used to indicate part or all of a business's name and that is directly related to the business's reputation and goodwill. Trade names are protected under the common law (and under trademark law, if the name is the same as the firm's trademarked property).

Trade secret

Information or a process that gives a business an advantage over competitors who do not know the information or process.

Trademark

A distinctive mark, motto, device, or implement that a manufacturer stamps, prints, or otherwise affixes to the goods it produces so that they may be identified on the market and their origins made known. Once a trademark is established (under the common law or through registration), the owner is entitled to its exclusive use.

Transfer warranties

Implied warranties, made by any person who transfers an instrument for consideration to subsequent transferees and holders who take the instrument in good faith, that (1) the transferor is entitled to enforce the instrument, (2) all signatures are authentic and authorized, (3) the instrument has not been altered, (4) the instrument is not subject to a defense or claim of any party that can be asserted against the transferor, and (5) the transferor has no knowledge of any insolvency proceedings against the maker, the acceptor, or the drawer of the instrument.

Transferee

In negotiable instruments law, one to whom a negotiable instrument is transferred (delivered).

Transferor

In negotiable instruments law, one who transfers (delivers) a negotiable instrument to another.

Traveler's check

A check that is payable on demand, drawn on or payable through a bank, and designated as a traveler's check.

Treasure trove

Money or coin, gold, silver, or bullion found hidden in the earth or other private place, the owner of which is unknown; literally, treasure found.

Treasury shares

Corporate shares that are authorized by the corporation but that have not been issued.

Treaty

An agreement formed between two or more independent nations.

Treble damages

Damages consisting of single damages determined by a jury and tripled in amount in certain cases as required by statute.

Trespass to land

The entry onto, above, or below the surface of land owned by another without the owner's permission or legal authorization.

Trespass to personal property

The unlawful taking or harming of another's personal property; interference with another's right to the exclusive possession of his or her personal property.

Trespasser

One who commits the tort of trespass in one of its forms.

Trial court

A court in which trials are held and testimony taken.

Trust

An arrangement in which title to property is held by one person (a trustee) for the benefit of another (a beneficiary).

Trust indorsement

An indorsement for the benefit of the indorser or a third person; also known as an agency indorsement. The indorsement results in legal title vesting in the original indorsee.

Trustee

One who holds title to property for the use or benefit of another (the beneficiary).

Tying arrangement

An agreement between a buyer and a seller in which the buyer of a specific product or service becomes obligated to purchase additional products or services from the seller.

U

U.S. trustee

A government official who performs certain administrative tasks that a bankruptcy judge would otherwise have to perform.

Ultra vires (pronounced uhl-trah vye-reez)

A Latin term meaning "beyond the powers"; in corporate law, acts of a corporation that are beyond its express and implied powers to undertake.

Unanimous opinion

A court opinion in which all of the judges or justices of the court agree to the court's decision.

Unconscionable *(pronounced un-kon-shun-uh-bul)* **contract or clause**

A contract or clause that is void on the basis of public policy because one party, as a result of his or her disproportionate bargaining power, is forced to accept terms that are unfairly burdensome and that unfairly benefit the dominating party. *See also Procedural unconscionability; Substantive unconscionability*

Underwriter

In insurance law, the insurer, or the one assuming a risk in return for the payment of a premium.

Undisclosed principal

A principal whose identity is unknown by a third person, and the third person has no knowledge that the agent is acting for a principal at the time the agent and the third person form a contract.

Unenforceable contract

A valid contract rendered unenforceable by some statute or law.

Uniform law

A model law created by the National Conference of Commissioners on Uniform State Laws and/or the American Law Institute for the states to consider adopting. If the state adopts the law, it becomes statutory law in that state. Each state has the option of adopting or rejecting all or part of a uniform law.

Unilateral contract

A contract that results when an offer can only be accepted by the offeree's performance.

Union shop

A place of employment in which all workers, once employed, must become union members within a specified period of time as a condition of their continued employment.

W

Waiver

An intentional, knowing relinquishment of a legal right.

Warehouse receipt

A document of title issued by a bailee-warehouser to cover the goods stored in the warehouse.

Warehouser

One in the business of operating a warehouse.

Warranty

A promise that certain facts are truly as they are represented to be.

Warranty deed

A deed in which the grantor guarantees to the grantee that the grantor has title to the property conveyed in the deed, that there are no encumbrances on the property other than what the grantor has represented, and that the grantee will enjoy quiet possession of the property; a deed that provides the greatest amount of protection for the grantee.

Warranty disclaimer

A seller's or lessor's negation or qualification of a warranty.

Warranty of fitness

See Implied warranty of fitness for a particular purpose

Warranty of merchantability

See Implied warranty of merchantability

Warranty of title

An implied warranty made by a seller that the seller has good and valid title to the goods sold and that the transfer of the title is rightful.

Waste

The abuse or destructive use of real property by one who is in rightful possession of the property but who does not have title to it. Waste does not include ordinary depreciation due to age and normal use.

Watered stock

Shares of stock issued by a corporation for which the corporation receives, as payment, less than the fair market value of the shares.

Wetlands

Areas of land designated by government agencies (such as the Army Corps of Engineers or the Environmental Protection Agency) as protected areas that support wildlife and that therefore cannot be filled in or dredged by private contractors or parties.

Whistleblowing

An employee's disclosure to government, the press, or upper-management authorities that the employer is engaged in unsafe or illegal activities.

White-collar crime

Nonviolent crime committed by individuals or corporations to obtain a personal or business advantage.

Whole life

A life insurance policy in which the insured pays a level premium for his or her entire life and in which there is a constantly accumulating cash value that can be withdrawn or borrowed against by the borrower. Sometimes referred to as straight life insurance.

Will

An instrument directing what is to be done with the testator's property on his or her death, made by the testator and revocable during his or her lifetime. No interests in the testator's property pass until the testator dies.

Willful

Intentional.

Winding up

The second of two stages involved in the termination of a partnership or corporation. Once the firm is dissolved, it continues to exist legally until the process of winding up all business affairs (collecting and distributing the firm's assets) is complete.

Workers' compensation laws

State statutes establishing an administrative procedure for compensating workers' injuries that arise out of—or in the course of—their employment, regardless of fault.

Working papers

The various documents used and developed by an accountant during an audit. Working papers include notes, computations, memoranda, copies, and other papers that make up the work product of an accountant's services to a client.

Workout

An out-of-court agreement between a debtor and his or her creditors in which the parties work out a payment plan or schedule under which the debtor's debts can be discharged.

Writ of attachment

A court's order, prior to a trial to collect a debt, directing the sheriff or other officer to seize nonexempt property of the debtor; if the creditor prevails at trial, the seized property can be sold to satisfy the judgment.

Writ of certiorari (pronounced sur-shee-uh-rah-ree)

A writ from a higher court asking the lower court for the record of a case.

Writ of execution

A court's order, after a judgment has been entered against the debtor, directing the sheriff to seize (levy) and sell any of the debtor's nonexempt real or personal property. The proceeds of the sale are used to pay off the judgment, accrued interest, and costs of the sale; any surplus is paid to the debtor.

Wrongful discharge

An employer's termination of an employee's employment in violation of an employment contract or laws that protect employees.

Z

Zoning

The division of a city by legislative regulation into districts and the application in each district of regulations having to do with structural and architectural designs of buildings and prescribing the use to which buildings within designated districts may be put.

INDEX